MW01536747

THE RULES OF COMPETITION
IN THE
EUROPEAN ECONOMIC COMMUNITY

THE RULES OF COMPETITION

IN THE

EUROPEAN ECONOMIC COMMUNITY

A study of the Substantive Law on
a Comparative Law Basis

WITH SPECIAL REFERENCE TO
PATENT LICENCE AGREEMENTS AND
SOLE DISTRIBUTORSHIP AGREEMENTS

by

R. GRAUPNER, LL. B. (London)

Solicitor in London
Member of the Berlin Bar

THE HAGUE
MARTINUS NIJHOFF
1965

ISBN 978-94-011-8709-1   ISBN 978-94-011-9542-3 (eBook)
DOI 10.1007/978-94-011-9542-3

Copyright 1965 by Martinus Nijhoff, The Hague, Netherlands
Softcover reprint of the hardcover 1st edition 1965
All rights reserved, including the right to translate or to reproduce
this book or parts thereof in any form.

TABLE OF CONTENTS

TABLE OF CASES

GERMAN COURT DECISIONS

FRENCH COURT DECISIONS

DUTCH COURT DECISIONS

BELGIAN COURT DECISION

UNITED KINGDOM COURT DECISIONS

TABLE OF STATUTES

Regulations issued by the Council of Ministers of the E.E.C.

GERMANY

LIST OF ABBREVIATIONS

I

BOOKS

Baumbach-Hefermehl	Baumbach, A. & Hefermehl, W., *Wettbe- werbs- und Warenzeichenrecht*, 8th ed. (1960)
Brewster	Brewster, Kingman, Jr., *Antitrust and American Business Abroad* (1958)
Campbell	Campbell, Alan, *Restrictive Trading Agree- ments in the Common Market* (1964)
Deringer	Deringer, Arved, *"Das Wettbewerbsrecht der Europäischen Wirtschaftsgemeinschaft. Kommentar zu den EWG-Wettbewerbsregeln (Art. 85-94) nebst Durchführungs- Verord- nungen und Richtlinien" (unter Mitarbeit weiterer Autoren)* (1962–....) (not yet completed), appears in *Wirtschaft und Wett- bewerb (WuW)*
Fugate	Fugate, Wilbur L., *Foreign Commerce and the Antitrust Laws* (1958)
Gleiss-Hirsch	Gleiss, Alfred and Hirsch, Martin, *EWG- Kartellrecht, Kommentar* (1962)
v. Gamm	von Gamm, O.-F. Frhr., *Das Kartellrecht im EWG-Bereich, Kartellrundschau (Heft 3)* (1961)
Handler	Handler, Milton, *Antitrust in Perspective – The Complimentary Roles of Rule and Discretion* (1957)
Honig a.o.	Honig, F., Brown W. J., Gleiss, A., Hirsch, M., *Cartel Law of the European Economic Community (based on EWG-Kartellrecht by Gleiss-Hirsch)* (1963)
Jellinek	Jellinek, G., *Allgemeine Staatslehre*, 3rd ed. (1914)

* Books, articles and other publications which are referred to on one occasion only, are not contained in the above list but are fully quoted in the note in which the citation appears.

Langen	Langen, E. (in co-operation with H,–U. Wilke), *Kommentar zum Kartellgesetz, Gesetz gegen Wettbewerbsbeschränkungen mit Erläuterungen für die Praxis*, 3rd ed. (1958)
Lieberknecht	Lieberknecht, O., Patente *Lizenzverträge und Verbot von Wettbewerbsbeschränkungen. Eine vergleichende Darstellung der Rechtslage in Deutschland, Grossbritannien und den Vereinigten Staaten* (1953)
Lüdecke-Fischer	Lüdecke W. und Fischer, E., *Lizenzverträge* (1957)
Magen	Magen, A., *Lizenzverträge und Kartellrecht* (1963)
Gemeinschafts-kommentar	Müller-Henneberg, H. und Schwartz, G. (in co-operation with other authors), *Gesetz gegen Wettbewerbsbeschränkungen - Gemeinschaftskommentar* - 2nd ed. (1963)
Neale	Neale, A. D., *The Antitrust Law of the United States of America. A Study of Competition Enforced by Law* (1960)
Oppenheim-Lauterpacht	Oppenheim, L., *International Law. A Treatise*, Vol. I, *Peace*, 8th ed., edited by Lauterpacht, H. (1955)
Oppenheim	Oppenheim, S. Chesterfield, (assisted by Richard W. Pogue) *Federal Antitrust Laws – Cases and Comments*. 2nd ed. (1959)
Plaissant-Lassier	Plaissant, R. et Lassier, J., *Ententes et Marché Commun* (1959)
Schwartz	Schwartz, Ivo E., *Deutsches Internationales Kartellrecht. Der Anwendungsbereich des Gesetzes gegen Wettbewerbsbeschränkungen unter vergleichender Heranziehung des amerikanischen Antitrustrechts* (1962)

Note. The Organisation for Economic Co-operation and Development (OECD), 2 Rue André-Pascal, Paris 16e has published (since 1959) the *Guide to Legislation on Restrictive Business Practices* (a loose leaf service) which contains the relevant legislation currently in force in sixteen O.E.C.D. countries (Austria, Belgium, Canada, Denmark, Eire, France, Federal Republic of Germany, Italy, Netherlands, Norway, Portugal, Spain, Sweden, Switzerland, United Kingdom, United States of America as well as in the E.E.C. and the E.C.S.C.) with annotations, short reports of important Court cases and summaries of the various national laws and those of the Communities in this field. In 1964, O.E.C.D. issued *"Restrictive Business Practices – Comparative Summary of Legislation in Europe and North America."*

Wohlfarth a.o.

Wohlfarth, E., Everling, U., Glaesner, H. J. Sprung, R., *Die Europäische Wirtschaftsgemeinschaft. Kommentar zum Vertrag* (1960)

II

ARTICLES IN PERIODICALS

Baruch

Baruch, W., "Zum Anwendungsbereich des GWB", 11 *WuW* (1961), pp. 530–540.

Buxbaum

Buxbaum, R. M., "Patent Licensing: A Case Study on Antitrust Regulation within the European Economic Community", 9 *The Antitrust Bulletin* (1964), pp. 101–144 b.

Buxbaum

"The Applicability of the German Patent Law to Licenses of Foreign Patents", 8 *The Antitrust Bulletin* (1963), pp. 925–940 (also published in German translation "Die Anwendbarkeit des GWB auf Lizenzverträge über ausländische Patente", *WRP* 1963, pp. 288–291).

Deringer

Deringer, A., "Inhalt und Auswirkungen der ersten Kartellverordnung der Europäischen Wirtschaftsgemeinschaft", *GRUR (AIT)* (1962), pp. 283–295.

Gleiss-Hirsch

Gleiss, A. & Hirsch, M., "EWG-Kartellrecht: Bereichsausnahme für den Verkehr", *Aussenwirtschaftsdienst des Betriebsberaters* (1963), pp. 34–36.

Jansse, Oudemans & Wolterbeck

Jansse, P., Oudemans, G., & Wolterbeck, J. "Der Einfluss der Wettbewerbsregeln auf die gewerblichen Schutzrechte", *GRUR (AIT)*, (1961), pp. 276–284.

Kellermann

Kellermann, A., "Die gewerblichen Schutzrechte im Gesetz gegen Wettbewerbsbeschränkungen" Part I, *WuW* 1958, pp. 643–655, Part II, *WuW* 1960, pp. 603–618.

Ladas, Stephen P.,

"Antitrust Law in the Common Market with special Reference to Industrial Property Agreements", 23 *Ohio State Law Journal* (1962) pp. 709–751.

Mathély

Mathély, P., "Das Recht der Kartelle und der marktherrschenden Stellung in Frankreich", *GRUR(AIT)* 1964, pp. 14–21.

Ophüls

Ophüls, C. F., "Quellen und Aufbau des Europäischen Gemeinschaftsrechts", *NJW* 1963, pp. 1697–1701.

Schapiro

Schapiro, P. D., "The German Law against Restraints of Competition – Comparative International Aspects", 62 *Columbia Law Review*, (1962) pp. 1–48, 201–256.

Van Notten

Van Notten, M. M., "Know-how licensing in the Common Market", 38 *New York University Law Review* (1963), pp. 525–546.

III

PERIODICALS AND REPORTS

1. General

A.J.C.L.

The American Journal of Comparative Law (USA)

C.M.L. Rep.

Common Market Law Reports (U.K.)

C.M.L. Rev.

Common Market Law Review (The Netherlands and U.K.)

Der Betrieb

Der Betrieb (Germany)

Betriebsberater

Der Betriebs-Berater (Germany)

AWD

Aussenwirtschaftsdienst des Betriebs-Beraters – Recht der Internationalen Wirtschaft – (Germany)

GRUR

Gewerblicher Rechtsschutz und Urheberrecht (Zeitschrift der Deutschen Vereinigung für gewerblichen Rechtsschutz und Urheberrecht)

GRUR(AIT)

Gewerblicher Rechtsschutz und Urheberrecht – Auslands und Internationaler Teil – (Germany)

NJW

Neue Juristische Wochenschrift (Germany)

Recueil, Vol.

Recueil de la Jurisprudence de la Cour des Communautés Européennes (Reports of the Court of the European Communities)

WRP   Wettbewerb in Recht und Praxis (Germany)
WuW   Wirtschaft und Wettbewerb – Zeitschrift
                  für Kartellrecht, Wettbewerbsrecht und
                  Marktorganisation (Competition and Trade
                  Regulation) (Germany)

2. The European Economic Community

1. The Treaty for the Establishment of the
European Economic Community and Connected Documents (March 25, 1957).
The Treaty has been officially promulgated
in the Dutch, French, German and Italian
languages. (See Vols. 294, 295, 296 and 297
of the United Nations Treaty Series). For a
translation authorised by the Secretariat of
the Interim Committee for the Common
Market and Euratom in 1957, see 298
United Nations Treaty Series (1958). The
translation of the Articles of this Treaty
used in the following text is based on the
English version published by Her Majesty's
Stationery Office, London (1962), (known
as Foreign Office translation) which has
however in several places been amended by
the Author.

Treaty of Rome or Rome
Treaty or E.E.C. Treaty

2. Journal Officiel des Communautés Européennes (published in the four official
languages) (1958–....) (Official Gazette of
the European Communities)

J.O. (with year)

3. E.E.C. Commission, First (and subsequent
annual) General Report on the Activities of
the Community (1958–....)

General Report on the
Activities of the E.E.C.
(with year)

4. Articles 85 and 86 of the E.E.C. Treaty and

A Manual for Firms

the Relevant Regulations: A Manual for Firms (issued by European Community Information Service, 1962) (Guide pratique concernant les articles 85 et 86 du traité instituant la C.E.E. et leurs règlements d'application)

FOREWORD

The creation of the European Economic Community and the gradual achievement of a Common Market in connection with this Community raises not only economic but numerous legal problems as well. In fact, the Treaty of Rome and the various regulations, directives and decisions enacted for its implementation are bringing into being a new legal system which has a great influence not only within the frontiers of the Community but also on all European States which are in economic contact with the Community and indeed on the entire world. This applies particularly to the provisions on the laws of competition laid down by the Treaty and its implementing regulations. These provisions must be known and taken into consideration not only by Common Market enterprises but also by large firms outside the Community.

The very comprehensive literature on the European Economic Community has therefore laid special stress on this subject. The large number of commentaries published in the various languages of the Community on the Rules of Competition indicates the great interest taken not only by the commercial world but also by the world of jurisprudence.

A whole series of publications has also appeared in English. In view of the publications already existing, many people might feel that the attention given to these questions by Mr. GRAUPNER, the author of the present work, is unnecessary, but I believe such an opinion to be unjustified. Apart from the fact that the laws of competition of the European Economic Community are in a continual state of development so that every new work on the subject acquaints the reader with the latest position, Mr. GRAUPNER, who has tackled this subject in the most thorough fashion from both a theoretical and a practical point of view has the merit of viewing these problems as a practising English lawyer, particularly from the point of view of comparative law, taking into particular consideration the cartel laws of the United States, Great Britain, the Federal Republic of Germany and France. Thus, this work gives a very clear picture of the whole of legislation on competition in the most important Western industrial States.

For this purpose, the author not only refers to the entire literature on the subject but, true to Anglo-Saxon tradition, also bases himself on the most important court decisions. Even if decisions on these questions by the Court of Justice of the European Communities in Luxemburg are not as yet very numerous, they nevertheless are of fundamental importance and are being supplemented by decisions of the national courts of the Member States. From a practical point of view, decisions issued in the meantime by the Commission are also of special importance.

The present work also deserves special notice, however, because of the detailed attention it pays to a number of questions connected with the laws of competition. This applies particularly to questions concerning exclusive agency agreements, the significance of which is evident from the fact that, of the 35,000 registrations received by the Commission under Regulation No. 17, 30,000 relate to such agreements.

The book also examines in an extremely thorough manner the questions of licence agreements and patents. A very large number of licence agreements have been concluded in connection with trade between the United States and Great Britain on the one hand and the Common Market on the other hand, on account of the highly technical development of the economy of these States.

The last chapter, in which the author deals with the question of Community law in general and its relationship to the legal system of the individual Member States, is in my opinion also of very great merit. Mr. GRAUPNER argues in a striking manner that, although the Community's legal system is closely related to the national laws of the individual Member States, its validity cannot be tested by its agreement with the standards of national law, and not even by the constitutional provisions thereof. If it had been at all possible to doubt the author's opinion on this point which, for that matter, I have always shared myself, the question was finally settled by the decision (preliminary ruling) of the Court of Justice of the European Communities in Luxemburg on 15th July, 1964 in the case of Costa v. E.N.E.L. (Matter No. 6/64) (*Recueil* Vol. X, p. 1141 (1964) ; C.M.L. Rep. 425 (1964)).

Where there is a conflict between law enacted by the institutions of the Community and the provisions of national law, Community law takes, within the scope of its competence, precedence over national law and cannot be altered or restricted in its operation by a subsequent law of the national legislator.

The present work by Mr. GRAUPNER on the law of competition in the European Economic Community offers not only a statement of the

actual rules of competition and related problems, but also an introduction to the problem of Community law which has so far received
little attention and consequently represents something completely
new, since such law emanates not from a national legislator but from
the institutions of an international or, as it is often termed, supra-
national Community.

The book is therefore well suited to kindle an appreciation of the
problem in jurists concerned with this subject, and I wish the author
and his work every success.

ERNST WOHLFARTH

Legal Adviser of the Council of Ministers
of the European Communities.

PREFACE

Ducunt fata volentem,
nolentem trahunt.

The plan to write this book was conceived when Great Britain contempleted accession to the European Economic Community; it was prepared after the breakdown of the negotiations between the six Member States and Great Britain; it is published when, after severe political tensions between the Member States had been overcome, the economic integration of the Common Market has made substantial progress and interest in a *rapprochement* between the United Kingdom and the Six is being revived.

As far as the subject of this book is concerned, even during the difficult period in 1963/64 the legal machinery which had been set up to create and regulate the Common Market appeared to have been only little impeded by the events on the political scene. This is particularly true of the operation of the Rules of Competition of the Rome Treaty. If their implementation must still be considered as rather slow, this is due to several factors. In the first place, the law against restrictive trade practices is everywhere a sensitive and controversial subject and meets with constant and sometimes pertinent criticism under both economic and legal aspects in each stage of its application. Secondly, this rather novel body of law is laid down in an international treaty and operated on a supra-national level. Thirdly, a large number of practical cases of great variety have to be dealt with by the organs of the E.E.C. through implementing legislation and administrative acts which are both subject to judicial review by the Court of Justice of the European Communities. Fourthly, many cases in which the effect of Articles 85 and 86 becomes an issue are decided by national administrative cartel authorities (in so far as such exist) or national Courts which have thus been burdened with the task of taking part in the creation of the new European law against restraints of competition. Taking all these factors into consideration, one may assert without undue diffidence that through application of the Rules of Competition the idea and execution of an effective law against restrictive trade practices on a wide scale is being firmly established in Western Europe. There can be little doubt that the introduction of this law in the supra-national sphere will gradually also show an influence on national legis-lation not only in those Member States in which such law does not so far exist or is only of a rudimentary nature but also in non-Member States, as is shown by the present legislation in the United Kingdom, and might even bring life into Article 15 of the EFTA Convention.

Although this book has been written primarily for English lawyers and businessmen for whom the extensive references to United States law might afford a somewhat easier understanding and appreciation of the system and the working of the Rules of Competition, the inter-ested reader on the European Continent who is more familiar with this subject should here and there find some aspect which has not or has only casually been discussed elsewhere, for instance, the possible appli-cation of antitrust law to trade union activities and the treatment of a genuine as distinct from a mere sham agency in American law in the field of exclusive distributorship agreements, or some aspects of cross-licensing and patent pools and of trade secrets and know-how.

As the manuscript was completed at the beginning of October, 1964, certain recent developments in the field of European and national cartel law could not be dealt with in the text. In the field of Community law, the decision in the *Grundig-Consten* case[1] was the first negative ruling by which a typical international sole distributorship agreement has been condemned, and it must be said, in a rather sweeping manner. Even though the Commission emphasised in a Press Release[2] that from the large number of exclusive distribution agreements of which notifi-cation has been given, many might be declared compatible with the Rules of Competition, the prohibition of the entire agreement including the use of a trade mark owned by Grundig raises the question whether even a sole distributorship agreement which does not contain an abso-lute territorial protection as that embodied in the *Grundig-Consten* Agreement would be eligible for a declaration of inapplicability under Article 85 (3). It is understood that an appeal against this decision has been lodged with the European Court. The forthcoming Regulation by the Commission pursuant to Regulation No. 19/65 CEE of the Council

---

[1] *J.O.* 1964, pp. 2545–2564; re-printed *infra*, Appendix E, p. 261.
[2] Text in Board of Trade Journal No. 3525 of October 9, 1964, p. 830.

of Ministers will very probably have a bearing on the question whether and how far stipulations of the nature laid down in the *Grundig-Consten* Agreement will be treated as permissible.

This Regulation 19/65 CEE[1] is merely an enabling regulation by which the Commission has been empowered to issue both exemption declarations in specific individual cases and so-called "block exemptions" by special regulations for two types of agreement, namely sole distributorship agreements (or resolutions or concerted practices) and industrial property licensing rights agreements if only two parties are involved – provided that such agreements fulfil the requirements of Article 85 (3). The Commission will have to classify these agreements (or resolutions or concerted practices respectively); when a regulation by which exemption for a particular class of transactions has been granted is issued, the parties need no longer notify it to the Commission but may still apply for a clearance certificate under Regulation No. 17. Further Articles contain provisions for the safeguard of the economic interests of enterprises affected by these exemptions and, on the other hand, for the control by the Commission of the operation of these transactions in order to insure the observance of the requirements of Article 85 (3).[2]

In the field of national law, the judgement of the French *Cour de Cassation* of October, 1964, in the matter *Etat Français and Société Brandt*, by which this important case was finally determined, should be quoted.[3] On the German scene, mention should be made of the Bill for the amendment of the Cartel Law which contains, *inter alia*, a provision for an enlargement of the Government's power to intervene if sole distributorship agreements (section 18) result in an unreasonable restrictions of access to the market for other enterprises unless such restriction is negligible in relation to the possibilities of offer and demand. The principle that such agreements are lawful will, however, not be changed. In the United States, the now well-known case of U.S. v. White Motor Co.[4] was settled by consent decree[5] according to which the White Motor Company has to refrain from inserting any clause

---

[1] Of March, 2, 1965, *J.O.* 1965, pp. 533–535; English text in Board of Trade Journal, No. 3552 of April 16, 1965, p. 870.
[2] *Cf.* the Information Memorandum issued by E.E.C. on February 5, 1965, Board of Trade Journal, No. 3544 of February 19, 1965, p. 431.
[3] *See infra*, pp. 111, 124, 125.
[4] See *infra*, pp. 63, 97, 98.
[5] Of September 8, 1964; 1964 CCH Trade Cases, Par. 71, 195.

into the agreements with its distributors or other dealers with the object "to limit, allocate or restrict the territories in which, or the persons or classes of persons to whom, any distributor or other person may sell trucks." The principal question whether stipulations of this type are prohibited *per se* or merely subject to the Rule of Reason has therefore not been finally determined.

A few words must be said on the linguistic aspect. The Treaty of Rome itself is drawn up in a single original in the French, German, Italian and Dutch languages, all four texts being equally authentic.[1] The same principle applies to the legislative instruments but in the case of directives and decisions frequently only the language of the party or parties concerned is stated to be authentic. The English versions are always merely unofficial or, at the most, semi-official translations. As regards the Articles of the Treaty, I have used the translation issued by Her Majesty's Stationary Office in 1962 (the so-called Foreign Office translation) but have altered it freely where I though it necessary or expedient, sometimes relying on the translation published in *The American Journal of International Law*, Vol. 51 (1957), pp. 865–937, and, in one instance, on the suggestion made by Prof. E. J. Cohn in *The International and Comparative Law Quarterly*, Vol. 13 (1964), p. 1468. The translations of the Regulations issued by the Council of Ministers and the Commission as well as the Announcements and the decisions of the latter (reprinted in Appendix E) are Crown copyright; they were made for the convenience of Parliament and the public and appeared either in the Board of Trade Journal or as special publications of the Board of Trade. The translations of the sections of the Treaty establishing the European Coal and Steel Community (Appendix E) and of the French laws (Appendix C) are reproduced by kind permission of the Organisation for Economic Co-operation and Development in Paris. As for the German Law against Restraints of Trade (Appendix B), I have used, with some alterations, the translation issued by the United States Department of Commerce, Bureau of Foreign Commerce, published in *World Trade Information Service*, Part 1, No. 58–1.

---

[1] On the rules governing the languages of the institutions of the Community, see Article 217 of the Treaty. As to the practice of the Court of the European Communities, see Articles 29, 30 and 31 of the *Règlement de procédure* (Rules of Procedure) of the Court of March 3, 1959 (*J.O.* 1959, pp. 350 f.) and Regulation No. 1 of the Council of Ministers of October 6, 1958 on the Use of Languages in the E.E.C. (*J.O.* 1958, pp. 385–386).

Lastly, I wish to thank all those who have assisted me in the preparation of this book. The Index was prepared by Mr. N. March Hunnings of the Middle Temple who was able to use the preparatory work done by my former pupil Dr. Gesine Wacup. Miss Hilary Cartwright of the Middle Temple supervised the manuscript under the linguistic aspect. Mrs. Zelda Horn has typed the various drafts and the final manuscript carefully and efficiently in her spare time.

I would especially like to express my sincere gratitude to Herrn Ernst Wohlfarth for his encouragement to publish this study and for having written the Foreword.

3 & 4, Clement's Inn, Strand,   R. GRAUPNER
London, W. C. 2.   March, 1965

PART ONE

I. Preliminary Observations

In the summer of 1962 when the United Kingdom was engaged in negotiations with a view to joining the European Economic Community (E.E.C.) I ventured to write a paper on Articles 85 to 90 of the Treaty of Rome which contain the Rules of Competition operative in the E.E.C. The fairly wide interest in this subject at that juncture was not only due to the expected entry of this country into the Community but also to the fact that the first Regulation issued by the Council of Ministers of the E.E.C. on the application of these Articles had come into force on March 13, 1962 and was implemented by a Regulation issued by the Commission on May 3, 1962 relating to the form, contents and other particulars of the applications and notifications which had now become necessary. Furthermore, on the 6th April of the same year, the Court of the European Communities had rendered its first Judgement (in the so-called *Bosch* case[1]) in the field of European Cartel Law by which the Court confirmed, though with some qualifications, the immediate applicability of Article 85. As a result of the publication of the Regulations, attention was focused on their meaning and effect, that is to say, on matters of procedure, whereas efforts to understand and interpret the substantive law of the Rules of Competition were lacking. A discussion of their substantive contents would seem to be all the more necessary because the far-reaching and sweeping character of the provisions would, more often than not, leave even a commercial lawyer at a loss to understand which actual relationships are or are not caught thereby, so that he would frequently be in doubt as to when applications or notifications have to be submitted to the E.E.C. Commission. I therefore tried to give an account of the Rules, limited in principle to the substantive law.[2] Since that contribution appeared, this aspect of the cartel law of the E.E.C. has been dealt with in numerous publications in Great Britain and elsewhere. Nevertheless, in comparison with the abundant legal and economic literature devoted to this subject by Continental writers, there still appears to be some reluctance on the part of lawyers in the United Kingdom to concern

---

[1] *Robert Bosch G.m.b.H and another v. Kleding-Verkoopbedrijf de Geus en Uitdenboogerd (Matter 13/61), Recueil,* Vol. VIII, p. 89; (1962) 1 C.M.L. Rep., p. 1.
[2] *The Law Society's Gazette,* (London) 1962, July (pp. 372–381), August (pp. 450–455) and September (pp. 515–521).

themselves with problems pertaining to the substantive law contained
in these Rules. This cannot probably be explained merely by the fact
that the United Kingdom is not or not yet a member of the E.E.C.,
although this part of the Treaty of Rome has a direct impact on the
trade between the United Kingdom and the countries belonging to the
E.E.C., but would also seem to be due to other considerations. In the
first place, the absence of a comprehensive body of law of restraint of
competition in the United Kingdom[1] might create an obstacle to the
understanding of the implications of the Rules. Secondly, the lack of
decisions by the European Court on Articles 85 and 86 (except the
one in the Bosch case) and the difficulty of gaining access to and
appreciating the numerous decisions in this field rendered by national
Courts of the Member States of the E.E.C. must necessarily make any
attempt at an explanation of their meaning a hazardous task, which
lawyers in the United Kingdom who are apt to rely chiefly on precedents are not wont to undertake. Further, the fact that the Articles
were drafted by lawyers trained in different legal systems is a handicap
to any approach without further authoritative guidance. Finally, the
non-participation of the United Kingdom in the legislative and administrative work of the Community has, understandably enough,
created a feeling of aloofness that also extends to the Rules of Competition which come more and more to be regarded as a *res inter alios
acta* in which active co-operation is, at least for the time being, not
called for. However, in spite of these difficulties and considerations the
business world and especially the legal profession in Great Britain
should make a serious effort to understand the significance of the
European cartel law not only because this law will occasionally have
a direct impact on private law relationships between traders in the
United Kingdom and in the Member States of the E.E.C. but also
because the prevalence of this part of the European Community Law
will in many instances have to be taken into account in the shaping of
Great Britain's export and foreign investment policy.

These considerations apply equally to those other European and
non-European Countries whose commercial communities carry on
trade with the Member States of the E.E.C. It is the practical concern
of these parties outside the Common Market that has been made a
special feature of this study.

---

[1] In comparison with the antitrust law of the United States and the German Cartel
Law of 1957, United Kingdom legislation against restrictive trades practices and monopolies covers a rather limited field.

Conversely, the operation of a fairly strict and comprehensive law against restrictive trade practices in the major European industrial countries will probably eventually have repercussions in the legislative regulation of trade and industry in the United Kingdom, as the hitherto existing legislation against restrictive trade practices can only be regarded as a first step.[1]

The importance to be attached to the new European Community Law and the Rules of Competition in particular has been manifested by the legal profession in the United States where a voluminous body of legal literature on this subject has been built up. Being able to profit from long experience in United States antitrust law, American writers have made valuable contributions to the creation, development and understanding of its European counterpart.[2]

As mentioned before, I had limited my discourse in the Law Society's Gazette to the substantive law of the Rules of Competition, as the procedural side had at that time even in the United Kingdom been fairly widely discussed. On its present (considerably enlarged) re-publication I had to consider whether a detailed discussion of the procedural provisions, in particular the regulations issued by the Council of Ministers and by the Commission, should be included. I have decided against such extension for various reasons. First, the regulations have been extensively publicised and commented upon in trade journals, legal periodicals and recently in two books which deal with this aspect fairly comprehensively,[3] particularly with the notification of "existing" and "new" agreements and the exclusive competence of the Commission to declare paragraph 3 of Article 85 applicable. Secondly, in regard to the important provisions in Regulation No. 17 on

---

[1] On the present intentions of the British Government in this field, see the White Paper (Cmnd. 2299) of March 1964 on "Monopolies, Mergers and Restrictives Practices." This new policy has so far only been implemented by the Resale Prices Act, 1964 (see *infra*, Appendix D).

[2] Apart from the books and articles quoted in the text, the following publications may be mentioned: Stefan A. Riesenfeld, "The Protection of Competition" (pp. 197–342) in Vol. II, Stein & Nicholson, *American Enterprises in the European Common Market – A Legal Profile*, Ann Arbor, 1960; the same, "Antitrust Laws in the European Community: A Sequel," *50 California Law Review p. 829* (1959) (containing a bibliography of the more important literature on this subject); "Symposium, Antitrust and the Common Market," *38 New York University Law Review (1963), p. 435*. A major current publication is the *Common Market Reporter* (loose leaf service) published by Commerce Clearing House, Inc., Chicago, Ill., in which most of the laws and other material including (annotated) Court decisions in the field of the E.E.C. Rules of Competition are also reprinted.

[3] Honig a.o., *op. cit.*, esp. pp. 42–84; 91 f.; Campbell, *op. cit.* A fairly thorough explanation of the rules of procedure is contained in "Practical Guide – A Manual for Firms," reprinted in Appendix E, *infra*, pp. 232–250.

Requests for Information from Governments, authorities and, in particular, private enterprises,[1] not much can at present be said pending judicial rulings. Lastly, I believe that a reader who is not specialised in this subject-matter will prefer to peruse an, as I hope, fairly readable survey of a new legal subject which has already become so overladen with procedural technicalities that a full presentation may understandably cause a serious obstacle and even an aversion to a study of the more important substantive law. The exclusion of a comprehensive treatment of the procedural rules does not mean, however, that they will be entirely neglected. They will in fact be referred to in so far their application has a bearing on the understanding or the effect of substantive provisions.

On the other hand, I have included in this enquiry a discussion of Articles 90 and 91 of the Rome Treaty. It is somewhat surprising that the special legal literature in the United Kingdom devoted to the cartel law of the E.E.C. is limited to annotations to Articles 85 and 86 and the following three Articles which contain the provisions for the enforcement of the substantive law.[2] Such omission can hardly be justified as far as Article 90 is concerned since this qualifies the application of Articles 85 and 86 to a very important class of traders in the commercial field and belongs, systematically, to Section 1, "Rules applying to Enterprises," of the Chapter "Rules of Competition." As regards Article 91, it is true that it deals with a special problem, that of "Dumping Practices," but as it does apply to transactions regulated by private law and moreover, its paragraph 1 is addressed to both Member States and enterprises alike, I have thought it imperative to discuss it. By contrast, I have omitted to comment upon the third Section of the Rules of Competition, "Aids granted by States" (Articles 92–94). Even though both private enterprises and public undertakings may be the recipients of public subsidies and such subsidies may in turn facilitate dumping practices (in which case the Commission or the Council of Ministers of the E.E.C. will have to proceed in accordance with

[1] Arts. 11–16 and Regulation No. 99/63 issued by the Commission on July 25, 1963 (*J.O.* 1963, p. 2268; unofficial English translation in *Board of Trade Journal* of August 30, 1963, p. 484, and in *The Law Society's Gazette, 1963, p. 683).* The Regulation came into force on August 30, 1963. For a general discussion of this topic, see Wohlfarth, "The Right of the Commission to Ask Information" in *Doing Business in the Common Market*, p. 36 (published prior to the issue of Regulation No. 99/63), and H. Würdinger in *WuW* 1964, pp. 579–588.

[2] E.g., Honig a.o., *op. cit.*, Campbell & Thompson, *Common Market Law*, 1961 (with First Supplement, 1963). Campbell, *op. cit.*, devotes only a few lines to the annotation to Art. 90 (at p. 2) and disregards Art. 91 altogether.

Articles 93 and 94[1]), the practitioner, especially a lawyer practising outside the area of the Common Market, will hardly be concerned with this issue.

In concluding these preliminary observations I have to refer to a particular aspect of the establishment of the European Economic Community, *viz.*, the creation of a novel legal system through which the integration of the economy of the Member States shall be furthered. This is the so-called Community law which is distinct from the municipal law of the various Member States but is not public international law in the traditional sense. The nature and operation of this Community law becomes most apparent in the chapter of the Treaty on Competition (Articles 85 to 94). This means that anyone who really wishes to understand the system and functioning of the Rules of Competition must become familiar with the concept of Community law. Although a thorough discussion of this topic must necessarily remain outside the scope of this book, the basic principles and effects of Community law will be conveniently set out in a separate part, Part III.

Before I deal with the proper subject of this study I have to make a few observations on linguistic points. Dealing with institutions belonging to a foreign sphere of law and discussing them largely on the basis of what has become known as "comparative law," questions of terminology are of particular moment. I shall in due course have regard to such questions. Here, I should only like to say a few words on the description of the subject-matter of this study. The relevant chapter in the Treaty of Rome has been correctly translated from the four authoritative texts as Rules of Competition (Fr.: *Les règles de concurrence;* G: *Wettbewerbsregeln;* It.: *Regole di concorrenza;* Dutch: *Regels betreffende de mededinging*). This heading might be considered as too wide as it could be understood to include the regulation of "unfair competition," a clearly defined legal subject of great importance in many Continental countries. In fact, the Rules of Competition embody only a branch of the law relating to competition which is differently described in those countries which have provisions regulating it. In the United States it is generally termed antitrust law (or in short "antitrust") although it comprises restraints of competition on both horizontal and vertical levels. The French name is *"entente."* In Germany the relevant statute is the "Law against Restraints of Competition" of 1957 but this legal subject is commonly known as cartel law *(Kartellrecht),* and the Statute is usually referred to as the *"Kar-*

---

[2] See Wohlfarth a.o., *op. cit.,* n. 1 to Art. 91, p. 268.

tellgesetz".[1] In the United Kingdom the statutes directed against restraints of trade are the Monopolies and Restrictive Practices (Inquiry
and Control) Act, 1948, the Restrictive Trade Practices Act, 1956 and
the recently enacted Resale Prices Act, 1964; colloquially, one usually
speaks of restrictive trades practices law. This variety of descriptions
for the one and same legal institution poses the question whether I
should only choose one description applicable to this law in all the
countries where it exists or whether I should follow the description
applied by each country for its own system. I thought it best to adopt
– as a rule – the second alternative. As regards the E.E.C., I have used
either the technical term Rules of Competition or spoken of European
cartel Law or cartel Law of the E.E.C., expressions which are today
generally accepted in Continental legal and economic literature. This
method also appeared to me useful for the description of special institutions and terms within the framework of the main subject.[2]

II. Origin and Background of the European Cartel Law

The wide scope of Articles 85–90 and the technique of their formu-
lation can only be understood by reference to American antitrust
legislation and judicial practice since the enactment of the Sherman
Act in 1890. When the United States emerged from the last War as the
strongest world power, it became apparent that it was determined to
see its cherished principle of free competition in trade and commerce
accepted in all economic organisations of which it was a member.[3]
Furthermore, the Allied Occupation legislation of 1947 on the de-
concentration and decartelisation of German industry widely reflects
the principles of American antitrust policy.[4] In turn, the Federal

---

[1] All references to Germany and German law are references to the Federal Republic
of Germany (and West Berlin) and to the law prevailing in these territories only.
Needless to say, in a communist society competition between private enterprises does
not exist and there is consequently no room for a law against restrictive trade practices.
The much propagated "socialist competiton" is a mere competition to achieve the
maximum output by State owned enterprises in a completely planned and controlled
economy.

[2] Arts. 85 to 91 of the Treaty of Rome and Regulations. Nos. 17 and 27 will hereinafter
only be referred to as such without any further addition.

[3] *Cf.* Chapter V of the (abortive) Havana Charter of March 24, 1948, and the efforts
to create an international control of cartels through GATT (General Agreement on
Tariffs and Trade) of October 30, 1947 in the amended form effective as from October
10, 1957 (*cf.* Cmd. 9413); see E. Guenther, "The Problems Involved in Regulating
International Restraints of Competition by means of Public International Law" in
Cartels and Monopoly, Vol. II, p. 579.

[4] Military Government Law No. 56 (U.S. Zone) and Order No. 78 (British Zone) on
Prohibition of Excessive Concentration of German Economic Power. In the French

German Law against Restraints of Competition of July 27, 1957 embodies Allied legislation to a considerable extent. In a comparison with the cartel law of other Member States of the E.E.C.,[1] the German law is by far the most comprehensive, in regard to both the substantive law and its administration. Even though it cannot be said that the Rules of Competition in the Treaty of Rome were an adaptation from German Cartel Law (which, like the Treaty of Rome itself, came into force on January 1, 1958), the Allied decartelisation legislation in Germany and the extensive deliberations which preceded the introduction of the German Cartel Law no doubt influenced the framing of the Rules of Competition in the E.E.C. Treaty. One will therefore probably not go wrong in assuming that the administration of these Rules by the organs of the E.E.C. and their judicial interpretation by the Court of the European Communities will to a significant degree be influenced by American and German experience in this field.[2] How far other European national laws against restraints on competition will bear upon the development of the European Cartel Law cannot be foreseen; such national laws include the wide-scale prohibition of resale price maintenance in France and the interpretation of Article 59*ter* of the French Decree of August 9, 1953, which served as the model for Article 85 (3), as well as the impending rather stringent new Italian Law already referred to. In attempting at this stage to understand the meaning and effect of the Rules, guidance can therefore be found in the, albeit comparatively short, tradition in this specialised legal province. It is assumed that the Council of Ministers and the Commission of the E.E.C. as well as the European Court will be influenced by the same considerations.

III. The Substantive Law of Articles 85 to 91

A. Article 85

(1) The following practices shall be prohibited as incompatible with the Common Market: all agreements between enterprises, all decisions by associations of enterprises and all concerted practices which are capable

Zone a similar though less stringent Order was also issued. All three enactments were due to American initiative.

[1] At present such laws are in force in France, the Netherlands, West Germany and Belgium. There is none in Luxembourg. An Italian law against restrictive trade practices is in preparation.

[2] Such influence is, *e.g.*, clearly discernible in the Announcement of the Commission of the E.E.C. of December 24, 1962 on Patent Licences (*J.O.* 1962, p. 2922), see *infra*, p. 59.

of affecting trade between Member States and which are designed to prevent, restrict or distort competition within the Common Market or which have this effect. This shall, in particular, include:

(a) the direct or indirect fixing of purchase or selling prices or of any other trading conditions;

(b) the limitation or control of production, markets, technical development or investment;

(c) market-sharing or the sharing of sources of supply;

(d) the application of unequal conditions to parties undertaking equivalent engagements in commercial transactions, thereby placing them at a competitive disadvantage;

(e) making the conclusion of a contract subject to the acceptance by the other party to the contract of additional obligations, which, by their nature or according to commercial practice have no connexion with the subject of such contract.

(2) Any agreements or decisions prohibited pursuant to this Article shall automatically be null and void.

(3) The provisions of paragraph 1 may, however, be declared inapplicable in the case of:

– any agreement or category of agreement between enterprises,

– any decision or category of decision by associations of enterprises, and

– any concerted practice or category of concerted practice

which helps to improve the production or distribution of goods or to promote technical or economic progress, whilst allowing consumers a fair share of the resulting profit and which does not:

(a) subject the enterprises in question to any restrictions which are not indispensable to the achievement of the above objectives;

(b) enable such enterprises to eliminate competition in respect of a substantial part of the goods concerned.

The present main difficulty in arriving at a reasonable interpretation of Article 85 lies in the very far-reaching provisions of its paragraph 1, and the equally very general and wide power of granting exemptions, now exclusively conferred upon the Commission by Article 9 (1) of Regulation No. 17 (subject, of course, to review by the European Court). Whereas it must therefore be borne in mind that in principle any transaction prohibited under paragraph 1 may be permitted under paragraph 3, it is the effect of paragraph 1 upon a transaction that is of decisive importance, not least in view of the provisions of the said Regulation.[1]

We now turn to a closer examination of the transactions prohibited under paragraph 1.

1. THE GENERAL CLAUSE IN PARAGRAPH (1)

(a) The following practices shall be prohibited as incompatible with the Common Market: all agreements between enterprises, all decisions by associations of enterprises and all concerted practices...

Articles 85 and 86 speak of "enterprises." This is not a legal term found in the general law of any of the Member States nor is it defined in the Treaty. It is now however recognised as referring to any economic unit – either a single individual or several individuals combined in a partnership or corporation – which is concerned with the production or distribution of goods or the provision of services.[2]

Where a concern (combine) comprises formally independent legal enterprises, it is probably an association of enterprises, but in the case of a very close interdependence, when the restrictive agreements *etc.* originate from a direction of the management of the concern, the concern may be classified as one enterprise.[3] Again, whether restrictions on competition imposed by a parent company on its subsidiary either by agreements or provisions to that end in the latter's articles of association are or are not subject to Article 85 will depend on both the legal and factual relationship between parent company and subsidiary.

The prohibition applies to agreements between enterprises, or between associations of enterprises, or between an enterprise and an association of enterprises; an agreement must have been entered into with the intention of creating legally binding obligations. Associations of enterprises can, for the purpose of Article 85 of the Treaty, also act through a decision, *i.e.*, usually by way of resolutions with binding effect on the members of the association; mere recommendations or suggestions do probably not come within this term. However, a possible

---

[1] See especially its Arts. 1 to 9 and 15 and 16. Whether transactions which fulfil the conditions of paragraph (3) are valid *ipso lege* or only when paragraph (1) has been declared inapplicable under paragraph (3), is a question that has not been determined by the Regulation, which speaks of a notification only and not of an application for granting exemption (Arts. 4 and 5).

[2] Public undertakings are subject to special treatment under Art. 90.

[3] See for a detailed review of this problem, Deringer, *op. cit.*, n. 13 to 16 to Art. 85(1.)

gap is closed by the application of the prohibition to concerted practices (the "concerted actions" of American antitrust law). Briefly,
concerted practices are so-called "gentlemen's agreements," *i.e.*, understandings intended to be acted upon without being legally binding, and
other consciously effected co-operation, for example by way of a
recommendation; but they probably do not include mere "price
leaderships" or the so-called "parallel actions."

It is generally stated that contracts between employers and employees (including collective bargaining agreements), as well as agreements
relating to terms of employment on a horizontal level are not within
the ambit of a law against restraints of competition[1] although the
Rules of Competition as such know no "exemption areas." In Germany,
the reasons given for the nonapplication of the Cartel Law are, first,
that an employee is not an enterprise in the meaning of the statute
since independence is a necessary element for such qualification and,
secondly, that supply of labour is not rendering commercial services
in the meaning of sections 1, 15 and 18 of the Cartel Law even if such
agreements result in restraint of trade.[2] But it may be questioned
whether such sweeping generalisation is justified. The fact that an
agreement falls into the sphere of industrial law should not *per se*
exempt it from the application of the law against restrictive practices.
Legislators and Courts in the United States have been concerned with
problems of this kind for many decades. It would now seem to be established that commercial restraints brought about by labour groups
(especially trade unions) through strikes and/or measures of boycott
of opponents' goods or services are not within the antitrust law but if
labour groups combine for such purpose with non-labour groups, the
Sherman Act might be violated.[3] As regards Article 85, the apparent

---

[1] See, *e.g.*, Honig a.o., *op. cit.*, p. 9.

[2] See thereon decision of the *Kammergericht Berlin* of January 12, 1960, *WuW* 1960,
p. 446, and Letter of the Federal Cartel Office of August 6, 1962, *WuW* 1962, p. 716.
For further references, see *Gemeinschaftskommentar*, pp. 131, 154, 1163.

[3] Through s. 6 and 20 of the Clayton Act, 1914 and the Norris-La Guardia Act, 1932
labour disputes in a wide sense were excluded from the compass of antitrust law. The
non-applicability of the Sherman Act and of the Norris-La Guardia Act to labour
disputes fought on traditional lines was confirmed in *Apex Hosiery Co. v. Leader*, 310
U.S. 469 (1940) and *United States v. Hutcheson*, 312 U.S. 219 (1941). However, in several
other cases it was established that if an organised labour union combines with non-
labour groups, it loses its immunity and its activities can be judged under antitrust law.
The principal rule was laid down in *Allen Bradley Co. v. Local No. 3*, 325 U.S. 797 (1947).
The facts of this most illustrative case are as follows. The defendant trade union had
been successful in obtaining closed-shop agreements with manufacturers and dealers
of electrical equipment in New York. The latter had also undertaken to buy such
equipment only from local manufacturers who had closed-shop contracts and the
former were bound only to sell to dealers who employed members of this union. The

difficulty arises from its wording, as this Article prohibits certain restrictive practices carried on by enterprises. In the United States the law as found by the Supreme Court also obtained legislative approval in certain sections of the Taft-Hartley Act (Labor Management Relations Act, 1947[1]) relating to labour boycotts. An organised labour group, *i.e.*, as a rule a trade union, can thus be treated as an enterprise in the meaning of this provision. Though this will in principle have to be denied if a trade union is concerned with the defence of the interests of dependent labour, its participation in restrictive trade practices by way of co-operation with commercial enterprises in the capitalistic sector operating in the sphere of business competition should permit its classification as an enterprise *pro tanto*. Such characterisation would not be dissimilar to the position of a public authority which is exempted from the application of cartel law if it acts in the exercise of its governmental functions but is within such law if it performs commercial transactions in the sphere of private law, for instance if a Government department or public authority sells goods or renders services (unless every activity of such body is expressly exempted[2]).

Supreme Court found in this arrangement a combination which "intended to and did restrain trade in and monopolise the supply of electrical equipment in the New York City area to the exclusion of equipment manufactured in and shipped from other States, and did also control its price and discriminate between its would-be customers." The Court concluded: "It is true that victory of the union in its disputes, even if the union had acted alone, might have added to the costs of the goods, or might have resulted in individual refusals of all their employers to buy electrical equipment not made by Local No. 3. So far as the union might have achieved this result acting alone, it would have been the natural consequence of labor union activities exempted by the Clayton Act from the coverage of the Sherman Act, *Apex Hosiery Co. v. Leader, supra* 503. But when the unions participated with a combination of businessmen who had complete power to eliminate all competition among themselves and to prevent all competition from others, a situation was created not included within the exemption of the Clayton and Norris-La Guardia Acts."

See Oppenheim, *op. cit.*, pp. 45–51, and Neale, *op. cit.*, pp. 5 f. Having regard to Article 85 it should however be emphasised that the Sherman Act declares "every contract, combination in the form of trust or otherwise, or conspiracy, in restraint of trade" illegal (subject to certain qualifications) and does thus not limit its application to such relations or co-operation between enterprises.

In a quite recent case *(Jewel Tea Co. Inc. v. Local Unions Nos. 189 etc. Amalgamated Meat Cutters and Butchers Workmen of North America AFL – C10, et al.*, CCH Trade Reg. Rep. (1963) 70, 713) the District Court of Illinois, N.D. declared the Sherman Act inapplicable to a collective bargaining agreement which apart from regulating hours of work also contained the stipulation that the employers have to prevent the sale of fresh meat after 6 p.m. The Court held that even if antitrust law were applicable, this part of the agreement was to be sustained as it was an ancillary restraint that was reasonable in the circumstances of the case. In German law the legal position would seem to be the reverse, see the note in *WuW* 1963, p. 715.

[1] 29 U.S.C.A. p. 158, s. 8(b) (4) and (6).

[2] See *infra*, p. 35 For the merely limited application of the Rules of Competition to agricultural products and traffic, see *infra*, pp. 34–36 and on the position of public authorities in the German Cartel Law, see *Gemeinschaftskommentar*, pp. 1164 ff.

(b) ... which are capable of affecting trade between the Member States...

The trade in this connection is not merely the exchange of particular goods or services but the entire field of inter-Member State trade between at least two, but not necessarily more, Member States. It is presumably sufficient for such trade to be affected – not necessarily disadvantageously[1] – yet the effect must be real and not too remote. Transactions which affect trade within one Member State only are outside this provision, even through they may be prohibited by the national cartel law of the State concerned; but if such agreements *etc.*, though *prima facie* limited to a single national market, affect or are capable of affecting other markets too, they are within the scope of Article 85. This extended interpretation of Article 85 has been justified on the ground that it is necessary for the creation of a common market. The demarcation between prohibited and permitted agreements will no doubt be difficult in practice. The impact on the trade between Member States can also be brought about by a transaction in which one of the enterprises concerned is situate in a non-Member State or by one in which all the parties are resident outside the Common Market area. Such situations are dealt with in a separate chapter.[2]

(c) ... and which are designed to prevent restrict or distort competition within the Common Market or which have this effect.

"Design" or "effect" connotes more than a mere possibility; unless a transaction has in actual fact had one of the consequences against which Article 85 is aimed, it must be intended and be objectively apt to have such consequences. The very important concept of "competition" is not defined, but no definition should be necessary since it could in any event only be a formal one.[3] The Treaty is based on the principle of free economic competition, expressly laid down or inherent in the political and economic constitutions of the Member States, under which their nationals can in principle freely determine the price and the conditions of delivery of goods or of the provision of services and freely enter into contracts thereon. Yet this is not considered sufficient. It must also remain possible for other participants in the

---

[1] This interpretation gains support from the decision of the Commission in the Grundig-Consten case of September, 23, 1964, II, 2 (see *infra*, Appendix E, p. 261).

[2] See *infra*, pp. 37–47.

[3] For the German Cartel Law, competition has been defined as "efforts to maintain and if possible to increase the range of his own customers (including suppliers) at the expense of others" (Baumbach-Hefermehl, *op. cit.*, p. 2) or as "the effort through one's own performance to surpass others in quality or price and thereby to achieve the highest possible profit" (Government Justification of the German Cartel Law).

market to have access to and avail themselves of other sources of supply or to change the outlet for the sale of their goods or the supply of their services. The importance of this element in the concept of free competition can hardly be exaggerated, as it will in cases of doubt often be the test of whether competition is substantially unhampered or, on the other hand, prevented, restricted or distorted. Whereas cartel law is designed to safeguard freedom of competition in the interests of the public in general and for the creation and maintenance of the Common Market in particular, the Common Market law is not to be used for the protection of unfair competition which is partly the subject matter of the general law (e.g., in France and Italy), and partly of special ancillary legislation (e.g., in Germany[1]). Article 85 would in any case not be concerned with unfair competition in its traditional sense.[2]

As with the term "competition" itself, there is no definition in Article 85 of the terms "prevention," "restriction" and "distortion." This Article gives, however, instances of activities which prevent, restrict or distort competition (paragraph (1) (a) to (e)). Although this list is expressly set forth only for guidance on the interpretation of the general rule ("... in particular consisting in ..."), the examples themselves are so widely framed that it may be doubted whether any other important method of interference can legitimately be added to this list (e.g., prohibition of mergers of enterprises or a general prohibition against discrimination). The Commission has however indicated that it will impress upon the Member States and trade associations that concentrations of enterprises which are not justified economically shall in any event not be promoted artificially.[3]

Before dealing with the catalogue of examples, it must be emphasised that the prohibited transactions can either be carried out on the same trade level, for example by agreements between enterprises or decisions by associations of enterprises which are manufacturers of goods of the same or a similar nature and which pursue thereby an aim

[1] In the United States, violation of antitrust law may in special cases amount to unfair competition, see Neale, op. cit., pp. 4 f.

[2] Cf. Gemeinschaftskommentar, p. 1454: "Only fair competition should be the subject of protection of the Rules of Competition... consequently, agreements across the frontiers relating to the observance of provisions against unfair competition should not be considered a violation of Art. 85. Difficulties may however arise from the divergency in the legal treatment of questions of competition in the various countries."

[3] See Memorandum of the Commission of the E.E.C. in regard to the Action Program for the Second Stage of October 24, 1962, KOM (62) 300 Ch. 2, pp. 29/30, 35; see on the discussion thereon, General Report on the Activities of the E.E.C., 1962/1963 (English Edition), p. 25.

common to them all (the cartel proper), or by agreements between enterprises operating on different trade levels, for example between manufacturers and distributors whose business interests are as a rule in some respects opposed to each other. The first type are commonly described as "horizontal agreements" (concerted practices are generally found in this sphere), and the second type as "vertical agreements" (of which resale price maintenance is an important instance). There cannot be any doubt that both types are covered by Article 85.[1]

2. THE CATALOGUE OF EXAMPLES

(a) the direct or indirect fixing of purchase or selling prices or of any other trading conditions.

On the horizontal level, this prohibition applies to simple price fixing cartels, the so-called "calculation cartels," in which the parties agree to observe cost values (which are in fact their own minimum cost values), and cartels dealing with the uniform application of terms of trade, of deliveries or of payments, including trade discounts ("condition cartels"), cartels stipulating rebates in various forms ("rebate cartels"), cartels by which parties bind themselves to observe a minimum price on tenders for the execution of work or supply of goods on invitation for public tender ("submission cartels").

On the vertical level, the insertion of the price into an individual simple contract for sale is unobjectionable but resale price maintenance is unlawful. Although this institution may be of minor importance in relation to inter-Member State trade as distinct from home market trade, there may be trade sectors, for example the book trade, in which approval of resale price maintenance (under paragraph 3) would be generally welcomed. Vertical resale price maintenance may come within Article 85 if it is connected with an export prohibition. Agreements directed against the re-importation of exported goods which are subject to resale price maintenance only in the exporting Member State are probably illegal under Article 85, as their observance might enable the exporting manufacturer to maintain in his home market a price level that is higher than in other Member States, but tenable arguments have been advanced against this view.

---

[1] See Art. 4, paragraph (2)(a) and (b) of Regulation No. 17 where certain vertical agreements are exempted from notification only if not more than two enterprises are involved, and the decision in the *Bosch* case (see *supra*, p. 3).

(b) the limitation or control of production, markets (distribution), technical development or investment.

The types of cartel in question are mainly the following: cartels dealing with uniform application of standards and types ("standardisation cartels"), cartels aiming at "the rationalisation of the economic processes for the purpose of substantially raising the efficiency or productivity of the participating enterprises from a technical, economic or organisational point of view and aiming thereby to satisfy demand more effectively."[1] Such cartels may include "specialisation cartels" which provide for a division of production and/or distribution of certain goods among the parties of the cartel, and, further, "syndicates" which are cartels with a joint purchasing or marketing agency. Lastly, "quota cartels" by which production and/or distribution of goods or services is restricted in order to prevent overproduction. The future will show whether the Council or the Commission will take a liberal view towards those of these types which are considered as unavoidable in view of conditions of present day requirements of industrial research and its high costs for long-term investments and of operational expenditure.

On the vertical level, important instances are (a) agreements between enterprises (*e.g.*, manufacturers and distributors) by which the purchaser is bound to deal with the goods obtained by him in a certain manner only (*e.g.*, to sell them in a restricted territory, or to stock a certain minimum amount of his supplier's goods, or not to distribute third parties' similar goods) or to submit to tie-in clauses; (b) the appointment of a "sole distributor" or "sole importer" in one Member State by an enterprise in another Member State.[2]

(c) market-sharing or the sharing of sources of supply.

The main instances are the market-sharing cartels. Agreements to this effect often form part of other cartels or of vertical agreements, for instance patent licence agreements. Their prohibition would seem to be especially necessary in the Common Market as such cartels could stultify the (gradual) abolition of customs and trade frontiers which is one of the foremost aims of the E.E.C. As regards vertical restrictions, the European Court held in the *Bosch*[3] case that a contractual stipulation prohibiting the export of goods from one Member State to another may be a violation of Article 85.

---

[1] This definition is taken from s. 5 of the German Cartel Law.
[2] See on these types of restrictions Part II "Sole Distributorship Agreements," *infra*, pp. 91 ff.
[3] See *supra*, p. 3.

*(d) the application of unequal conditions to parties undertaking
equivalent engagements in commercial transactions, thereby placing them
at a competitive disadvantage.*

This is one of the few instances of the prohibition of discriminatory
measures in the Treaty, another being laid down in Article 7, where,
subject to other special provisions in the Treaty, every discrimination
on the ground of a person's or corporate body's nationality (not residence) is forbidden. However, in contrast to the European Coal and
Steel Community Treaty of 1952 (Article 4(b) and Article 60(1) (i)) the
Rome Treaty does not contain a general prohibition of discrimination.[1]
It follows, therefore, that this example, and (by way of conclusion)
also the general clause in Article 85, must in this connection be understood to apply only to agreements *etc.*, on the horizontal level, so that
in respect of the equivalent delivery of goods or provision of services
to their customers, individual enterprises may stipulate unequal terms
that fall short, possibly, of a demand for an exclusive dealing arrangement and, certainly, fall short of boycott-like practices. It would
seem to be expedient in this connection to refer to Article 86, paragraph
(2) (c) according to which such practices are illegal if adopted by a
market-dominating enterprise.

*(e) making the conclusion of a contract subject to the acceptance by the
other party to the contract of additional obligations which by their nature
or according to commercial practice have no connection with the subject of
such contract.*

An absolute prohibition of contractual tie-in clauses applies only to
cartels and not to individual enterprises (on the vertical level), except
again in the case of a market-dominating enterprise (Article 86 (2) (d)).
It would seem that, by virtue of these qualifying words, manufacturers,
for example, of machinery might legitimately insist on its assembly
and erection at the purchaser's factory, or the acceptance of specified
materials, when the proper use of the machinery is only secured by
such supply, or when, in general, the supplier's goodwill would otherwise seriously suffer. This qualification is at variance with American
judicial practice which is generally hostile to tie-ins.[2] Each case will

---

[1] For a rather wide interpretation of this provision see decision of the *Kammergericht
Berlin* of May 4, 1962, (1963) 2 C.M.L. Rep., pp. 336, 344; *WuW* 1963, p. 697 ("*Fensterglas* III").

[2] *Cf. Standard Oil Co. of California and Standard Stations, Inc. v. United States*, 337
U.S. 293 (1949); *United Shoe Machinery Corp. v. United States*, 258 U.S. 451 (1922) but
cf., in contrast, *United States v. Jerrold Electronics Corp.*, 187 F. Supp. 545 (E.D. Pa.

have to be decided on its special facts and a liberal interpretation by the European Court should not be taken for granted.

3. GRANTS OF EXEMPTION

Paragraph (3) of Article 85 reads as follows:

The provisions of paragraph 1 may, however, be declared inapplicable in the case of:

– *any agreement or category of agreement between enterprises,*

– *any decision or category of decision by associations of enterprises, and*

– *any concerted practice or category of concerted practice*

which helps to improve the production or distribution of goods or to promote technical or economic progress, whilst allowing consumers a fair share of the resulting profit and which does not:

(a) subject the enterprises in question to any restrictions which are not indispensable to the achievement of the above objectives;

(b) enable such enterprises to eliminate competition in respect of a substantial part of the goods concerned[1].

1960), affirmed *per curiam*, 365 U.S. 567 (1961). The German practice is not so stringent, *cf.* decision of the Cartel Office in a film distributors' case, Annual Report of the Activities of the Federal Cartel Office for the Year 1959, p. 42.

[1] As observed *supra*, p. 9, Art. 59*ter* of the French Decree of August 9, 1959, served as a model for Art. 85(3). It reads as follows:

"The provisions of Article 59*bis* shall not apply to any concerted action, convention or combine:

(1) arising out of the application of a legislative provision or regulation;

(2) whose promoters are able to prove that its effect is to improve and extend the market for their products or to ensure further economic progress by means of rationalisation and specialisation."

It will be noticed that these requirements for obtaining exemptions are less stringent than those in the Rome Treaty. It must be borne in mind that the emphasis in the French restrictive trade practices law lies heavily on the prevention of the manipulation of prices, whereas the scope of Arts. 85 ff. is wider. The administration of cartel law in France is entrusted to the criminal jurisdiction of the ordinary Courts (Art. 419 *Code pénal* as amended on December 3, 1926) and the Decree No. 45–1483 of June 30, 1945 as amended by Laws 53–704 of August 9, 1953 and 58–545 of June 24, 1958 and Law 65–628 of July 2, 1963. By Art. 59*quater* which was enacted by the Law of June 24, 1958, a *Commission Technique des Ententes*, which was re-styled *Commission des Ententes et des Positions Dominantes* by the Law of July 2, 1963, was set up. This Commission is not a judicial body but has only to examine individual cases on which it has to render opinions which may serve as a basis for criminal prosecutions. The Commission, which has been active since 1955, publishes its opinions in Annual Reports. (See on the practice of the Commission, Mathély, *loc. cit.*). The functions of the Commission were discussed in the case of *Etat Français v. Nicolas et Société Brandt* by the *Cour d'Appel d'Amiens* of May 9, 1963, (1963) 2 *C.M.L. Rep.*, pp. 239, 248.

Whereas one is able to venture to list the more usual agreements, decisions and concerted practices that may be be caught by paragraph (1) of Article 85, it is well-nigh impossible to give instances of transactions exempted under paragraph (3) with any degree of certainty. It must therefore suffice to try to elucidate the principles on the basis of which an application for exemption may with some confidence be submitted.

As regards the parties to the transactions, paragraph (3) – in contrast to paragraph (1) – also mentions classes (categories) of agreements, classes of decisions and classes of concerted practices (French: *catégories de*...; German: *Gruppen von*...). This enlargement of the type of (prohibited) transactions is apparently merely designed to enable the competent administrative and/or judicial organs of the Community to grant exemptions not only for individual transactions but also for whole classes of similar or comparable transactions where such exemptions could perhaps not otherwise be given.[1]

In regard to the transactions themselves, the prohibitions may be removed if the transactions contribute

(1) to the improvement of production; or
(2) to the improvement of the distribution of goods or services; or
(3) to the promotion of technical progress; or
(4) to the promotion of economic progress – provided, however, that they

(a) reserve to users an equitable share of the profit resulting therefrom and

(b) do not impose on the enterprises concerned any restrictions which are not necessary for the attainment of one (or more) of the above objectives, and

(c) will not enable such enterprises to eliminate competition in respect of a substantial proportion of the products concerned.

Having regard to these conditions, it is rather difficult to enumerate any types of agreements, *etc.*, which would thus pass the test of being unobjectionable.[2] Nevertheless, the standardisation cartels and ration-

---

[1] See Franceschelli in *Cartel and Monopoly*, Vol. 1, pp. 297, 303. It seems that the grant of "class exemptions" by the Commission requires an enabling Regulation by the Council of Ministers by virtue of Art. 87(2) (b), see Deringer, *op. cit.*, ns. 16–19 to Art. 85(3). A Regulation to that affect has quite recently been issued, see Preface.

[2] A valuable interpretation of the (affirmative) application of paragraph 3 of Art. 85 can be found in the decision of the German Cartel Office of February 1962 (*WuW* 1962, pp. 555, 568 ff.) in which a know-how licence agreement containing a prohibition of

alisation cartels mentioned above[1] may qualify for a grant of exemption, especially if such agreements do not lead to a price increase or even cause a price reduction. A reduction in price is the main instance of the equitable share of profits to be reserved to users, but it would seem not to be exclusively so since every other advantage, for instance better and more regular distribution or the better quality of the goods concerned should be sufficient. "Users" (in French: *utilisateurs*) in this connection are not the enterprises involved but the public at large, *i.e.*, consumers, though not necessarily the ultimate consumers since the accrual of an equitable share of the profits to intermediate manufacturers and/or distributors should be of equal significance. Requirements (b) and (c) above are intended to secure that any restrictions upheld when exemptions are granted are proportionate to the approved objective and, finally, that the exempted transaction does not lead to the creation of a monopoly or part-monopoly in respect of the goods concerned. Attention must also be drawn to Article 8 of Regulation No. 17, which limits the period for which such a grant of exemption shall be valid and also provides for its revocation or alteration in certain circumstances.

While no more precise analysis would seem to be possible at the present stage, one important issue might legitimately be considered in this discussion of the function of paragraph (3) of Article 85. Is it likely that the Commission and/or the European Court, when determining the validity or invalidity of a transaction under paragraph (1), and perhaps also when making a decision to issue a declaration under paragraph (3), will apply the principle of the "Rule of Reason" and, (on the other hand), the *"per se* doctrine"?[2] It has indeed been suggested that paragraphs 1 and 3 of Article 85 should be read together and thereby a result akin to the establishment of the Rule of Reason be achieved. It seems that this question can only be resolved by the European Court.[3]

It is well known that since the decision in the leading case of *Standard*

---

exports of machines to the Netherlands was held to be subject to Art. 85(1) but approved under paragraph 3 of this Article on the ground that the prerequisites of this paragraph were considered to have been met. As this decision was rendered before Art. 9 of Regulation No. 17 came into force, the (German) national Authority was competent to apply paragraph 3 (see *infra*, p. 23). It is expressly stated in the decision that the Directorate-General for Competition of the Commission of the E.E.C. had been consulted in this case (at p. 558).

[1] *Supra*, p. 16.
[2] See on these conceptions the discussion in the text below.
[3] See Kelleher in *Doing Business in the Common Market*, p. 146.

Oil Co. of New Jersey v. U.S.,[1] the United States Courts have interpreted the Sherman Act and subsequent antitrust legislation as being subject to the Rule of Reason, that is to say, the Acts were not held to have been violated by mere insignificant restraints on competition which have an undoubtedly minor effect on the market in all its relevant aspects.[2] Thus, this Rule applies to horizontal agreements if a restraint is merely ancillary or incidental to a legitimate business transaction, and to vertical agreements if the restraint is not wider than is necessary for the protection of the lawful interest of the covenantee, taking into consideration the effect both on the covenantor and on the public.[3]

The Rule of Reason, which is essentially one of evidence, is however not applicable if a transaction is subject to the *per se* doctrine, *i.e.*, the rule that certain transactions are always illegal if it is their immediate purpose "to restrain commerce." In practice, price-fixing and market-sharing transactions are generally treated as illegal *per se*, whereas in regard to "close-knit combinations" and in the important field of patent agreements there is still room for the application of the Rule of Reason.[4] It would appear that the very wide scope of Articles 85 (1) and 86, on the one hand, and the narrowness of the requirements for granting exemptions on the other call for the application of the Rule of Reason. The preferential treatment of the transactions listed in Article 4(2) of Regulation No. 17 is perhaps a pointer in this direction. As regards procedure, according to Article 9 of Regulation No. 17(1) only the Commission shall have power to declare Article 85 (1) inapplicable pursuant to Article 85(3). Thus, national Authorities and Courts have lost such competence as from March 13, 1962 when this Regulation came into force. The Commission's ruling is subject to revision by the European Court to which an aggrieved party may appeal.

---

[1] 221 U.S. 1 (1911).

[2] In contrast thereto, in modern English law the function of the Rule of Reason in cases of restraint of trade is different. If a restraint is considered reasonable as between the parties (and this is rather liberally accepted) it is generally difficult to establish that it is injurious to, and therefore unreasonable in, the interests of the public; see *Att.-General for Australia v. Adelaide Shipping Co. Ltd.* (1913) A.C. 781, 797.

[3] See P. D. Schapiro: "The German Law against Restraints of Competition – Comparative and International Aspects," 62 *Columbia Law Review* (1962), pp. 1, 13, 204.

[4] Whilst in the German Decartelisation Law the Rule of Reason was applied, it has not been accepted into the German Cartel Law since this Law is meant to have taken account of all the situations in which the stringent American antitrust law called for its mitigating effect (Baumbach-Hefermehl, *op. cit.*, Introduction, n. 12). As regards the Rules of Competition, this question is hotly discussed. See Honig a.o., *op. cit.*, pp. 15 f; *contra*, E. Wolf, *A.J.C.L.* (1962), pp. 539–559 who argues for the application of this Rule. Spengler in *Gemeinschaftskommentar*, p. 1448 favours the adoption of at least the narrower doctrine of ancillary restraint of trade as developed in United States antitrust law (see thereon Oppenheim, *op. cit.*, pp. 2–5).

4. THE SANCTION OF NULLITY

Article 85(2) reads as follows:

Any agreements or decisions prohibited pursuant to this Article shall be automatically null and void.

In spite of the simple wording of this provision, its interpretation and application bristle with difficulties.

(a) The sanction of nullity only applies to agreements or decisions. Thus, concerted practices are not covered; this would seem correct in legal logic since these are mere factual relationships and the sanction of nullity can only apply to a legal relationship, *i.e.*, one which is intended to create a binding obligation which the sanction destroys. The necessary absence of the sanction of nullity here does not, however, exclude other measures being taken and Article 87(2) (a) as implemented by Article 15(2) (a) of Regulation No. 17 authorises the Commission to impose fines for infringements of Article 85(1) and infringements include the carrying out of concerted practices.

(b) The nullity of a prohibited agreement or decision will as a rule be declared by the Commission and/or the European Court or, though now to a rather reduced extent, by the Cartel Authorities or Courts of the Member States. The declaration of nullity is not however limited to ex officio actions; a private party concerned, for example a member of a cartel or a party to a licence agreement, can plead the illegality of the agreement in question in a private law suit before a national Court. In this connection the problem may arise as to how far negative clearance certificates (Article 2 of Regulation No. 17) or the exemptions of certain prohibited transactions according to Articles 4(2) and 5(2) of Regulation No. 17 are binding on national Courts.

(c) Even before the issue of Regulation No. 17 the effect of paragraph (2) was by no means clear. There was no doubt that the sanction of paragraph (2) was closely bound up with paragraph (3). Did paragraph (2) make all transactions of the type described in paragraph (1) void *ab initio* until they were permitted in accordance with paragraph (3), *i.e.*, were they illegal until expressly permitted by the act of an Authority (formerly by a national cartel authority but now by the Commission only: Article 9 of Regulation No. 17); or were they legal if they complied with the requirements of paragraph (3) so that the decision of such Authority (or of a Court) had merely a declaratory effect? Furthermore, the question was raised whether a national Court, which had such an issue before it, would first have to request a

decision by a (then national) administrative office that was competent to give a ruling under paragraph (3). Regulation No. 17 has disposed of some of these problems, but has done so in a manner that has created new complications which became quite apparent through the decision of the European Court in the *Bosch* case.[1]

Briefly, the present position would seem to be as follows. In the first place, when reading Article 1 of Regulation No. 17, one might have thought that Articles 85 and 86 became immediately operative as from the date on which the Rome Treaty came into force, *i.e.*, January 1, 1958, subject only to the qualifying provisions of Articles 6 and 7 of the Regulation and the further proviso that exemptions granted under paragraph (3) by the competent national Authorities of Member States (by virtue of Article 88 of the Treaty) shall remain valid, but may become invalid if an exemption under Article 85(3) is not granted. Yet the effect of the Regulation, as interpreted by the European Court in the *Bosch* case, amounts, as far as "existing agreements" ("old agreements") are concerned, on the one hand to a limitation of the absolute effect of the sanction of nullity, and on the other hand to an automatic declaration of nullity if "existing agreements" have not been notified to the Commission within the prescribed time, even if they are eligible for a grant of exemption under Article 85(3). Thus, the so-called "existing agreements" were unqualifiedly valid until March 13, 1962 (when the Regulation came into force), because, as the Court pointed out, Article 85(1) could not be understood as being intended to invalidate such transactions, when (at least in several Member States) there was no possibility of having them validated in accordance with Article 85(3); however, if such a transaction had in fact been declared invalid by a competent Authority of a Member State,[2] or by the Commission itself,[3] it became and remained invalid. If "existing agreements" are notified before November 1, 1962[4] they become valid for the time being,[5] but will only become finally

---

[1] See *supra*, p. 3 n. 1.

[2] The German Cartel Office could have done this; see decisions of the Cartel Office of August 23, 1960 ("Terazzo" case), *WuW* 1960, p. 805, and of June 20, 1960, *ibid.*, p. 818; see, further, judgement of the District Court of Düsseldorf of December 6, 1960, *ibid.*, 1961, p. 566. (In the two decisions of the Cartel Office exemption under Article 85(3) was granted).

[3] The Commission had apparently given no such ruling but, for a recommendation by the Cartel Office to the Commission, see Annual Report of the Activities of the Federal Cartel Office for the Year 1960, p. 61.

[4] Art 5 of Regulation No. 17 as amended by Regulation No. 59 of July 3, 1962. The original date was August 1, 1962.

[5] In a decision of May 30, 1963 the Appeal Court of Munich (*WuW* 1963, p. 626) has held that this is also the case even if their violation of Art. 85(1) is to be presumed.

valid when the Commission approves them under Article 85(3); if due notification is omitted they become retrospectively invalid as from March 13, 1962. As regards the more favourably treated transactions set forth in Article 5(2) of the Regulation (which refers to Article 4(2) thereof), they would seem to be valid unless and until declared prohibited by the Commission, and then from the date of the declaration onwards.[1] In order to remain valid they must be notified by the end of 1966 (Article 7(2) of Regulation No. 17 as amended by Regulation No. 118).[2] However, in view of the language in the decision in the *Bosch* case, it is not clear whether their validity ends in case of non-notification *ex tunc* or retrospectively as from March 13, 1962.

In regard to "new agreements," *i.e.*, transactions which came into existence after March 13, 1962, they are invalid prior to notification, but become temporarily valid afterwards. They may become finally[3] valid when exemption is granted under Article 85(3); if exemption is refused, they are treated as invalid *ab initio*.

The privileged transactions (Article 4(2) of Regulation No. 17) are valid unless and until prohibited (under Article 85(1) of the Treaty).[4]

Lastly, Regulation No. 17 provides for the issue of negative clearance certificates (Article 2). While the national Authorities appear to be bound by them, it is by no means certain that national Courts have lost the right to examine whether transactions of the type listed in Article 85 are nevertheless caught by Article 2 and therefore prohibited unless exempted under Article 85(3). This uncertainty can presumably only be resolved by a decision of the European Court whose ruling would in this respect be binding on the Courts of the Member States.[5]

(d) If an agreement or decision is or becomes invalid under Article

---

[1] Gleiss-Hirsch (*AWD* 1962, pp. 121 ff.) submit that the reasoning of the Court in the *Bosch* case permits the conclusion that these transactions are finally valid. This interpretation would seem to be unwarranted as the exemption from notification ought not to affect the question of their substantive validity. On the other hand, Deringer in *GRUR (AIT)* 1962, at p. 287, takes the view that for these (privileged) agreements, *etc.*, the exemption can be granted with retrospective effect from a date prior to the date of notification which may be the date of their coming into existence (thus apparently denying that the Commission may declare them invalid only from the date of the declaration onwards as stated in the text above).

[2] Of November 5, 1963, *J.O.* 1963, p. 2696.

[3] *I.e.*, always subject to the provisions of Art. 8 of Regulation No. 17.

[4] Whether, and if so in what circumstances, national Authorities and Courts retain jurisdiction in respect of these transactions is a rather difficult problem which is outside the scope of this study; in any event, the scope of this jurisdiction would now be narrow.

[5] Such a decision would be rendered in the proceedings provided for in Art. 177 of the Treaty. Although a decision of the European Court would only be binding in the case submitted to the Court, its determination of a point of general importance would necessarily settle the same authoritatively.

85(2), the consequences of the invalidity are determined by the law of the country which governs the agreements or the decision (which need not necessarily be that of a Member State). Particular regard must be had to the relevant domestic laws on the question of the severability of the lawful parts of an agreement from its illegal parts;[1] the rules of frustration of contracts, in so far as they be applicable to the discharge of contracts by supervening illegality, and the express or implied obligation of the parties to apply for governmental validation of illegal agreements, even if such validation can only be obtained by an alteration of the terms of the agreement (see in this connection, Articles 7 and 8 of Regulation No. 17), will be relevant. Lastly, the domestic law will have to determine whether and how far third parties who have entered into contracts with an enterprise that is a party to a prohibited transaction are affected, and especially whether the invalidity of a prohibited agreement has the effect of releasing them from their contract and/or entitles them to damages.[2]

B. Article 86

1. THE GENERAL CLAUSE IN PARAGRAPH (1)

Any abusive exploitation by one or more enterprises of a dominant position on the Common Market or on a substantial part of it shall be deemed to be incompatible with the Common Market and shall be prohibited, in so far as trade between Member States could be affected by it.

(1) Like Article 85, Article 86 contains a general prohibition and the subsequent catalogue of examples is merely a guide for the interpretation and application of the general rule, though this enumeration would raise a presumption against the admissibility of an extension of the general rule to a new set of facts. Likewise, Article 86 is also addressed to, and is of immediate effect on, the enterprises in the Member States of the Community. As distinct, however, from the transactions covered by Article 85, the abuse of a dominant position cannot be made the subject-matter of a grant of exemption, except perhaps that if the principle of the operation of the Rule of Reason is adopted minor instances might not be deemed to be caught by Article 86; such would not be the case, of course, if the *per se* doctrine should prevail.

---

[1] For a view on the relevant position in English law, see Honig a.o., *op. cit.*, p .29.

[2] See the detailed study of this special problem by H. van den Heuvel, "Civil Law Consequences of Violation of the Antitrust Provisions of the Rome Treaty," in 12 *A.J.C.L.* (1963), pp. 172–193.

(2) It has to be emphasised that the prohibition is not only directed against monopolistic enterprises but also against the abuse of a dominant position by more than one enterprise, *i.e.*, so-called oligopolies. It is not clear whether there must be any legal relationship between such oligopolies or whether at least co-operation between them by parallel actions or price leadership has to be proved. If there is a legal relationship, or if the oligopolies have acted through concerted practices, Article 85 would also be applicable in so far as the provisions of Article 86 are not exhaustive for the suppression of practices condemned by either Article. It has to be borne in mind that Article 85 is directed against both horizontal and vertical agreements *etc.* as such, whereas Article 86 is designed to prevent the exploitation of the customers of enterprises holding a market-dominating position.

(3) The term "dominant position" is not defined. Assistance in its interpretation might perhaps be gained from Article 66(7) of the European Coal and Steel Community Treaty which is concerned with "enterprises which, in law or in fact, have or acquire on the market... a dominant position which protects them from effective competition in a substantial part of the Common Market." Section 22(1) of the German Cartel Law defines a market-dominating enterprise as one that has no competitor or is not exposed to any substantial competition in a certain type of goods or commercial services. Subsection 2 deals with the so-called oligopolies: "Two or more enterprises are considered as market-dominating as far as, in regard to a certain type of goods or commercial services, no substantial competition exists in fact between them in general or in specific markets, as far as they jointly meet the requirements of subsection (1)."[1] Enactments against abuses by market-dominating enterprises are also found in the Dutch Law on Economic Competition[2] and in the Belgian Law on the Abuse of a Position of Economic Power.[3] In France, market-dominating as such was not the object of legal regulation until Art. 59[bis] was amended by Law of July 2, 1963. The relevant subs. 4 of Article 59[bis] reads as follows: "The activities of an enterprise or group of enterprises holding

---

[1] According to Campbell, *op. cit.*, pp. 3 and 16 "it is understood that over 50% of the market of the goods in question in the area will be treated as a "dominant position"" but the source of this assertion is not mentioned, In the British White Paper on "*Monopolies, Mergers and Restrictive Practices*" (Cmnd. 2299), 1964 p. 4 a monopoly (in the case of mergers) is assumed to exist if there is "control of at least one third of the market."

[2] Art. 1 of the Law of June 28, 1956 as amended by the Law of July 16, 1958, *Staatsblad* 1956, No. 401; 1958 No. 412.

[3] Law of May 27, 1960, *Moniteur Belge*, 1960, p. 4674.

a dominant position on the domestic market which is characterised by
a monopoly situation or by a manifest concentration of economic
power, if such activities have the purpose of, or may result in, interference with the normal operation of the market, shall also be prohibited." In other words, one or more enterprises would appear to be
in a dominant position if it, or they, suffer virtually no competition
or no substantial competition for all or part of their products within
the relevant area with the consequence that such enterprise or enterprises can determine their sales policy, and particularly the fixing of
prices, without regard to competition. In practice, the extent of their
share in the market for the type of products concerned would be an
important factor for ascertaining whether one or more enterprises
occupied a dominant position. It is irrelevant whether an enterprise is
located and produces in one Member State only, if its dominance
prevails, even without foreign subsidiaries, in another Member State.
The market-dominating enterprises which are subject to Article 86
may, in principle, be either monopolies or oligopolies in fact or created
by law in the Member States; the latter are however specially dealt
with in Article 90(2) and their position will therefore be discussed in
connection with that Article.[1]

The prohibition laid down in Article 86 is an immediate one, *viz.*,
its operation and effect are not conditional upon a Regulation or Order
issued by the Commission or by a national Authority. These bodies
and the European Court would in a given case only determine whether
a situation had been created by which Article 86 has been violated.

(4) Article 86 prohibits the abuse of a dominant position "on the
Common Market or in any substantial part thereof." This is merely a
geographical demarcation. In spite of this limitation there is unanimity
that the exercise of dominant power must take place in a "relevant
market" in order to make this Article applicable.[2] This "relevant
market" is the delimitation in relation to both the geographical area
and the class of goods or services concerned. For it follows from the
very notion of a dominant position that this cannot be determined in
the abstract but must be ascertained in relation to certain goods sold
(or bought) within a certain area, and, frequently, also within a certain
time. As regards the territory, it is not the place of production but only
the area of sales which is material. Whether such dominance must

---

[1] See *infra*, pp. 47–50.
[2] See Honig a.o., *op. cit.*, p. 37. For a comprehensive review of the present discussion
of this topic, see Deringer, *op. cit.*, Art. 86, ns. 10–19.

prevail in the territory of more than one Member State, or whether it
is sufficient if it is restricted to one Member State or even part thereof
only, is a much debated point[1] which can ultimately only be decided
by the European Court. However, the effect of such a position of an
enterprise will probably have to be judged by reference to the whole
of the Common Market.

More difficult is the determination of the second element, *i.e.*, the
class of goods or services concerned. The German, Dutch and Belgian
interpretations differ considerably from that adopted by some French
lawyers. According to the former, which appear to have been strongly
influenced by judicial practice in the United States,[2] dominance in a
market is based on a conception of a market in a legal sense, *i.e.*, a
market situation existing at the moment the purchaser has made his
choice of the kind of goods which he wants to buy or the services he
wishes to be rendered to him, and is then faced with a variety of goods
belonging to the same category. These goods (or services) may be
"reasonably interchangeable by consumers for the same purposes"[3]
but such interchangeability will have to be a real and practical and
not merely a theoretical one. In order to test the possibility of interchangeability, American antitrust law has developed the principle of
"crosselasticity of demand," which is, in effect, the responsiveness of the
sales of one product to price changes of the other.[4] The relevant market
will then have to be more clearly ascertained from a variety of factors,
for instance the range of potential buyers or the nature of the goods,
especially whether they are saleable on special markets only or on the
general market. It appears however that some French writers refuse
to make the relevant market a determining factor for the existence of
a dominant position and would primarily see the test in the size of the
enterprise and not necessarily in its market behaviour with its economic effects.[5] As Article 86 does not give any indication of how the
concept of market-dominating enterprise is to be defined, the Commission and ultimately the European Court will have to undertake
this task.

(5) A position of monopoly or oligopoly as such is not sufficient for

[1] See Deringer, *op. cit.*, Art. 86, n. 12, and Spengler in *Gemeinschaftskommentar*, p. 1429.
[2] See Oppenheim, *op. cit.*, pp. 397 ff., 414 ff. See also note in 54 *Columbia Law Review* (1954), p. 580.
[3] *U.S. v. E.I. Dupont de Nemours & Co.*, 351 U.S. 377 (1956), at p. 395.
[4] *Ibid.*, at p. 400.
[5] See Spengler in *Gemeinschaftskommentar*, p. 1430 with references to French legal literature.

the application of Article 86 as there must be an exploitation by the abuse of such position. The test for this would be the imposition of unreasonable conditions, and particularly the charging of unjustifiably high prices, on the strength of the dominant position.

2. THE CATALOGUE OF EXAMPLES

The following practices may in particular constitute such abuse:

(a) the direct or indirect imposition of unfair buying or selling prices or of any other unfair trading conditions.

By contrast with Article 85(1) (a), the prices charged must be both unreasonable (*i.e.*, they must be out of proportion to the real economic value of the goods supplied or services rendered) and imposed (in the sense of dictated) on the customer; the same applies to other terms. The difference between these two Articles is, of course, due to the policy of the law which condemns (in Article 85) price-fixing terms agreed upon in horizontal or vertical agreements, *etc.*, whereas it is left to a market-dominating enterprise to determine the prices of its products or services or to stipulate trade conditions (unless they are, on the vertical level, prohibited under Article 85), provided that they are not unreasonable or unfair. Resale price maintenance may fall under this prohibition.

(b) the limitation of production, markets (distribution) or technical development to the disadvantage of consumers.

For similar reasons such practices are here only forbidden if they result in damage to consumers, because otherwise a manufacturer or distributor, as distinct from cartels, should remain free to decide his own business policy. This would also seem to be the ground on which control and limitation of investments, which are mentioned in Article 85(1) (b) are left out here. The determination of damage to consumers will doubtless be very difficult since it must be damage going beyond a detriment which results normally from such limitation and, probably, this effect must have been intentional.

(c) the application of unequal conditions to parties undertaking equivalent engagements in commercial transactions, thereby placing them at a competitive disadvantage.

The provision is identical with that in Article 85(1) (d). It is an instance of discrimination which is however only prohibited when brought about by abusive exploitation of a dominant position and must in itself be unjustified in the light of the circumstances of the relevant transaction.

(d) making the conclusion of a contract subject to the acceptance by the other party to the contract of additional obligations which by their nature or according to commercial practice have no connection with the subject of such contract.

The wording of this example is the same as that in Article 85(1) (e) and the observations thereon apply here too.

It will be noticed that the example in Article 85(1) (c) is left out since market-sharing or the sharing of sources of supplies presupposes an understanding between at least two enterprises. In the case of oligopolies Article 85(1) (c) could of course apply.

The infringement of Article 86 does not authorise the Commission or the European Court to take measures for the abolition of the dominant position of the enterprises concerned,[1] as the prohibition is directed only against the abuse of a monopoly or oligopoly. Pending the issue of another Regulation on the basis of Article 87(2) (a), the Commission can at present act only within the limits of the competence conferred upon it by Article 3 of Regulation No. 17. However, by virtue of Article 88, the authorities of the Member States have power to determine whether a violation of Article 86 has taken place. As the scope of co-operation between the organs of the E.E.C. and the Authorities of the Member States and the delimitation of their respective competences have not yet been officially clarified as far as Article 86 is concerned, it must suffice to state that, having regard to the immediate effect of Article 86, the only present practical consequence of this prohibition is the possible invalidity of the prohibited contracts which the dominant enterprise has concluded with its customers. Like those of Article 85(2), the consequences of this invalidity would be determined by the law of the country which governs the contract.[2]

---

[1] In the United States, the Courts have power to order the dissolution of an offending "close-knit combination" (usually a holding corporation); see *U.S. v. Dupont Nemours & Co.*, 188 Fed. 127 (C.C.D. Del.) (1911); *Standard Oil Company of New Jersey v. U.S.*, 221 U.S. 1 (1911); *U.S. v. American Tobacco Company*, 221 U.S. 106 (1911). *Cf.* also Neale, *op. cit.*, pp. 405 ff.

[2] Wohlfahrt a.o., *op. cit.*, n. 10 to Art. 86, p. 252, and Baumbach-Hefermehl, *op. cit.*, n. 6 to Art. 86, p. 1506 express the view that such contracts may be void under s. 134 of the German Civil Code which provides that legal transactions which violate a statutory provision are void. According to Plaissant-Lassier, *op. cit.*, p. 37 the position in French law is said to be similar. On the other hand, v. Gamm, *op. cit.*, pp. 39/40, infers from the absence of a sanction in Art. 86 corresponding to that of Art. 85(2) that

C. Articles 87, 88 and 89

ARTICLE 87

(1) Within three years of this Treaty coming into force, the Council shall issue the appropriate regulations or directives to put into effect the principles set out in Articles 85 and 86. The Council shall decide on these unanimously, on a proposal of the Commission and after consulting the Assembly.

If such regulations or directives have not been adopted within the specified period they shall be issued by the Council by qualified majority vote on a proposal of the Commission and after consulting the Assembly.

(2) The regulations or directives referred to in paragraph 1 shall be designed, in particular:

(a) to ensure, by the institution of fines or penalties, the observance of the prohibitions referred to in Article 85(1) and in Article 86;

(b) to decide exactly how Article 85(3) is to be applied, taking into account the need both one the one hand to ensure effective supervision and, on the other, as far as possible to simplify administrative control;

(c) to define. where necessary, the extent to which the provisions of Articles 85 and 86 are to be applied in the various economic sectors;

(d) to define the respective functions of the Commission and of the Court of Justice in giving effect to the provisions referred to in this paragraph;

(e) to determine how domestic legislation is to be reconciled with the provisions of this Article and with any Rules made thereunder.

ARTICLE 88

Until the regulations or directives issued in pursuance of Article 87 shall have come into force, the competent authorities in Member States shall determine to what extent they will permit agreements (decisions, concerted practices) or the abusive exploitation of a dominant position on the Common Market. The said competent authorities shall so determine in accordance with their domestic law and the provisions of Articles 85 (especially para. 3) and 86.

such contracts are not void in German law and that the protection of a customer could only be achieved by treating the carrying out of such a prohibited contract as a tort entitling the injured party to claim damages, (s. 823(2) of the German Civil Code). See also van den Heuvel, *ut supra*, p. 26. n2.

ARTICLE 89

(1) Without prejudice to the provisions of Article 88, the Commission shall, upon assuming its duties, see that the principles laid down in Articles 85 and 86 are put into effect. It shall, of its own volition or at the request of a Member State, investigate any alleged infringement of the principles mentioned above. It shall do so in co-operation with the competent authorities of the Member States, who shall give it their assistance. If it finds that such infringement has taken place, it shall propose appropriate measures for bringing it to an end.

(2) Should such infringement continue, the Commission shall, by means of a reasoned decision, confirm that such an infringement of the principles is taking place. The Commission may publish its decision and may authorise Member States to take the necessary measures, the conditions and details of which it shall determine, to remedy the situation.

1. GENERAL OBSERVATIONS

As this book is concerned only with the substantive law of the Rules of Competition in the Rome Treaty (matters pertaining to procedure having merely been referred to in so far as they are more or less closely connected with the substantive law), a comprehensive comment on Articles 87, 88 and 89 may be omitted since these Articles relate to the procedure for the application of the substantive law. Suffice it therefore to say that Article 87 deals with the enactment by the Council of Ministers of regulations and directives for enforcing Articles 85 and 86; that Article 88 contains arrangements for the transitional period[1] until

---

[1] Art. 88 has lost much of its relevance through the issue of Regulation No. 17. Nevertheless, the competence of the national Authorities and Courts has not been entirely abolished. Although only the Commission can now declare that paragraph (1) of Art. 85 shall not be applicable on account of the provisions of paragraph (3) of Art. 85, the national Authorities and Courts still remain competent to apply Arts. 85(1) and 86 as long as the Commission has not initiated any procedure pursuant to Arts. 2, 3 or 6 of Regulation No. 17 (Art. 9(3), *ibid.*). It appears, however, that this competence is severely restricted in that the national Authorities and Courts will, if they are seized with such a case, have to give the enterprises concerned the opportunity to ask the Commission to issue a declaration of the inapplicability of paragraph (1) of Art. 85. Consequently, the issue of a negative clearance certificate (Art. 2, *ibid.*) presupposes the initiation of a procedure according to Art. 9(3), and therefore binds the national Authorities, but it is doubtful whether such certificate also binds the national Courts (see Deringer, *WuW* 1962, pp. 81, 90, and Gleiss-Hirsch, *loc. cit.*, p. 126) On the other hand, Schlieder, *Betriebsberater*, 1952, p. 308, denies such binding effect on either national Authorities or Courts. It should be emphasised that the national laws against restraints of competition remain unaffected by Arts. 85 ff. and Regulation No. 17. Lastly, Regulation No. 17 (with amending Regulation No. 27 as amended by Regulation No. 153 of May 3, 1962, *J.O.* 1962, p. 2921) and Regulation No. 26 (as amended by

the organs of the Community take full charge of the application of the Rules of Competition by enjoining the Authorities of the Member States to administer them in conformity with their own law, *i.e.*, national laws against restraints of competition, while Article 89 confers upon the Commission rights of supervision and of the adoption of suitable measures for the enforcement of the Rules of Competition.

It would, however, seem appropriate in this context to refer to two aspects relating to the scope of the application of the Rules, namely

(1) as to the sectors of trade and commerce to which the Rules do not apply or apply only to a limited extent;

(2) as to whether enterprises incorporated, residing or principally carrying on business in non-Member States are subject to the jurisdiction of the organs of the Community if their activities infringe Articles 85 and 86 (and in practice the former especially).

Lastly, as already mentioned in the Preliminary Observations, a full appreciation of the operation of the Rules of Competition will be difficult without a basic knowledge of the concept and nature of what is called the supra-national law of the European Communites. Owing to the length of this subject it will be dealt with in a separate part.[1]

2. EXCEPTIONS TO RULES OF COMPETITION

The Rules of Competition apply to the entire field of industry, trade and commerce within the Common Market with the following exceptions:

(a) Under Article 232(1) of the Rome Treaty an exception is made in the case of such restraints of competition as are governed by the *European Coal and Steel Community Treaty* of 1952 (which contains special rules in Articles 60, 65 and 67)[2];

(b) Under Article 42 of the Rome Treaty, Articles 85 and 86 apply to *agricultural production and trade in agricultural products* only to the extent determined by the Council. By Regulation No. 26 of April 4,

---

Regulation No. 49 of June 29, 1962, *J.O.* 1962, p. 1571) implement only paragraph 2(a) and (b) of Art. 87, and (b) perhaps only partly.

[1] See *infra*, Part III, p. 133.

[2] Whether Arts. 85 ff. do apply to the economic sphere regulated by the E.C.S.C. Treaty in so far as the latter's special cartel law does not prevail or whether these two cartel law systems actually exclude each other's applicability altogether is not settled (see v. Gamm, *op. cii.*, pp. 17 f; *Gemeinschaftskommentar*, p. 1407).

1962,[1] the Council, *inter alia*, made Articles 85 and 86 applicable to this sector of the economy (Article 1 of the Regulation), with the proviso, however, that Article 85(1) shall not apply to agreements, *etc.*, of the kind listed in that Article, namely, agreements which form an essential part of a national market scheme or are necessary for the achievement of the objects set forth in Article 39 of the Treaty (laying down the aims of the agricultural policy of the E.E.C. and the methods of their pursuance). Consequently, Articles 85 and 86 do not, *prima facie*, apply to such agreements, *etc.*, entered into by agricultural producers or producers' organisations or associations of such producers' organisations in one Member State, if those agreements, without fixing prices, concern the production or the sale of agricultural products or the user of joint installations for the storage, treatment or working up of such products; nevertheless, it is always open to the Commission to determine that competition is excluded by such agreements or that the aims set out in Article 39 of the Treaty are endangered thereby (Article 2 of the Regulation). This part of Regulation 26 came into force on July 1, 1962 (Article 5).

(c) By Article 90(2) of the Treaty exemption from the Rules of Competition is granted to public undertakings, *i.e.*, mostly *public utility undertakings*, or private enterprises which have been entrusted with the performance of services of general economic interest or which have the character of a fiscal monopoly, in so far as the application of the provisions of the Treaty, and especially of the Rules of Competition, would in law or in fact prevent them from accomplishing their special task; otherwise they are subject to these Rules.[2]

(d) Whilst it had been for some time uncertain whether the Rules of Competition apply to the *common transport policy* as laid down in Articles 74 to 84 of the Treaty, Regulation No. 141 issued by the Council of Ministers on November 26, 1962[3] would seem to have confirmed (although this is not expressly stated) that rail, road and inland water traffic as well as sea and air transport are subject to the provisions of Articles 85ff.[4] By this Regulation Regulation No. 17 shall not apply to agreements *etc.* relating to traffic "which have the object

[1] See *infra*, Appendix E, p. 215.
[2] For a more detailed discussion of Article 90, see *infra*, p. 47–50.
[3] *J.O.*, 1962, p. 2751.
[4] This would seem to be the leading opinion (see Deringer, *op. cit.*, n. 31, 33 to Art. 87). The same view is taken by Gleiss-Hirsch, *AWD* 1963, pp. 34, 35 (it is therefore surprising that in *Cartel Law of the European Community*, 1963, p. 91, of which the same writers are co-authors, the opposite opinion is expressed). Spengler in *Gemeinschaftskommentar*, p. 1454 considers the issue as still undecided.

or effect of fixing the costs or terms of carriage or of dividing traffic markets, nor shall it apply to dominant positions in the traffic market within the meaning of Article 86 of the Treaty". Thus agreements *etc.* in restraint of trade outside this express provision of the Regulation (such as exclusive dealing agreements, tie-in clauses and patent licence stipulations), insofar as they are prohibited under Articles 85ff., remain subject to Regulation No. 17.[1] Incidentally, in so far as Regulation No. 17 has been declared inoperative, this also holds good, as a matter of course, for all such Regulations issued by the Commission for the purpose of carrying the former into effect (*e.g.*, Regulation No. 27). As regards procedure, it need only be mentioned that in consequence of Article 1 of Regulation No. 141 both the national Authorities and Courts remain competent to declare an agreement *etc.* prohibited by the Rules of Competition as invalid or to sanction it under paragraph 3 of Article 85.[2] The somewhat difficult problem whether the belated enactment of this Regulation has the effect of making all existing agreements in this sphere which were not notified to the Commission by October 31, 1962 invalid and reviving them automatically,[3] or whether they must be treated as merely temporarily invalid with retroactive confirmation of their validity *ab initio*,[4] and the consequences in private law flowing therefrom, will only be mentioned here.[5]

(e) The Rules of Competition do not apply to the production of and trade in *arms, ammunition and war material* within the limits set forth in Article 223 of the Treaty.

(f) Rather difficult to answer is the question of the extent to which Articles 85ff. apply to the banking and insurance business. There is no doubt that these branches of economy are within the purview of the Rules of Competition[6] but it seems to be the unanimous view that

---

[1] See Deringer, *op. cit.*, Art. 87 n. 331; Gleiss-Hirsch, *AWD* 1963, pp. 34, 35.

[2] By virtue of Art. 88 or Art. 89(2) respectively (which thus remain operative) and confirmed by the judgment of the European Court in the *Bosch* case, see *supra*, p. 3.

[3] As maintained by Deringer, *op. cit.*, n. 34 to Art. 87.

[4] As suggested by Gleiss-Hirsch, *AWD*, 1963, pp. 34–36.

[5] The provisional character of this Regulation appears from both the Preamble and Arts. 2 and 3. Whereas the exemption of rail, road and inland water traffic is limited until 1965 by which date the Council of Ministers shall have issued suitable provisions for the application of the Rules of Competition to rail, road and inland water traffic, no such legislation is at present intended in regard to air and sea traffic. It is understood that the Commission is working on a Regulation on rail, road and inland water traffic. Air and sea traffic remain unqualifiedly subject to the Rules of Competition. The special provision of Art. 90(2) has always to be taken into account. Both in German and United States antitrust law the sphere of transport belongs to the "exemption areas," but it is not entirely outside that law (see *Gemeinschaftskommentar*, p. 1172; Oppenheim, *op. cit.*, pp. 28 ff.).

[6] See *A Manual for Firms*, Parts I, VI, (Appendix E, *infra*, pp. 232, 236).

their application is only possible with substantial qualifications. The organs of the E.E.C. are faced with difficulties similar to those experienced by United States administrative authorities and Courts in respect of their so-called "regulated industries," *i.e.*, "regulatory agencies charged (by Congress) with certain duties of limited supervision of the economic activities of particular industries engaged in interstate commerce.[1] Some of the statutes administered by these agencies contain provisions analogous to the prohibitions of the antitrust laws but are sometimes more lenient than the Sherman Act or the Clayton Act. As regards Europe, both banking and insurance are in several Member States a business controlled (regulated) by the State. It appears that unless the Council of Ministers regulates these economic spheres by a Regulation issued under Article 87(a, c) or by granting "block exemptions" under Article 85(3), banking and insurance transactions which are within the reach of Article 85(1) can, as the law stands at present, only be validated under Article 90(2). It seems that the anxiety over the effect of Article 85 is greater in the insurance business than in banking circles, as "co-insurance contracts between insurers aiming at the acceptance of certain risks according to terms agreed beforehand which exceed the co-insurance of one definite risk" (if they affect trade between Member States), certain re-insurance contracts and insurance pools can fall within the ambit of Article 85.[2] Probably, as distinct from banking, the problems of the insurance business in regard to the Rules of Competition cannot be solved by reliance upon Article 90(2) except for such branches of insurance as are entrusted with public duties, for example compulsory third party liability insurance, so that legislative acts based on Article 87(2)(c) or "block exemptions" by virtue of Article 85(3) are being demanded.[3]

3. ENTERPRISES OUTSIDE THE COMMUNITY

The second question posed above was whether Articles 85 and 86

[1] See Oppenheim, *op. cit.*, pp. 29–45, 52/53. In the recent case of *Pan American Airways, Inc. v. United States*, 371 U.S. 296 (1963) the Supreme Court held that the Federal Aviation Act of 1958 impliedly repealed the antitrust laws partly and that s.411 of that Act, which condemns unfair methods of competition, prevailed.

[2] See Salomonson, next note.

[3] The reader who is interested in a fuller discussion of these problems is referred to *Gemeinschaftskommentar*, pp. 1446, 1271–1274, and with regard to insurance only, to "Insurance Law in Europe and the United States," *British Institute of International and Comparative Law, Special Publication* No. 4 (1964), with contributions on cartel law concerning insurance companies by F. Salomonson, M. Grossmann and Spencer L. Kimball.

apply to the activities of enterprises in non-Member States. In the special case of the United Kingdom it concerns enterprises situate there only if that country does not join the E.E.C., but if it does, the question still remains of considerable importance for the members of the British Commonwealth and therefore for their representatives in the United Kingdom who transact their European trade.

Neither the Rules of Competition nor any other provision in the Rome Treaty contain a conflict of laws rule relating to the application of Articles 85ff. to the transactions prohibited in those Articles.[1] Nevertheless, the absence of such an express rule must not lead to the assumption that the Rules of Competition are not applicable to such transactions entered into by enterprises of which one (or more) carry on business in a Member State and one (or more) in a non-Member State, or even between enterprises in non-Member States, since the wording of Articles 85(1) and 86 and their purpose make it imperative to include such transactions within the orbit of these Articles.[2] The test as to whether they apply is, if stated in general terms, fairly simple. It is neither the place where an agreement has been concluded nor where it is to be performed nor the place where a concerted action is started, since it is exclusively the effect within the territory of the Common Market which is relevant.[3] Conversely, any transaction of the nature listed in Article 85 which is agreed upon and/or carried out by enterprises situate within the Member States or by enterprises of which one (or more) are situate within and one (or more) situate outside is innocuous from the point of view of Community law if its effect, and this means its direct effect, only takes place outside the Common Market.[4] Whether consequential economic repercussions in the sphere

---

[1] This position is the same as in the restrictive trade practices laws of Belgium, France, Eire, Canada, Netherlands, Sweden, Switzerland, South Africa, United States of America, the European Coal and Steel Community and the European Free Trade Association. On the other hand, the pertinent laws of Norway, Austria, Denmark and the Federal Republic of Germany do contain such a rule. As regards the United Kingdom, s. 10(4), in conjunction with ss. 2, 3 and 4, of the Monopolies and Restrictive Practices (Inquiry and Control) Act, 1948 and s. 6(1) (with the proviso in s. 36(3) of the Restrictive Trade Practices Act, 1956), are provisions which amount to such a (limited) conflict of laws rule (see Schwartz, *Cartel and Monopoly*, Vol. II, pp. 707, 711–712).

[2] See *Cartel and Monopoly*, Vol. II, Schwartz, pp. 707–708 and Hug, pp. 652–653.

[3] See *Gemeinschaftskommentar*, p. 1415; Schwartz, *op. cit.*, p. 3 (with further literature) and *passim*.

[4] Thus, the German Federal Cartel Office by an Order of June 28, 1961 (*WuW* 1961, p. 737) approved an export cartel concluded between a number of German enterprises by which these stipulated minimum prices for half-finished goods for export to foreign markets with the exception of the other E.E.C. Member States (and some other countries).

of competition resulting therefrom within the Common Market, for example exclusion of non-members of an export cartel from export facilities, are also caught by Article 85 is an open question which cannot be answered before the Commission and ultimately the European Court have had an opportunity to give a ruling on this point.[1][2]

When discussing this question further one has to keep in mind the legal nature of the Rules of Competition. It is characteristic of the law against restrictive trade practices that it is, especially under the jurisdictional aspect, a combination of administrative law (as understood in Continental law), private law and, if it contains penal sanctions (which is usually the case, although not so in the United Kingdom) criminal law.[3] Consequently, transactions by enterprises in non-Member States are subject to these different legal aspects. Thus, in the sphere of private law, no party to any such transactions can rely on a proscribed transaction before a Court of a Member State or *vis-à-vis* an Authority of a Member State; whether a third party may do so will depend on the particular circumstances of the case, whereby it must be borne in mind that rights of innocent third parties may have to be protected. In a non-Member State, the legality or illegality of such a transaction will be determined in accordance with its private international law, whereby a distinction might be made according to whether the transaction (usually an agreement) is governed by its own law, by the law of another non-Member State or by that of a Member State. In the first two cases, the Court of the non-Member State will have to consider, on the basis of its own domestic law, whether the agreement is intended to contravene Community law[4] or whether the

---

[1] This important problem is still not settled in Germany (see *Gemeinschaftskommentar*, p. 1167, 1169, 1170), whereas under United States antitrust law such consequences are treated as affecting United States trade (see Fugate, *op. cit.*, p. 114, esp. pp. 118, 119), except where the Webb-Pomerene (Export Trade) Act, 1918 sanctions combinations for the purpose of engaging in export trade (see Fugate, *op. cit.*, pp. 162 ff., and at p. 182 for the limits of the scope of transactions permitted by that Act).

[2] The significance of this principle for patent licence agreements and exclusive dealings agreements is discussed in the two chapters on this type of transactions, see *infra* Part II, pp. 83–84.

[3] The "criminal" law may be the classical criminal law as in the United States or a quasi-criminal law as in the German Cartel Law, where the violation of its provisions is punished, not as a crime in the traditional sense, but as a so-called administrative offence, in the meaning of the Law on Contraventions against Good Order of 1952, to which no stigma, such as is normally incurred by punishment for criminal offences proper, is attached. Similarly, Art. 15(4) of Regulation No. 17 states that the fines (Fr. *amendes*) which the Commission may impose by virtue of Art. 87 of the Treaty and Art. 15 of Regulation No. 17 have no such penal character. The "penalties" (Fr. *astreints*) in Art. 16 of Regulation No. 17 are mere administrative measures without any criminal or quasi-criminal connotation.

[4] It should be emphasised that the Rome Treaty forms part of the municipal law

choice of the law of a non-Member State would exclude the taking into account of Community law. But even if the governing law is that of a Member State, the Court of a non-Member State might disregard the Community's Rules of Competition on the ground that they belong to the province of administrative and therefore public law and are not designed to protect private interests of individuals as distinct from the furtherance of the Community's economic policy.[1]

The legal positions in regard to administrative and criminal law are preferably discussed together as their determination belongs primarily to the sphere of public international law. Whereas the existence or application of the Rules of Competition may produce automatic consequences in the sphere of private law (*e.g.*, a party's reliance on the invalidity of a prohibited agreement in a private law suit), any effects of administrative acts of the Commission (or national Authorities) including imposition of fines or penalties (by the Commission or the European Court) can only be brought about by an explicit order issued by these organs. The question therefore arises whether and, if so, how far these organs are permitted to exercise their powers against non-Member State enterprises. While the Commission or the European Court may wish to justify such jurisdiction on the basis of the Treaty, its validity is determined by public international law, of which the so-called international criminal law, which is here in point, forms only a part.

It is to be expected that when the administration of the Rules of Competition is in full swing the question as to their extra-territorial effect on non-Member State enterprises will become a serious problem. Again, one has first to look to judicial practice in the United States to find guidance on possible developments in this direction in the Common Market.

Based on the Sherman Act of 1890,[2] which is generally held to have

---

of the Member States and that the decisions of its organs, including the European Court, are to be treated as such in the respective Member States. As regards the United Kingdom, the decision of the House of Lords in *Regazzoni v. K.C. Sethia (1944) Limited*, (1957) 3 All. E.R., p. 286, might be in point.

[1] According to Hug, *loc. cit.*, pp. 669–670, Swiss Courts would neither pay regard to the intention of the parties, apparently even if one or both belong to Member States, to act in contravention of Community law nor to the actual violation of that law; similarly, they would not recognise a judgment of a Court of a Member State by which a foreign law against restraint of competition is sought to be enforced.

[2] The relevant s. 1 of this Act (26 Stat. 209 (189)) reads as follows: "Every contract, combination in the form of trust or otherwise, or conspiracy, in restraints of trade or commerce among the several states, or with foreign nations, is hereby declared illegal... Every person who shall make any contract or engage in any combination or conspiracy hereby declared illegal shall be deemed guilty of a misdemeanor, and, on conviction

been enacted within the power conferred on Congress by the Constitution "to regulate Commerce with foreign Nations...,"[1] the American Courts have gone to considerable lengths in extending the antitrust provisions to foreign enterprises. Lack of space permits merely a bare reference to some of the more important cases[2] and a short discussion of two, admittedly rather extreme, cases, namely, the often quoted decision handed down by Judge Learned Hand in *U.S. v. The Aluminum Company of America*[3] and that in *U.S. v. Imperial Chemical Industries Limited*.[4]

It has been rightly observed[5] that the lower courts have gone much further than the Supreme Court in the extension of United States jurisdiction to foreign companies but it would seem that the relevant ruling in the *Aluminum* case has become the established principle of United States extension of extra-territorial jurisdiction.[6]

thereof, shall be punished by fine not exceeding fifty thousand dollars, or by imprisonment not exceeding one year, or by both said punishments, in the discretion of the court."

[1] Article 1, section 8, clause 3.

[2] *American Banana Co. v. United Fruit Co.*, 213 U.S. 347 (1909); *U.S. v. American Tobacco Co.*, 221 U.S. 106 (1911); *U.S. v. Pacific and Arctic Railway and Navigation Co.*, 228 U.S. 87 (1913); *Thomson v. Cayser*, 243 U.S. 66 (1917); *U.S. v. Sisal Sales Corp.*, 279 U.S. 268 (1927); *Steele v. Bulova Watch Co.*, 344 U.S. 280 (1952); *Timken Roller Bearing Co. v. U.S.*, 341 U.S. 593 (1951); and the following cases decided by lower courts: *U.S. v. National Lead Co.*, 63 F. Supp. 513 (S.D.N.Y. 1945), affirmed 332 U.S. 319 (1947); *U.S. v. Minnesota Mining and Manufacturing Co.*, 92 F. Supp. 947 (D. Mass. 1950); *United States v. The Watchmakers of Switzerland Information Center*, 133 F. Supp. 40, D.C.S.D. N.Y. (1955); *U.S. v. Holophane C. Inc.*, 119 F. Supp. 114 (S.D. Ohio, 1954), affirmed 352 U.S. 903 (1956). In all these cases American citizens or companies were held to have violated American antitrust law by activities outside the United States, in several cases by co-operation with foreign companies, or foreign companies to have committed the infringement by carrying on business in the United States.

[3] 148 F. 2d. 416 (2d. Cir. 1945), 91 F. Supp. 333 (S.D.N.Y. 1950).

[4] 100 F. Supp. 504 (S.D.N.Y. 1951); F. Supp. 215 (1952). In these two cases foreign companies which did not carry on business in the United States (at least not in the generally accepted sense) were made parties to the proceedings. Another case belonging to that category is *U.S. v. General Electric Co.*, 82 F. Supp. 753 (D.N.J. 1949), involving the Dutch Philips Corporation.

[5] By H. Smit, "International Aspects of American and Netherlands Antitrust Legislation," 5 *Nederlands Tijdschrift voor Internationaal Recht* (1958), p. 274. This article and that of Prof. J. H. W. Verzijl, "The Controversy regarding the so-called Extra-territorial Effect of the American Anti-Trust Laws," *ibid.*, 8 (1961), p. 3, present an excellent survey of the American practice, combined with a critical examination of this practice in the light of public international law. For American sources, see Brewster, *op. cit.*, and the recent survey by Kirkpatrick, "U.S. Antitrust Law and its Relations to American Firms Doing Business within the E.E.C." in *Doing Business in the Common Market*, p. 152. For a critical discussion see George W. Haight, "The Sherman Act, Foreign Operations and International Law" in *Legal Problems in International Trade and Investment*, New York, 1962 and, under political aspects, Thomas E. Dewey, Antitrust Barriers to Foreign Policy Goals, 33 *New York State Bar Journal* (1961), p. 21.

[6] See the review of post-World War II cases in the lecture by Kirkpatrick, *supra* previous note, at pp. 164 ff. He suggests that even activities of non-American enterprises outside the United States foreign trade can be made subject to that country's antitrust law (at pp. 157 f.).

In the *Aluminum* case the United States Government had commenced criminal antitrust proceedings against both American and foreign companies (the Canadian Aluminum Ltd. being, however, a subsidiary of the American Aluminum Co.) in respect of an alleged conspiracy in restraint of interstate and foreign commerce. It asked for an injunction against the American Company ordering it to leave the European cartel and for an order of divestiture of its foreign holdings. The issue relevant to our discussion is whether the Sherman Act did apply to a conspiracy between foreign enterprises only (*i.e.*, to which no American company was a party) entered into and executed outside the United States so that the Court could give an order to a foreign company, the Canadian Aluminum Limited, to leave the European cartel. Judge Learned Hand, made, *inter alia*, such an order on the assumption that the offending agreements amounting to a conspiracy "were extended to affect imports into the United States and did affect them." He held that "any State may impose liabilities even upon persons not within its allegiance for conduct outside its borders that has consequences within its borders which the State reprehends." It has to be noted that the Judge emphasised that such power should only be exercised in respect of such foreign agreements as are intended to affect foreign commerce, *i.e.*, export and import, and do affect it, but not otherwise. Subject to this qualification he thought that his ruling complied with international law.

The second case, *United States v. Imperial Chemical Industries Ltd.*, concerned agreements between I.C.I. and the Du Pont Company in America, providing, *inter alia*, for world wide market-sharing of their products through grants of patent licences by Du Pont to I.C.I. The Court found a violation of the Sherman Act and directed I.C.I. "to refrain from asserting rights which it may have in Britain, since the enforcement of those rights will serve to continue the effects of wrongful acts it has committed with the United States affecting the foreign trade of the United States." In other words, it ordered I.C.I. to grant immunity, subject to charges of reasonable royalties, to any American manufacturer who had made goods under I.C.I.'s United States patents. However, in view of the questionability of such an order under international law, the New York Court expressed the hope that the British patent authorities and courts would recognise its order as a matter of comity between nations although they need not do it under positive international law.

As to the jurisdictional aspect, in contrast with the *Aluminum* case, the Court assumed jurisdiction in personam on the ground that Imperial Chemical Industries had a subsidiary company in New York by which it was operating itself.[1] In the subsequent well-known English case of *British Nylon Spinners v. Imperial Chemical Industries*[2] in which B.N.S. as licencees of I.C.I. resisted the re-assignment of the (Dupont) patents assigned to them by I.C.I. the Court of Appeal politely but bluntly refused to implement the American Court's order.[3]

Two special questions in the sphere of antitrust law relating to American business activities abroad are not only of considerable importance to American traders but may in due course also become the concern of enterprises in the Common Market. They are, firstly, the relevance of foreign law (*i.e.*, non-United States law and non-Common Market Member States law respectively) for the application of antitrust law and, secondly, what has been aptly described as "activities required by foreign trade 'realities'")[4]. Both situations have been judicially determined in the U.S.A. As regards the first one, the Supreme Court held in *United States v. Sisal Sales Corp.*[5] (distinguishing and in fact overruling *American Banana Co. v. United Fruit Co.*)[6] that reliance on foreign (Mexican) law of a discriminatory character enacted in favour of the defendant company could not be pleaded in defence to a prosecution for violation of antitrust law. In the later *Watchmakers'* case,[7] decided by a lower Court, a like defence based on the act-of-State doctrine was rejected, subject to the qualification that if "the defendants' activities had been required by Swiss law, this Court could indeed do nothing." Where, however, a party concludes an agreement which, though governed and valid by foreign law, violated American antitrust law or where there is no "direct foreign governmental action compelling the defendants' activities unless due to a defendant's own

---

[1] As had been said in the earlier case of *U.S. v. United States Alkali Transport Association*, CCH Trade Reg. Rep. (1946 Trade Cases) par. 57, 481 (S.D.N.Y. 1946): "I.C.I. (New York) is the *alter ego* of I.C.I. (London) for which it exists and acts. Formally, the two are separate legal entities but actually they are one in all that pertains to the activities of I.C.I. (London) in alkali business in the United States."

[2] (1952) 2 All. E.R. 780 (C.A.).

[3] In the "strange case" of *Cattermole v. Borax & Chemicals Ltd.*, (1946) 31 Report of Tax Cases 202, a fine (legally voluntarily but economically unavoidably) paid by an English subsidiary of an American company indicted for violation of the Sherman Act on the compromising of the antitrust proceedings with the U.S. authorities was not allowed as a deductible trade expense.

[4] By Kirkpatrick, see *supra* p. 41 n. 5, at pp. 160 f.

[5] 279 U.S. 268 (1927).

[6] 213 U.S. 347 (1909).

[7] *United States v. The Watchmakers of Switzerland Information Center Inc.*, (1963) Trade Cases 70, 600, F. Supp. S.D.N.Y. (1962).

machinations", foreign law cannot successfully be pleaded.[1] In respect of "activities required by foreign trade 'realities'," with which American firms trading abroad consider it necessary to conform in order to remain in business there, United States Courts have hitherto shown little sympathy to lessen the strict application of antitrust law[2] (unless, of course, they fall within the reach of the Robinson-Patman Act of 1936).[3] Whether such a situation would today give rise to a more liberal interpretation in the light of the Rule of Reason is an open question.

This part of American antitrust law requires comment in several respects. In the first place, in regard to private international law, the issue which usually falls to be determined in conflict of laws cases, as to which law governs the contract and whether it is legal or illegal thereunder, is entirely immaterial in antitrust law, as this is treated as a matter of public policy;[4] American courts seem not even to have discussed this question.[5] Secondly, and more important from the point of view of public international law, the assumption of this far-reaching jurisdiction by the United States courts has led to an extensive discussion as to whether these judgments and the efforts of United States Government officials to obtain information in foreign countries in connection with antitrust proceedings, are admissible in international law or constitute an international delict. We must limit our observations thereon to a few short remarks. As long as the United States confined itself to taking action against its own nationals when taking part in a prohibited transaction entered into and executed abroad but with disadvantageous effect on the American market, it had internationally valid jurisdiction on account of the "active nationality principle." Similarly, if foreigners are parties to unlawful agreements concluded and/or actively carried out in the United States, they can be punished there in accordance with international law. But what is the position if foreign nationals (including corporations) which are not resident (or incorporated) in the United States commit what, under American antitrust law, is termed a conspiracy outside the United States, and implement such co-operation with the intended conse-

---

[1] For a similar ruling see the recent decision by the Supreme Court in *Continental Ore Co. v. Union Carbide and Carbon Corp.*, 370 U.S. 690 (1962).

[2] See *United States v. Minnesota Mining and Manufacturing Company*, 92F. Supp. 947 D. Mass (1950); *United States v. The Watchmakers of Switzerland Information Center, Inc., ut supra*, p. 43 n. 7.

[3] 49 Stat. 1526.

[4] See Rabel, *The Conflict of Laws*, Vol. 2 (1947), p. 300.

[5] This is not only due to the fact that most of the antitrust suits are in the nature of criminal prosecutions; in cases of civil antitrust proceedings also it is without importance whether the offensive agreement is legal under its "proper law of the contract."

quence that the American market is affected thereby in so far as, say, the import of certain goods into or the export thereof from the United States is prevented or reduced? Under positive public international law the American authorities and Courts could only justify measures in the field of criminal law if the so-called "principle of protection" (of the State affected) applied, but it is generally held that this principle only prevails in cases where the social existence or the security of the State claiming jurisdiction is thereby endangered, or if the acts concerned are connected with common crimes committed or attempted to be committed in that State. In spite of the opinion expressed in United States Court decisions, and supported by American legal literature, it can hardly be said that such transactions fall within any of the aforementioned categories. However, it does not necessarily follow from this that the relevant American Court decisions, and the administrative practice in obtaining information in other countries in connection with such transactions, constitute a violation of international law. Such would merely be committed if the decisions or administrative acts were carried out in disregard of the territorial sovereignty of another State, *i.e.*, by attempts to enforce the orders of the Courts or the administrative measures in another State without its consent; or if the persons or corporations against which prosecutions have been carried through were punished, *i.e.*, in the case of individuals on a visit in the United States, or if their goods, after lawful importation into the United States, were confiscated, or, in the case of maritime trade, if their ships were seized. It is submitted that it might also be a violation of international law if the United States were to achieve or try to achieve the enforcement of such Court decisions or administrative orders by directly or indirectly compelling the officers or managers, be they United States citizens or aliens, of United States subsidiary companies in other States to comply with them, for example, by handing over documents or by breaking agreements valid under the law of the subsidiary's country of incorporation or prevailing at its seat or place of management or in the country where the agreements are to be performed.

While this United States legal practice has become quite firm and consistent, there would seem to be no corresponding experience in the judicial practice or administration of any other national law against restrictive trade practices. In the German Cartel Law, section 98(2) provides that the statute shall apply to all restraints of competition which become effective in the area in which it is in force, even if these restraints of competition result from acts done outside such area. A literal interpretation of this section might enable German Cartel Authorities and Courts to accept the American practice but so far there are no precedents from which the scope of its application can be gathered, especially in regard to imposing fines (by virtue of section 38) on foreign enterprises or taking administrative measures against them.[1]

German legal writers seem inclined to construe this section rather widely but stop short of applying it to foreign enterprises which do not transact business within Germany itself.[2] However, it is common ground that the fact that the agreement in question is subject to non-German law, either by the choice of the parties or by the ordinary conflict of laws rules, does not take it out of the application of the German Cartel law.[3] This view is identical with the American exclusive application of United States antitrust law to agreements that are as such not subject to any law prevailing in the United States.

The last enquiry to be undertaken in this section is a particularly difficult and controversial one and, at that, may one day become an important issue. Are transactions of the kind prohibited under Article 86 caught by this Article if they emanate from an enterprise (or more than merely one) that possesses neither the "nationality" of one of the Member States nor has its seat or centre of control and management within the Common Market? That enterprises of this character which have branches or subsidiaries within the Common Market are in principle within the orbit of the Rules of Competition can hardly be doubted if the parent enterprise exploits thereby its market-dominating position contrary to that Article. Yet is an outside enterprise which has no such representation nevertheless to be treated similarly? One important opinion[4] denies this, chiefly on the basis of the construction of the wording of Article 86(1) which speaks of "a dominant position *on* (Fr. *sur*; G. *auf*; It. *sul*; D. *op*) the Common Market" which is understood to demand a "territorial relation of such intensity that mere radiations from a position of power rooted outside this Market

---

[1] For a case in point, see p. 24 n. 3 *supra*, where the Cartel Office found that an agreement between a Dutch and German enterprise violated s. 1 of the Cartel Law and Art. 85(1) of the Treaty but confined itself to requesting the Commission to take action against the Dutch enterprise.

[2] See *Gemeinschaftskommentar*, p. 1171 and Schwartz, *op. cit.*, pp. 164–241.

[3] Schwartz, *op. cit.*, pp. 205–210; *Gemeinschaftskommentar*, pp. 1170/71; Baumbach-Hefermehl, *op. cit.*, p. 1216.

[4] Expressed by Spengler in *WuW* 1961, p. 509, 514, and in *Gemeinschaftskommentar*, p. 1429, n. 44.

can certainly not be sufficient." But most writers are agreed that if it is the effect within the Common Market which is the decisive element[1] so that enterprises whose seat and/or centre of control and management is outside that area can still acquire a dominant position on the Common Market with the consequential subjection to Article 86. It would seem that nothing can be gained from the aforementioned construction of the (inconclusive) text of Article 86, but whether the extension of Article 86 to outside enterprises can be justified on the same ground and to a similar extent as the far-reaching application of Article 85 is in reality a matter of legal policy ultimately to be determined by the European Court.

As regards the probable practice of the E.E.C. Commission and the European Court, nothing can be said at present with any degree of certainty. However, in view of the great importance which the Administration of the Community attaches to the Rules of Competition on the ground that the highest possible degree of free competition is a necessity for the creation and proper functioning of a Common Market, the possibility cannot be excluded that these organs will, after an initial period of grace, go to great lengths of preventing any harm to the Common Market, even if this is caused by outsiders, and that they might, at least to some extent, adopt American judicial practice.

D. Article 90

(1) In the case of public undertakings and enterprises to which they grant special or exclusive rights, Member States shall neither introduce nor maintain in force any measure contrary to the Rules contained in this Treaty, in particular to those Rules provided for in Article 7 and Articles 85 to 94 inclusive.

(2) Any undertaking entrusted with the management of services of general economic interest or having the character of a fiscal monopoly shall be subject to the Rules contained in this Treaty, in particular to the Rules of Competition, in so far as the application of such Rules does not obstruct the de jure *or* de facto *fulfilment of the specific tasks entrusted to such undertaking. The development of trade shall not be affected to such an extent as would be contrary to the interests of the Community.*

---

[1] Gleiss-Hirsch, *op. cit.*, p. 84 (n.1); Deringer, *op. cit.*, Art. 86 n. 13, footnote 6; to the same effect the Swiss writer Hug in *Cartels and Monopoly*, 1961, Vol. II, p. 639, esp. pp. 652 ff.; French experts on this branch of law, Plaisant-Laissier, *op. cit.*, p. 27, are undecided.

(3) The Commission shall see that effect is given to the provisions of this Article and shall, where necessary, issue appropriate directives or decisions to the Member States.

The modern State participates in the economic activities of the Community to a large and ever growing degree. Such participation consists not only of legislative and administrative measures regulating trade and commerce for the purpose of preventing criminal or otherwise undesired abuses by individuals or enterprises or of safeguarding the interests of economically weaker groups, but also of direct participation in economic life through enterprises of its own. These may be trading or non-trading corporations financially entirely in the hands of the State[1] (including a municipal authority, *e.g.*, a town), or corporations which belong partly to the State and partly to private individuals, or privately owned enterprises which the State has entrusted with the performance of public services, conferring upon them for the proper and efficient discharge of their duties the right of exercising public executive functions.[2] Having regard to the variety of these enterprises and their great importance for the national economy, they were to some extent accorded special treatment under the Rules of Competition. Whereas the provisions of Articles 85 and 86 are addressed only to the enterprises concerned, paragraph 1 of Article 90 is directed to Member States, but this does not mean that the public undertakings and enterprises mentioned therein are exempted from being subject to Articles 85 and 86.[3] On the contrary, Article 90(1) imposes an additional duty by enjoining Member States, on account of their being in control of these undertakings, not to take or maintain any measures that might be in conflict with the rules of competition. This general rule is qualified in certain circumstances as laid down in paragraph 2 of Article 90 which will be dealt with below.

As public undertakings are not, in regard to restraint of competition, treated differently from private enterprises, no detailed dis-

---

[1] The State in this context is not only the State proper as represented by the central government, but also by inferior public bodies like the component members of a federal State or municipal authorities.

[2] This last-mentioned class plays a considerable role in France and Germany (Fr. *établissements privés de service public*; G. *Beliehene Unternehmen*). Examples are: concessions granted to private railway companies for public service, public authority conferred on private utility companies supplying water, gas or electricity to the public at large; a recent instance is the functions exercised by private banks in the administration of exchange control (both in Germany and in the United Kingdom) by delegation of the Government (*Halsbury's Laws of England*, 3rd ed., Vol. 27, pp. 114–115).

[3] See Wohlfarth a.o., *op. cit.*, p. 264, and v. Gamm, *op. cit.*, pp. 42, 44.

cussion of the categories of enterprises which bear the character of those mentioned in paragraph 1 of Article 90 would seem to be called for. It should be sufficient to note that enterprises do not belong to that class merely because they are financially controlled, partly or even entirely, by the State. Yet if they are public undertakings in the sense that they are constituted in a form known to private (company) law but are owned by the State and exercise functions for the benefit of the public at large and therefore belong to the sphere of public law,[1] they fall into the category of public undertakings set out in Article 90.[2] However, this is not the case if a public authority acts exclusively as such (*e.g.*, a municipality in the discharge of its proper functions of local government).

The private enterprises which the States has entrusted with the performance of public services have just been mentioned. It is only these which would appear to be meant by the second class of undertakings in Article 90(1) and not enterprises carrying on a trade for the exercise of which a special concession or permission is required (*e.g.*, pharmacies, banks, insurance companies).

The limitation in paragraph 2 of Article 90 applies only to those public undertakings and private enterprises entrusted with the performance of public services which are charged with the rendering of services of general economic interest or have the character of a fiscal monopoly. The task of rendering such services must have been conferred by a legislative or administrative act, so that mere private corporations, albeit their services may be of no less advantageous economic importance, cannot rely on this provision. Probably the main instances of a type of undertaking which can rely on this limitation are the public utility undertakings (water, gas, electricity). The enterprises that bear the character of a fiscal monopoly can belong to either of these types. A fiscal monopoly is created by the State by virtue of its prerogative *(iura regalia)* to assume a monopoly in regard to a certain trade or to grant a concession to an enterprise; examples of this in Germany are the State monopolies in respect of spirits and matches, in France the State monopolies in regard to tobacco, matches, paper for newspapers, crude oil, potash, explosives and in Italy in

---

[1] The distinction between private law and public law is common to all continental legal systems, going back to Roman law: "*Publicum ius est, quod ad statum rei Romanae spectat, privatum quod ad singulorum utilitatem pertinet,*" Inst. I, 1, 4.

[2] The equivalent enterprises in Great Britain are certain public authorities and so-called national corporations, see *Halsbury's Laws of England*, 3rd ed., Vol. 30, pp. 682, 683, and Vol. 9, p. 6.

regard to matches, tobacco, cigarette paper, quinine, salt and flint lighters.[1] It should be observed that all the provisions of the Treaty and not merely the Rules of Competition apply to these special undertakings only to a limited extent, namely in so far as the performance of their task is not impeded thereby; but this exceptional treatment must not unduly and disadvantageously affect trade within the Community. Article 90(2) is addressed to the undertakings concerned as well as to the Member States. It follows therefore that an undertaking in this category can rely on this statutory exemption and need not apply for a declaration under Article 85(3).[2]

Paragraph 3 of Article 90 imposes upon the Commission the duty of supervising the proper application of this Article, including the balancing of conflicting interests that may arise under paragraph 2; the Commission may for this purpose issue regulations or directives addressed to the Member State in accordance with Article 189 of the Treaty but it has, presumably, to refrain from taking direct steps against the undertakings concerned.

E. Article 91

(1) If, during the transitional period, the Commission, at the request of a Member State or of any other interested party, determines that dumping practices exist within the Common Market, it shall send recommendations, designed to end these, to the originators of such practices. Should such dumping practices continue, the Commission shall authorise Member States adversely affected thereby to take protective measures in respect of which the Commission shall lay down the conditions and the methods to be followed.

(2) Immediately this Treaty comes into force, any products which originate in or are entitled to free circulation in one Member State and have been exported to another Member State shall be admitted free of all customs duties, quantitative restrictions or measures having equivalent effect when re-imported into the territory of the first-mentioned State. The Commission shall make appropriate Rules for giving effect to this paragraph.

---

[1] Pursuant to Art. 37 of the Treaty, the Commission issued three recommendations to France to transform the tobacco, matches, potash and spirits monopolies (*J.O.* 1962, pp. 1500, 1505, 1506; 1963, p. 2858), one to Italy regarding the monopoly of the trade in matches (*J.O.* 1962, p. 1505) and one to Germany in respect of the monopoly in spirits (*J.O.* 1963, p. 2857).

[2] See v. Gamm, *op. cit.*, p. 45.

While Articles 85 to 90 are provisions contained in Section 1 of the Chapter "Rules of Competition" with the caption "Rules applying to Enterprises," Article 91 is the only provision of Section 2, bearing the heading "Dumping Practices." For the reasons stated in the Preliminary Observations[1] this Article is still within the province of our discussion because paragraph 1 is addressed to States as well as to enterprises and makes the adoption of remedial measures by the Commission dependent upon requests by either a Member State or any other interested party, *viz.* an enterprise. On the other hand, in paragraph 2 only duties of the Member States are laid down.

Article 91 condemns dumping practices within the Common Market and empowers the Commission to take measures with a view to putting an end to them.

Although dumping practices have the effect that goods imported into a country at a dumping price will reduce the price level of such goods and as a rule also of similar goods and therefore operate in the same direction as the prohibition of price-fixing and other anti-competitive practices, dumping is nevertheless discouraged and has been made the object of preventive measures because it is considered as an unfair process of competition which is outside the international protection of fair competition.[2] Article 91 merely refers to "dumping practices" without any further definition. The question therefore arises whether this is an established and generally recognised legal term or merely an economic concept open to legal definition by the Commission and ultimately by the European Court. It seems to be the

[1] See *supra*, p. 6.

[2] The term "dumping" is limited to transactions in interstate trade and not applied to practices in a State's home trade, especially to sales below the vendor's own costs (of production or purchase). The legal treatment of the latter belongs in principle to the law of unfair competition but such practices become frequently also an issue in restrictive trade practices law. In Germany, sales below cost price are as such not unlawful; they will only be considered as infringing the Law against Unfair Competition of 1909 (as amended) if such sales are *contra bonos mores*. The main instance of transactions of this kind are sales below cost price with the aim of destroying a competitor's business. To this extent such business behaviour is very similar to boycott practices and may be caught by the provisions in the Cartel Law, particularly by s. 1 (agreements to sell at a price lower than that charged by one or more competitors) or s. 26(2) (prohibition of discrimination by market-dominating enterprises and cartels through "unfairly hindering" another enterprise (*cf.* Baumbach-Hefermehl, *op. cit.*, n. 155 to *UWG*, p. 276 and ns. 39, 40, 41 to s. 26 of the Cartel Law, p. 1391 f.)). In the United States, s. 2 of the Clayton Act, 1914 as amended by the Robinson-Patman Act, 1936, and s. 5 of the Federal Trade Commission Act, 1914 are enactments to much the same effect (*cf.* Oppenheim, *op. cit.*, pp. 662–664, and, on the relation of these two Acts to each other, pp. 18–20, where the purpose of the relevant section of the Clayton Act is understood as chiefly to maintain competition and that of the Federal Trade Commission Act mainly to regulate competition). For English law, *cf.* s. 3 of the Resale Prices Act, 1964 ("loss leaders").

general understanding that this Article of the Rome Treaty refers to the definition of dumping in GATT[1] of which all Member States of the E.E.C. are members.

In Article VI ("Anti-Dumping and Countervailing Duties"), Dumping is defined as the introduction of products from one country into the commerce of another country at less than the normal value of the products, and is condemned if it causes or threatens material injury to an established industry in the territory of a country which is a party to GATT or materially retards the establishment of a domestic industry. Goods are imported below the normal value

if the price of the product exported from one country to another

> *(a) is less than the comparable price, in the ordinary course of trade, for the like product when destined for consumption in the exporting country, or,*

> *(b) in the absence of such domestic price, is less than either*

>> *(i) the highest comparable price for the like product for export to any third country in the ordinary course of trade, or*

>> *(ii) the cost of production of the product in the country of origin plus a reasonable addition for selling cost and profit.*

Due allowance shall be made in each case for differences in conditions and terms of sale, for differences in taxation and for differences affecting price comparability.

Article VI(1).[2]

This is not the place for a disquisition on the correct economic determination of the concept of Dumping or for a suitable definition for legal purposes. Only two or three short observations would seem to be necessary for a fuller understanding of this concept. It is important to appreciate that it is the difference between the home and the foreign price which is the characteristic mark of Dumping so that the export of goods at less than production cost does not as a rule constitute Dumping if the price in the country into which the goods are imported is not lower than in the exporting country. The rule in Article VI(1)

---

[1] General Agreement on Tariffs and Trade of October 30, 1947, see *supra*, p. 8 n. 3 and Art. 10 of the O.E.E.C. Code of Liberalisation, New Edition brought up to July 1, 1960, O.E.E.C., Paris (1960), see Appendix F, *infra*, p. 272.

[2] See for a comprehensive treatment of this subject the publication of GATT, *Antidumping and Countervailing Duties*, Geneva (1958). (GATT/1958–2).

(9) (ii) must therefore be considered as based on a presumption of last resort. Yet neither ought the other two tests (subsection 1(a) and (b)) to serve as an entirely safe guide for the determination of an important element in dumping practices.[1] Even though Article VI of GATT has been accepted as authoritative guidance, it seems that the Commission of the E.E.C. will in a given case consider whether the export price is indeed an abnormally low one and causes or may be likely to cause severe damage to a competitor in a Member State. The Commission will consider the relevant facts within the framework of the whole policy of competition in the Community and, in particular, under the aspect that a discrepancy between home and export prices is in principle unobjectionable.[2] The Commission has repeatedly taken action in pursuance of complaints lodged under Article 91(1). According to the General Report on the Activities of the E.E.C. for the Year 1962/63,[3] out of 20 complaints so far lodged, 18 were finally determined; a Dumping with injurious consequences was found in two cases and recommendations to the enterprises causing it were issued, whereas in six cases the enterprises concerned had ceased to employ such practices before action was taken. The Commission attributes this result to the "moral pressure" of the complaints based on Article 91.

By Article 3 of Regulation No. 26 of April 4, 1962 issued by the Council of Ministers of the E.E.C.,[4] Article 91(1) is made applicable to trade in agricultural products (the right to levy countervailing import duties in accordance with Article 46 of the Rome Treaty remaining unaffected).

The application of paragraph 1 is limited to the transitional period of 15 years laid down in Article 8 of the Rome Treaty because it is assumed that the expected integration of the Common Market after that period will, through the abolition of customs and trade barriers, render such practices uninteresting and superfluous.[5]

The Commission will only intervene in pursuance of a complaint by an aggrieved party, which may either be a Member State or an enter-

[1] Neither the so-called "social dumping" which is caused by very low wages in the exporting country, nor the export of goods which are State subsidised in the home market with a consequential low export price are Dumping in the meaning of either Art. VI of GATT or Art. 91 of the Rome Treaty (see Wohlfarth a.o., *op. cit.*, n. 1 to Art. 91, p. 268).

[2] See v.d. Groeben in *WuW* 1961, pp. 373, 393 ff., and General Report on the Activities of the E.E.C., 1962/1963, pp. 67 ff.

[3] See previous note.

[4] *J.O.* 1962, p. 993.

[5] See v. Gamm, *op. cit.*, pp. 47 f; Wohlfarth a.o., *op. cit.*, n. 3 to Art. 91, p. 269.

prise in such State. The Commission will first issue a (non-binding) recommendation (Article 189(f)) addressed to the originating party, which may again be an offending Member State or an enterprise; as Article 91 is intended to protect the area of the Common Market, an enterprise in a third State which exports goods into a Member State can also be requested to cease such practice. If the recommendation is of no avail, the Commission cannot adopt compulsory measures against the Member State or the enterprise concerned but it may authorise the Member State affected by Dumping to take appropriate protective measures for which it prescribes the conditions and methods of implementation. This will have to be done by a decision (Article 189 (4)) which, although binding on the State to which it has been directed, is only of an enabling character. The remedies in question will be either imposition of (equalising) import duties, introduction of import quotas or, possibly, price determination.

Paragraph 2 of Article 91 deals with the re-introduction of goods from a Member State into the commerce of the Member State from which they had previously been exported into the former. It is irrelevant whether the goods in question were intended to be sold at dumping prices, but the provisions in this subsection will in practice probably only gain importance in cases of goods exported at dumping prices. Although not expressly stated, paragraph 2 is equally of a merely temporary character since after full integration of the economy within the Common Market it will become meaningless. The Commission has to secure its implementation by the Member States by any of the measures which are at its disposal under Article 189. In order to clarify the rather succinct text of this provision and to enable Member States to operate this legislative piece of market automatism, the Commission has issued a Regulation[1] in which several of the legal terms in paragraph 2 are authoritatively interpreted and detailed regulations are laid down for its application by the Member States, especially by their customs and tax authorities. This enactment was accompanied by an Explanatory Memorandum by the Information Office of the E.E.C.[2]

With respect to our enquiry, it is of particular interest to know whether paragraph 2 applies to private contractual prohibitions of the

[1] Regulation No. 8 of the Commission for Carrying into Effect Article 91(2) of the Treaty establishing the European Economic Community of March 11, 1960, *J.O.* 1960, p. 597, see *infra*, Appendix E, *infra*, p. 222. This Regulation has been amended (in regard to a minor point) by Regulation No. 13(2) of March 15, 1961, *J.O.* 1961, p. 585.
[2] See *WuW* 1960, p. 702.

re-import of goods which exporting suppliers frequently impose on their distributors in other Member States.[1] As paragraph 2 lays down the duties of the Member States in this particular field of trade policy and is exclusively addressed to their Governments, the view has been expressed that this paragraph cannot be relied upon for protection from re-imports in the sphere of private law with the consequence that contractual stipulations to a contrary effect are invalid.[2] Support for this opinion is sought in the aforementioned Regulation No. 8 of the Commission, which does not in fact refer to such contractual prohibition of re-imports.[3] While it must be admitted that neither Article 91(2) nor Regulation No. 8 is directly operative, the policy laid down in these provisions could very well quite legitimately be taken into account in the construction of Articles 85 and 86 when the problem of their application to agreements with distributors in another Member State containing a prohibition of re-import clause arises. Such interdependence has been emphasised by the Federal Cartel Office in the following words; "The re-import serves the purpose of contributing to the harmonisation of the markets; its protection is derived from the general legal principle underlying the Treaty which has found expression in Article 91(2) and has also to be taken into account when restraints of competition in the meaning of Articles 85 and 86 are considered."[4] It appears that so far neither the Commission of the E.E.C. nor the European Court has had an opportunity to give a ruling on this point.

---

[1] This problem is discussed at some length in the chapter on Sole Distributorship Agreements, see *infra*, Part II, pp. 109 f., 123 f.

[2] See Lutz-Basson, *"Re-Importverbot und der EWG-Vertrag,"* *NJW* 1963, pp. 385, 388 f.; v. Gamm, *op. cit.*, p. 48.

[3] *Ibid.*

[4] Statement of a representative of the Federal Cartel Office (submitted in Court proceedings under s. 90 of the German Cartel Law) of December 12, 1960 (*WuW* 1961, p. 303). This statement was submitted in the proceedings *Braun v. Ruhrland* in the Court of first instance. The case was finally decided by the German Supreme Court on June 14, 1963 (see Part II, *infra*, p. 123). However, in none of the three judgments was the relationship between Art. 85 and Art. 91 discussed.

PART TWO

SPECIAL AGREEMENTS

Introductory Observations

In (b) of the Catalogue of Examples in Article 85 reference was made to Sole Distributorship Agreements and in (c) to Patent Licence Agreements. These two types of agreements are of very frequent occurrence and it is therefore not surprising to find that they are the first ones on which the Commission has issued an Amending Regulation (No. 153) to Regulation No. 27[1] (in regard to so-called "Exclusive Concession Agreements") and two Announcements (one on "Exclusive Agency Contracts made with Commercial Agents" and one in regard to "Patent Licence Agreements"), all of December 21, 1962 and published on December 24, 1962.[2]

The general importance of these classes of agreements for the business world and their legal advisers both inside and outside the Member States of the Community justifies a separate and somewhat more detailed treatment.

I. Restrictions in connection with Patents, Registered Designs, Trade Secrets, Trade Marks and Copyright

Although industrial property rights are not expressly mentioned in the Rules of Competition, it cannot any longer be doubted that these legal rights are subject to the application of Art. 85[3]. Despite the fact that they are monopolies, their existence and use as such is not prohibited by the Rules but restrictions are placed on them which may appear to be rather severe, especially to the English lawyer who knows only the statutory restrictions of sections 57 and 58 (as well as sections 37 and 38) of the Patents Act, 1949.[4] As appears from Article 4(2) (ii)

---

[1] *J.O.* 1962, pp. 2921 ff.; see Appendix E, *infra*, p. 225.

[2] *Ibid.*

[3] Art. 36 of the Treaty provides expressly that, *inter alia*, industrial and commercial property, thus the national laws of patents, registered designs, trade marks, copyright and the law against unfair competition shall remain unaffected. This Article therefore guarantees the maintenance of these legal institutes, subject, however, to the prohibition in case of abuse by way of arbitrary discrimination or disguised restrictions on trade between Member States. There is unanimity today that Art. 36 has not the effect of taking such property rights out of the application of the Rules of Competition of the Treaty. See on the problems arising out of the relationship between Art. 36 and Arts. 85, 86, VerLoren van Themaat, *GRUR (AIT)*, 1964, p. 14.

[4] Furthermore, under the Restrictive Trades Practices Act, 1956 (sec. 6(1)(d)) patent licence agreements, especially exclusive licence agreements and agreements for the

(b) of Regulation No. 17 and from the Announcement of December 24, 1962, the Commission subjects these rights to Article 85. Because of the omission of any reference to the treatment of these rights in the Rules, the Commission has in the said Announcement stated its view on the scope of the application of Article 85 – with the proviso, however, that the last word thereon will lie with the European Court. One may safely assume that that Court will, at least in principle, confirm this view. The Commission's Announcement gives some guidance in this respect (stating, however, expressly in paragraph III of the Announcement that a large field in the sphere of industrial property rights may be dealt with at a later date), but any real understanding and appreciation of the position of these rights in the Rules of Competition can only be gained if one is aware of the great influence of both the antitrust law of the United States and the German Law against Restraints of Competition of 1957 on the practice of the Commission in this particular province of the Community's law of restrictive trade practices.[1] It would therefore appear to be expedient to give a short outline of the basic principles of the treatment of patents and similar proprietary rights in the antitrust law in these legal systems. Moreover, some familiarity with the large body of case law in the United States and the administrative practice of the German Cartel Authorities and the Court decisions based on a fairly detailed statute will not only assist in the understanding of this special application of Article 85 but also enable the interested parties to avoid entering into or maintaining agreements that might in time be held invalid.

A. The Legal Position in the United States and in Germany

The examination of this subject will be divided into five parts, namely in regard to restrictions
  (1) on simple patent licences
  (2) on cross-licences and patent pools

exchange of information relating to the operation of processes of manufacture including know-how are registrable in the register of restrictive trading agreements unless they are exempted under sec. 8(4),(5). The exemptions are, however, rather narrow.
  [1] *Cf.* the Address by Lee Levinger, Director of the Antitrust Division, Department of Justice, on "Solving Antitrust Problems including those of the Common Market" before the New York State Bar Association on January 25, 1962, *New York State Bar Association, Antitrust Law Symposium* (1962), pp. 29–44; extract in *WuW* 1963, p. 44. Timberg in *Doing Business in the Common Market* comments (at p. 125) on this part of the Rules of Competition as follows: "In my opinion the philosophy that will be followed by the Common Market will to a large extent duplicate the philosophy of the German cartel legislation."

(3) on know-how licences

(4) on trademarks

(5) on copyrights

1. SIMPLE PATENT LICENCES (ONE-WAY LICENCES)

Prima facie (vertical) agreements in regard to the acquisition or use of patents are prohibited if they impose on the acquirer or licensee respectively restrictions on his normal course of business that exceed the scope of the patent protection. The limitation may either be contained in the patent law itself (as, *e.g.*, in section 57 of the Patents Act, 1949 or in the United States patent law under the concept of misuse of a patent[1]) or form part of antitrust law directed against the creation of obligations by contract. The difficulty arises in determining what is the proper scope of the grant. In the first place, the scope of the grant must be ascertained from patent law and its interpretation in the respective national statutes; as regards the Member States, this part of patent law shows considerable differences.[2] These differences are however of minor significance in comparison with the contractual stipulations which are found in licence agreements, and we shall be primarily concerned with these only.

A patent owner may legitimately sell his patent outright or grant exclusive or non-exclusive licences. Such licences may be limited as to time or to territory or to both, or granted for certain purposes only, for example for the manufacture and/or distribution of certain goods, and they may also be limited as to quantity or as to the category of customers who alone are to be supplied. These principles are subject to several qualifications. As to time, the licence must not exceed the term of the patent, and covenants for non-competition exceeding that term or securing other benefits to the patentee beyond this period (*e.g.*, prolonged payment of royalties) are void. Nor can this result be achieved by extending this period by way of providing royalties for the presumed subsisting know-how connected with the licensed use of the patent.[3] In regard to territorial limitations, both in American and

---

[1] As regards the United States, see Neale, *op. cit.*, pp. 262 ff.; Brewster, *op. cit.*, pp. 141 f.

[2] Whereas in Germany and the Netherlands patents are only granted after a thorough examination of the novelty of the subject-matter applied for, no such examination takes place in France, Belgium, Luxembourg and Italy, so that the scope of the patent obtained must ultimately be determined by the respective national Courts. This difference is of considerable importance for the computation of royalties payable to the patent owner.

[3] This is the rule laid down in *U.S. v. Timken Roller Bearing Co.*, 83 F. Supp. 284

German law such limitations are valid short of restrictions of resale of the (patented) article, and if the licence relates to a process patent, the sale of the product made under patented process must not be restricted.[1] An obligation imposed on the licensee to require his customers not to sell the goods outside his licensed territory is equally invalid. Under German law, a licensee may be bound not to export into, or manufacture in, another country where no patent protection exists, and the payment of royalties for the manufacture or sale of such articles in such country may be agreed upon. The position in American law seems not to have been finally determined.[2] Different considerations apply however in the case of grants of parallel multiple licences. Although a patentee can certainly grant non-exclusive licences of one patent to a number of licensees limited to certain territories, he must not insert a price fixing provision into one or more of such licences and thereby create a system whereby he could control a large field of industry.[3] An agreement or understanding among the licensees themselves relating to price fixing or entering into other restrictions will be subject to the same considerations as one concluded between patentees and would come under the prohibition of the Sherman Act. The important question whether and how far the licensor can determine the price at which the licensee may sell the article covered by the patent and whether the licensor can even bind the licensee to impose a certain price (or other terms) on the latter's customers have been more or less similarly answered in American and German law. If there is only one patentee he can fix the price to be charged by his licensee,[4] but if there is more than one patentee or more than one licensee, such a price fixing arrangement is invalid in American law;[5] in Germany, the fact that there are multiple licensees would seem to be irrelevant but a combination of several patentees might be treated as a cartel and be subject to the provisions applicable to horizontal agreements. The imposition

at p. 313; see also Brewster, *op. cit.*, p. 163. In Germany, this question appears not to have been finally decided; Lüdecke-Fischer, *op. cit.*, N. 40, pp. 750 f. advocate the legality of the extension of the know-how. In any case, according to s. 20(3) and s. 21 of the Cartel Law, a term to this effect can be permitted by the Cartel Authorities.

[1] *U.S. v. Univis Lens Co. Inc.*, 316 U.S. 241 (1942); Germany: see Kellerman, *loc. cit.*, p. 604.

[2] See Brewster, *op. cit.*, p. 146.

[3] *U.S. v. Paramount Pictures, Inc.*, 334 U.S. 131 (1948) (a copyright case) and *Newburgh Moire Co. v. Superior Co., Inc.*, 237 F 2d. 283 (1956).

[4] *U.S. v. General Electric Co.*, 272 U.S. 476 (1926); Germany: s. 20 (II) (2) of the Cartel Law.

[5] *U.S. v. Line Material Co.* 333 U.S. 287 (1948); *Interstate Circuit Inc. v. U.S.*, 306 U.S. 208 (1939). See on the "whittling away" of the General Electric principle, Neale, *op. cit.*, pp. 263 ff.

of price fixing conditions on the licensee's customer (who purchases an article which thereby becomes free from patent protection) is prohibited in both laws.[1]

Tie-in clauses are generally held to be invalid in America as a misuse of the patent grant itself or as a violation of section 3 of the Clayton Act.[2] Evidence of tie-in clauses has often with success been advanced as a defence in suits by the licensor when sued for infringement of a patent. The sale of an unpatented product tied to a patented article is a *per se* violation of antitrust law.[3] The Courts have even disallowed obligations imposed on a licensee which the licensor thought necessary for maintaining the goodwill of his patent, as, for example, provisions that the licensee of a patented machine or of a process must purchase certain materials from the licensor which he could not obtain of equal quality elsewhere.[4] Probably this prohibition does not apply to a foreign licensee of an American patentee, except perhaps in a stark monopoly situation.[5] In the German Cartel Law, however, by section 20(1) no. 1 such obligations on the part of the acquirer of a patent or of a licensee are permitted in so far as they are justified by the interest of the patentee in a technically faultless exploitation of the patented invention, but they are unlawful if the licensor has merely a financial interest in such undertaking. This exemption applies in principle to every kind of obligation as far as it is objectively necessary for the said purpose. Thus, undertakings to purchase raw material or even partly or fully manufactured articles[6] from the licensor or from a third party for production with a licensed machine, restrictions providing for supply to certain limited groups of purchasers only (unless this amounts

[1] See for German law, Kellerman, *loc. cit.*, p. 615. In the United States, prohibition follows from the prohibition of fixing the price of unpatented products, see Neale, *op. cit.*, pp. 264 f. In Germany, regard must however be had to s. 16 of the Cartel Law which permits re-sale price maintenance of branded articles subject to certain statutory conditions.

[2] This is shown by a long line of Supreme Court and lower Courts' decisions as, *e.g.*, *United Shoe Machinery Corporation v. U.S.*, 247 U.S. 32 (1918); *International Business Machines Corporation v. U.S.*, 298 U.S. 131 (1936). See thereon also Neale, *op. cit.*, p. 286, and Brewster, *op. cit.*, pp. 174 ff.

[3] *Mercoid Corp. v. Mid-Continent Investment Co.*, 320 U.S. 661 (1944); *Mercoid Corp. v. Minneapolis-Honeywell Regulator Co.*, 320 U.S. 680, (1944); *International Salt Co. v. U.S.*, 332 U.S. 392 (1947); *The White Motor Company v. U.S.*, 374 U.S. 174 (1963).

[4] *United Shoe Machinery Corporation v. U.S.*, 247 U.S. 32 (1918); *International Business Machines Corporation v. U.S.*, 298 U.S. 131, 138 (1936).

[5] See Brewster, *op. cit.*, p. 149.

[6] The obligation to obtain spare parts for repairs is probably an obligation belonging to the exploitation within the scope of the patent grant, see Kellermann, *loc. cit.*, p. 611. The contrary view had, however, been held by the German Supreme Court under the Allied Decartelisation Laws (decision of October 5, 1951, *NJW* 1952, p. 101, at p. 102; *WuW* 1952, p. 218).

to a non-justified discrimination), and provisions as to maintenance of "minimum quality and after sale service" are valid.[1] On the other hand, a condition that the licensee will not manufacture and/or sell competing products would be invalid. Sometimes the licensor makes the grant of a licence for one specific patent conditional upon the licensee also taking a licence in regard to one or more other patents, the so-called "package licensing." The question of the validity of such arrangements appears not to have been finally settled in the United States although the tendency is to hold it invalid, especially if it appears to be an attempt to monopolise a substantial field of industry.[2] The position under the German Cartel Law is still more uncertain as this question has so far not been judicially determined; most writers think that such a term is permitted.[3] The combination of licences for the exploitation of a patent and of a trade secret is legally possible in German Law and such licences may also cover a trade mark for the goods thus produced.[4]

Many licence agreements contain a clause by which, in some way or other, the licensee undertakes to grant back to the licensor either the complete title to, or an exclusive licence of, any improvement patent which could be obtained on the strength of an additional invention made by him; frequently, the licensor gives an undertaking to extend the licence to any future improvement patent made by him. In the leading case of *Transparent-Wrap Machine Corp. v. Stokes & Smith*,[5] the exclusive licensee of Transparent-Warp's patented machine had agreed to transfer improvement inventions relating to the machine made by him in order to enable the licensor to have them patented if he wished to do so. If Transparent-Wrap availed themselves of this option, the existing licence should extend to this additional patent without increased royalty payment. If the licensor did not exercise this option, the licensee had the right to obtain patent protection

---

[1] Thus, many of the tie-in clauses declared invalid in the aforementioned American cases would be upheld under the German Cartel Law. Moreover, s. 20(3) provides that the Cartel Authorities may, upon application, grant permission of an (otherwise prohibited) tie-in clause if the economic freedom of movement of the acquirer or licensee or other enterprises will not be unduly restricted and if the competition on the market will through the moderate extent of the restrictions not be substantially restricted.

[2] *Automatic Radio Mfg. Co. v. Hazeltine Research*, Inc. 339 U.S. 827, 831 (1950); *U.S. v. Paramount Pictures, Inc.*, 334 U.S. 131 (1948). Such prohibition would, however, as a rule not apply to a foreign licensee, see Brewster, *op. cit.*, pp. 153 f.

[3] Lieberknecht, *op. cit.*, pp. 240 f., 306 f; Baumbach-Hefermehl, *op. cit.*, p. 1362, n. 3.

[4] Baumbach-Hefermehl, *op. cit.*, p. 1365, n. 18, p. 1372, n. 1, p. 759, n. 6.

[5] 329 U.S. 637 (1947). There was a further stipulation to the effect that improvements by either party were to be included in the licence with the proviso that Transparent Wrap would use the licence and grant sublicences of the licensee's inventions also outside the licensed territories.

thereon and, if granted, the licensor would obtain a non-exclusive licence outside the licensed territories. On the action of Transparent-Wrap for its enforcement, the Supreme Court upheld this agreement as neither constituting a misuse of the patent grant nor a violation of antitrust law. It is true that in several later decisions (by lower Courts[1]) similar clauses were declared invalid but these were cases in which such terms were a part of grants of cross-licences and amounted to a division of markets, or were, at least in the opinion of the Courts, attempts to control a large sector of industry. In any event, a clause of this kind is not illegal *per se* but subject to the application of the Rule of Reason. These principles would also apply to transactions with foreign parties.[2] Similar considerations apply to the inclusion of grants of future patents in a licence agreement but probably not to grants of licences under (future) patents that are not closely related to the existing patent; furthermore, the American patentee must not undertake to refrain from exporting articles to be manufactured under future patents.[3] As regards non-U.S. patents, such arrangements would seem to be outside the antitrust law unless they constitute a substantial restraint on American domestic or foreign commerce.[4]

In Germany, the Supreme Court held in a decision rendered in 1955 when the Decartelisation Order was still in force that the licensor could not demand the grant back of the title to an improvement patent based on the licensee's invention but only obtain a non-exclusive licence thereon under which the licensee would in turn obtain a (non-exclusive) licence.[5] The Cartel Law of 1957 has dealt with this question in section 20 (2) no. 3 which lays down that obligations of the transferee of a patent or of a licensee to exchange experience or to grant licences, including exclusive ones, for improvements *(Verbesserungs- oder Anwendungserfindungen)* are permitted if these correspond to similar obligations on the part of the licensor. Thus, an obligation on the part of the licensee to transfer the patent concerning the improvement itself is not covered by this exemption and is therefore invalid.[6] Nor

---

[1] *U.S. v. General Electric Co.*, 80 F. Supp. 989 (S.D.N.Y. 1948); *U.S. v. General Electric Co.*, 82 F. Supp. 753 (D.N.J. 1949); *U.S. v. Imperial Chemical Industries Ltd.*, 105 F. Supp. 215 (S.D.N.Y. 1952). In *U.S. v. United States Gypsum Co.*, 340 U.S. 76 (1950) the Supreme Court's refusal to approve a similar clause was apparently due to the fact that it formed part of widely framed conspiracy to violate the Sherman Act.
[2] See Brewster, *op. cit.*, p. 158; Fugate, *op. cit.*, pp. 202–204.
[3] See Brewster, *op. cit.*, pp. 151 ff.
[4] See Brewster, *ibid.*
[5] *NJW* 1955, p. 829. In this case the Supreme Court did not apply the Rule of Reason although it could have done so under the Decartelisation Law.
[6] Decisions of Federal Cartel Office, December 1960, *WuW* 1961, p. 297 and of the

does the exemption extend to other inventions, including so-called parallel inventions (in kindred fields of industry).[1] The observance of the principle of reciprocity is of decisive importance. By subsection 3 of this section the Cartel Authorities can grant exceptions and they have frequently done so, sometimes subject to modifications in order to prevent the accumulation of patents in the hands of the (original) patentee, who might otherwise extend and perpetuate his control over a whole field of industry, or create patent pools, or exclude third parties from acquiring new technical knowledge.[2] These rules also apply to international licence agreements in so far as such agreements take effect within Germany, which is usually the case if the licensee is an enterprise in Germany; it is irrelevant whether the agreement is governed by German or foreign law.[3]

The licensee is as a rule not entitled to challenge the patent in respect of which he has obtained a licence unless a licence agreement contains a price fixing condition the legality of which depends on the validity of the patent[4] or unless another violation of antitrust law would otherwise exist.[5] A licensee may, however, in any event challenge the validity of a patent which is not the basis of the licence granted to him.[6] Section 20(2) no. 4 of the German Cartel Law permits an agreement by which the licensee is not permitted to attack the validity of the patent of which he holds a licence, but the challenge of other patents must not be restricted. However, if both parties are aware of the weakness of the patent which might lead to its being declared invalid, an agreement not to challenge it would presumably be bad.[7]

Court of Appeal of Düsseldorf of September 11, 1962, *WuW* 1963, p. 360. A problem which has hitherto apparently not been discussed, is dealt with in the Annual Report on the Activities of the Federal Cartel Office for the Year 1963, p. 68. The Federal Cartel Office holds that an obligation by the licensee to transfer a patent in addition (G. *Zusatzpatent*; F. *brevet de perfectionnement*) to the licensor is not valid. However, if the licensee makes an invention of this kind which can only be protected as an additional patent by a grant in favour of the original patentee (*i.e.*, the licensor), the licensee can be obliged to agree to the making of the grant in favour of the licensor who has however afterwards to transfer the additional patent to the licensee but may reserve the right to acquire a licence thereunder.

[1] Decision of Federal Cartel Office of December 1960, *WuW* 1961, p. 297.

[2] See Kellermann, *loc. cit.*, p. 616.

[3] By virtue of s. 98(2) of the Cartel Law; see the author's "The Law relating to Restrictive Trade Practices in Western Germany and in the Treaty establishing the European Economic Community," *Br. Inst. Int. Comp. Law, Suppl. Publ. No. 2* (1961).

[4] *Sola Electric Co. v. Jefferson Electric Co.*, 317 U.S. (1942); *Chikago Metallic Mfg. Co. v. Edward Katzinger*, 329 U.S. 394 (1947); *MacGregor v. Westinghouse Electric and Mfg. Co.*, 329 U.S. 402 (1947).

[5] *Scott Paper Co. v. Marcalus Mfg. Co.*, 326 U.S. 249 (1945).

[6] *Pope Mfg. Co. v. Gormully*, 144 U.S. 224 (1892).

[7] See Kellermann, *loc. cit.*, p. 616.

Excursus: Effect of Antitrust Law on International Licence Agreements

Licence agreements of which one or more of the parties thereto are non-resident enterprises (which may be called "international agreements") may relate to a United States or German patent respectively. In both laws the legal position in regard to such licence agreements in so far as they are one-way licence grants is somewhat uncertain as the decided cases in the international field mostly deal with cross-licensing and patent pools. Nevertheless, in view of the importance of this situation, a few observations are necessary.

It is the question of territorial limitations which is probably the most important in this connection. An American patentee can determine the territorial limits of the exploitation of his United States and foreign patents respectively. Yet he would violate the antitrust laws if he bound a licensee in the United States not to export the goods manufactured under the licence,[1] and it is very doubtful whether he may make provision for territorial restrictions upon import into and export from the United States in an agreement with a foreign licensee of United States patents.[2] As regards a licence under a foreign patent, there appears to be complete lack of judicial guidance, but Brewster has expressed the view that, "given the power of the patent, any restraint going beyond it is likely to have an even more anti-competitive effect than if no patent existed at all."[3] Of course, a corresponding United States patent would enable the patentee to prevent imports into the United States, but even then would a covenant to that effect be incompatible with antitrust law.[4]

Consequently, a patentee will have to rely on his patent rights only.

The German Cartel Law provides in section 20(2) no. 5 that restrictions beyond the scope of the patent grant may be imposed upon the licensee to the extent that they concern the regulation of competition on markets outside Germany. Kellermann[5] considers the following restrictions as permitted:

(a) the prohibition to manufacture (and/or use) and/or sell the licensed article in foreign countries where it does not enjoy patent protection;

(b) the prohibition to export such articles to foreign countries where they are not protected by a patent;[6]

---

[1] Fugate, *op. cit.*, p. 199.
[2] *Ibid.*, 201 f., and Brewster, *op. cit.*, pp. 143, 146 f.
[3] *Op. cit.*, at p. 144.
[4] See Fugate, *op. cit.*, p. 199.
[5] *Loc. cit.*, p. 617.
[6] To this may be added the right to prohibit the purchaser of a foreign licensee to

(c) undertakings by the licensee to pay royalties for production and distribution in such foreign countries.

On the other hand, Kellermann maintains[1] that the following trans-actions are outside the exemption of section 20(2) no. 5:

(aa) contractual restraints of competition preventing the foreign licensee from selling on the German market classes of goods that are not covered by patent protection;

(bb) obligations to purchase such unpatented goods from an enter-prise in Germany for sale abroad, or to manufacture by virtue of a licence granted by another German enterprise;

(cc) entering into obligations in respect of supply in so far as a foreign licensee would be restricted in the purchase of raw materials and other goods required for the manufacture of the patented article.[2]

However, under section 20(3) the Cartel Authorities can in individual cases grant exemptions from the prohibition. The question whether licence agreements in respect of patents granted in a foreign country are subject to section 20 cannot be regarded as finally settled. The fact that this section speaks of patents generally is not conclusive since such reference in a German law might well apply only to German patents. On the other hand, the protection of free competition might neces-sitate the extension of the application to non-German patents. This would seem to be the attitude of the Federal Cartel Office,[3] which is supported by Reimer[4] and Buxbaum[5], whilst Gleiss-Hootz[6] and Magen[7] take a different view.

Lastly, if an agreement contains both elements of a patent know-how licence and exclusive sales provisions, the Federal Cartel Office

---

re-export into third countries (except – as a rule – for re-importation into Germany), see also Schwartz, *op. cit.*, pp. 82 ff., and Magen, *op. cit.*, pp. 139 f.

[1] Kellermann, *loc. cit.*, p. 617.

[2] The obligations referred to in bb) and cc) show a peculiar feature in that their effect is a mere repercussory one to restrictions imposed on a foreign licensee and is to take effect abroad. Kellermann's view is based on the practice of the Federal Cartel Office (see Magen, *op. cit.*, p. 137). See also Order of the Federal Cartel Office, *WuW* 1961, p. 217, but in a recent Advice (August 15, 1962, *WuW* 1963, p. 440) that Office has clarified its attitude by emphasising that the effect within Germany must be a real one, mere theoretical possibilities being insufficient.

[3] Notification of a permission under s. 20(3) of a licence agreement in regard to know-how (*WuW* 1959, p. 648).

[4] *Gemeinschaftskommentar*, p. 593.

[5] 9 *WRP* (1963), p. 288.

[6] *Betriebsberater* 1962, p. 1060.

[7] *Op. cit.*, p. 139.

will only apply section 20 if the licensing provisions are of substancial importance.[1]

2. CROSS-LICENCES AND PATENT POOLS

It would seem expedient to distinguish between these two kinds of exchange of patent rights. In the case of cross-licensing agreements the parties grant to each other non-exclusive or exclusive licences in respect of their patents which, as a rule, also cover improvements or even future patents in a certain technical field; such agreement may be concluded by two or more parties. Sometimes, these agreements contain stipulations to the effect that a party may grant (non-exclusive) licences to an outsider only with the consent of the other parties. Patent pools in the strict sense are bodies,[2] often in the form of a company created for such purpose, to which patent owners transfer their patents or grant an exclusive licence, (frequently, however, retaining the right to exploit the patent themselves), authorising the body to grant non-exclusive licences to the other members of the organisation and to exclude non-members from the right to use the patent. In spite of this theoretically fairly clear distinction between these types of patent exchanges, the Courts, and particularly the American ones, have not kept them apart so that it is not possible to say that clear antitrust law principles distinguishing these different types have been laid down.

Under both United States patent law and antitrust law the grant of cross-licences is as such not illegal.[3] However, agreements providing for a mere exchange of licences are apparently somewhat rare since the contracting parties, especially if they are larger enterprises, wish by such transactions to make arrangements in the field of price policy, for the demarcation of territorial spheres of interest and the regulation of competition in regard to the range of their products. It is these features which have become the object of the Courts' determination. As a rule, the American Courts have held such agreement invalid even if a stipulation found in a cross-licensing agreement would be legal in a one-way grant of a licence. Thus, it was held in *U.S. v. Line Material*

---

[1] Annual Report on the Activities of the Federal Cartel Office for the Year 1961, p. 57; *Gemeinschaftskommentar*, p. 578.

[2] A patent pool may, on the other hand, also be created by a mere agreement to pool patents without further restrictions and to divide royalties, each patentee being permitted to retain the right to grant licences, as was the (lawful) arrangement in *Standard Oil Company (Indiana) v. U.S.* 283 U.S. 163 (1931).

[3] *Standard Oil Company (Indiana) v. U.S.*, 283 U.S.. 163 (1931).

Co.[1] that two (or more) patentees who had combined their patents for joint use by way of cross-licensing must not try to fix the price of the articles sold under those patents. In the later case of *United States. v. New Wrinkle Inc.* this rule was applied to a patent pool proper.[2] Many important decisions[3] relate to agreements on division of territories in which one or more of the parties were foreign enterprises. The Courts have, however, particularly under the aspect of attempted monopolisation of a field of industry, denied the legality of such arrangements. An arrangement between cross-licensors about exclusive allocation of types of products to be manufactured by each of them is equally prohibited.[4]

As with a simple cross-licensing agreement, a patent pool, and especially a rather loose one with the participants retaining the right to grant licences to third parties within their discretion, is unobjectionable.[5] But in practice patent pools usually show features of market sharing, price fixing, attempts to exclude outside competitors and often also a tendency to create a monopoly. In view of these aspects they violate the antitrust law.

In German law both cross-licensing and patent pools are covered by the Cartel Law. Cross-licensing is subject to section 20 and, to the extent that the patentees-licensors enter into obligations, to section 15. However, if a cross-licensing agreement is accompanied by stipulations to divide territories or to limit output (subject to the proviso of section 20(2) no. 5 concerning foreign markets), they may amount to a cartel proper and are to be judged by section 1 (and sections 2 to 14) of the Cartel Law. The strict patent pools which are created by "horizontal agreements" may either appear as a simple association governed by sections 705 et seq. of the Civil Code or, in a higher form, as a juristic person like a limited company *(Gesellschaft mit beschränkter Haftung* or an *Aktiengesellschaft)* and are then an "institutionalised" cartel. By section 1 of the Cartel Law such a cartel is invalid and, if merely created for this purpose, would have to be dissolved unless the Cartel

---

[1] 333 U.S. 287 (1948); see on this case Neale, *op. cit.*, p. 266. The same principle was applied in *U.S. v. General Electric Co.*, 80 F Supp. 989 (S.D.N.Y. 1948) *(Carboloy* case), in which one of the holders of a United States patent was the German firm of Krupp.
[2] 342 U.S. 371 (1952); see thereon Neale, *op. cit.*, pp. 268 f.
[3] *E.g., U.S. v. National Lead Co.*, 63 F Supp. 513 (S.D.N.Y. 1945), aff'd 332 U.S. 319 (1947); *U.S. v. Imperial Chemical Industries* Ltd., 100 F. Supp. 504 (S.D.N.Y. 1951). In *U.S. v. Timken Roller Bearing Co.*, 341 U.S. 593 (1951), the inclusion of future patents and unpatented information seems to have been an additional fact which made the agreement illegal.
[4] *Hartford-Empire Co. v. U.S.*, 323 U.S. 386 (1945).
[5] *Standard Oil Company (Ind.) v. U.S.*, 283 U.S. 163 (1931).

Authorities saw fit to approve it under one or more of the exempting provisions laid down in sections 2 to 8 of the Cartel Law[1].[2]

3. LICENCES RELATING TO TRADE SECRETS AND KNOW-HOW

In both American and German law a distinction is made between a secret process (or trade secret) on the one hand and the so-called know-how (or technology) on the other. A secret process is a technical secret the nature of which is similar to an invention for which patent protection could be but is not granted either because it does not fulfil the factual or legal requirements of a relevant patent law or because its owner has for some reason or other not obtained such grant, whereas know-how is merely the experience or special technical or managerial knowledge of the handling of a patented invention.[3]

The importance of these two types of industrial property which are not protected by express statutory provisions[4] is considerable and this all the more so in international commerce since an invention may either not be patentable at all (e.g., cultivating processes in the agricultural field[5]) or may be patentable in one country but not in another so that a resident in the latter country might only be able to obtain a licence of a secret process or mere know-how.

As regards licences of secret processes, the position in American law is far from definitely settled. It had been recognised in Dr. Miles' case that "the secret process may be the subject of confidential communication and of sale or licence to use with restrictions as to territory or prices."[6] In a number of more recent cases, licences on secret processes

---

[1] See thereon the author's publication referred to on p. 66, n. 3, supra.

[2] The French Commission des Ententes et des Positions Dominantes (see supra, p. 19) has advised that contractual obligations in a patent licence agreement by which a tie-in clause concerning purchase of material has been imposed upon the licensee, amount to a (prohibited) entente (Magnesium case, Ann. 1960, 253, 271; see Mathély, loc. cit., p. 20).

[3] But know-how might also relate to an (unpatented) secret process.

[4] As distinct from this "industrial know-how" there also exists so-called "commercial know-how" (e.g., advertising schemes, customer lists, analysis of chemical substances, see Turner, Trade Secrets, 1962, pp. 11 f.). One often finds these two kinds of know-how interwoven in licence agreements. In the following discussion the term "know-how" is, as a rule, meant to comprise both know-how in the narrower sense and trade secrets unless a distinction is specifically mentioned.

[5] E.g., in the United Kingdom as to brands of cultivated plants until the passing of the Plant Varieties and Seeds Act, 1964.

[6] Dr. Miles Medical Co. v. John D. Park and Sons Co., 220 U.S. 373 (1911). The Supreme Court nevertheless declared the fixing of resale prices of Dr. Miles Company's proprietary medicines illegal on the ground that "the present case is not analogous to that of a sale of goodwill, or of an interest in a business, or of the grant of a right to use a process of manufacture" and "whatever rights the patentee may enjoy are derived from statutory grant under the authority conferred by the Constitution," but "that

with territorial restrictions were upheld,[1] thus applying the principles governing grants of patent licences proper. Needless to say, antitrust principles governing grants of crosslicences, patent pools and situations of monopoly apply also to secret process licences, and even more strictly.[2]

Still scarcer and therefore still less clarified is the antitrust law position of know-how in the narrower sense, namely the licence relating to mere expert knowledge in the application of patented articles. It appears that restrictions might be upheld if closely connected with the patent and necessary or expedient for the proper use within the scope of the grant; but such restrictions must not be a device to secure an extension of the use of the patent, especially to divide territories by way of a contractual arrangement. The same holds good for prolongation of the licence beyond the duration of the patent,[3] unless, perhaps, the know-how has independent value.[4]

In German law the position is however less uncertain as this very point is explicitly determined by a statutory provision. Section 21 of the Cartel Law reads as follows:

(1) *Section 20 shall apply, as appropriate, to agreements concerning the transfer or exploitation of legally unprotected inventions, manufacturing processes, technical designs and other technological achievements, as well as legally unprotected achievements towards cultivation in the field of plant breeding, if such achievements constitute business secrets*

the complainant has not seen fit to make the disclosure required by the statute, and thus to secure the privileges it confers." Dr. Miles Company's medicines were manufactured under a secret process, and the licensee for their distribution did not acquire secret information but only the secretly processed goods. The significance of this distinction drawn by the Court can probably only be understood in the light of the earlier decision in *Bement v. National Harrow Co.*, 186 U.S. 70 (1902) in which it had been held that an owner of a patented article could legitimately grant a licence to manufacture or sell it "upon the condition that the assignee shall charge a certain amount for such article." It is, however, doubtful whether this straight-forward doctrine would still prevail in the generally more complex factual situation today, in spite of the affirmation in *United States v. General Electric Co.*, 272 U.S. 476 (1926), see Neale *op. cit.*, pp. 264 f. In essence, *Dr. Miles'* case should be understood as merely prohibiting resale price maintenance.

[1] *Thomas v. Sutherland*, 52 F. 2d 592 (3d Cir. 1931); *Foundry Services. Inc. v. Beneflux Corp.*, 110 F. Supp. 857 (S.D.N.Y. 1953), reversed on other grounds, 206 F. 214 (2d Cir. 1953); *U.S. v. E.I. Dupont de Nemours & Co.*, 118 F. Supp. (D. Del. 1954), affirmed 351 U.S. 377 (1956), without adjudication on the question of the legality of the territorial restriction which was not in issue.

[2] See on this aspect, Brewster, *op. cit.*, p. 167.

[3] See *United States v. Timken Roller Bearing Co.*, 83 F. Supp. 284, at 313 (Court of first instance).

[4] That this is the exception can perhaps be inferred from the language in *U.S. v. General Electric Co.*, 82 F. Supp. 753, at 846 (D.N.J. 1949), the so-called *Incandescent Lamp* case.

(2) *Section 20 shall apply, as appropriate, to agreements concerning seed brands entered into the special list of sorts (section 37 of the Seed Law) between a plant breeder engaged in the maintenance of parent stock and a multiplier or a multiplying enterprise.*

This provision requires only a short comment. In the first place, this section comprises both the secret processes and the know-how (in the narrower sense), and adds the special achievements in the field of plant breeding (in so far as they are not protected by a patent) and, secondly, a licence can be granted for the period in which the secret process or the know-how remains secret; once it becomes known to third parties, *i.e.*, outsiders (which is a question of fact), all restrictions become invalid and licence fees need no longer be paid.[1] In the case of the grant of a know-how licence this probably comes to an end too if the patent to which it relates expires. In both cases the Cartel Authorities have power to permit restrictions beyond the scope of the grant (section 21 in conjunction with section 20 (3) of the Cartel Law).[2] It must, however, be emphasised that section 21 relates to so-called industrial trade secrets only; licences of commercial trade secrets and non-secret know-how are governed by sections 15 to 18 of the Cartel Law.[3]

4. TRADEMARKS

While a patent gives its owner the legal monopoly in the sense that he can exclude others from using or exploiting an invention protected by patent, a trade mark gives no such right as its purpose is merely to prevent what is known as "unfair competition" by securing for a trader the source of origin of goods sold by him and by protecting those goods and his goodwill generally from the sale of other similar

---

[1] See Baumbach-Hefermehl, *op. cit.*, p. 1373. It appears, however, from several decisions of the Federal Cartel Office that the test of secrecy is fairly leniently applied if the know-how can be considered to have a real value (*WuW* 1960, p. 818; 1961, p. 217; 1962, p. 555).

[2] By an Order of September 2, 1963 the Federal Cartel Office declared a contractual prohibition to manufacture and sell competitive goods imposed by a German licensor of know-how on a Portuguese licensee unobjectionable under s. 20(2) (5) since this restriction applied only in distant territorial areas (Portugal and Portuguese overseas possessions) and would not have an effect in Germany (*WuW* 1964, p. 345). (Probably, if on the same facts the licensor had been a Member State of the E.E.C., the ruling would have been different).

[3] Non-industrial, *i.e.*, commercial, know-how may be secret and eligible for legal protection. This appears to be sometimes overlooked, *e.g.*, by Magen, *op. cit.*, pp. 41 ff., 52, 61 f. See however the divergent opinions in *Gemeinschaftskommentar* § 18, n. 11 (p. 528) and § 21, n. 1 (p. 613).

goods by another trader as his, the trade mark owner's, goods; in short, it is designed to prevent "passing off."

Although a trade mark is less suitable for monopolisation of a whole or a substantial part of a specific industry or trade or for substantially stifling competition, experience has shown that, particularly in the international field, trade marks can indeed be used to similar ends if made the vehicle for agreements for market sharing or excluding competition.

In many countries the owner of a trade mark can prevent such goods as bear his trade mark from entering his country.[1] In the so-called Perfume cases the U.S. Government charged United States-French interdependent perfume manufacturing companies with intentional monopolisation by excluding competitors through improper use of Article 526 of the Tariff Act of 1930, but although the Court of first instance supported the suit, the Government withdrew it when the defendants appealed.[2] If the exclusive American distributor of a foreign manufacturer registers the latter's trade mark in the United States, he can on the authority of older cases keep out goods of the same kind[3] under section 526 of the Tariff Act, but the Commissioner of Patents has recently restricted the interpretation of that section if the importer is merely an exclusive distributor without an American business and goodwill apart from that of the foreign manufacturer.

The important instance of the application of antitrust law on trade marks is, however, the use of trade marks for the purpose of division of markets and attempts at monopolisation. In the famous *Timken* case[4] the Supreme Court held that the American Timken Company which owned the relevant trade mark could not, by registering or

---

[1] *United States:* (Lanham) Trade Mark Act of 1946, 60 Stat. 427, 446, as amended, 15 U.S.C.A. 1951–1127; see thereon Fugate, *op. cit.*, pp. 224 ff.
Germany: Warenzeichengesetz (Trade Mark Law) of May 5, 1936 (as amended), s. 28, and Law on Accession to the Madrid Convention relating to the Suppression of False Indications of Origin on Goods of March 21, 1925 (*BGBl.* II, 115).
United Kingdom: Merchandise Act, 1887 s. 16(1) (9); Customs and Excise Act, 1952 s. 320, Sched. 12 Pt. 1; Merchandise Act, 1953, s. 3(1) (a).
[2] *U.S. v. Guerlain, Inc., Civ.* 93–267, S.D.N.Y. (1954), CCH 1954 Trade Reg. Rep. No. 66, 128; *U.S. v. Parfums Corday, Inc., Civ.* 93–268, S.D.N.Y. (1954), CCH Trade Reg. Rep. No. 66, 128; *U.S. v. Lanvin Parfums, Inc. Civ.* 93–269, S.D.N.Y. (1954), CCH 1954 Trade Reg. Rep. Nr. 66, 128. See thereon Fugate, *op. cit.*, pp. 226–229, and Neale, *op. cit.*, p. 292.
[3] *Sturges v. Clark D. Pease Inc.*, 48 Fed. 2d 1035 (2d Cir. 1931); *Scandinavia Belting Co. v. Asbestos & Rubber Works*, 257 Fed. 937 2d Cir. 1919), cert. denied, 250 U.S. 644 (1919); see Fugate, *op. cit.*, pp. 228 f.
[4] *U.S. v. Timken Roller Bearing Co.*, 83 F. Supp. 284 (N.D. Ohio 1949) modified and affirmed, 341 U.S. 593 (1951). This is the only Supreme Court case dealing with trade marks under an antitrust law point of view. See also the similar case of *U.S. v. Bayer Co. Inc.*, 135 F. Supp. 65 (S.D.N.Y. 1955).

direct or indirect licensing of the trade mark or the trade name "Timken" in several European countries and by making agreements with subsidiary or contractually bound companies in Europe, achieve a division of markets since "a trademark cannot be legally used as a devise for Sherman Act violation."[1] Another infringement of antitrust law may be the grant of a licence of an enterprise's trade mark to a competitor if this does or may result in excluding competition "by seeking to have established a standard which only they (*i.e.*, the two competitors) were able to meet.[2]

In the German Cartel Law trade marks (or trade names) are not specifically mentioned at all. Section 20 is not applicable, either directly or by way of analogy. The owner of a trademark is therefore entitled to use this (full) right freely. However, sections 15 to 18 of the Cartel Law do apply to licences of trade marks so that, for example, price fixing stipulations and the imposition of conditions on resale are governed by section 15, and restrictions of the freedom of the use of trade mark protected goods or in regard to the mode of their resale can be prohibited by the Cartel authorities under section 18(1) nos. 1 and 3.[3] In this way, the use of trade marks is controlled by the general provisions of the Cartel Law in German law too.

In a recent decision the German Supreme Court[4] has given a ruling on the basic question whether a trade mark can be used for the purpose of market-sharing by way of exclusive dealing agreements. Although this decision makes no references either to the Cartel Law or to the Rules of Competition and the Court's opinion is only based on sections 1, 15 and 24 of the *Warenzeichengesetz*,[5] the effect of this judgment must undoubtedly have far-reaching consequences for the use of trade marks in the Common Market, at least as far as German enterprises are concerned. A Spanish soap manufacturer sells this product under the description "Maja" which is registered as a trade mark both in Spain and Germany. The sale in Germany is effected by a German

[1] 341 U.S. 593, at 599.

[2] *U.S. v. General Electric Co.*, 82 F. Supp. 753 (D.N.J. 1949), concerning an agreement between General Electric and Westinghouse on the trade mark "Mazda" for an incandescent lamp with the exclusion of its use by other traders.

[3] See Busse, *Warenzeichengesetz*, 3rd ed., 1960, p. 18, and Baumbach-Hefermehl, *op. cit.*, p. 759, n. 6, p. 891, n. 14.

[4] Of January 22, 1964 ("*Maja* case") *AWD* 1964, pp. 122 ff.; *GRUR (AIT)* 1964, p. 202. In a judgment of July 14, 1964 (re "*Revlon*" trade mark), the *Düsseldorf* Appeal Court applied the ruling of the Supreme Court to a case in which the plaintiff, the German subsidiary of an American parent company, based its claim not on a German trade mark registered in favour of a foreign company as in *Maja*, but on the trade mark registered in its own favour in Germany. (*WuW* 1965, p. 147 ff).

[5] See *supra*, p. 74 n. 1.

firm as sole distributor which is the registered user of the trade mark registered in Germany and which is also authorised to make claims for infringements of the German trade mark. When a German importer bought Maja soap (produced by the same Spanish manufacturer) from Spanish wholesalers and sold it in Germany at a cheaper price than that charged by the sole distributor, the latter brought proceedings against the importer for infringement of the German trade mark, claiming damages. The Supreme Court dismissed the action on the ground that no infringement had been committed. It pointed out that it was the main object of a trade mark to designate the goods concerned as originating from the owner of the trade mark but that the trade mark must not be used by him for the control of the re-sale of the trade mark protected goods by making differentiating provisions for sales in other countries. Consequently, the German importer could legitimately sell in Germany Maja soap once it had been brought on the market in Spain by the manufacturer irrespective of the sole distributorship agreement with a German registered user of the (identical) German trade mark. As the importer had not exploited a breach of contract between other parties (*i.e.*, between the manufacturer and sole distributor), the plaintiff could not alternatively maintain that the defendant had committed a tort by inflicting damage on him in a manner prohibited by section 1 of the Law against Unfair Competition[1] and section 826 of the Civil Code. There is reason to believe that this decision will show considerable influence on the expected ruling by the Commission in the fields of trade mark licences and sole distributorship agreements.

5. COPYRIGHT LICENCES

The use of a copyright in literary, dramatic, musical and artistic work, being a monopoly similar to a patent of an invention, may in various ways conflict with antitrust law. The principle of such possible misuse of a copyright as distinct from a patent has been aptly explained in the case of *Alfred Bell & Co. v. Catalda Fine Arts*[2] in the following words:

> In the patent cases, typically the legal monopoly is misused to obtain illegal monopoly over other non-patented goods. In the copyright cases the claimed illegality is the combination of holders of legal monopolies to do something in concert which they might have done separately as to individual copyright articles. They are not accused of attempting to extend the monopoly to articles not copyrighted.

[1] Of June 7, 1909 as amended *(Gesetz gegen den unlauteren Wettbewerb)*.
[2] 74 F. Supp. 973, at 978 (S.D.N.Y. 1947), affirmed as modified, 191 F. 2d 99 (2nd Cir. 1951); see also Oppenheim, *op. cit.*, p. 904.

In any event, as the Supreme Court stated in *Strauss v. American Publishers' Association*,[1] "the rights of the copyright owner are no greater than those of the patentee." Thus, resale price fixing of copyrighted books was condemned,[2] and a (prohibited) conspiracy was found in an agreement between copyright owner-licensors (distributors of motion picture films) and their licensees (motion picture exhibitors) relating to admission prices for picture performances.[3] Whereas in one case "understanding between or parallel business behaviour" by motion picture producers and distributors towards a suburban exhibitor who was refused "first-run" pictures was not proved,[4] monopolisation and attempts at monopolisation in violation of sections 1 and 2 of the Sherman Act by producers and their affiliated distributors and exhibitors and by distributors was found in the case of *United States v. Paramount Pictures*.[5]

Perhaps the most important and certainly a very illustrative case on the effect of antitrust law on copyright is *United States v. The American Society of Composers, Authors and Publishers*[6] (called ASCAP) which was disposed of by consent decree. ASCAP, the leading performing rights society which controls 90% of the copyrighted music in the United States, has thereby obtained a virtual monopoly in licensing the public performance for profit of musical compositions (except as part of a dramatic performance) and collects the royalties due thereon. The formation of ASCAP (and corresponding organisations in many other countries) became necessary for the protection of musical composers and also served the interest of the performers of the composers' music. The members of ASCAP assign their non-dramatic performing rights to this Society, retaining, however, the rights of mechanically recording, printing, publishing and selling them.

[1] 231 U.S. 222 (1913).

[2] *Bobbs-Merill Co. v. Strauss*, 210 U.S. 339 (1908); *Strauss v. American Publishers Association*, 231 U.S. 222 (1913).

[3] *Interstate Circuit Inc. v. United States*, 306 U.S. 208 (1939). The Supreme Court concluded its ruling by saying: "A contract between a copyright owner and one who has no copyright, restraining the competitive distribution of the copyright articles in the open market in order to protect the latter from the competition, can no more be valid than a like agreement between two copyright owners or patentees."

[4] *Theatre Enterprises, Inc. v. Paramount Film Distributing Corporation*, 346 U.S. 537 (1954).

[5] 334 U.S. 131 (1948). On remand, the District Court (85 F. Supp. 881 (S.D.N.Y. 1949)) held that the defendants by way of a vertical integration achieved exclusion of competition and established price fixing and restrictions in the field of distribution. It decreed separation of the defendants' business of producers and distributors from that of exhibitors of motion pictures.

[6] S.D.N.Y. 1950, 1950–1951. Trade cases 62.595. See also *Alden Rochelle, Inc. v. A.S.C.A.P.*, 80 F. Supp. 888 (S.D.N.Y. 1948).

ASCAP licenses these compositions to users on a so-called blanket licence, *i.e.*, its entire musical repertoire, this has proved necessary both in order to avoid the reproach of discrimination against ASCAP members and to prevent the existence of chaotic conditions in the use of copyrighted music on the performers' side. The revenue from the royalties collected by ASCAP is distributed amongst its members. It is apparent that this scheme, though no doubt necessary for the parties involved and ultimately not contrary to the interest of the public, contains many features which would seem to be incompatible with the traditional antitrust law, for instance the blanket licensing system which corresponds to patent licence packaging and, further, the elimination of competition and the monopolisation of a whole industry. Litigation ensued through complaints by the motion picture exhibitors[1] but dissatisfaction with its policy was also expressed by film producers and broadcasting stations. Proceedings against ASCAP were instituted by the U.S. Government in 1934. They were settled by consent decree in 1941 and by a subsequent amended consent decree of 1950 which amounts to a virtual piece of legislation on the rights and duties of ASCAP in regard to both its members and third parties. ASCAP, however, remained in being and is still the monopolistic protection organisation of composers of music.[2] Although the ASCAP cases deal with purely domestic United States issues, the facts underlying them and the factual and legal problems raised in them are of general interest to all countries in which a law against restrictive trade practices may become applicable to similar protection societies, thus also in particular to the Member States of the E.E.C.

In Germany, the Allied Decartelisation Laws were also applicable to agreements concerning copyright.[3] The Cartel Law of 1957 does, however, not contain any special provisions or references relating to copyright.[4] These are nevertheless subject to the general provisions such as the prohibition of actual cartel agreements or resolutions

---

[1] *Alden Rochelle v. ASCAP*, 80 F. Supp. 888 (S.D.N.Y. 1948).

[2] For a comparatively short but nevertheless very informative discussion of the case of *U.S. v. ASCAP* (80 F. Supp. 900 (S.D.N.Y. 1948) including the consent decree of 1950 and its social aspect, see Neale, *op. cit.*, pp. 412–418. For a detailed and thorough treatment of this whole subject see S. Timberg, "Antitrust Aspects of Merchandising Modern Music; the ASCAP Judgment of 1950" in *Law and Contemporary Problems*, Spring 1954 (Duke University School of Law, Durham, North Carolina).

[3] See Ulmer, *Urheber- und Verlagsrecht*, 2nd ed., 1960, p. 35.

[4] The silence of the Cartel Law on copyright is not due to an accidental omission on the side of the legislator, as the question whether this statute should deal with them expressly had been discussed before it came into force, see Heydt in *GRUR* 1952, p. 493 and Lieberknecht, *op. cit.*, p. 303.

(sections 1 to 14), the supervision of market-dominating enterprises (sections 22 to 24), the illegality of measures of boycott and discrimination (section 26) and the power given to the Cartel Authorities to enforce the acceptance by a trade organisation of an enterprise (within the meaning of the Cartel Law) as member (section 27); market-dominating enterprises (section 22) which own copyrights can be ordered to grant compulsory licences.[1]

The prohibition of resale price maintenance (section 15) does not apply, inter alia, to the sale of publications in the fields of literature, music, fine art and photography in the form of books, periodicals, printed pictures *etc.* or gramophone records, irrespective, incidentally, of whether they enjoy copyright protection or not (section 16(1) no. 2). Resale price maintenance through one or more stages in the sale of books and kindred products is thus permitted. German legal writers are well aware of the precarious position of performing rights societies (of the American ASCAP type) from a restrictive trade practices point of view. Such organisations have for a long time been treated as monopolistic enterprises which are not at liberty to refuse the conclusion of contracts with authors or performers (known as the principle of *Kontrahierungszwang*). The question whether they are cartels or, in a given case, market-dominating enterprises with the consequences ensuing from such a position under the Cartel Law has only quite recently engaged the attention of both the Federal Cartel Office and the Commission in Brussels.

The Federal Cartel Office had in 1960 commenced proceedings against the *Gesellschaft für musikalische Aufführungs- und mechanische Vervielfältigungsrechte (Gema)* and the *Bureau International de L'Edition Mécanique (Biem)* (as well as against some other associations) for alleged violations of the Cartel law by fixing prices of gramophone records and stipulating conditions to be maintained on the sale of these articles. After thorough investigations the Federal Cartel Office abandoned these proceedings in July 1963 as no unlawful co-operation between the incriminated organisations could be found. In these investigations the Office had however had an opportunity to examine the legal nature of the two above mentioned societies from the point of view of the Cartel Law. It held that each of them was an association of enterprises in the meaning of section 1 of this Law since authors

---

[1] By s. 22 of the Law on Copyrights on Works of Literature and Music of June 19, 1901; such remedy belongs, however, to the law of copyright proper and not to the cartel law.

(both composers and script writers) who exploit their creative powers in the economic field are to be treated as enterprises; but whereas both *GEMA* and *BIEM* are in a position to influence the relevant market and are therefore market-dominating enterprises within the meaning of section 22 of the Cartel Law, they do not restrict competition so that section 1 of this Law does not become applicable. This ruling is all the more remarkable as *GEMA* itself had argued that *BIEM*, as distinct from the national copyright protection societies, constituted a cartel in accordance with the requirements of section 1. It appears from the complaints made by *GEMA* against the Federal Cartel Office about the abandonment of these proceedings that the Commission of the E.E.C. had initiated investigations against *BIEM* (and that the Federal Cartel Office ought therefore to have awaited the outcome of those proceedings commenced by the Commission.)[1] It will be interesting to learn in due course which view the Commission and, possibly, the European Court will adopt.

B. The Legal Position in the European Economic Community[2]

It was stated at the beginning of this chapter that the rights of industrial and commercial property are in principle subject to the application of Articles 85 ff.[3] This is also the opinion of the Council of Ministers and of the Commission, as appears explicitly from Article 4 (2,b) and (3) and Article 7 of Regulation No. 17.[4] In view of the frequency and great practical importance of licence agreements in international commerce and because of the difficulties of ascertaining with any degree of certainty the legal implications of the effect of cartel law on patent law, the Commission has published an Announcement[5] on Patent Licence Agreements which, as stressed repeatedly therein, is to be understood as a mere expression of its opinion on these implications without prejudice to the interpretation of this part of restrictive trade practices law either by any other (national or Community) Authority or by a Court. As such guide the Announce-

---

[1] See *"Deutsche Zeitung"* (newspaper) of July 27/28 and 31, 1963, p. 7, and *"Die Welt"* (newspaper) of November 2, 1963, p. 8. The findings of the Federal Cartel Office on the position of GEMA, BIEM and other foreign and German copyright managing societies are summarised in Annual Report on the Activities of the Federal Cartel Office for the Year 1963, pp. 57–58.

[2] For a thought-provoking discussion of this subject mainly from a procedural point of view, see Buxbaum, *loc. cit.*, pp. 101–144b.

[3] See *supra*, p. 59.

[4] See Appendix E, *infra*, pp. 205, 206, 208.

[5] See *supra*, p. 59.

ment should be accepted as a very welcome step in the process of necessary clarification of this subject-matter. Apart from these reservations, the Announcement limits its scope to what has been termed in this study the "one-way licence," and, even in respect of this type, only to the terms usually found in licence agreements (clause II paragraph 1), and it expressly refrains from any opinion on "agreements relating to: 1) joint ownership of patents (patent pools), 2) reciprocal licences, 3) multiple parallel licences." Valuable as this limited guidance may be, the fact that many patent licence agreements contain reciprocal grants and not a few fall into both the first and second category makes their investigation on the basis of their treatment under the hitherto known law against restrictive trade practices indispensable. Whether this Announcement will in time be supplemented by another statement dealing with the types of agreements so far not mentioned in the present one is doubtful. The Director-General of the Department of Competition of the Commission, VerLoren van Themaat in his address to the International Chamber of Commerce in Paris on March 14, 1963 has commented on the two Announcements of December 24, 1962 as follows:[1]

> Some prominent representatives of industry have raised the question whether it is not the duty of the Commission to determine for the benefit of the whole economic community which agreements and which modes of behaviour are prohibited or permitted according to Articles 85 and 86 respectively. In its Announcement of December 24, 1962 the Commission has taken an important step in this direction, particularly in the field of exclusive distributorship agreements and patent licence agreements. Quite generally, however, I do not think that this is a good solution either for the enterprises or for the Common Market. As regards the enterprises, a general interpretation of Articles 85 and 86 in respect of various kinds of agreements can neither do justice to the general economic relations nor to the special conditions of the individual case. A comprehensive condemnation of specific types of agreements might well be unjustified in the case of the one or the other individual agreement or for this or that economic region. This is, incidentally, also the reason why no condemnation is contained in the Announcement of December 24. Any inference to the contrary from these Announcements would be an erroneous one.

A comparison of the operative part of the Announcement (clauses I A to D) with section 20 of the German Cartel Law (and its interpretation by the Cartel Authorities, the Courts and writers) shows the strong influence of that part of German Cartel Law. An exhaustive exposition of the application of Art. 85 to patent licence agreements in the light of the said Announcement would by far exceed the scope of this study and we must therefore limit our observations to some

[1] Published in *WuW*, 1963, pp. 555 ff., at p. 557.

points of major importance which have either not been fully dealt with in the Announcement or would appear to be necessary for the proper understanding of the Commission's intended practice.[1]

Clause A of the Announcement lists those restrictions which fall within the proper scope of the patent and raise therefore no antitrust questions, at any event if forming part of a mere one-way licence; the statement of the Commission only confirms a legal position which has been accepted in both United States and German law. A few annotations may, however, be useful.

(1) Generally, restrictions must not be extended to unpatented goods; if an article has been lawfully sold to a third party, the patent protection has ceased to be effective. Thus, articles manufactured with a patented machine are outside patent protection, but if the machine has only been hired out to a manufacturer for his use or if merely the exploitation of a patented process has been licensed, the articles produced in this way may still remain under patent protection.[2]

(2) Restrictions as to the time of a licence agreement cannot be circumvented by dressing up the licence for the use of a patent as one for the know-how of its exploitation – unless perhaps the know-how has a substantially independent value.

(3) Restrictions in respect of territory are probably those which require the closest scrutiny under antitrust law. In conformity with the law of both the United States and Germany, the Commission considers territorial restrictions, *i.e.*, restrictions for a part or the whole of the territory for which a patent protection exists, or providing for the use of the patent by a particular manufacturer or seller only, as being within the scope of the patent grant;[3] one could, however, assume that an agreement to that effect with a competitor-licensee might be treated as a prohibited market sharing.[4]

A distinction had to be drawn between such restrictions as apply to the territory of another Member State of the E.E.C., and to that of a

---

[1] Agreements or other arrangements in regard to patent licences and know-how between parent companies and their subsidiaries which contain restrictions which would be caught by Art. 85 if they were made between independent enterprises are therefore not discussed in this chapter since the determination of their validity belongs to the special problem whether companies combined in a concern are independent enterprises under Art. 85, see *supra*, p. 11.

[2] Lüdecke-Fischer , *op. cit.*, D. 54, p. 414; Baumbach-Hefermehl, *op. cit.*, p. 1363, n. 8, and p. 1364, ns. 11, 14.

[3] Announcement cl. I A, 4b, c.

[4] On the principles laid down in the case of *United States v. Masonite Corporation*, 316 U.S. 265 (1942), and *United States v. General Electric Co.*, 82 F. Supp. 753, at 846 (D.N.Y. 1949); see also *infra*, p. 99.

non-Member State. In the first situation, a patent protection of the article concerned in another Member State in favour of the licensor has the effect of making restrictions of manufacture or sale or a prohibition of export into that State permissible since the lawfulness of such restriction would in any event be based on the protection provided by a patent which would enable the patentee-licensor to prevent the sale there. If however the patentee in the other State is a third party, the legal position would seem to be different. Whether the export of an article patented in Member State A into Member State B where no patent protection exists can be contractually prohibited is doubtful. According to the view expressed by the majority of German writers, this question has to be answered by reference to the relevant provisions of the national patent laws prevailing in those Member States from which the export is to be prohibited. For instance in Germany, the putting of the patented article on the market (section 6 of the Patent Law) has the effect of making an export prohibition lawful as an element of the proper scope of the patent protection.[1] On the other hand, the absence of a corresponding provision in the national patent law of another Member State from which an export is to take place would have the effect of making a contractual prohibition of export unlawful provided that commerce between Member States is affected thereby.[2]

As regards the second situation, it would seem to be irrelevant whether patent protection does or does not exist in a non-Member State in which a licensee residing there has been put under restrictions, for Article 85 will only suppress restrictive trade practices "capable of affecting trade between Member States and which are designed to prevent, restrict or distort competition within the Common Market or which have this effect." In other words, according to the principle that only such restrictions are subject to Articles 85 and 86 as take effect inside the area of the Common Market,[3] restrictions upon the exercise of licences exploited in non-Member States are outside the ambit of the Rules of Competition. Yet this statement is subject to an important qualification. Restrictions imposed on a licensee in a non-Member State may have a repercussive effect in the State of the licensor or in another Member State, e.g., a term compelling the licensee to purchase

---

[1] Deringer, op. cit., Article 85(1) n. 36 with further references; ibid., Regulation No. 17. Art. 4, n. 16; Magen, op. cit., p. 135; Hootz in NJW, 1963, pp. 232, 233. Contra: revised practice of the Federal Cartel Office, see Annual Report of the Federal Cartel Office for the Year 1962, p. 70.

[2] Magen, op. cit., p. 141; Jansse, Oudemans & Wolterbeck, loc. cit., p. 282 (example g).

[3] See supra, pp. 38–39, 45–47.

all the material necessary for the production of the patented goods will prevent the licensee from obtaining suitable supplies of such material from other sources within the Common Market. Whether such indirect effects lead to the application of Articles 85 and 86 is a matter of hot controversy. The Federal Cartel Office has answered this question (which arises on the interpretation of section 20 of the German Cartel Law) in the affirmative but has made known that "not every merely potentially possible repercussion on the domestic market which might in certain circumstances occur in the future... will be taken into account; in fact, effects within the area in which the Cartel Law prevails must be discernible, at least in an inchoate state, at the time when the agreement under review is examined under the provisions of the Cartel Law."[1] Although this ruling is rather vague it shows the intended restraint which the Federal Cartel Office will exercise in cases of this kind. Moreover, in its practice the Federal Cartel Office has liberally granted permission for the imposition of such terms, when they were not too comprehensive and seemed to be justified by the licensor's legitimate economic interests. Whether the interpretation of Article 85 will be similar cannot yet be said; the Announcement does not deal with this point and rulings by the Commission (or by national authorities or Courts) have not yet been published. It is however probable that the view of the Commission will not be stricter than that of the Federal Cartel Office.[2] The last word will of course lie with the European Court.

It is somewhat surprising that the Announcement does not say whether the licensor can fix the price of the patented article when sold by the licensee. As such restriction is expressly allowed in section 20(2) no. 2 of the German Cartel Law, one might infer that the omission is a deliberate one with the effect that such restriction is not allowed. On the other hand, the absence of any reference to this very important point and the emphasis in clause IV of the Announcement that the list in clause I(A) is not an exhaustive enumeration of the rights conferred by the patent, would justify the view that this question has

---

[1] Letter of the Federal Cartel Office of August 15, 1962, *WuW* 1963, p. 440. This practice of the Federal Cartel Office – Court decisions seem not to have been rendered – has been severely criticised by several writers on the ground that s. 20(2) no. 5, s, 98(2) and s. 6(1) of the Cartel Law (which are those dealing with the export trade), must necessarily be understood to accept repercussions on the domestic market as possible and outside the application of the Cartel Law, see Magen, *op. cit.*, pp. 137 ff.; Schwartz, *op. cit.*, pp. 40 ff., 78–92.

[2] Support for this assumption can perhaps be gained from the ruling of the Commission in the Sole Distributorship Agreement Grosfillex-Fillestorf, see *infra*, p. 128.

been intentionally left open. In principle, both United States and German law permit the licensor to fix the price.[1] If, however, the licensor imposes different price structures upon his several licensees in Common Market territories this might lead to a prevention, restriction or distortion of competition and must be considered as prohibited by Article 85 (1). Difficult questions however remain if, as it often happens, the price determination applies to goods that are composed of both patented and unpatented elements and sold as single units, since vertical price fixing in respect of unpatented goods is, subject to certain exceptions,[2] illegal in both United States and German law.

Clauses B, C and D concern restrictions that exceed those which are covered by a patent grant but shall nevertheless be permitted on grounds of economic expediency or because their disadvantageous effect on competition would in any event be minimal.

Clause C corresponds to section 20(1) no. 1 of the Cartel Law but is somewhat more exact in that it explicitly mentions undertakings as to observance of quality standards and as to purchases of supplies so far as they are indispensable for the technically perfect exploitation of the patent. The wording in the Announcement is narrower than the similar provision in the German Cartel Law so that other restrictions imposed for the purpose of a perfect exploitation of the patent are not permitted. Thus, a condition that the licensee must not manufacture and/or sell competing products could not be lawfully agreed upon (whereas in German law such a condition, although in principle not permitted, could, and in suitable cases would, be sanctioned by the Cartel Authority by virtue of the power conferred on it by section 20(3)). The same applies to other tying clauses, e.g., package licensing. The combination with the licensed user of a trade mark would however be perfectly lawful.[3]

---

[1] The opinions of the writers are divided: Jansse, Oudemans & Wolterbeck, loc. cit., pp. 276, 282; Kleemann, Die Wettbewerbsregeln in der EWG, 1962, p. 47; Gleiss-Hirsch, op. cit., Art. 85 n. 57; Honig a.o., op. cit., p. 23; and Magen, op. cit., p. 164 consider such price determination as permitted whereas Deringer, op. cit., Art. 85 n. 37 expresses the opposite view.

[2] Resale price maintenance is in German law only permitted in the circumstances set forth in s. 16 of the Cartel Law (branded goods) and in the United States under the Fair Trade Legislation of many States as sanctioned by the Miller-Tyding Act, 1937 (50 U.S. Stat. 693) and the McGuire Act, 1952 (66 U.S. Stat., 631) also in respect of branded articles, cf. Oppenheim, op. cit., p. 207–211. The Federal Cartel Office has recently ruled (Annual Report of the Activities of the Federal Cartel Office for the Year 1961, p. 58) that if the patented portion of a composite product is the characteristic and main part, the price of the total article may be fixed. As regards the United Kingdom, see s. 1 of the recently enacted Resale Prices Act, 1964 (Appendix D, infra, p. 180).

[3] See supra, p. 64.

Clause D is similar to section 20(1) no. 3 but somewhat more exact. It allows (as stated in the explanation thereto) the imposition on the licensee of non-exclusive undertakings only. The licensee who has made an improvement invention and obtains patent protection for it (in accordance with the relevant national patent law), may only grant to the licensor a non-exclusive licence.[1]

Incidentally, it may be asked whether these rules apply to foreign patents, *i.e.*, to agreements concerning a licence to exploit a patent registered in a country other than that whose antitrust law controls the agreement. The Announcement is silent on this question. However, since at least the interpretation of sections 20 and 21 of the German Cartel law in regard to foreign patents and unpatented trade secrets is in favour of the applicability of these provisions if restrictions of a nature which would be prohibited in a purely domestic agreement might produce a reaction on the German Market,[2] it can probably be presumed that the Commission might, if occasion arises, adopt the same attitude.

Clause E deals with certain obligations of the patentee-licensor. Such obligations are outside the scope of the patent grant and must therefore be scrutinised under antitrust law provisions. The exemption from Article 85(1) of an undertaking on the part of the licensor not to authorise any third person to exploit the invention confirms the legality of the grant of an exclusive licence; it follows from such grant that the licensor, by necessary implication, is prevented from exploiting the licensed invention himself. To this extent, no. 2 of clause E can be regarded as declaratory only. On the other hand, may the licensor of one or more non-exclusive licences agree not to exploit the invention in question? Whereas in United States law such an undertaking would be invalid,[3] and in the German Cartel law its lawfulness not free from doubt,[4] the Announcement would seem to answer this question in the affirmative since the undertaking of the licensor not to exploit the invention has not been made dependant upon whether the grant relates to an exclusive or to a non-exclusive licence. As regards other restrictions accepted by the licensor, *e.g.*, not to manufacture and/or sell

---

[1] That the licensee's "grant back" must be limited to a non-exclusive licence had already been decided by the German Supreme Court under the Allied Decartelisation Laws, see decision of *the Supreme Court* of March 18, 1955, *NJW* 1955, p. 829 (*Kokillenguss* case). See also *supra*, p. 65 n. 5.

[2] See *supra*, p. 68.

[3] *Mason City Tent Awning Co. v. Clapper*, 144 F. Supp. 754, at 767 (W.D. Mo. 1956) with further references; see also Oppenheim, *op. cit.*, p. 822.

[4] Lüdecke-Fischer, *op. cit.*, n. 36, p. 733.

competing goods, these are prohibited by Article 85(1) as they are in United States law[1] and in German law, in the latter under section 15 or 18 respectively of the Cartel Law. The Announcement is silent on an agreement in respect of licences for the use of *registered designs*. This is surprising, as this kind of industrial property plays an important part not only in Germany but also in many other States. Grants of licences of registered designs are possible and the relevant rules are, at least in German law,[2] the same as those relating to licences under patents. As a registered design is essentially a monopoly of the same nature as a patent and has therefore in German Cartel Law (section 20) been subjected to the same restrictive trade practice provisions as patents, agreements for licences of registered designs must be considered as coming within the orbit of Article 85, and the principles set forth in the Announcement should *mutatis mutandis* be applicable to such agreements.

As mentioned above, the Announcement, as stated in clause III, expressly refrains from dealing with the more complex and difficult cases of patent pools, reciprocal licences and multiple parallel licences, although it is very often these types which are the main subject of international agreements. Since it is understood that guidance on such agreements will not be forthcoming in the near future, the parties concerned will be wise to study the experience gained in the United States and Germany in order to avoid the conclusion of agreements which might later be declared unlawful. The same consideration holds good for grants of licences of trade marks and copyrights.

Similarly, in regard *know-how*, it is merely stated in the Announcement that it might be dealt with in a later ruling.[3] This is all the more surprising as in the First Statement on the Application of Article 85 of the Treaty to Certain Patent Licence Agreements of November 9, 1962[4] (which is now obsolete), the Commission had indicated its intention to declare, in accordance with paragraph 3 of Article 85, that the provisions of its paragraph 1 were not applicable to, *inter alia*, "reciprocal agreements between the licensor and the licensee about exchange of know-how." In fact, neither in the Announcement referred to nor in any other publication has the Commission up to the present time expressed its views on such an exchange or on the treatment of know-how from a restrictive trade practices' angle in general.

[1] Oppenheim, *op. cit.*, p. 822, n. 86.
[2] Lüdecke-Fischer, *op. cit.*, n. 36, pp. 731–736.
[3] Clause III.
[4] *J.O.* 1962, p. 2627.

This negative attitude is rather regrettable since licence agreements of know-how, either combined with patent licence agreements or as separate contracts, play an ever-growing role in the international commerce of our industrial society. It has therefore so far been left to legal science to work out the legal principles which govern know-how licences under the Rules of Competition and thereby to prepare the ground for later official rulings by the E.E.C. organs.

Although American antitrust and German cartel law will afford guidance in this field also, the scarcity of specific statutory provisions as well as the still not quite settled concept of know-how[1] and of its legal status in the relevant national laws permit the expression of any firm views on its position under Articles 85 and 86 only with a high degree of diffidence. In the first place, having regard to Article 36 and the wide scope of Article 85 it may be assumed that both industrial and commercial know-how are treated as being within the purview of the Rules of Competition.[2] Secondly, the national laws on the legal protection of trade secrets and know-how in general, which are to some extent at variance, have to be taken into account when their licensing is scrutinised under Article 85.[3] Thirdly, the basic difference between the nature of a patent (as well as that of registered designs, trade marks and copyrights) and of know-how (which is not a statutorily protected monopoly) must not be lost sight of.

Whilst the scope of a patent follows from the statutory patent monopoly, it may be asked whether one can attribute a corresponding quality to know-how. As legally protected know-how is a proprietary right or, through the protection under the law of tort, a quasi-pro-

---

[1] See *supra*, pp. 72 ff. Timberg in *Doing Business in the Common Market* (at p. 125) vividly, though perhaps with some exaggeration, describes this position as follows: "This whole problem of know-how is still a largely unexplored area. The legal contours for the protection of know-how is something which has not been resolved even within the Common Market. The problem of defining know-how, the problem of giving commercial protection to know-how and, above all, the problem of what restrictions may validly relate to know-how, these have not yet been developed to a satisfactory state. And yet they may, in industry after industry, be more important than the problem of patent licensing."

[2] Van Notten, *loc. cit.*, p. 529, n. 16, aptly observes that "in the Member States, with the exception of the Netherlands, there is indeed a tendency in law and doctrine to distinguish between the protection of industrial and commercial trade secrets." It should be noted that Art. 4(2), (2,b) of Regulation No. 17 concerns industrial know-how only so that licences of commercial know-how are not privileged.

[3] For instructive reviews of the – in principle – resembling protection of know-how in the law of the Member States, see van Notten, *loc. cit.*, p. 541–546, and Charles S. Maddock in 2 C.M.L.R. (1964) pp. 36, 48–64. It has to be emphasised that know-how as defined in Article 4(2) (2,b) of Regulation No. 17 need not be secret – as distinct from the concept of the (technical) *"Betriebsgeheimnis"* in s. 21 of the German Cartel law (see Deringer, *op. cit.*, n. 17 on Regulation No. 17 Art. 4; Ladas, *loc. cit.*, p. 744).

prietary right, certain legal consequences, called "inherent rights" of the owner of know-how, have to be recognised. Such rights are the capacity to grant licences upon it and to oblige the licensee not to make it public or allow other persons to do so inasmuch as such acts would destroy the very nature of the legally protected and protectable right of know-how. On the other hand, a "no contest" clause, corresponding to a term directed against forfeiture of the patent in patent licence agreements, would seems to be prohibited since the licensee should be able to prove that the know-how in question has (during the currency of the agreement) become public knowledge; such a provision, may however, be validated under Article 85(3). Next, are restrictions imposed on the licensee as to territory, quantity and volume, singly or cumulatively, still within these inherent rights? In the Manual for Firms,[1] Article 4(2) (2,b) is declared applicable to technical know-how. Van Notten[2] rightly points out that the language of the Manual does not make it clear whether its general discussion of "inherent rights" refers to patents only or also to know-how. Owing to the lack of statutory protection of know-how he concludes that restrictions both as to area and largely as to use are caught by Article 85, which means that such restrictions in a know-how licence agreement are to be judged differently from similar ones contained in a patent licence agreement. He relies for this view on an illustrative and carefully reasoned decision of the Federal Cartel Office.[3] It can however be doubted whether this decision really supports his opinion, for the Cartel Office has only held that a prohibition of production in, and export into, another Member State (the Netherlands) is invalid under Article 85(1) when the know-how (in this instance a technical trade secret) becomes public.[4] Since, in spite of the undoubtable conceptual differences between patents (and therefore also patent licences) and know-how (and know-how licences), the economic and legal affinities are very close, it may be asked whether the scope of a patent and the inherent rights of the owner of know-how should not be largely equated. Such a method would be justified all the more in that many, if not

[1] Parts II, III, 3 (pp. 10/11). See also *supra*, p. 5 n. 3.
[2] *Loc. cit.*, pp. 532 f.
[3] Of February 1962, *WuW* 1962, p. 551, 568–571. It is expressly mentioned in this decision that the Directorate-General, Commission of the E.E.C., had been consulted in this case (at p. 558).
[4] *Ibid.*, p. 569. The Cartel Office approved the licence agreement in question by virtue of Art. 85(3) which it had power to do before the coming into force of Art. 9 of Regulation No. 17. The reasons given for this exemption supply an interesting commentary on the prerequisites for the application of Art. 85(3) as understood by a national Authority.

most, patent licence agreements contain corresponding provisions for know how related to the patent to be exploited.[1]

In so far restrictions are not within the inherent rights, they are caught by Article 85(1) but may of course be sanctioned under paragraph 3 of this Article. One such restriction is the obligation undertaken by the licensor to grant to the licensee an exclusive licence. Such a grant may have a threefold significance. First, the licensor may confer upon a sole licensee a licence unlimited as to territory; secondly, such licence may be limited as to a specific area; thirdly, the licensor may, in addition to either grant, undertake not to exploit the know-how himself, either generally or in relation to the area in question. It would seem that on the basis of an analogy with patent licence agreements[2] and the German Cartel Law[3] such a restriction is outside the reach of Article 85(1).[4]

As regards the restrictions imposed on the licensee, it has already been suggested that those which belong to the inherent rights of the owner of know-how should not be regarded as coming within Article 85(1).[5] It should be added that the licensor should be able freely to determine the price of goods manufactured and sold under the know-how licence just as the licensor in a patent licence agreement may do, short only of differentiating between prices to be charged by several licensees in different territories of the Common Market.[6] Tie-in clauses are generally caught by the prohibition, except, probably, the obligation to obtain supplies of certain materials, especially raw material "in so far as they are indispensable for the technically perfect use of the know-how."[7] Restrictions with respect to use and distribution should, as a rule, be permitted as being the exercise of the inherent rights of the know-how's owner – except if they involve restrictions

---

[1] If this view prevails, restrictions as to quantity and volume, which are also mentioned in the *Manual for Firms*, would also have to be regarded as covered by the inherent rights of the owner of the know-how.

[2] See Announcement on Patent Licence Agreements of December 24, 1962, *J.O.*, p. 2922, clause I.E.

[3] Decision of the Federal Cartel Office of February 1962, see *supra*, p. 89 n. 3 at pp. 563, 568 ff.

[4] Accord, Ladas, *loc. cit.*, p. 745; van Notten, *loc. cit.*, pp. 535 f. The latter suggests however that in a grant of an exclusive licence to be developed in the future, such restriction undertaken by the licensor might stifle his incentive for further research and would thus have to be considered as violating Art. 85(1).

[5] See *supra*, pp. 89–90.

[6] See *supra*, pp. 84 f. Both Ladas, *loc. cit.*, p. 746, and van Notten, *loc. cit.*, p. 537, take the opposite view, subject only to the qualification that if the licensor sells identical goods in the same market and has a legitimate interest in not becoming the victim of his own creation, permission under Art. 85(3) should be given.

[7] *Cf.* the Announcement of December 24, *J.O.* 1962, p. 2922, cl. I.C.

upon the licensee's freedom to manufacture by use of the know-how in another Member State.[1] Output and control of sales are not permitted restrictions but according to Ladas,[2] the facts that the know-how is of substantial value and that but for its acquisition the licensee's manufacture would have been impossible, may justify such restrictions. A clause preventing the licensee from manufacturing and/or dealing in competitive goods is bad but a restriction can probably be placed on the licensee's use of the granted know-how in the manufacture of a line of goods other than those which are the subject-matter of the specific licence agreement. Doubts have been expressed as to whether a licensee may be obliged to affix the licensor's trademark or trade name markings to the goods sold under a know-how licence as distinct from such permitted restriction on a patent licensee.[3] Lastly, the grant of non-exclusive licences of know-how is outside the purview of Article 85 as are non-exclusive licences of patents.

If, as it very often occurs, an agreement contains both terms relating to grants of patent licences and licences of know-how, the Commission will probably, in accordance with the German practice,[4] apply the rules governing the former unless, perhaps, the latter are in fact the more important.

II. Sole Distributorship Agreements

In his review of the development of "exclusive dealing" and the administrative and judicial attitude towards such business arrangements under United States antitrust law, one of the greatest American authorities on this subject, Professor Milton Handler of Columbia University, expressed the view: "Exclusives are not of transcendent importance either legally or economically. There are other practices of infinitely greater antitrust concern."[5] It is not unlikely that one will in due course be justified in repeating this statement in respect of the antitrust law of the E.E.C., but at the moment it seems that the control of exclusive distributorship contracts is one of the major concerns of the Commission. Having regard to the very wide range of the prohibition of such agreements under Article 85(1) as expressed in

[1] See the decision of the Federal Cartel Office, *supra*, p. 89 ns. 3 and 4.
[2] *Loc. cit.*, p. 746. It is not clear whether that writer wants in such case to exclude such restrictions from the prohibition of paragraph 1 or thinks of the application of paragraph 3 of Art. 85.
[3] See Buxbaum, *loc. cit.*, pp. 115 f.
[4] See decision of the Federal Cartel Office, *supra*, n. 1, at pp. 558 ff.
[5] *Op. cit.*, p. 46.

the Announcement,[1] it seems expedient to refer in some detail to the relevant legal position both in the United States and the Member States of the E.E.C., especially in Germany and France, in order to understand and appreciate the creation of this new rule in European commerce which to a considerable extent also affects enterprises in non-Member States. These agreements are, generally without any difference in meaning, also described as exclusive dealing contracts, exclusive dealing and tying contracts, exclusive agency contracts, exclusive agency contracts made with commercial agents, exclusive representation contracts, exclusive distribution contracts, exclusive territorial distributorship contracts, exclusive concession contracts (or, in all these instances, agreements respectively).[2] In American legal literature, they are often referred to merely as 'exclusive dealing(s)' or 'exclusive(s),' amongst others also by Handler.[3] In this study, changes in the use of this varied terminology are without material significance and are only made for linguistic reasons. In Germany, the expression usually used is *"Alleinvertriebsverträge,"* but sometimes they are referred to as *"Ausschliesslichkeitsverträge," "Exklusivverträge," "Alleinvertriebsbindungen," "Ausschliesslichkeitsbindungen."* In French, they are known as *"contrats de représentation exclusive"* or *"contrats de concession exclusive de vente"* or *"contrats d'exclusivité"* or *"contrats comportant une exclusivité."*

Again, in this study, the two parties involved in an exclusive dealing agreement are throughout called supplier and distributor. A supplier may be a manufacturer or wholesaler of any goods who sells them through an independent party which may either be a single trader, partnership or limited company, irrespective of whether such party carries on a business as mere "representative" for one or more suppliers or acts as distributor only in addition to or incidentally to a business of a similar or different nature. An employee or, as a rule, an agent (in the legal sense of the term)[4] of the supplier is not a distributor for the purposes of antitrust law.

---

[1] Announcement on Exclusive Agency Contracts made with Commercial Agents of December 21/24, 1962, *J.O.* 1962, pp. 2921 ff.

[2] Attempts can be found to distinguish the various restrictions on the supplier and distributor respectively, see, *e.g.*, the references by Oppenheim, *op. cit.*, p. 682, but useful as they may be no such distinctions from a terminological point of view have been generally accepted.

[3] *Op. cit., passim.*

[4] See however, *infra*, pp. 93–95 as to the United States law and pp. 117–120 as to the Cartel Law of the E.E.C.

1. UNITED STATES OF AMERICA

In the United States exclusive dealing agreements were at first not severely affected by the Sherman Law but this position changed after the enactment of the Clayton Act in 1914, section 3 of which proscribes exclusive dealing and tying arrangements where their effect "may be to substantially lessen competition or tend to create a monopoly in any line of commerce." Although this section is the specific one enacted to make such undesired agreements unlawful, the Sherman Act is still applicable to certain contracts of this type so that an agreement may contravene both statutes.

Exclusive dealing agreements usually contain one or more of the following contractual stipulations:

(a) an undertaking by the distributor not to handle competing goods;

(b) an undertaking by the distributor to limit his sales to a certain geographical area or to a certain group or certain groups of customers;

(c) an undertaking by the supplier to refrain from making supplies available to any other distributor in such geographical area or to one competing in sales to a certain category or categories of customers.

Frequently, supplier and distributor give reciprocal undertakings. At the outset, the legal character of the two parties involved in such agreements must be scrutinised. Whereas "supplier" comprises manufacturers and wholesalers but patent owners only in so far as they sell their patented articles otherwise than through licensees of their patent (when to some extent different rules come into play), in regard to the "distributor" the important question arises whether and if so how far, agents of the supplier (in the legal sense of the term) fall into this category with the effect that the antitrust law provisions do not extend to such relationship.[1]

A supplier may, from the legal point of view, effect all transactions of sale which he has power to do himself through one or more agents, without offending the antitrust law as the acts of an agent are in law deemed to be those of the principal. Needless to say, in a given case a Court will have to be convinced that a contract denominated as one

[1] See *Federal Trade Commission v. Curtis Publishing Co.*, 260 U.S. 568 (1923) in which the Supreme Court said: "Judged by its terms, we think this contract is one of agency, not of sale upon condition and the record reveals no surrounding circumstances sufficient to give it a different character. This, of course, disposes of the charges under the Clayton Act."

of agency does satisfy all the essential requirements of the concept of agency and does not turn out on close analysis to be one of sale.[1] But whilst in the economically lower levels of industry and commerce distribution through the medium of genuine agency will as a rule be accepted,[2] situations have occurred in more powerful economic strata where Courts were called upon to decide whether distribution through an agency, even if this complied with the necessary elements of this institution, was nevertheless incompatible with antitrust law. In *United States v. General Electric Co.*[3] the Supreme Court held that the Company could lawfully, through a large net of wholesale and retail merchants (even though these had previously bought the lamps and sold them as their owners but had not to pay for them until they were sold), control resale prices provided they were agents in the full legal sense, which included *del credere* agents. According to the Court, the usual private law tests as to the delimitation between sale and purchase between independent firms on the one hand and agency on the other are also decisive in the province of antitrust law. As the Court found that the arrangements withstood the test of agency, the Government's allegation of violation of the Sherman Act was not sustained. However, no reliance can today be placed on this decision since in *United States v. Masonite Corporation*,[4] where the facts were similar, the Supreme Court distinguished, in truth virtually overruled, the decision in the *General Electric Co.* case, apparently mainly on account of the stipulation of a *del credere* agency.[5] Mr. Justice Douglas said:

> Del credere agency has an ancient lineage and has been put to numerous business and mercantile uses... But however useful it may be in allocating risks

[1] As was held by the Supreme Court in *Standard Fashions Co. v. Margrane-Houston Co.*, 258 U.S. 346 (1922) where it was found that "full title and dominion (of the goods concerned) passed to the buyer" the contract with whom had been framed to appear as a genuine agency agreement.

[2] See *e.g., Federal Trade Commission v. Curtis Publishing Co.*, 260 U.S. 568 (1923); Oppenheim, *op. cit.*, pp. 685 f.

[3] 272 U.S. 476 (1926). The opinion of the Court was delivered by Taft, C. J. The case involved two issues, namely first, the sale of General Electric's electric lamps and, secondly, the validity of a licence granted to the Westinghouse Lamp Company to manufacture and sell electric lamps protected by a patent in favour of General Electric Co. Although General Electric Co. was also the patentee of the lamp sold by it, the problem relating to agency is of a general applicability.

[4] 316 U.S. 265 (1942). For other aspects of this case, see *infra*, p. 99. On the other hand, when the same contracts which were the subject-matter of the aforementioned General Electric Co. case of 1926 became an issue in *United States v. General Electric Co.*, 82 F. Supp. 753 (D.N.J. 1949), they were upheld as genuine and as such unobjectionable contracts of agency with reference to the previous decision (at p. 827).

[5] This case also involved the sale by a patentee but, as in the *General Electric* case, the Court's ruling and observations on the agency aspect are equally applicable to exclusive distributorship agreements, see Oppenheim *op. cit.*, p. 685, n. 19, p. 207 n. 38.

between the parties and determining their rights inter se, its terms do not necessarily control when the rights of others intervene, whether they be creditors or the sovereign... Certainly, if the del credere agency device were given broad approval, whole industries could be knit together so as to regulate prices and suppress competition... Doubtless, there is a proper area for utilisation by a patentee of a del credere agent in the sale or disposition of the patented article... But where he utilises the sales organisation of another business – a business with which he has no intimate relationship – quite different problems are posed since such a regimentation of a marketing system is peculiarly susceptible to the restraints of trade which the Sherman Act condemns.

Handler's comment on these two cases is as follows:[1]

The props from the first part of this decision (*i.e.*, in the General Electric case) were removed in *U.S. v. Masonite Corp.*, 316 U.S. 265 (1942), where the Court pierced the conceptualistic veil of agency and invalidated price fixing among those who are in reality independent businessmen.[2]

Yet the ruling in the *Masonite* case very probably does not apply to an agency agreement between a supplier and one or more independent businessmen if the transactions in question are on a small scale and are not reasonably likely "to substantially lessen competition or tend to create a monopoly."[3] Lastly, the presence of a genuine agency will not be relevant if two or more suppliers sell at fixed prices through a common agent as such a device violates section 1 of the Sherman Act.[4]

Having tried to clarify the legal character of the parties to these agreements we shall now turn to their treatment by the Courts and the administrative agency created for the enforcement of antitrust law.

In the first important case decided by the Supreme Court,[5] an agreement of the type set forth under (a) above between a New York Company manufacturing and supplying fashion patterns, which controlled 52,000 so-called pattern agencies in the entire country amounting to a control of two-fifths of the whole market, and one retail store in Boston, was declared invalid on the ground that it might probably substantially lessen competition or tend to create a monopoly. The Court added however that section 3 of the Clayton Act "was not intended to reach every remote lessening of competition" in view of the

---

[1] Handler, *op. cit.*, p. 82, n. 73.

[2] See to the same effect, *United States v. General Electric Co.*, 80 F. Supp. 989 (S.D.-N.Y. 1948) (the *Carboloy* case) where the Court said: "The agency arrangement, as applied to the manufacturing operations of the agents, was a pure sham, designed to invoke the rule of *United States v. General Electric Co.*, 272 U.S. 476 (1926), but came short of falling within its protection because of the nature of the agents' activities."

[3] See *Federal Trade Commission v. Curtis Publishing Co.*, 260 U.S. 568 (1923); Oppenheim, *op. cit.*, pp. 685 f.

[4] *Virginia Excelsior Mills v. FTC*, 256 F. 2d 538 (4th Cir. 1958).

[5] *Standard Fashion Co. v. Magrane-Houston Co.*, 258 U.S. 346 (1922).

requirement that such lessening must be substantiated. In the *Standard Stations* case,[1] the Supreme Court by a majority of five to four con-demned an exclusive supply agreement which Standard Oil Company had concluded with nearly 6,000 independent petrol filling stations. These agreements covered 16% of the total of all such stations in the western States of the U.S.A; 23% of all petrol sold in that area was supplied by Standard Oil, about 7% of the whole by Standard's own and the same percentage by contractually bound independent filling stations, the balance being sold direct to industrial users. Standard's leading six competitors who accounted for 42.5% of the total sales, employed similar exclusive dealing arrangements. Most of Standard's contracts were running from year to year with a renewal clause, a few for longer periods. Although the majority of the Court conceded that such arrangements might have economic advantages that might also be in the general public interest, it nevertheless con-sidered that owing to the severe restrictions of competition section 3 of the Clayton Act would apply, whereas the minority opinion relied on the Rule of Reason under which the evaluation of economic issues would be decisive.[2] It appears from these decisions that the Supreme Court[3] based its rulings not on evidence and appreciation of economic facts and forseable consequences but applied the test of a prima facie presumption of a substantial lessening of competition if the exclusive dealing agreement covered a quantatively substantial portion of the products affected thereby, so that it was immaterial to prove that competition had been actually reduced.

In contrast with the attitude of the Courts, the Federal Trade Commission,[4] true to the task for which it was created, namely to

---

[1] *Standard Oil Co. of California and Standard Stations, Inc. v. United States*, 337 U.S. 293 (1949).

[2] See for a similar case in which such agreements were also invalidated, *Richfield Oil Corp. v. United States*, 343 U.S. 922 (1952).

[3] The lower Courts followed this practice, sometimes applying it even more rigor-ously, see Handler, *op. cit.*, p. 38, 123, ns. 42-44.

[4] The Federal Trade Commission (F.T.C.) which was created by the Federal Trade Commission Act of September 26, 1914 (c. 311, 38 Stat. 317), is an administrative agency of the United States Government with far reaching tasks and powers in the fields of antitrust and unfair competition. It cannot only prosecute or institute civil proceedings in the Courts but has also jurisdiction to act as a tribunal rendering judicial decisions, especially in cases of violation of s. 2, 3, 7 and 8 of the Clayton Act. If the F.T.C. issues a "cease and desist order" (*i.e.*, one or more injunctions) which is not observed by the party concerned, the Commission can apply to a Circuit Court of Appeals for its enforcement. Correspondingly, the aggrieved party may apply to this Court (within a specified time) for the Order to be set aside. The F.T.C.'s finding as to the facts, if supported by evidence, shall be conclusive, subject however to the Court granting leave to adduce further evidence (s. 5(6) (c)). Its decisions are published.

examine, evaluate and appraise complex economic situations, after some earlier oscillation approached the question of the lawfulness of exclusive distributorship agreements from the opposite angle, *i.e.*, applying the test of whether such agreement not only substantially fulfilled the prerequisite of quantity but also was likely to lead to an actual lessening of competition in the relevant market. Even though in the *Maico* case[1] and several later cases based on *Maico*[2] agreements of this kind were not upheld, these cases show the different construction put by the F.T.C. on section 3 of the Clayton Act. However, it appears from the F.T.C. ruling in *Mytinger & Casselbery*[3] that it is now more or less prepared to follow the Supreme Court's attitude.

It should be emphasised that the foregoing observations only concern the distributor's undertaking listed under (a).[4] In regard to the undertakings described under (b) and (c)[5] relating to geographical restrictions or restrictions in dealings with certain groups of potential customers, the legal position is today rather unsettled. As distinct from the obligation of the distributor not to deal in goods competitive with those of the supplier, the obligations (b) and (c) are not governed by the Clayton Act but by the Sherman Act. Both under common law and later under the Sherman Act such restrictions were – by way of application of the Rule of Reason – considered as ancillary restraints designed to further a legitimate business purpose. If there was no monopolistic dominance on the part of the supplier nor a tendency to create a monopoly for the distributor, and if there was no real danger of injury to the public, they were, as a rule, upheld.[6] The whole problem has, however, quite recently been reviewed (though not finally decided) in the case of *United States v. White Motor Company* in which

---

[1] *Maico Co., Inc.*, Docket 5822, CCH Trade Reg. Rep. (9th ed.), par. 11, 577 (1953).
[2] *E.g.*, *Harley Davidson Motor Co.*, Dkt. 5698 Trade Reg. Rep. 10th ed.), par. 25, 108 (1954); *Revlon Products Corp.*, Dkt. 5685, *ibid*; par. 25, 184 (1954); *Outboard Marine & Mfg. Co.*, *ibid.*, par. 25, 594 (1955) and par. 26, 087 (1956); *Beltone Hearing Aid Co.*, *ibid*; par. 25, 397 (1955). See on these cases Oppenheim, *op. cit.*, pp. 715 f. and Handler, *op. cit.*, pp. 38, 124–126 (n. 47–50).
[3] 29091 at 37529 (28–9–1960), CCH Trade Reg. Rep. (10th ed.).
[4] See *supra*, p. 93.
[5] See *supra*, p. 93.
[6] *E.g.*, *Boco Corp. v. General Motors Corp.*, 124 F. 2d 822 (2d Cir. 1942), rehearing denied, 130 F. 2d 196 (2d Cir. 1942), cert. denied, 317 U.S. 695 (1943) (territorial limitation on establishing a used car outlet, lot or saleroom outside distributors' "zone of influence," but simple prohibition of resale outside thereof); *U.S. v. Bausch & Lomb Optical Co.*, 321 U.S. 707 (1944) (limitation of resale by excluding sales of tinted glass or lenses to certain groups of customers, *i.e.*, to manufacturers or members of the optical trade). The F.T.C. has recently, however, adopted a more hostile view of such restrictions, particularly if coupled with other restrictive practices, see Handler, *op. cit.*, p. 129 n. 60.

the numerous distributors of the White Motor Company were restricted to selling the company's motor lorries only within a defined area at fixed prices and were forbidden to sell to the U.S. Government; White had undertaken not to supply other dealers or ultimate producers in the relevant territories. The District Court[1] had condemned these agreements, not because exclusive dealing contracts were unlawful as such, but because the agreements in question showed features which amounted to a concerted action for the purpose of a refusal to deal and, as between the distributors themselves, to a (horizontal) market sharing agreement, both of which are *per se* unlawful. The fixing of the resale price was an additional obnoxious aspect. In its appeal against this decision to the Supreme Court of the United States, White Motor Company confined itself to a complaint against the condemnation of the restrictions as to the geographical area and of the exclusion of the U.S. Government from sales by the distributors, abandoning the attack against the ruling that the price fixing terms were unlawful. The Supreme Court, in a six to three decision,[2] reversed the lower Court's finding that the restrictions under appeal were unlawful *per se*. It held, in the first place, that the combination of these restrictions with the fixing of resale prices was not so close and comprehensive as to make the whole of the contracts illegal since the price fixing terms only applied to a comparatively smaller part of the sales by the distributors. Secondly, and this is the more important part of the decision, the Supreme Court declined to apply the principles governing the prohibition of horizontal agreements[3] to vertical agreements in as much as the lawfulness of the latter type will depend on whether they are designed and amount to a lessening of competition or are a mere justified protection for a smaller enterprise against powerful competitors. Since however the District Court had determined the issue by summary judgment only, the Supreme Court, stating that it would not express any view on the merits of the case, ordered a trial in which the question will be decided whether the vertical agreements in fact constitute, having regard to the Rule of Reason, a violation of antitrust law will be decided.

[1] N.D. Ohio 194 F. Supp. 562 (1961).
[2] 374 U.S. 174 (1963). For a thorough discussion of this judgment see Milton Handler, "Recent Antitrust Developments" in 112 *University of Pennsylvania Law Review* (1963), pp. 159–189.
[3] Said the Supreme Court: "Horizontal territorial limitations like group boycotts or concerted refusals by traders to deal with other traders *(Klor's Inc. v. Broadway-Hale Stores*, 359 U.S. 207–212) are naked restraints of trade with no purpose except stifling competition."

Whatever the legal position may be in a "normal" exclusive dealing agreement, the appointment by an enterprise of a competitor as distributor is illegal, being considered as an agreement not to compete.[1] The same may be true of the agreed appointment of one common distributor by two competitors for their products unless they have chosen him independently of each other.[2]

This chapter will be concluded by a short reference to foreign distributorships, *i.e.*, restrictions placed on the foreign distributor of an American supplier and, correspondingly, on the American distributor of a foreign supplier. As to the first type of case, there would seem to be nothing objectionable to the appointment of a foreign exclusive distributor;[3] but how far territorial limitations can be safely imposed on foreign distributors has not been decided, and it can only be assumed that they are permitted at least within the same limits as they are lawful in domestic trade, provided, however, that they do not disadvantageously affect United States import or export trade, in which event they would have to be judged under the Sherman Law.[4] An undertaking by the foreign distributor not to deal in goods competitive with those of his suppliers is not subject to section 3 of the Clayton Act,[5] but the Sherman Act does apply and situations may occur in which other United States suppliers have virtually no possibility of selling their goods in the relevant area. Lawfulness of resale control including price fixing will have to be determined by the same consideration; Brewster rightly points out that for all practical purposes such restrictions can hardly have repercussions on United States trade, but a naked agreement not to export would be *per se* unlawful.[6] The foregoing observations on the appointment of a competitor as exclusive distributor also hold good if the appointee is a foreign enterprise[7] and, likewise, if an American and foreign supplier use a common distributor.[8] Frequently, international agreements of this kind contain recipro-

---

[1] *Cf. United States v. Masonite Corp.*, 316 U.S. 265 (1942), at p. 279 which, though a patent licence case, is also relevant to the position referred to in the above text (see Oppenheim, *op. cit.*, p. 1011, and Fugate, *op. cit.*, p. 115).

[2] *United States v. General Dyestuff Corp.*, 57 F. Supp. 642 (S.D.N.Y. 1944). In this case, the condemned agreement had been made by an American and a foreign firm, but the principle would probably also prevail in domestic cases.

[3] *United States v. Keystone Watch Co.*, 218 Fed. 502 (E.D.Pa. 1915).

[4] The various decisions on s. 3 of the Clayton Act are therefore not in point as this statute does not extend to foreign commerce, see Fugate, *op. cit.*, p. 119.

[5] See the foregoing note.

[6] *Op. cit.*, pp. 122, 132 ff.

[7] See Fugate, *op. cit.*, p. 155.

[8] *United States v. General Dyestuff Corp.*, 57 F. Supp. 642 (S.D.N.Y. 1944); Fugate, *op. cit.*, pp. 155 f.

cal undertakings. These are generally held to be unlawful conspiracies not to compete, often by way of market division.[1] Lastly, as regards the position of an American distributor of a foreign supplier, the general rules of United States interstate antitrust law apply.

2. GERMANY

The German Cartel Law[2] does not expressly mention exclusive dealing agreements but such relationships are governed by section 15 (with the qualifying provisions of section 16) and section 18 of that Law.[3] As both sections speak of "agreements between enterprises" *(Unternehmen)*, the question arises as to which types of representatives acting for a principal (both terms being used here in their widest commercial meaning) are within these provisions. Employees of an enterprise are clearly outside but what is the position in regard to those auxiliaries of a supplier who are independent traders but act on his instructions and entertain transactions at his financial risk, such as commercial agents, *Kommissionäre* including *Kommissionsagenten* and brokers *(Makler)*.[4] According to the Official Reasoning of the Bill of the Cartel Law, which has found the unanimous approval of legal writers, agreements between such parties are not caught by the regulation of so-called "individual agreements" in the Cartel Law. One leading commentator[5] characterises this relationship and approves its exemption as follows:

> Freedom of determination [*i.e.*, of prices and/or terms of contract] exists only if this is not contrary to institutions which are recognised by the legal order... Their [*i.e.*, the commercial agents' *etc.*] activity is characterised by being concerned with another party's interests. They are not restrained in a competitive business of their own since this is, in so far as they have to take charge of the interests of the party that has instructed them, necessarily an alien one as far as they are concerned. It is the mandator who in truth determines his own prices and terms. It is in this respect not decisive whether the mandatory acts in his own name or in that of another or whether the property has already been transferred to him.

---

[1] *United States v. Timken Roller Bearing Co.*, 341 U.S. 593 (1951).

[2] In the following discussion of the legal position in Germany the impact of Arts. 85 ff. will be disregarded. As far as necessary, reference to German Cartel Law under this aspect will be made in the part dealing with the Cartel Law of the E.C.C.

[3] See Appendix B, *infra*, pp. 164 ff.

[4] Ss. 86 and 384(1) of the German Commercial Code. For a detailed discussion of the general German law on Agents and Sole Distributors, see E.J. Cohn, "An Introduction to the German Law on Agents and Sole Distributors" in *Commercial Agency and Distribution Agreements in Europe, The British Institute of International and Comparative Law, 1964*, pp. 1–23.

[5] Baumbach-Hefermehl, *op. cit.*, s. 15, n. 16, p. 1310.

As a consequence of this position, the "principal" may not only insert in his (unilateral) instructions to his commercial agents or in agreements with them the conditions set forth in section 18 without having to fear the sanction of their invalidation, but he can also fix the prices of the goods or services with which the purchaser, *i.e.*, the party which acquires them from him through the commercial agent, is to be charged. It should be emphasised for the sake of clarity that this holds good for the fixing of prices generally and not only for those goods which are privileged under section 16, a provision permitting resale price maintenance within certain limits.

Radically different from the position of a commercial agent is that of the "independent trader acting for his own account" whom we shall call "independent distributor" or, shortly, simply distributor (*Eigenhändler*, sometimes also called *Zwischenhändler*). In contrast to commercial agents (in the wider sense), the independent trader purchases the goods from his supplier for his own account and re-sells them in his own name and for his own account with the intention of making a profit; he also bears the legal and commercial risk in regard to such goods (even if the scope or amount of the risk may be reduced under an arrangement with his supplier, for example, by his right to return unsold goods or to receive monetary allowances on goods which he is unable to dispose of). The fact that he has an agreement with his supplier by which he alone is authorised to sell the supplier's products within a certain geographical area or to a certain class of customers only and that such agreement is to last for a defined period does not affect his position as independent trader[1] in civil and commercial law. Correspondingly, for the purposes of the Cartel Law he is an enterprise strictly separate from that of his supplier so that his relations with the latter are governed by sections 15 to 19 (of which the important ones are sections 15, 16 and 18) and, in certain circumstances, also by sections 22 and 26.

The circumstance that this relationship is subject to a variety of statutory provisions makes a few observations on the structure of the relevant part of the German Cartel Law necessary. Chapter 1 (of Title I), (sections 1 to 14) of the Law deals with "Cartel Agreements and

---

[1] See Würdinger in *RGR Kommentar zum Handelsgesetzbuch*, 2nd ed., Vol. I (1953), s. 84, ns. 1 and 5, pp. 681/682. Such independent traders are often called *"Generalagenten"* or *"Generalvertreter"* (general agents or general representatives) or *"Alleinvertreter"* (sole agents or sole representatives), but such descriptions are legally without significance if they carry on their business in the manner described above, see Würdinger, *ibid.*, n. 1, p. 681.

Cartel Resolutions," *i.e.*, with so-called horizontal agreements between, and resolutions of, enterprises or associations of enterprises "for a common purpose." Chapter 2, (sections 15 to 21), which is headed "Other Agreements," regulates vertical agreements concluded between enterprises belonging to different economic levels (for instance between manufacturer and wholesaler, manufacturer and distributor, wholesaler or distributor and retailer or ultimate customer, distributor and wholesaler or retailer or ultimate customer). The statute distinguishes between two different types of restriction imposed on either party to a vertical agreement, namely, 1) those restricting one of the parties in its freedom to charge prices or insert terms in a contract on the *resale* of goods acquired from the other (vendor) party or from a third party, or in a contract for rendering commercial services (section 15), and those restricting one of the parties generally in regard to goods sold and commercial services rendered to it or obtained by a third party (section 18). Both types of restrictions are frequently combined. The sanctions in either section are different. Section 15 constitutes an absolute prohibition the violation of which makes the agreement null and may, if a party acts upon such invalid agreement, render it liable to quasi-criminal prosecution under section 38. By contrast, the restrictions listed in section 18 can be lawfully stipulated but are subject to supervision and invalidation by the Cartel Authorities. The contravention of an order invalidation by a Cartel Authority is equally punishable.

We have now to examine the significance of these sections for exclusive dealing agreements.

Under section 15, the supplier cannot lawfully lay down the price or conditions of contract which the distributor would have to observe on the resale of the goods supplied to him.[1][2] Only such restraint as has been made a term of the contract is prohibited although the restriction may be a merely indirect and, so to speak, imperfect one, for example inserting a condition to the effect that the distributor (of a manufacturer) must only resell or grant a rebate to such customers who, as wholesalers, voluntarily – without entering into a legally enforceable agreement – promise to keep the price suggested to them.[3]

---

[1] The prohibition may extend to services if these are connected with the resale of goods. A case in point arose in the linoleum industry when the price for the laying of linoleum had also been fixed by the manufacturers.

[2] Whether the inclusion of one or more illegal terms makes the agreement entirely or only partially void is determined by the general private law, *i.e.*, s. 139 of the Civil Code.

[3] See Langen, *op. cit.*, p. 144, quoting the Government Justification to s. 10 of the bill (now s. 15 of the statute).

On the other hand, a mere recommendation is not illegal unless it results in uniform conduct on the part of several distributors and then becomes a contravention under section 38(2).[1] The rather severe prohibition laid down in section 15 is, however, substantially qualified by section 16 which constitutes an exemption from the prohibition of price fixing for trade marked goods (including agricultural products) and for the trade carried on by publishing enterprises in respect of books and other publications, provided such agreements are in writing (section 34) and the Federal Cartel Office is duly notified thereof. The Federal Cartel Office has, however, power to invalidate any price fixing if either the prerequisites set forth in section 16 have ceased to exist or if the resale price maintenance is being abused or becomes economically unbearable (section 17). As section 16 allows only price fixing and not the imposition of conditions of contract, the latter remain unqualifiedly prohibited under section 15.

Occasionally, a German or foreign manufacturer or an importer may be interested in binding his wholesaler–distributor to impose such conditions as he, the wholesaler, has to observe, also upon the latter's retailers. A restraint by the manufacturer or importer imposed upon the wholesaler in the choice of business partners (retailers) is not a prohibited restriction in the meaning of section 15[2] but in principle permitted under section 18 subsection 1 no. 3. Yet in so far as the contents of the wholesalers agreements with his customers are concerned, stipulations to that effect are, as a rule, unlawful. Thus, the Federal Cartel Office has condemned the uniform imposition of terms by importers upon domestic dealers who had in turn to bind their sub-dealers to the same extent, except for a customers' service and a repair service. Prescribing prices to be charged for repair work to be carried out by the sub-dealers (except for the price of spare and exchange parts if these can be fixed under section 16)[3] remains however, unlawful. On the other hand, in a previous ruling the Federal Cartel Office had sanctioned a provision whereby a manufacturer had obliged a wholesaler of his goods to insert a territorial restriction in his agreements with his retailers since the (lawful) territorial restriction imposed upon

---

[1] The prohibition of s. 15 applies only to the home market so that for goods exported abroad resale prices and conditions of contract can be lawfully set. This section is of course inapplicable in so far as Arts. 85 ff. of the Rome Treaty prevail. see also *infra*, p. 108.

[2] See *Gemeinschaftskommentar*, sec. 15 n. 7, p. 391.

[3] See Annual Report on the Activities of the Federal Cartel Office for the Year 1962, Bonn 1963, p. 28.

the wholesaler could only be made effective by such (corresponding) stipulation.[1]

There may also be reverse cases, though instances in practice are probably rarer. Sometimes, one finds that a supplier has undertaken to sell other goods which correspond to those supplied to the distributor to a third party at a fixed price only. Such a contractual term would be caught by the prohibition of this section and be void,[2] unless, of course, it is protected under section 16. Whatever the general importance of section 15 may be, its effect on exclusive dealing arrangements is apparently of little moment. This seems to be due to two factors. In the first place, it appears that many ranges of goods which are the subject-matter of such arrangements are trade marked[3] and, secondly, that the supplier is generally not interested in the imposition of contractual terms on his distributor's customer.

Thus, it is not so much section 15 as section 18 which is the real *sedes materiae* of the control of exclusive dealing agreements from a restraint of trade point of view. It provides that the Cartel Authority may invalidate agreements between enterprises and prohibit the application of a new agreement relating to goods or commercial services and the substitution of a new similar restriction in so far as such agreements

(1) restrain one of the parties (*i.e.*, enterprises) in its freedom to use the goods received or other goods or commercial services, or

(2) restrain one of the parties in the purchase or sale of other goods or other commercial services from or to third parties respectively (not necessarily enterprises), or

(3) restrain one of the parties in the resale of the goods delivered to it to third parties (not necessarily enterprises) or,

(4) oblige one of the parties to accept goods or services that are not related by their nature or by the custom of the trade to the goods contracted for,

and thereby unreasonably restrict the freedom of business activities of the party concerned or of other enterprises, if through the extent

---

[1] *Ibid.* for the Year 1961, Bonn 1962, p. 21 f.

[2] See Langen, *op. cit.*, p. 144.

[3] S. 15 may, however, gain greater significance in this field also if the resale price maintenance permitted under and within the framework of s. 16 is more and more held inapplicable on account of the lack of an effective uniform enforcement without showing a gap of the price fixed for the goods which is a prerequisite for upholding a valid resale price maintenance system, see Lieberknecht, *NJW* 1963, p. 609. See also *infra*, p. 109.

of such restrictions competition in the relevant market is substantially affected. It must be stressed again that such restrictions are *prima facie* lawful but subject to invalidating measures by the Cartel Authorities in case of misuse or on the ground of substantial limitation of free competition.[1]

Although section 18 is fairly detailed and clear, a fuller understanding of it still requires a few observations. It has first to be rembered that it regulates only vertical agreements; horizontal agreements or mere gentlemens' agreements or uniform behaviour caused by a recommendation are governed by sections 1 and 38 respectively of the Cartel Law. We now urn to the four instances of restrictions listed in section 18.

As to (1). Restriction on use of goods and commercial services.

This is the case when the restriction is placed on the distributor's own use of goods or services (with the exception of acquisition or disposition as these are dealt with under (2)), irrespective of whether he has obtained them from his supplier or from a third party. Thus, this clause covers the case in which the distributor may be bound not to keep goods purchased from the supplier for himself but to resell them to the former if he is unable to sell them to third parties within a specified time. This clause is however of minor interest compared with the next clauses 2) and 3) which go to the core of the essential features found in exclusive dealing agreements.

As to (2) and (3). Restrictions on sales and purchases of goods and commercial services.

Clause 2 concerns restraints in dealing with goods or supplying services other than those delivered or rendered respectively by the supplier, whereas clause 3) relates to the goods sold by the supplier to the distributor, in respect of which he obliges the distributor to abstain from re-selling these goods outside a certain district or to certain groups of potential customers or binds him to resell them to certain defined groups of customers only.

The usual sole distributorship agreements for the sale of goods

---

[1] Like many other provisions of the Cartel Law, ss. 15 ff. are not applicable in the following economic sectors: public transport (s. 99), agricultural and forestry production (s. 100), the activities of the German Federal Bank and the Land Central Banks, the Bank for Reconstruction and State Monopoly Institutions (s. 101); in regard to banks, insurance companies and certain kindred institutions, s. 1 and s. 15 are declared inoperative but not s. 18.

contain a combination of both types of restrictions, *ie.*, the geographical and/or personal area of distribution (no. 3 of subsection 1 of section 18) and the provision of exclusivity (no. 2 of subsection 1 of section 18).[1] They are in principle lawful, both in regard to the obligations undertaken by the distributor and those of the supplier, subject only to governmental intervention in the event of misuse (section 18 subsections 1 and 2).

To conclude the review of the restrictions specified in section 18, it can be stated that clause 4 is of no practical relevance for exclusive dealing agreements.

On the other hand, two other sections of the Cartel Law may have an important bearing on the question whether an exclusive dealing agreement would be upheld. These are section 22, which defines what is a market-dominating enterprise and provides for governmental intervention in case of abusive practices by such enterprise, and section 26, which deals with a boycott against other enterprises (subsection 1) and other discriminatory measures by a market-dominating enterprise or an enterprise which is entitled to bind prices in accordance with section 16 (subsection 2). The relevance of these provisions is obvious as the existence of an exclusive dealing agreement necessarily results in the exclusion of hitherto existing or potential competitors from the sale of the class of goods which are the subject-matter of the agreement. As exclusive dealing agreements are in principle legal, section 26(1) is only applicable if the contracting parties, or one of them, do not primarily wish to further their own economic interests but only or chiefly intend to force certain individual competitors out of the market. If such a purpose can be proved, the exclusive dealing agreement is treated as a concealed boycott measure and therefore illegal (sections 26(1), 38(1), (8)) and void by virtue of section 134 of the Civil Code.[2]

Whereas an exclusive dealing agreement will probably seldom be concluded for the purpose of boycotting competitors, and proof of such intention will in any event be very difficult, the prohibition of (wilful) discrimination by enterprises that are market-dominating or entitled to fix prices under section 16 may indeed in particular instances affect an exclusive dealing agreement. The German Supreme Court quite recently had an opportunity to render a judgment in a case which can be considered as typical for a large class of exclusive dealing agreements

---

[1] Commercial services are not mentioned in sec. 18(1)(3) as, by their very nature, they cannot be made the subject of a restriction in the field of distribution (see *Gemeinschaftskommentar* § 18, n. 26, p. 538).

[2] See Baumbach-Hefermehl, *op. cit.*, s. 26 n. 15, p. 1385.

in modern commerce.[1] The defendant company, a manufacturer of motor cars, sells its products through a large chain of distributors and entertains a customers' service through numerous owners of service stations, both being independent traders. These are bound by agreements in which they have undertaken to buy spare and exchange parts, special accessories and special tools from the manufacturer and are forbidden to use any other supplemental parts, being restricted to the use of original spare and exchange parts produced by the manufacturers. The prices for a number of the spare parts are fixed. The plaintiff was a wholesaler in spare parts and accessories for motor vehicles, including those suitable for the defendant company's motor cars, which he partly bought from the latter and partly from other manufacturers of such vehicles. He attacked the validity of the said terms of the agreement on the ground that they violated both subsections of section 26. Whereas the lower Court (the first Appeal Court) found in favour of the plaintiff, the Supreme Court reversed that judgment and upheld the exclusive dealing agreement. Discussing the relations between section 18 on the one hand and section 26 on the other, the Court held in concurrence with general legal opinion that the power of invalidation built into section 18 does not prevent the application of section 26 to exclusive dealing agreements. Yet the unavoidable consequence that third parties are excluded from selling to the sole distributor or purchasing from the supplier must, in view of the sanctioning of the legal institution of exclusive dealing agreements by section 18, not be treated as either a boycott or a discrimination under section 26. The abuse of this institution as contemplated by the legislator can only be remedied by the intervention of the Cartel Authorities as provided by, and in the circumstances of, section 18 itself. The situations which these two sections are designed to regulate are, irrespective of certain possible overlapping, not the same, and so are not the consequences of their application. A violation of section 26 may only result in the commission of a quasi-criminal offence against, or claim for damages by, one or several individual competitors, whereas a measure taken by the Cartel Authority under section 18 would remove the restriction as such. The test whether or not the subsections of section 26 have been violated is whether the harming of competitors (subsection 1) or the discrimination (subsection 2) was unreasonable. The Court found that this very element was absent from the present case. Reviewing in considerable detail the exclusive dealing agreement

[1] Decision of October 6, 1963, *WuW* 1963, p. 247.

against the background of the practice in the field of the sale of motor cars and taking into account the interest of the public in general in an efficient customers' service, the Supreme Court upheld the attacked terms of the agreement (not even distinguishing between the various kinds of spare parts or exchange parts). As regards the danger of monopolistic price fixing, the Court referred to the very keen competition between the various motor-vehicle manufacturers, which must necessarily, at least indirectly, extend to the trade in spare parts. However, as the Supreme Court observes finally, its decision rests on the facts submitted and proved in the case at issue and does not foreclose a re-examination of the whole position by the Cartel Authorities under the power given to them by section 18(1) and (2) with the result that the Cartel Authorities' finding may form the basis of a different view, namely that the practice of the manufacturer was after all unreasonable in the meaning of section 26.

Excursus: International Aspects

It only remains now to discuss the international aspects of exclusive dealing agreements. According to section 98(2) all restraints of trade are subject to the Cartel Law if they take effect in Germany even though they may result from acts done outside German territory. This also applies to vertical agreements, including sole distributorship agreements. Thus, an agreement of this kind between a foreign supplier and a German distributor whose field of activity is the German home market, is subject to section 15 or section 18, as the case may be.[1] But what is the position if the distributor's territory also comprises other countries, for example, if an English manufacturer appoints a German distributor for Germany and/or one or more other countries on the Continent of Europe? As regards the prohibitions laid down in section 15 (irrespective of whether the goods in question are privileged under section 16), they apply only to sales inside Germany either by virtue of section 98(2) or of section 15 itself which speaks of agreements "relating to markets located within [Germany]" and thus to that area only.[2] According to leading opinion, the same principle holds good in respect of section 18, so that a German manufacturer may lawfully oblige a German distributor not to export his, the manufacturer's, goods abroad, even if such restriction has an unfavourable effect on the distributor's business and would in the case of a purely domestic

[1] See Schwartz, *op. cit.*, p. 66.
[2] See W. Baruch, *WuW* 1961, pp. 530, 535/36.

transaction be regarded as unreasonable.[1] In the converse case in which a German supplier appoints a distributor in another country, neither section 15 nor section 18 applies to an exclusive agreement across the frontiers.[2]

Not infrequently, the foreign distributor is a competitor of the supplier and the agreement between these parties has been concluded for the purpose of removing undesired competition in the relevant territories. It would seem that this special position of the distributor, whether he be the foreign distributor of a German supplier or the German distributor of a foreign supplier, does not alter the legal position as already described. If, however, a German and a foreign enterprise appoint each other reciprocally as sole distributors for their respective territories, such arrangement might well be considered as a (horizontal) cartel agreement for market sharing with the effect that it is void to the extent that it takes effect on the German market. Similarly, the appointment of a third party as a common agent might be considered as a device to achieve the same result.[3]

Finally, another important restriction in the international sphere should be mentioned, *viz.* the condition imposed by the supplier on his foreign distributor not, by way of export, to re-import the goods supplied to the latter into the supplier's own country. As regards Germany, a term to that effect would be of the greatest importance for those goods which the supplier sells on the German home market at fixed prices with a lawful resale price maintenance proviso. Since resale price maintenance (provided, of course, that the statutory conditions of section 16 are complied with) can only be enforced if such enforcement is uniform and without gaps,[4] re-import of such goods which would then be sold by the German importers below the fixed price would destroy the otherwise permitted system of resale price

[1] See Schwartz, *op. cit.*, pp. 62 ff. W. Baruch, *loc. cit.*, pp. 538 ff., and Würdinger, *WuW* 1960, pp. 313, 322 advance the opposite view. This question has so far not yet been decided by the Cartel Authorities or by a Court.

[2] See Schwartz, *op. cit.*, p. 65; decision of the Federal Cartel Office of June 26, 1959, *WuW* 1959, p. 756 (emphasising the significance of the "relevant market"). It may be mentioned in this connection that under s. 6 (horizontal) export cartels are, subject to certain safeguards, exempted from the general prohibition of cartels laid down in s. 1. If such an export cartel necessarily also encompasses inland trade, it shall be approved by the Cartel Authorities and vertical agreements incidental thereto shall not be affected by s. 15.

[3] See Schwartz, *op. cit.*, pp. 66/67.

[4] See *supra*, p. 104 n. 3. It may be added that this rule belongs in principle to the Law against Unfair Competition *(Gesetz gegen den unlauteren Wettbewerb)* of June 7, 1909 (as amended), see Baumbach-Hefermehl, *op. cit.*, pp. 355 ff., ns. 279–299, pp. 315, 318.

maintenance. Economic justification does of course not exempt such a contractual term imposed on the foreign distributor from the application of section 18, as his economic freedom to effect sales in Germany is thereby restricted, but the Cartel Authorities will probably only intervene in extreme cases.[1]

3. FRANCE

In this chapter a short reference to French law appears to be called for as the present treatment of exclusive dealing agreements in Regulation No. 17 and in the practice of the Commission is due to French insistence on their importance in the antitrust law of the European Community,[2] an attitude that has its origin in the relevant French domestic law.

By the Decree of June 30, 1945 (Decree No. 45–1483)[3] price control was introduced. This Decree was amended by Ordinance 53–704 of August 9, 1953 but this Ordinance was declared invalid by the *Conseil d'Etat* in 1958. It was replaced by Decree No. 58–545 of June 24, 1958, Article 1 of which has amended Article 37 of the Decree No. 45–1483 by making a refusal to deal *(refus de vente)* and discriminatory treatment (no. 1(a)) punishable, providing criminal sanctions for offences against horizontal agreements prohibited under Article 59bis of the said Decree (No. 3),[4] and introducing penalties for price fixing (No. 4).[5] It should be noted that the aim of all these provisions is the prevention of illicit price increases, and their application is determined by this aim. The prohibition of a refusal to deal is meant to have a very wide application to the trade between dealers on different vertical levels so that, for example, a manufacturer must not refuse to supply a retailer who is prepared to buy at the same conditions as a wholesaler, or a manufacturer must not exclude department stores or wholesalers, as the case may be. This leads in effect to a general duty to enter into contracts. It is obvious that such a rule must needs affect the conclusion

---

[1] *Cf.* the judgment of the German Supreme Court of June 14, 1963, *infra*, p. 123. Although in that case the chief problem was whether the prohibition of re-import into Germany was incompatible with Art. 85, the decisions of the Frankfurt Court of Appeal of January 19, 1962 (*WuW* 1963, p. 313) and of the Supreme Court contain valuable observations on the subject of re-import under the German cartel law.

[2] For details, see the section on the position of these agreements under Art. 85, *infra*, pp. 114 ff.

[3] Followed in respect of penalties by Decree No. 45–1484.

[4] See previous note. The discussion of horizontal agreements (No. 3) is outside the subject-matter with which we are concerned in this chapter.

[5] The text of the relevant Nos. 1(a) and 4 is set out in Appendix C, *infra*, p. 170.

of sole distributorship agreements *(contrats de concessions exclusive de vente)* since its proper performance must result in a refusal by the supplier to deal with third parties direct if one or more distributors have been appointed for a territorial district, or if all sales by a certain supplier have to be effected through one or more distributors. On the other hand, the legislator did not intend to forbid sole distributorship agreements as such, since such agreements could not in every case be considered as leading to the undesired result of price increases or to have been made for the purpose of circumventing prohibited price fixing. Further, this institution was, acknowledged as necessary for both national and international commerce. The Government therefore issued a Directive to the public prosecutors to whom the supervision and enforcement of these orders has been entrusted.[1] This Directive, which is however a mere commentary on the aforementioned statutory legal provisions, has been submitted to repeated judicial tests. The basic problem of whether and under what conditions a supplier may thus discriminate and therefore conclude a sole distributor agreement was discussed in the important decision of the *Cour de Cassation* (Criminal Chamber) of July 11, 1962.[2] The French Supreme Court in principle approved the interpretation by the Government and summarised its opinion in the following language:

A sole distributor agreement by which the parties have reciprocally restricted their freedom to enter into contracts and from which it appears that it has neither been made with the intention nor has the indirect effect of restricting the distributor in the fixing of the resale prices but, on the contrary, results in the improvement of the service to his customers, may make the goods of, and kept by, the vendor inalienable in the legal sense. Such a practice can, in regard to goods the sale of which requires special expert knowledge, or to articles of special quality, fulfill the requirements of a trade customer in the meaning of Article 37 no. 1(a). The (criminal) judge seized with the case will have to examine in each individual case whether the sole distributorship agreement, on which a defendant relies as a defence to the charge of refusing to deal, falls into the aforementioned category and does not show the intention of excluding the rights of third parties and of restricting competition in a manner disapproved by the legislation in the economic field.[3]

[1] Directive of March 31, 1960, (French) *Journal Officiel* 1960, p. 3048 (known as *Circulaire Fontanet*).

[2] *Etat Français v. Nicolas and Société Brandt : Société Photo Radio Club v. Nicolas and Société Brandt, Juris Classeur Périodique*, 1962 II, No. 12799; *Dalloz* (1962) *Jurisprudence*, p. 497; (1962) 1 C.M.L. Rep., p. 93.

[3] The *Cour de Cassation* partly quashed and annulled the judgment of the *Cour d'Appel* of Paris and remitted the case for a partial new determination by the *Cour d'Appel* of Amiens *(Etat Français v. Nicolas and Société Brandt : Société Photo Radio Club v. Nicolas and Société Brandt (No. 2)*, 1963 (2) C.M.L. Rep., p. 239). This Court found Nicolas, the Director-General of *Société Brandt Frères* guilty of the criminal offence of refusal to sell and the company civilly liable for its Director-General (in

The result of the interpretation of the law relating to refusals to deal by the Government and the effect of the decision by the *Cour de Cassation* in relation to sole distributorship agreements can therefore be summarised as follows. If the distributor has merely to fulfil certain conditions in connection with the resale, except of course observance of the price fixed by the supplier, no difficulty arises. If, however, the distributor is limited to sales in a certain clearly defined territory, he must agree not to handle competitive goods and the supplier must not sell through other channels; in any event, the agreement must lead to an improvement in the delivery of the goods concerned for the benefit of the ultimate customer. The agreement must not be a cloak for price fixing or even for price recommendations. The parties to the agreement must perform it strictly, as any laxity in this respect may raise the suspicion that it is in fact only a device for the circumvention of the prohibition of price fixing or price recommendation.[1] It appears from the Judgment of the *Cour de Cassation* that the determination whether a sole distributorship agreement is lawful will largely depend on the facts of each individual case, the onus to justify such agreement, being upon the party who seeks to maintain it. Incidentally, the question whether a sole distributorship agreement concluded between a parent and a subsidiary company is caught by these provisions has not yet been determined by a Court decision.

Looking at the French system of control of sole distributorship agreements, its great difference from both the American and the German approaches to this problem becomes apparent. Whereas price fixing is condemned by all three laws (subject, however, to the French law indicated here,[2] to the fair trade laws in some States in the United States and to the privileged treatment of trade marked goods and publications in Germany), prohibition of market sharing as a means of safeguarding free competition as it exists in the United States is not only absent from the French system but, on the contrary, a necessary

substantial accord with the judgment of the *Cour d'Appel* of Paris). Certain other important opinions contained in this judgment are referred to elsewhere in this study (*infra*, pp. 124f,, 150). The *Cour de Cassation* also confirmed that a party to the proceedings which claims to have suffered damage through the accused's action is not entitled to bring either a concurrent or an independent civil action, since the relevant Decrees were issued for the benefit of the whole community and not for the protection of individual users or consumers; the civil claim of Photo Radio Club was therefore dismissed. The appeal against this judgment of the *Cour d'Appel* of Amiens was dismissed by the *Cour de Cassation* on October 22, 1964 (*Recueil* Dalloz, 1964, p. 753).

[1] Resale price maintenance is in principle prohibited in France. Exemptions may be granted by Joint Ministerial Orders for a prescribed time by virtue of Art. 37*quater* of Decree No. 45–1483 as amended (see *infra*, Appendix C, p. 170).

[2] See previous note.

condition for the legality of such agreements. As regards Germany, the prohibition of refusals to deal is only contained in section 26(2) of the Cartel Law which is designed to prevent abuses by market-dominating enterprises or those that are allowed to fix resale prices (section 16).

Sole distributorship agreements between a French supplier and a foreign distributor, irrespective of whether they are governed by French or a foreign law, would seem to be outside the application of the law against price fixing and refusal to sell, since its aim is exclusively to protect the public on the home market against unjustified price increases. The considerations which caused the United States Courts to examine the possible effect of international agreements on American foreign trade through the possible exclusion of other American competitors from a foreign market, especially if they provided for market-sharing[1] or the appointment of a foreign competitor as sole distributor,[2] play no part in French law.[3]

Conversely however, an agreement by which a foreign supplier appointed the other party to be his sole distributor in France would seem to be fully subject to the relevant French law on price fixing and refusal to sell (irrespective of whether the agreement itself be governed by French or foreign private law), even though a French Court of first instance has indicated that a foreign supplier of a French sole importer-distributor could not be taken to do acts which would be classified as a refusal to sell within the meaning of French law.[4] These observations

[1] See *U.S. v. Imperial Chemical Industries Ltd.*, Opinion on Relief, 105 F. Supp. 215 (S.D.N.Y. 1952).

[2] *U.S. v. Timken Roller Bearing Co.*, 341 U.S. 593 (1951), at 596.

[3] According to Art. 62 of Decree No. 45–1483 (as amended, see *supra*, p. 110), the whole export trade is exempted from the application of this Law.

[4] *Cf.* the decision of the *Tribunal de Commerce de la Seine* of May 21, 1962, in the case of *Consten v. U.N.E.F.* The French firm of Consten, which was the sole distributor of radio and tape recorder sets produced by a German firm, had instituted proceedings for unfair competition against a French importer, U.N.E.F., which, in disregard of Consten's sole distributorship agreement, had managed to import products of the same German firm and sold them in France. The *Tribunal de Commerce* decided in favour of the plaintiff as the defendant had acted unfairly by availing itself of the work done and the expenses incurred by the distributor through the introduction of the goods in France. The defendant had unsuccessfully pleaded the illegality of the sole distributorship agreement both under French domestic law and under Art. 85 (as well as Arts. 86 and 91) of the Rome Treaty, and had asked the Court to stay the proceedings in accordance with Art. 9(3) of Regulation No. 17, or to submit the question of the legality of the agreement to the European Court in accordance with Art. 177 of the Rome Treaty. On appeal, the *Cour d'Appel* of Paris (judgment of January 26, 1963, see (1963) 2 C.M.L. Rep. p. 176) reversed the decision on the ground that the proceedings had to be stayed until the Commission of the E.E.C., which had been notified of the sole distributorship agreement by the defendant U.N.E.F., could render a decision under Art. 9(1) of Regulation No. 17. (This is the application which was determined by the

should not be concluded without a short reference to the significance of trade mark protected articles as the subject–matter of sole distributorship agreements. Justification of such agreements is frequently pleaded on the ground of the trade mark protection accorded to the goods concerned. While several writers[1] deny that this argument is well founded, as the trade mark is only intended to protect its owner against his trade mark being forged or falsely applied by other persons, but not to allow him to deal with trade mark protected goods in a privileged manner, several Courts have so far upheld exclusive dealing agreements in regard to trade mark protected goods even in the absence of the other requisite conditions.[2] The *Cour de Cassation* has not yet had an opportunity to give its ruling on this problem.

4. EUROPEAN ECONOMIC COMMUNITY

Although arguments that exclusive dealing agreements are not caught by Article 85 are still advanced,[3] there can today be no real

Commission of the E.E.C. on September 23, 1964 (re-printed *infra*, in Appendix E, V, 6)) The *Cour d'Appel* did not express any opinion on the question raised in the text above. See also the decision of the *Tribunal de Commerce de la Seine* of June 25, 1962, *Société Arlab Import-Export (Sarie) v. Société Union Nationale des Economies Familiales (U.N.E.F.)*, (1963) 2 C.M.L. Rep., p. 185 in which the facts were very similar to those of the aforementioned *Consten v. U.N.E.F.* case, except that the foreign supplier was a United Kingdom enterprise.

The important question whether a foreign supplier of a sole distributor in France is subject to the French (criminal) law of refusal to sell, has been examined by Mezger in *Revue critique de droit international privé*, 1963, p. 43 who answers it in the affirmative: "*La maison française qui ne reçoit aucune réponse à sa demande légitime au sens de l'article 37, alinéa 1er 1° (a), et à plus forte raison la maison qui reçoit une réponse négative à sa demande adressée à une maison étrangère, se trouvant donc en face d'un refus de vente commis et punissable en France.*" See, however, on this problem also the Submissions of the Rapporteur in *Etat Français v. Nicolas and Société Brandt etc*, Cour de Cassation, July 11, 1962, (1962) 2 C.M.L. Rep., p. 93, at pp. 103–106.

[1] H. Desbois in *La propriété industrielle et le Marché Commun*, Colloque des Facultés de Droit, Lille, 1959: "Les problèmes juridiques et économiques du Marché Commun, pp. 199 ff., 209, and the same in Dalloz *1960*, p. 567.

[2] E.g., *Cour d'Appel d'Aise*, October 14, 1958, *Juris Classeur Périodique* 1958, II, 10924; *Tribunal de Commerce de Nice*, March 30, 1960, *Dalloz*, Jurisprudence, 1960, p. 567 (with critical note by Desbois). On the other hand, in the (international) case *Société Comptoir National de Contrôle v. Société Contrôle Typesales* (a similar case of unfair competition), the *Cour d'Appel* of Paris in its decision of June 22, 1960 *(Juris Classeur Périodique*, 1960, II, 11857) expressed the opposite view.

[3] See, *e.g.*, the publication by Soelter, *Vertriebsbindungen im Gemeinsamen Markt*, 1962, in which this subject is discussed under both economic and legal aspects. This opinion had also been expressed by lower French Courts, see *Etablissements Consten v. U.N.E.F.* (see (1963) 2 C.M.L. Rep., p. 176 n. 1) and *Société Arlab Import-Export v. U.N.E.F.* (both decided by the *Tribunal de Commerce de la Seine*), (1963) 2 C.M.L. Rep., p. 185 but as the first mentioned case has been overruled (see (1963) 2 C.M.L. Rep., p. 176) and a stay of proceedings by virtue of Regulation No. 17 Art. 9(3) ordered, the ruling of the Courts of first instance cannot be taken to represent the prevailing legal opinion in France.

doubt that this Article also comprises vertical agreements and understandings, of which exclusive dealing agreements are one class. This is the view of the organs of the E.E.C. as manifested in Regulation No. 17 issued by the Council of Ministers, the subsequent executory orders of the Commission, and particularly by the decision of the European Court in the *Bosch* case.[1] Because the whole agreement between the *Robert Bosch G.m.b.H* (the supplier) and its dealers, in which the relevant clause relating to the prohibition of exports to another country was contained, had not been submitted to the Court, which therefore felt unable itself to make enquiries in the proceedings which were instituted under Article 177 of the Rome Treaty, it had to decline to adjudicate on the question whether the clause in the agreement in issue was prohibited by Article 85. Nevertheless, the Court went so far as to give its opinion in the following language: "In these circumstances the Court must confine itself to a declaration that the possibility that the prohibitions on export to which the (Dutch) Appellate Court refers may fall within the definition of Article 85(1), especially within the words 'agreements... which are capable of affecting trade between Member States' cannot be excluded." In spite of this guarded language, it seems clear that the Court has indicated with sufficient clarity and certainty that in principle exclusive dealing agreements are subject to the application of Article 85. The Court's ruling has also been universally understood in this sense.

As exclusive dealing agreements are not explicitly mentioned in Article 85, the question arises whether such legal relationships are indeed governed by this Article and, in particular, whether they fall within one of the examples set out in paragraph 1 of Article 85 or only within the general rule laid down in its first sentence.[2] It goes without saying that such agreements will only be caught by Article 85 if they "are capable of affecting trade between Member States." This contingency will exist primarily if the supplier appoints a sole distributor in another Member State, but it may also arise if a sole distributor in the supplier's own State is bound not to export the latter's products. It would seem that examples (b) and (c) are especially in point. Example (b) mentions the practice of "limitation or control of production,

---

[1] See *supra*, pp. 3, 17.

[2] Whether an agreement between two (or more) independent trading enterprises amounts to an exclusive distributorship agreement in the true legal sense or merely contains restrictive terms short of such agreement (which is sometimes difficult to decide), is to be determined by the law of the country which governs such relationship according to its national private law, including conflict of laws rules.

markets, technical developments or investment." An exclusive dealing agreement might limit or control principally production and/or markets since third parties, *i.e.*, other dealers, are necessarily excluded from distributing the goods which are the subject-matter of the agreement in the sole distributor's territory. Such an agreement has therefore the effect of controlling a market and may lead to a limitation of marketing and possibly also of the amount of production if – in the absence of such agreement – a multiplicity of dealers could promote a larger sale of the goods concerned. It must however be admitted that such considerations will in most cases be purely theoretical, because in practice the supplier will appoint a sole distributor for the very purpose of increasing the sale of his goods which, in his experience, he would otherwise be virtually unable to market in special areas, particularly in a foreign country to which he is often a newcomer. The Commission has given its reasoning for the application of Article 85 to such agreements in its "Announcement on Exclusive Agency Contracts made with Commercial Agents"[1] in the following language:

> In the case of such exclusive contracts the restriction of competition lies either in the limitation of supply, when the vendor undertakes to supply a given product only to one purchaser, or in the limitation of demand, when the purchaser undertakes to obtain a given product only from one vendor. In the case of reciprocal undertakings there will be such restrictions on both sides. The question whether a restriction of competition of this nature is liable to affect trade between Member States depends on the circumstances of the case.

As regards example (c), "market-sharing or the sharing of sources of supply,"[2] this also applies because an exclusive agreement involves a division of markets, since the sole distributor is not allowed to sell to customers resident outside his contractual territory; this aspect is of particular importance in view of the intended creation of one common market of the Member States.

[1] Of December 24, 1962, clause II, see Appendix E, *infra*, p. 253. Exclusive distributorship agreements (with independent traders) do not enjoy the privilege of Arts. 4(2) (2,a) and 5(2) of Regulation No. 17. Accord, Gleiss-Hirsch, *op. cit.*, pp. 114 f.; Honig a.o., *op. cit.*, pp. 52 f.

[2] This translation of the French text *"répartir les marchés ou les sources d'approvisionnement"* which corresponds to the German text *"die Aufteilung der Märkte oder Versorgungsquellen"* and to the Italian *"ripartire i mercati o le fonti approvigionamento"* and to the Dutch *"het verdelen van de markten of van de voorzieningsbronnen"* is inaccurate to the extent that the word "sharing" would only cover an agreement on a horizontal basis, *viz.*, sharing of a geographical area with other competitors trading on the same economic level, whereas in the case of a vertical agreement markets are divided by one supplier amongst two or more distributors (of whom the supplier himself may be one). It is therefore more accurate to render the words *répartir, Aufteilung, repartire* or *verdelen* respectively by "division" or "apportionment" which covers both horizontal and vertical agreements.

Finally, exclusive dealing agreements may be subject to Article 86 if the supplying enterprises has a dominant position on the Common Market or on a substantial part of it. An enterprise in such a position could thereby not only easily limit production and sales to the prejudice of customers (example (b)), but could also use the agreement for charging unfair ultimate selling prices for its products in a particular territory. The application of Article 86 would probably have to be considered if it is doubtful whether an exclusive dealing agreement would be caught by Article 85.

Having discussed the question whether and in what respect exclusive dealing agreements are encompassed by Articles 85 and/or 86, it is now necessary to ascertain the groups of persons which qualify as "sole distributors" within the meaning of these Articles. As regards the supplier's side, all that need be said is that the supplier must be an enterprise as understood by Articles 85 and 86.[1] This is usually a manufacturer or wholesaler trading in the form of a company or a partnership or as a single trader. On the distributor's side, the problem is, however, more complex, and the answer cannot merely be obtained by stating that it must also be an enterprise. When discussing the German law in point, we have seen that only dealers acting on their own account ("independent traders") as distinct from commercial agents are treated as enterprises to which the provisions of the Cartel Law apply (and at that only to a rather limited extent)[2]. Similarly, in France only exclusive dealing agreements with persons who sell on their own account are within the scope of the relevant French law. In the other Member States of the E.E.C., the restrictive trade practices law, if any, has no bearing on such agreements.[3]

The Commission in its aforementioned Announcement of December 24, 1962, has in principle adopted the German distinction between

---

[1] See thereon *supra*, p. 11.
[2] See *supra*, pp. 100 f.
[3] Rather strangely, by a Belgian law of July 27, 1961 *(Loi relative à la résiliation unilatérale des concessions de vente exclusive à durée indéterminée, Moniteur-belge* Nr. 238 of October 5, 1961, p. 7518) the hitherto prevailing right of either party to determine without notice an exclusive sale agreement *(monopole de vente; concessions de vente exclusive)* which had been concluded for an indefinite time, was changed by the introduction of a reasonable period of notice and a provision for compensation which will usually ensure for the benefit of the distributor *(concessionaire)*. This Law also applies to Belgian concessionaires of a foreign supplier *(concédant)*. By s. 4, Belgian courts have been accorded jurisdiction to entertain relevant claims by a Belgian concessionaire and Belgian law governs such agreements. The policy of this law would seem to be opposed to that of Art. 85 of the E.E.C. Treaty. See on this Law, Bricmont-Gysels, *Le Contrat de Concession de vente exclusive*, 1962, and A. Baetens, *Le Statut du Concessionaire Exclusif de Vente et la Législation de la Communauté Economique Européenne*, 1963.

mere commercial agents on the one hand and independent traders on the other. It has, however, found it necessary to refine that distinction by not merely distinguishing between these two categories according to their purely legal characteristics (as apparently German law still does) but to qualify them from an economic point of view, thereby creating two new legal categories, namely those commercial agents who do not incur or do not undertake to incur any financial risk and those who do.

The Commission sees the presence of such financial risk, with the consequence that the commercial agent in fact acts as an independent trader, in any of the following circumstances:

(a) that he is required to keep or does in fact keep as his own property a considerable stock of the goods that are the subject-matter of the agreement, or

(b) that he is required to organise, maintain and carry out at his own expense a substantial service to customers free of charge, or does in fact organise, maintain or carry out such a service, or

(c) that he is permitted to determine or does in fact determine the prices or terms of business (*i.e.*, on the resale of such goods).[1]

The Commission created this distinction between persons who are mere auxiliaries in commercial transactions and independent traders after it had ascertained that the legal position of commercial agents was more or less the same in the various national laws of the Member States, either by statutory provisions or by virtue of case law.[2] A brief review appears, however, to be necessary as the English business man in particular, will often be somewhat unfamiliar with the legal descriptions of the various types of commercial agents in the relevant Continental laws; he will in particular wish to know whether, if he enters into a sole distributorship agreement with a commercial agent (in the widest sense of this term), he merely avails himself of an auxiliary so that the agreement is outside Articles 85 and 86, unless, of course, the agent fulfills the conditions of running a financial risk in the aforementioned sense, or whether he has made an agreement with an independent trader.

In English law agency signifies a relationship between the parties which arises by an (express or implied) agreement (or, more rarely, as agency of necessity which can be disregarded for our purpose) whereby one party, the principal, grants authority to another party, the agent,

---

[1] Announcement of December 24, 1962, clause I.
[2] *Ibid.*, clause II(3).

to establish a direct relationship between him, the principal, and a third party. The agent may act either in the name of his principal or in his own name. He can be an independent contractor or a servant; he may be a general agent or a mere special agent whose authority is limited to special transactions. English law has, however also developed special categories of commercial agents like the mercantile agents, brokers, auctioneers and ship-masters, to whom, subject to certain special rules, the general principles of agency apply.[1]

In Continental law and especially in the legal system of the six Member States of the E.E.C., the position is somewhat different. The civil law also knows the concept of general agency,[2] but in regard to commercial agency the commercial codes or special laws have typified the commercial agencies and extended the social protection accorded to employees to those commercial agents who through their dependence on their principals are in a social position not too different from that of mere employees. Thus, in France one distinguishes the group composed of *représentants de commerce, commis-voyageurs* and *placiers* who act in the name and for the account of their principal on a commission basis and/or a fixed salary and the *agents commerciaux* who are independent businessmen not connected with their principal by a *"lien de subordination"*; even an independent trader acting on his own account is often described as an *agent commercial*. In Belgian law there is no comprehensive statutory regulation. The *représentant de commerce* can as a rule only negotiate for his principal with third parties on the basis of an agency agreement entered into for a longer and continuous period; the *commis voyageur* (commercial traveller), although he is an employee of an enterprise,[3] has no authority to conclude a contract. Italian law distinguishes between the agent who merely negotiates transactions for his principal with a third party and the *rappresentante* who may conclude a contract between his principal *(preponente)* and a third party. In practice however, a person may exercise both func-

---

[1] In England (see *Halsbury's Laws of England*, 3rd ed., Vol. I (1952), p. 147) as elsewhere (see *infra*, pp. 93–95 as to the law in the United States and pp. 100 ff. as to the law in Germany), the relationship between a supplier and independent distributor is in commercial language frequently called "agency," and the Courts have taken notice of such misdescription. Whether a contractual relationship is one of agency proper (including a *del credere* agency) or one of sale, however shrouded in terms and conditions, will be decided on an analysis of the true legal nature of the contracting parties' rights and obligations and not by mere reference to the expression used by them.

[2] *E.g.*, ss. 164 ff. of the German Civil Code.

[3] *Loi sur l'Emploi* of August 7, 1922 as amended, see Fredericq, *Traité de Droit Commercial Belge*, 1947, I, no. 212, pp. 361 ff., 291, and *Moniteur-belge*, March 20, 1954, no. 79, p. 2078.

tions.[1] Dutch law distinguishes between *"handelsagenten"* who on the basis of a long-term agreement negotiate or conclude contracts with third parties for their principal on a commission basis and/or fixed remuneration, and *"handelsreizigers"* (commercial travellers) who are employess of an enterprise.

All these countries know also the institution of the *commissionaire* and *agent commissionaire* which largely corresponds with the *Kommissionäre* and *Kommissionsagenten* in German law.[2]

A supplier who appoints a sole distributor in any of these countries will therefore have to examine carefully whether the appointee is a commercial agent or an independent trader trading on his own account and, if belonging to the former category, whether he carries or is intended to carry on his business in a manner which will or will not bring him within Article 85.

While the Announcement on Patent Licence Agreements indicates the Commission's view as to a number of terms in a one-way licence agreement that are not covered by the prohibition of Article 85(1) and expressly reserves the appraisal of patent pools, reciprocal licensing and multiple parallel licences, the Announcement on Exclusive Dealing Agreements is confined to one point, *i.e.*, agreements with one group of sole distributors which are subject to the application of Article 85, and agreements with another group which are outside this Article. The important question whether all such agreements across the frontiers of the Member States or even within one Member State only or between a supplier outside the E.E.C. and a sole distributor within a Member State or *vice versa* are covered by this Article, or whether certain types of sole distributor agreements are exempted from the prohibition of paragraph 1 of Article 85, is not mentioned at all. Unless the Council of Ministers or the Commission issue further Regulations, such questions can only be determined by the European Court. Furthermore, the Announcement does not indicate whether any type of agreement of this nature might be exempted from the prohibition by virtue of paragraph 3. It will therefore have to be seen whether, and if so to what extent, the experience gained in other countries, and particularly in France and in the United States, will influence the development of this new branch of the European law of restraints of competition. The lack of guidance in the Announcement and the

---

[1] Art. 1745 of the *Codice Civile.* See Rotondi, "The Contract of Agencia in the New Italian Civil Code and Judicial Decisions," 10 *A.J.C.L.* (1961), p. 1–18.

[2] See *supra*, p. 100.

absence of either an administrative practice on the part of the Commission or a judicial determination by the European Court (with the exception of the rather inconclusive *Bosch* case)[1] should, however, be no obstacle to the mentioning of a few special aspects of such agreements. They are, first, prohibitions imposed by a supplier in Member State A on a sole distributor in Member State B of the export of the supplier's goods to Member State C, and, secondly, prohibitions on export contained in a sole distributorship agreement concluded between a supplier and a sole distributor who both reside (or have their seat) within one Member State. Prohibitions of the re-import of the supplier's goods into his own State are frequently connected with such export prohibitions, especially in the last-mentioned type of agreements.

The imposition of a condition upon a sole distributor not to export goods to another Member State has in principle been condemned by the European Court in the *Bosch* case even though the Court merely observed that such a prohibition might violate Article 85(1), subject of course, to exemption being granted under paragraph 3 of that Article. This is today the general understanding of the European Court's decision. As regards the second case, several writers[2] deny that an agreement between two parties in one Member State can affect the trade between Member States and therefore be caught by Article 85. The District Court of Munich held in two judgments[3] that Article 85 did apply to an agreement in which a German supplier obliged his numerous German distributors to observe prices (of trade-mark protected goods) fixed by him and not to export the goods acquired from him and, further, not to resell them to any party which was not prepared to give an undertaking to refrain from exporting them. However, one of these judgments[4] was reversed by the Munich Appeal Court,[5] which overuled the lower Court both on the interpretation of the *Bosch*

---

[1] See *supra*, p. 3 n. 1.

[2] Deringer, *op. cit.*, Art. 85 n. 46; Hellmann, *Betriebsberater*, 1963, p. 168; Benisch, *Der Betrieb*, 1963, p. 301.

[3] Of January 14, 1963 (1963) 2 C.M.L. Rep. p. 268 (in re *Agfa-Optima*) in *Der Betrieb*, 1963, p. 301, and of February 25, 1963; *WuW* 1963, p. 428.

[4] *I.e.*, the first-mentioned decision (In re *Agfa-Optima*). The Court of first instance, looking at the price fixing and export prohibiting system as a whole, had considered it as amounting to a sharing of the territory of the Common Market and restricting competition therein since all the German purchasers of the supplier would then be excluded from that territory outside Germany. (Although in each individual case only two enterprises, the supplier and the distributor, had entered into an agreement, the Court treated each individual agreement as a mere part of a whole complex system and held Art. 4(2) (2a) in conjunction with Art. 5(2) of Regulation No. 17 inapplicable so that according to Art. 5(1) (1) (as amended by Regulation No. 59, Art. 1) the time for notification had expired on November 1, 1962).

[5] Judgment of May 30, 1963, (1964) 3 C.M.L. Rep. p. 87, *WuW* 1963, p. 626.

judgment and on the construction of Regulation No. 17, Article 5(1)
(1). The Appeal Court doubted whether Article 85(1) was violated if
German purchasers of the supplier's goods were prevented from exporting these goods, but decided that even if this view could not be
supported the contractual prohibition was to be upheld under Article
5 of Regulation No. 17, as, contrary to the District Court's opinion,
only two enterprises were concerned; further Article 4(2) (2a), by which
vertical agreements were privileged, and the wording of Form B introduced by Regulation No. 153, had to be taken into account. The
Court came to the conclusion that registration had been effected in
time and that the prohibition of exports was valid for the time being.
Finally, the Court refused the application to refer the case to the
European Court under Article 177(3) of the Rome Treaty since its
judgment, though final, was rendered in interlocutory proceedings so
that the plaintiff still had the right to commence proceedings for a
decision in a main action.[1]

Although as a matter of principle the fact that the parties to a sole
distributorship agreement are resident within one Member State only
can certainly not by itself take such agreement outside the scope of
Article 85, it will have to be most carefully examined whether it
is indeed likely to affect trade between Member States. A mere far
fetched possibility of such an effect should not lead to an affirmative answer. In the comparatively few cases in which Courts of the
Member States have so far had an opportunity to consider this problem, they have denied this effect.[2] Since, however, one important
(national) decision rests ultimately on procedural grounds[3] and since,
above all, the European Court has not yet been concerned with a case
of this kind, the question must still be considered an open one.

---

[1] In the present proceedings the plaintiff had asked for the issue of an injunction
restraining the defendant from dealing with his products in Germany because these had
been obtained by way of re-import from abroad. In such interlocutory proceedings the
decision of the Appeal Court is final, whereas in ordinary proceedings, subject to certain
prerequisites, a further appeal *(Revision)* to the Federal Supreme Court is allowed.
For a ruling to the same effect (concerning the possible application of Art. 86), see the
decision of the Netherlands Supreme Court of April 10, 1964 in a case of interlocutory
proceedings *(Kort geding)*, (1964) 3 C.M.L. Rep., p. 100.
[2] Judgment of the Appeal Court of Munich of May 30, 1963 (see *supra*, p. 121 n. 5);
District Court of Amsterdam of May 9, 1963, (1963) 2 C.M.L. Rep. p. 329, *WuW* 1964,
p. 436; Commercial Court of Brussels of March 23, 1962, (1963) 2 C.M.L. Rep., p. 28;
see also judgment of the Appeal Court of Berlin of May 4, 1962, (1963) 2 C.M.L. Rep.,
p. 336 *(Fensterglas III)*.
[3] The judgment of the Appeal Court of Munich of May 30, 1963 (see *supra*, p. 221
n. 5). As to substantive law, the reasoning of the Court of first instance (see *supra*,
p. 121 n. 3) appears convincing.

Whether the prohibition of the re-import of his goods which a supplier imposes upon his distributors in another Member State and/or the contractual prohibition of the re-sale of re-imported goods by his domestic distributors (often coupled with an export prohibition) is lawful under Article 85 has been hotly disputed. Quite recently however, a decision of the German Supreme Court has settled at least part of the problem involved.[1] Because of its importance for the interpretation of Article 85 and Regulation No. 17 the facts of this case and the Court's reasoning deserve a more detailed account. The German company *Braun A.G.* are manufacturers of electric shavers which they sell both in Germany and abroad; being trade marked goods, their selling price can be fixed by virtue of section 16 of the German Cartel Law. Braun had registered the domestic price-fixing system with the Federal Cartel Office and had notified the Commission in Brussels of the prohibition of re-import which they had imposed on their foreign distributors. The German wholesale firm of Ruhrland had however succeeded in re-importing electric shavers produced by Braun from Belgium and had sold them in Germany below the fixed price with the express statement that they had been re-imported into Germany. Braun thereupon commenced legal proceedings, asking for a declaration that Ruhrland should be ordered to cease dealing in Braun products and, in particular, be forbidden to sell re-imported goods below the fixed price. The Frankfurt Appeal Court, reversing the decision of the Court of first instance and incidentally also disapproving the opinion rendered by the Federal Cartel Authority in the same proceedings,[2] declared the imposition of such prohibition incompatible with Article 85 and therefore invalid unless and until a declaration pursuant to paragraph 3 of this Article be obtained; but even if no violation of Article 85 could be found, the plaintiffs had failed to prove that their price fixing system was uniformly enforced without gaps as required in order to be admissible under section 16 of the Cartel Law.[3] The Supreme Court reversed this judgment for two reasons. First, relying on the decision of the European Court in the *Bosch* case according to which restrictive trade agreements remain valid unless and until they have been declared invalid by the Commission or a national Authority of a Member State (and remain therefore provisionally valid)

---

[1] Judgment of June 14, 1963 *(Braun A.G. v. Ruhrland re "Braun Electric Razors")*, (1964) 3 C.M.L. Rep., p. 59; *Betriebsberater*, 1963, p. 1393; *NJW* 1964, p. 152; *WuW* 1964, p. 175.

[2] Declaration made according to s. 90(2) of the Cartel Law, see *WuW* 1961, p. 303.

[3] See *supra*, pp. 104, 109.

if duly registered with the Commission, it held that the prohibition of exports (i.e., of imports into Germany) imposed on the Belgian distributors was valid for the time being.[1] Secondly, the Supreme Court was not convinced that the evidence had shown that the enforcement of the price fixing system was not uniform without gaps, and therefore remitted the case to the Court of first instance for further examination of this point which now appeared to decisive importance.

In two French cases, similar problems arose. First, in the case of *Consten v. U.N.E.F.* to which reference was made earlier,[2] the *Cour d'Appel* of Paris had stayed proceedings as the defendants had pleaded that they had made an application to the Commission under Article 3 of Regulation No. 17.[3] This decision is thus at variance with the afore-mentioned judgment of the German Supreme Court, but it must be emphasised that in the German case no such application had been pleaded. The second case, *Etat Français v. Nicolas and Société Brandt*, however, the *Cour d'Appel* of Amiens[4] refused a stay of proceedings on the application of the defendant as the Commission had not yet initiated any action within the meaning of Article 9(3) of Regulation No. 17. As to the merits of the case, it held

(a) that sole distributorship agreements between French enterprises relating to the distribution of French goods on the French market are not affected by Article 85;

(b) that irrespective of whether they are or are not subject to Article 85, they can be determined by French national cartel law;

(c) a *refus de vente* may be justified if certain prerequisites are fulfilled, but the distributor must not be bound by fixed prices (as was found to be the case in this instance);

(d) sole distributorship agreements are not within the prohibition of Article 59bis of the Law of August 9, 1953, as such agreements are governed by Article 37 (1a) and (4) of Decree No. 45–1483 of June 30, 1945 as amended by Law No. 58–545 of June 24, 1958;

---

[1] As this study is in principle not concerned with the procedural problems relating to Art. 85 ff., the lengthy considerations of the Supreme Court on the effect of the *Bosch* judgment and Regulation No. 17 are not discussed.

[2] See *supra*, p. 113 n. 4 (the judgment is not final).

[3] See *supra, ibid.*

[4] As mentioned *supra*, p. 114 n. 3. This is the application which was determined by the Commission of the E.E.C. on September 23, 1964 (re-printed *infra* in Appendix E, p. 261).

(e) that the Court of the European Communities only has juris-diction to apply Community law proper but not to delimit apparent overlappings of Community law and national law.[1]

A special problem arises if a supplier of goods protected by a trade mark sells them to the public at large and requires one or more of his distributors not to export them into a territory in which he enjoys additional trade mark protection for the same type of goods. The basic question, which belongs, strictly speaking, to the province of the law of trade marks, is this: Is the sole distributor in country B, who has obtained from a supplier in country A goods which are protected by trade mark registration in both countries, *viz.*, in country A in favour of the supplier and in country B in favour of the distributor (who is authorised to pursue infringements in his own name), entitled to prevent a third party that has acquired such goods from dealers in country A (or elsewhere) from bringing them onto the market in country B? The answer turns on the legal nature and effect of a trade mark. Both Dutch and German Courts have recently decided that a trade mark only signifies the origin of the goods to which it relates, *i.e.*, it makes known that the goods so marked come from a certain industrial enterprise; a trade mark confers upon its owner neither the right to a monopoly of the sale of his goods bearing the trade mark nor the control of agreements relating to such goods. Once the owner has put them on the market, the protection of the goods is, *pro tanto*, exhausted so that, even according to the principle of the territoriality of a registered trade mark, the sale of goods bearing the trade mark is not unlawful, even though under an agreement between supplier and sole distributor the rights arising from the trade mark protection have also been vested in the latter. The Courts have thus limited the function of the trade mark to the protection of the public against being misled about the origin of the goods; as all these goods were produced by the same supplier there was no deception of the public, the manner of the marketing of the goods being for this purpose entirely irrelevant.[2]

---

[1] The appeal against this judgment was dismissed by the *Cour de Cassation* on October 22nd, 1964 (Dalloz 1964, p. 754; see also the note by Mezger in *AWD* 1964, p. 361). The *Cour de Cassation* substituted its own reasons for those of the lower Court by merely stating that, as the latter Court had found, trade between Member State had not been affected through transactions between two French domestic firms so that Arts. 85 ff did not come into play and that on these findings there was no need to adopt the procedure laid down in Art. 177. One may however ask whether such somewhat arbitrary disregard of the jurisdiction of the European Court is compatible with the spirit of the Treaty.

[2] Judgment of the German Supreme Court of January 22, 1964, *AWD* 1964, p. 122;

In view of these decisions, which are supported in legal literature,[1] a contractual prohibition agreed between a supplier and one or more distributors as indicated above would appear to be of the same category as an ordinary prohibition since the trade mark protection of the goods concerned does not confer on either party a right which could take the prohibition outside the application of Article 85.[2] It might, however, be otherwise if a licensee of a trade mark himself manufactures goods which bear the same trade mark since in such case these goods are not those actually produced by the licensor; in this case the licensor may lawfully prevent the licensee from exporting the goods manufactured by the latter to a territory in which he, the licensor, manufactures himself or has granted further licences. The trade mark used by the licensee is not exhausted in any territory other than his own. A prohibition of exports is therefore justified under the national trade mark laws, and as these are upheld in Article 36 of the Treaty of Rome this special legal protection should prevail against Article 85.[3]

Lastly, there remains to be discussed the rather intricate problem as to whether and, if the answer is in the affirmative, how far transactions to which enterprises situate outside the six Member States are parties, can be caught by Articles 85 and 86. Such transactions would, of course, only be those which fall within the orbit of these Articles if carried out between enterprises situate in two (or more) Member States or, more rarely, within one Member State.

The general aspect of this question has already been discussed in this study[4] so that we need now only deal with the effect of Articles 85 and 86 on exclusive dealing agreements.

Three main factual situations have to be distinguished:

(1) the supplier has his residence in one of the Member States whereas the distributor resides and carries on business in a non-Member State;

(2) the supplier resides and carries on business outside a Member-

GRUR(AIT) 1964, p. 202. Judgment of the *Hooge Raad der Nederlanden* of December 14, 1956 *GRUR(AIT)*, 1957, p. 259 (re "Grundig"); on the other hand, the sole distributor is entitled to take action against third parties who sell goods which are protected by a Dutch trade mark which is identical with a foreign one of which he is the registered user *(Gerechtshof te 's-Gravenhage* of December 4, 1957, *GRUR(AIT)* 1959, p. 557; of May 13, 1959, *ibid.*, 1961, p. 250; *Arrondissement Rechtbank te Arnhem* of April 18, 1959, *ibid.*, 1961, p. 249).

[1] See v. Gamm, 8 *WRP* (1962), p. 79.

[2] Of the same opinion are Gleiss-Hirsch, *op. cit.*, Art. 85, n. 48.

[3] See Gleiss-Hirsch, *op. cit.*, Art. 85, n. 48; Honig a.o., *op. cit.*, p. 21; see also *supra*, p. 59, and the decision of the Appeal Court of Hamm (Germany) of January 17, 1964, *AWD* 1964, p. 124 *WuW* 1964, p. 535; (1964) C.M.L. Rep., p. 509.

[4] See *supra*, pp. 37–47.

State whereas the distributor resides and carries on business within a Member State;

(3) neither supplier nor distributor resides within a Member State but the distributor's business activities are carried on in one or more Member States.

(If either supplier or distributor is a company, the location of the seat or centre of management is relevant).

In principle, Article 85 will only become operative if trade between Member States is affected by such an agreement. This means that an exclusive dealing agreement must have a direct effect on the inter-state trade of the E.E.C. It is therefore not sufficient that it affects only the market of one or more Member States (and might thus become subject to the national cartel law of such State (or States)). On the other hand, it is immaterial that the effect is brought about by an agreement between parties of whom one or even both are resident outside the Member States of the E.E.C. The application of the Rules of Competition of the Rome Treaty depends not on subjection of the parties concerned to the law of a Member State by virtue of territorial or personal jurisdiction, but solely on the test whether the inter-state trade between at least two Member States is affected. Whether administrative or judicial measures against any offending party can effectively be taken, and whether any such measure would be in conformity with public international law, is a different matter which must be clearly distinguished from the question whether this inter-state trade is affected. Conversely, agreements between enterprises resident within two or more Member States or between one enterprise within and one outside a Member State which do not affect inter-state trade are outside Articles 85 and 86. Having stated the basic principles of the application of the Rules of Competition of the Rome Treaty we will revert to the three instances set out above.

As to (1). The restrictions become material in the territory in which the sole distributor carries on his business as it is only there, in the words of the Announcement on Exclusive Agency Contracts, that "the restriction of competition either in the limitation of supply, when the vendor undertakes to supply a given product only to one purchaser or in the limitation of demand, when the purchaser undertakes t obtain a given product only from one vendor" occurs.[1] As both limitations of supply and demand take place in the distributor's market

---

[1] Clause II(1).

and thus in a foreign market, the inter-state trade between Member States is *prima facie* not affected,[1] but repercussions on the inter-state trade of the Member States remain possible. On the other hand, in the case of the usual reciprocal undertakings by supplier and sole distributor, the supplier is prevented from selling to another distributor or to ultimate customers in the distributor's territory; although such a restriction takes effect principally in the foreign market it will often reduce the potential amount of the supplier's manufacturing or selling capacity.[2] That this is also the opinion of the Commission appears from its first published ruling on a relevant Agreement[3] of which it had been notified under Article 5 of Regulation No. 17 and for which the supplier had applied for the issue of a negative clearance certificate. The applicant, a French Company (Grosfillex) had appointed a Swiss firm (Fillistorf) as sole distributor of the goods manufactured by it (Grosfillex) for the territory of Switzerland; the terms of the Agreement also contained a price fixing clause. Fillistorf undertook neither to manufacture nor to sell any articles of a competitive nature and, conversely, Grosfillex was bound not to sell any articles in Switzerland which were the subject-matter of the contract, except through Fillistorf. The Commission issued a negative clearance certificate, justifying this measure with the finding that on the facts of the case "the competition within the Common Market is not perceptibly prevented, restricted or distorted."[4] It would seem from this line of reasoning that the Commission indeed considers agreements between such parties as being within the orbit of Articles 85 and 86 even though the agreement in the case at issue was held to be innocuous. Consequently, such agreements will have to be submitted to the Commission for clearance and the refusal of a negative clearance certificate cannot be excluded

[1] Several writers take this view, see Gleiss-Hirsch, *op. cit.*, Art. 85, n. 30 (with further references) who hold that a prohibition by a supplier resident in a Member State, imposed upon his distributors in one or more Member States, of the export of products to countries outside the E.E.C., or a prohibition imposed upon a distributor in a non-Member State of the export of goods obtained by him to a Common Market country, is lawful, as trade between Member States would not thereby be affected.

[2] Whether the national law on restrictive trade practices treats such a repercussive effect as subject to its own legal provisions is a different matter. As regards German cartel law, this is denied by Schwartz, *op. cit.*, p. 59 as a matter of principle and by Baruch, *WuW* 1961, p. 535 on account of the express wording of s. 15 of the German Cartel Law.

[3] This (and another Agreement – *Nicolas Frères and Vitapro (U.K.) Limited –*) was officially published (*J.O.* 1963, p. 1853) for the purpose of affording third parties an opportunity to file observations thereon.

[4] *J.O.* 1964, p. 915. This decision is reprinted (in English) in Appendix E, *infra*, p. 256, and the decision granting a negative clearance in the *Nicolas and Vitapro* matter, *ibid.*, p. 258.

if an agreement contains different, and especially additional, terms. This might particularly be the case if the contractual parties grant to each other mutual sole distributorship rights;[1] if the sole distributor resides in a Member State, such arrangement would fall into the category with which we shall deal hereafter.

As to (2). In this case the effect of the trade restrictions takes place in the Member State in which the distributor resides and carries on his business, these two circumstances normally occurring in the same place. It is in the territory of the sole distributor's State where supply and/or demand would be limited. If this State by its national law prohibits such agreements or provides for their registration and/or supervision, agreements of this nature will be governed by its law. This is the legal position under German cartel law.[2] Yet the affirmative answer given on the basis of a Member State's national law does not necessarily determine the question whether such agreement, independently of an infringement of a provision in a national law, affects the trade between Member States. In principle, the answer is in the negative. Thus if, say, an English supplier appoints a sole distributor residing in one of the Member States for the whole of the Common Market territory, trade between Member States is not affected (irrespective of whether one or more Member States treat this agreement as affecting their respective home markets, consequently subjecting it to their national restrictive trade practices law). However, if an English supplier appoints sole distributors for more than one Member State's territory, the position is different if the several distributors are not allowed to sell to customers outside the areas allocated to them. In such a case the limitation of demand and/or supply in one area could not be remedied by deliveries of the goods concerned across the relevant territories of the Member States since trade between the Member States would thereby be affected.[3]

As to (3). As it is not the place of residence of the sole distributor

---

[1] In a letter of May 16, 1963 (replying to an enquiry by the Federal German Minister of Economics) the Director-General for Competition of the Commission of the E.E.C. had expressed his opinion on this question as follows: "... I agree that it is generally outside economic probabilities that sole distributors' agreements concluded by an enterprise whose seat is within the Community with independent traders outside the Community restrict competition within the Common Market and are capable of affecting trade between Member States. Nevertheless, such agreements may in special individual cases contain clauses which may be caught by Article 85 so that a notification to the Commission is necessary or at least advisable" (*WuW* 1963, p. 810).

[2] See Schwartz, *op. cit.*, pp. 57–71.

[3] Deringer, *op. cit.*, Art. 85(1), n. 46 denies the application of Art. 85 if the supplier (the obligor) resides outside the Common Market. He mentions a special case, namely

but the place where he carries on his business that is relevant so far as the effect created by the restrictive exclusive sales agreement to which he is a party is concerned, it is immaterial whether he resides inside or outside the Common Market. The observations on case 2 also hold good for this situation. Thus, if an English Company appoints a Swiss individual or company as sole distributor for the whole territory of the Common Market States, Article 85 will not apply to the sole distributor's agreement. If however under such an agreement the Swiss enterprise's activities are confined to one or more but not all of the Member States, Article 85 becomes operative.

It must be appreciated that the foregoing exposition of the legal position of exclusive agency contracts under Articles 85 *et seq.* is based on hitherto scant legislative material and rather inconclusive judicial interpretation. Furthermore, nothing can be said on the practice of the Commission in granting exemptions under paragraph 3 of Article 85 or its interpretation of Article 86 in relation to such agreements. As it will probably take a considerable time before a more comprehensive administrative practice and a body of case law comes into existence, interpretation of the basic Rules of Competition in the Rome Treaty at the present time has to be guided by principles established in kindred national laws even though many relevant problems have not found a final determination there either. One has further to bear in mind that the special legal nature of the European Economic Community, and in particular the limitation of the antitrust law to inter-state trade, must needs lead to a cautious adoption of principles developed in different factual situations. The purpose and function of the Rules of Competition might therefore result in a sometimes stricter and sometimes more lenient application of these Rules in comparison with the provisions of national laws. Finally, a probably more thorough investigation of the types of sole distributorship agreements and their economic evaluation than has been hitherto undertaken might well influence the Commission's policy in this sphere and also the European

the obligation of a sole distributor in one Member State to sell to certain groups of customers only (specialised dealers, exclusion of mail order houses) and argues with some diffidence that "in those cases such a term might in special circumstances affect the trade between Member States indirectly, *e.g.*, if a (third party) purchaser (for instance, a mail order house), were caused to order relevant goods from another Member State. Whether such indirect effect – irrespective of whether this effect is considered as positive or negative –, would be sufficient 'to affect the trade between Member States', appears more than doubtful as the element of 'liability to affect this trade' would then have no significance of its own beside the element of 'restriction of competition.'" It is difficult to follow this train of thought.

Court's final rulings. But until this special part of the law of the E.E.C. has been more firmly settled, the businessman concerned will be wise if he reckons with a rather strict interpretation, mainly in order to avoid entering into contracts which his opponent could, if it suits him, attack as being void under this law[1].[2]

[1] For an (unofficial) statement of the Commission's policy, especially on sole distributorship agreements, see the Address of P. VerLoren van Themaat before the International Chamber of Commerce in Paris on March 14, 1963, *WuW* 1963, p. 557, at pp. 563 f.

[2] A striking illustration of the effect of Art. 85 on an important international cartel is the far-reaching alteration of the exclusive dealing agreements which had been practised by the *"Convention Faïence"* in Brussels, an association of 30 enterprises of the tile-makers industry in the E.E.C. Member States (and one English company) and about 900 Belgian distributors and tile-laying contractors. These two groups were bound by agreements by which the distributors and tile-layers had to obtain supplies only from such producers as were members of the association whereas the latter had undertaken to sell in Belgium only to customers who were members of this association. This network of agreements had the effect that the Belgian Market was virtually closed to outsiders. When the Commission indicated that these agreements were incompatible with Art. 85 inasmuch as an exemption under paragraph 3 of this Article could not be granted, *Convention Faïence* deleted the mutual exclusive dealings clauses in their standard agreements so that the distributors and tile-layers will in future not be compelled to purchase from member manufacturers only, whilst the latter would sell to all those distributors and tile-layers who satisfy the Association of a certain business standard and register with the Association. The recommendation of the Commission is fully published in *WuW* 1964, p. 54 and in English in E.E.C. Bulletin, May 1964, p. 46. After further examination of the legality of the remaining restrictions, the Commission has published the application of the *Convention Faïence* for the issue of a negative clearance certificate (*J.O.* 1964, p. 1167 – English translation in *Board of Trade Journal* (London), 1964, p. 1253).

PART THREE

THE SUPRA-NATIONAL LAW OF
THE EUROPEAN ECONOMIC COMMUNITY

I. The Legal Nature of the European Economic Community

Although the scope of this book is confined to an analysis of the Rules of Competition in the Treaty of Rome, and then only substantive law at that, the proper understanding of both the contents and functions of these Rules would seem to require a short discussion of the legal character of the European Economic Community itself, and, in particular, of the method of legislation in the Community and the special feature of the immediately binding legal force of these Rules in the Member States.

This is not the place to say more than a few words on the legal nature of the E.E.C. In the first place, it must be remembered that the E.E.C. is only one of three European Communities, the two others being the European Coal and Steel Community and the European Atomic Energy Community.[1] Some of the organs of the three Communities were already unified in 1957,[2] so that, *inter alia*, the exercise of judicial review in regard to three Communities was conferred on one single Court, the Court of Justice of the European Communities. These three Communities form the basis for the intended economic integration of Western Europe which other countries may join or with which they may conclude treaties of association.[3] Secondly, as a distinct aim, they are the nucleus and starting point for a political union in some form or other.

[1a] The Treaty establishing the European Coal and Steel Community of April 18, 1951 (concerning the basic industries of coal and steel); (English translation in 261 *United Nation Treaty Series*, p. 140; 46 *A.J.I.L.* (1952), Suppl. p. 107).

[b] The Treaty establishing the European Atomic Energy Community of March 25, 1957 (Euratom) (concerning the economic side of the use of atomic energy, including research and protection against the effect of radiation); (English translation in 298 *United Nations Treaty Series*, p. 169; 51 *A.J.I.L.* (1957), Suppl. p. 955).

[2] By the Convention relating to Certain Institutions to the European Communities of March 25, 1957 (298 *U.N.T.S.* 267 (1958), reprinted in the Foreign Office translation of the E.E.C. Treaty, Appendices, p. 149). By Resolution of September 24, 1963 the Council of Ministers requested the Governments of the Member States to comment upon the merger of the Executives of the three Communities (with a view to the ultimate merger of the three Communities). For a recent detailed discussion of the problems relating to such mergers, see H. P. Ipsen and G. Nicolaysen in *NJW*, 1963, p. 2209.

[3] Such treaties have so far been concluded with Greece, 18 African States, and Turkey. Only the Treaties with Greece (Arts. 51, 53, 54, 56) and Turkey (Arts. 12 ff.) provide for the extension of the application of the Rules of Competition to those countries; their application is dependent on a decision of the Council of Association provided for in these Treaties of Association.

While the six States concluded these Treaties in accordance with their constitutions and in conformity with public international law, their contents are basically different from those of traditional treaties between sovereign States. It is true that almost every international treaty contains a self-imposed limitation of each contracting State's exercise of sovereignty. When such a treaty comes to an end, either by expiration of the time for which it was made, or by an event foreseen in the treaty itself, or for any other reason compatible with or provided for by international law (*e.g.*, by war or State succession[1]), or even by a breach committed by one party (even if such breach constitutes an international delict), the restriction upon the exercise of sovereign rights comes to an end too. In principle, a State's sovereignty itself is not affected by the conclusion of a treaty. On the contrary, as the Permanent Court of International Justice said in the Wimbledon case:[2]

> No doubt any convention creating an obligation of this kind places a restriction upon the exercise of the sovereign rights of a State... But the right of entering into international engagement is an attribute of a State's sovereignty and the Court declines to see in the conclusion of any treaty by which a State undertakes to perform or refrain from performing a particular act an abandonment of its sovereignty.

On the other hand, if a State concludes a treaty by which it gives up one or more essential elements of the traditional characteristics which are the prerequisites of sovereign Statehood, it loses its sovereignty in the legal sense. Such abandonment must be far-reaching, for instance by permission granted to another State or an international organisation to control its foreign and/or internal policy, but probably not the mere agreement to limit the scope of its defence, or by merger into another State or becoming a member State in a federal State. The Treaties establishing the European Communities do not belong to either category. Through them new special bodies politic have been created. These owe their origin to public international law but once they have come into being, they do not belong any longer to that legal sphere and their relations to the States which have set them up are not governed by the rules of international law. This is not so much due to

---

[1] Whether a treaty can be unilaterally terminated or comes automatically to an end under the doctrine *rebus sic stantibus* is not without doubt, see Oppenheim-Lauterpacht, *op. cit.*, pp. 938 ff.

[2] (1923) Series A, No. 1, at p. 25. See also McNair, *The Law of Treaties*, 1961, Appendix A" (Treaties and Sovereignty"), pp. 754 ff.; Ch. de Visscher, *Theory and Reality in Public International Law*, 1957, pp. 257 ff.

the fact that the Treaties establishing the European Economic Community and the Atomic Energy Community were concluded for an unlimited time (Articles 240 and 208 respectively[1]) although this manifests the desire to found a permanent settlement, but to the covenant whereby each Member State thereby irrevocably transfers part of its sovereign powers to the respective Communities,[2] to the majority principle in voting (subject to certain reservations) and, further, to the comprehensive and extensive "institutionalisation" of the Communities' competencies. As none of these powers hitherto transferred to the Communities is a vital attribute of a Member State's sovereignty in the aforementioned sense, the Member States' sovereignty has remained unimpaired. Nevertheless, although this investment of the Communities with sovereign powers is limited to a sector of the economic sphere, attempts have been made to analyse the novel legal nature of the Communities against the background of traditional public international law and the principles of constitutional law, in other words, to examine whether they are, seen as a whole, a mere confederacy of (sovereign) States (which is an international union of States in which these retain their complete sovereignty) or a federal State (which consists of non-sovereign component States). There is now general agreement that the Communities are different from any of the numerous international administrative bodies often created by States to perform tasks in the field of international co-operation in a large number of fields (e.g., postal services, health, science and the joint administration of large rivers) or from a political organisation like the United Nations or even from a confederacy, an organisation of States of which several instances can be found in the history of the last two centuries.[3] It is a characteristic element of a confederacy that the nationals of the Member States can only be bound or accorded rights by the Member States, but not by the confederation, in other words,

---

[1] The Treaty establishing the European Coal and Steel Community (which was the first) is limited to a duration of 50 years (Art. 97); the Convention by which joint organs for the three Treaties were created does not contain any relevant provision, which is understandable as it is of a more procedural nature and ancillary to the main Treaties.

[2] The expression "transfer" with its connotation of finality and irrevocability would seem to convey the legal nature of the renunciation of rights belonging to a sovereign State and their vesting them in the Community better than the term "delegate" which implies a mere temporary handing over and the reservation of revocation. (See on the conception of delegation, Wohlfarth a.o., *op. cit.*, p. 189, and Bebr, "The Relationship between Community Law and the Law of Member States" (*Br. Inst. Int. & Comp. Law, Special Publ. No. 4* (1962)).

[3] Although the United Nations are sometimes described as such a confederacy, the fact that it comprises members with quite divergent economic and political systems,

no central organ of the confederation has the power to legislate with
the effect of directly binding the nationals of the Member States. The
transfer of a sector of sovereign power by the Member States to the
Communities and the corresponding authority of the Communities to
enact laws immediately binding on the nationals of the Member States
is, however, the salient feature of these new bodies. On the other hand,
the Communities, either any single one or as a whole, are not a federal
State either, since they entirely lack sovereign rights in the political
field, especially in respect of foreign policy and defence, and also in
respect of all other branches of policy, including economic policy with

many of whom are utterly hostile to each other, and its tendency to universality with
the effect that the main purpose of the historical confederacies, *viz.*, defence against
external aggression, is absent, should exclude its description as a confederacy. Nor is
the British Commonwealth a good example since the relations between its members
are not embodied in a formal constitution and often difficult to determine; incidentally,
the British Commonwealth owes its origin not to international treaties but to legislative
acts by Great Britain, a unitary State wich transformed itself into a confederacy of a
special kind. For suitable illustrations one will have to refer to the classical confederacies, *viz.*, the United States between 1781 and 1787, the Swiss Confederation betwen
1815 and 1848, the *Rheinbund* (1806–1814), the *Deutsche Bund* (1815–1866) and the
(secessionist) Confederate States of America (1861–1865). As distinct from the mere
international organisations which, in spite of their institutionalisation and the right
conferred upon them to issue orders or judgments as the case may be that are immediately effective in the contracting States (*e.g.*, in the case of the European Danube
Commission (see Oppenheim-Lauterpacht, *op. cit.*, p. 23 with further references) and
the Statute on the Navigation of the Rhine of 1868 (*ibid.*, p. 471) by which an international Central Commission was set up as an Appeal Court against decisions of the
national special Courts), are mere administrative bodies administering very limited
subject-matters, the nearest comparable organisation is the German *Zollverein* (Customs
Union) in its organised form between 1867 and 1871. From its foundation in 1818 until
1867 the *Zollverein* consisted of a series of treaties concluded between most of the then
sovereign German States but it was reorganised (after the war of 1866) and fully institutionalised by the creation of organs corresponding to those of the *Norddeutsche Bund*,
namely a Federal Customs Council, a Customs Parliament and a *Zoll* Presidency (represented by the Crown of Prussia). The legal nature of this *Zollverein* was in dispute.
Whereas Martitz, *Betrachtungen über die Verfassung des Norddeutschen Bundes*, 1868,
p. 8, considered it as a federal State, Georg Meyer, *Grundzüge des Norddeutschen Bundes-
staatsrechts*, 1868, p. 178 thought it was merely a confederacy because it could legislate
(in a limited field) but had no power of either direct administration (except for its own
customs inspectors with mere supervisory powers) or of enforcement of its laws since
such measures remained within the exclusive competency of the Member States so that
it could not bind the subjects of Member States immediately; (there was no Customs
Court). Two other writers, Thudichum, *Verfassungsrecht des Norddeutschen Bundes und
des deutschen Zoll- und Handelsvereins*, 1870, pp. 581, 582, and Georg Jellinek, *Das
Recht der Staatenverbindungen*, 1887, pp. 169 ff., described it as a mere treaty relationship between sovereign States since it could be terminated by notice before January,
1876 (Art. 29 of the Treaty establishing the *Zollverein* of July 8, 1867). As the E.E.C.
Treaty is concluded for an unlimited time and does not provide for its termination
(which is thus excluded) and, furthermore, its organs can bind subjects of the Member
States directly, the considerations of the commentators on the *Zollverein* might after
all influence one's thought about the legal nature of the European Communities. (For
literature in English on the *Zollverein*, see W. O. Henderson, *The Zollverein*, 1939, and
G.W. Keeton, *"The Zollverein and the Common Market."* in *Current Legal Problems*, 1963,
pp. 1 ff.).

the mere exception in those limited sectors which have been expressly conferred upon them. If one wishes to classify the Communities, now seen as a whole, in the terms of traditional constitutional law theories, one could, at most, describe them as "a federal State in process of creation"[1] and as a "fragmentary State,"[2] *i.e.*, as a body that shows certain elements of a State, in this case of a federal State, which are, however, insufficient to allow one to regard them as fulfilling the minimum requirements of statehood. The Official Reasonings of the three main Treaties have therefore been rightly content to classify the Communities as "bodies of a constitutional character."[3] The impossibility of characterising them in accordance with the tenets of traditional international law and constitutional law has led to the creation of a new legal category, namely that of supra-national law. If one is aware of the implications of this term as they have been indicated in the foregoing lines, this term should be a useful one.[4]

These short observations should assist in the understanding of the conception of Community law as distinct from the national law of the Member States, and its validity and application.

1. THE HIERACHY OF THE NORMS IN THE LAW OF THE E.E.C.

The first distinction in the Community law is that between the *primary law* which comprises the provisions embodied in the Treaties themselves, and the *secondary law* which consist of the legal provisions enacted by the organs of the Communities by virtue of the authorisation conferred upon them in the Treaties.[5] Into the first category fall, firstly, all those provisions relating to the constitution of the Communities themselves, *i.e.*, concerning the basic principles, the organs, the

[1] See Jellinek, *op. cit.*, *("werdende Bundesstaaten")*

[2] *Ibid.*, pp. 653 ff., and the same, *Ueber Staatsfragmente*, 1896, pp. 275–279.

[3] Official Reasoning of a) the E.C.S.C. Treaty, p. 4, and b) the E.E.C. and Atomic Energy Treaty, p. 108. See thereon also Ophuels, *loc. cit.*

[4] The explicit term "supranational" is only used in the E.C.S.C. Treaty with reference to the High Authority (Art. 9(6). According to Ophuels, *loc. cit.*, p. 1698 n. 3, the omission of the further use of this description in the E.E.C. and Euratom Treaties was not intended to characterise these Treaties differently.

[5] This useful characterisation has been introduced by Ophuels, *loc. cit.* Doubts about the political reality of the supranational character of these bodies have frequently, been expressed. F. Rosenstiel, *Le Principe de "Supranationalité," Essai sur les Rapports de la Politique et du Droit*, Paris, 1962, denies a sovereign power of the Communities even in various Member States through the medium of these States since they have no executive organs of their own. Generally, he is sceptical of accomplishing European integration through a mere technical bureaucratisation. Erler (in 18 *Veröffentlichungen der Vereinigung deutscher Staatsrechtslehrer* (1959), p. 17) infers from the fact that the Communities have neither legal nor actual power to prevent a secession of a Member State so that the supremacy of each of the Member States therefore remains factually

relations between the Member States and the Communities, and between the Member States in regard to the Communities; secondly,
certain subject-matters of economic policy itself, *e.g.*, agriculture,
transport and, to be specially noted for our purpose, restrictive trade
practices in both the E.C.S.C. and the E.E.C. Treaties. As regards the
second class, it may be sufficient to say that, as far as the E.E.C.
Treaty is concerned, it comprises all those clauses, in effect enabling
provisions, which require national legislation to make them applicable,
especially the harmonisation of taxes[1] and the approximation of legislative and administrative provisions[2] in the law of the Member States.

Another distinction which is perhaps even more important for practical purposes, is that between Community law which operates directly
within the Member States and binds their nationals, and Community
law which only becomes effective through the medium of transformation into national law. Whether a provision in one of the Treaties
belongs to the one or the other class can only be ascertained from its
meaning and purpose within the aims of the Treaty in question.

Both primary and secondary Community law can become effective
within the Member States either directly or indirectly. The following
examples (taken from the Chapter "Rules of Competition") may illus-
trate this:

1. (a) Article 85, which is a primary law provision, is directly effective (see the judgment of the European Court in the *Bosch* case[3]);

(b) The Regulations Nos. 17, 59, 118 and 26 enacted by the
Council of Ministers,[4] and Regulations Nos. 27[5] and 99[6] issued by the
Commission, are secondary law and directly effective;

2. (a) Article 90(1) is primary law and indirectly effective (as it only

intact, that no supranational character can properly be attributed to them. Such a
conclusion would however not seem to be cogent since compulsion, though it is an
element of positive law, may in certain provinces of law, *e.g.*, in international law and
constitutional law, not be exercisable in the sense that, owing to incompleteness through
lack of the necessary legal machinery, the substantive norms cannot be executed (see
Kelsen, *General Theory of Law and State*, 1945, pp. 23–29, 143 f., 343 ff.). The same
principle would seem to apply to supra-national law. Jellinek, *op. cit.*, pp. 336 f., with
reference to both constitutional law and international law, says: "It is therefore not
compulsion but the guarantee, whereof compulsion appears only as a special feature,
which is an essential element of the concept of law. Legal norms are not so much
compulsory norms as guaranteed norms."

[1] Art. 99.
[2] Arts. 100–102.
[3] See *supra*, pp. 3. 24.
[4] See *supra*, pp. 23–26, 34, 53; *infra*, Appendix E.
[5] See *supra*, p. 3, *infra*, Appendix.
[6] Of July 25, 1963 (*J.O.* 1963, p. 2268) concerning Procedure at Hearings.

imposes a duty on the Member States not to take certain measures);
Article 91(2), first sentence) is primary law and indirectly effective
(for similar reasons);

(b) Article 90(3) and Article 91 (1, first and second sentences) are
enabling provisions for the enactment of secondary law. Regulation
No. 8[1] is secondary law with indirect effect since it is addressed to the
Member States only and requires them to take legislative and/or administrative measures.

These brief examples will become more comprehensible through the
following discussion.

The Treaties contain machinery for making both primary and
secondary law effective. Confining our observations to the E.E.C.
Treaty, legislation in respect of Community law is carried out by the
Council of Ministers (which is the federal organ[2]) and the Commission
(which is the Executive[3]). The Assembly, which is now the European
Parliament, has only consultative (and certain controlling) functions.[4]
The Court of Justice is designed to ensure the observance of the Treaty.[5]

Primary law, though it may sometimes be directly applicable e.g.,
as an element in the private law of the respective national laws, as a
rule requires executory instruments to make it effective. This is
achieved by the issue of a *regulation* (Fr. *le règlement*, G. *Verordnung*)
by the Council of Ministers. This expression is actually somewhat
misleading since such enactment is what in English constitution law
would be called a statute (Fr. *loi*; G. *Gesetz*), particularly if contrasted
with the inferior orders issued by the Commission (comparable with
statutory instruments) which, to make the confusion complete, bear
the same description.[6]

---

[1] See *supra*, p. 54 and Appendix E, *infra* p. 222.
[2] Arts. 145–154, 189.
[3] Arts. 155–163, 189.
[4] Arts. 137 ff.; by virtue of the Convention on Joint Organs for the European
Communities of March 25, 1957 (Arts. 1, 2), the powers and competencies of this Assembly have been conferred on the European Parliamentary Assembly (in Strasbourg).
This body, called the European Parliament, has to be consulted before the Council of
Ministers issues Regulations or Directives under Art. 87 (Art. 87(1)). Another consultative organ is the Economic and Social Committee (Arts. 193 ff.).
[5] Art. 164. According to the Convention on Joint Organs for the European Communities (Art. 3, 4), this Court is the Court of Justice of the European Communities (for
short: European Court). Its seat is at present in Luxembourg. Of particular importance
for the interpretation of Arts. 85 ff. are paragraphs 2 and 3 of Art. 177 which enable
the European Court to give rulings if the interpretation of these Articles has become
an issue in proceedings pending before Courts in the Member States.
[6] See thereon Ophuels, *loc. cit.*, p. 1700, ns. 14, 17.

The distinction between primary law and secondary law is of great importance for the manner of its operation. Primary law may be applicable directly, that is without intermediate measures designed to bring it into force. This holds good for those provisions which are laid down in the Treaties and are capable of having immediate effect.[1] As for such primary law as requires further measures to make it effective, these measures are carried out through legislation by the organs of the Community, thus through the medium of secondary law. Such legislative power is, however, not exclusively reserved to the Council inasmuch as Article 155 enables the Council to confer on the Commission (which is primarily an executive organ) the exercise of powers for the purpose of carrying into effect the provisions issued by the Council. It would seem that such legislative activity by the Commission must be expressly authorised in every particular instance.[2]

Somewhat more complicated is the method adopted in the E.E.C. Treaty for making the merely indirectly binding Community law effective. Here the procedure is a two-tiered one, similar to the classical transformation of international law into municipal Law, or, perhaps more appropriately, to the execution of federal statutes by legislative or administrative measures of a component State in a federal State (*e.g.*, under the German Constitution of 1919[3] or in accordance with Article 83 of the Basic Law of the Federal German Republic[4]). As a first act, the Community imposes a duty on one or more Member States to enact a national law; as a second act, the Member State concerned introduces a national law (through its ordinary legislative process) and imposes duties and/or bestows rights on its subjects. The E.E.C. Treaty deals with this procedure in Article 189 in which the various forms of the measures to be taken by the Council of Ministers and the Commission are laid down.[5]

---

[1] This was a hotly disputed question in regard to Arts. 85 and 86 before the European Court largely clarified the position in its judgment in the *Bosch* case, see *supra*, p. 24. In the case of *van Gend en Loos v. Nederlandse Belastingsadministratie* of February 5, 1963, (1963) 2 C.M.L. Rep., 1963, p. 105, concerning the effect of Art. 12 of the E.E.C, Treaty, the European Court attributed a direct effect to that Article.

[2] See Deringer, *op. cit.*, Art. 87, n.4.

[3] See Fleischmann in *Handbuch des Deutschen Staatsrechts*, I, 1930, p. 371, who holds that the component States *(Länder)* were even bound to enact statutes in order to comply with *Reich* law.

[4] See Maunz-Dürig, *Grundgesetz*, Art. 83, n. 24.

[5] It will be noted that the legislative power in the E.E.C. is vested in the Council of Ministers and the Commission which are non-parliamentary bodies, whereas the European Parliament can in this process only exercise a consultative function. This method falls short of a truly democratic process but seemed in the first stages of the development of the Community to be unavoidable.

Article 189 lists three different categories of such measures, namely the *regulation* (Fr. *le règlement*; G. *Verordnung*), the *directive* (Fr. *le directive*; G. *Richtlinie*) and the *decision* (Fr. *la décision*; G. *Entscheidung*). The regulation is a legislative act by which the primary law of the Treaty, unless it is fully and directly self-executing, is made effective. Article 189(2) provides: "A regulation shall have general application. It shall be binding in its entirety and directly applicable in each Member State." Such regulations are as a rule enacted by the Council of Ministers but they can also be issued by the Commission by virtue of a special authorisation under Article 155.[1] A regulation must apply to all Member States uniformly, otherwise the appropriate measure is the issue of a directive.[2] A regulation, being the equivalent of a statute in the constitutional terminology of the Member States, has the force of a national law and has to be treated as such by the Authorities and Courts of a Member State.[3] While, as stated before, regulations are the appropriate measure to make primary law effective, they cannot be used to make secondary law operative. This has to be done either by directives or decisions. As regards the former, Article 189(3) provides as follows:

A directive shall be binding in respect of the result to be achieved upon every Member State to which it is addressed but both the form and the manner in which it is to be carried through shall be a matter to be determined by the national Authorities concerned.

Thus, the directive is the legislative measure for the implementation of secondary Community law by either national legislation or national administrative practice as may be required by the national law of the Member State concerned. Directives may be given only to one or more Member States. They have the legal nature of a statute. As distinct from regulations and directives, decisions are of a complex nature. Paragraph 4 of Article 189 rather tersely reads:

A decision shall be binding in its entirety upon those to whom it is directed.

---

[1] See *infra*, Appendix E, p. 202.

[2] See Wohlfarth a.o., *op. cit.*, Art. 189, n.3, p. 516. Exceptionally, under Art. 226 the application of Treaty provisions in one particular Member State can be suspended, see *ibid.*, n. 5., p. 517. In its judgment of July 13, 1963 (Matter 13/63) the European Court upheld a decision by the Commission in which a Member State had been authorised to take preventive measures in accordance with Art. 226 against the import of electrical household refrigerators from another Member State, *Recueil*, Vol. IX (1963), p. 339.

[3] For a more detailed discussion on the relation between Community law and national law, see *infra.*, pp. 147–151.

Who are these addressees? It appears that decisions can be directed to Member States as well as to their nationals (individuals or legal entities). The issue of a decision directed to a Member State would seem to be the necessary legislative instrument if a directive, owing to its more general tenor, could not sufficiently take account of all relevant particulars of the individual case in question as, when it receives a directive, the State concerned will then have to comply with it by either enacting legislation or taking administrative measures. Yet decisions addressed to nationals are of a different nature: they are purely administrative acts.[1] Such an administrative act with immediately binding effect (*i.e.*, without being required to be transformed into national law) can therefore only be used to make primary law effective. It will, as far as the Rules of Competition are concerned, in principle be limited to the implementation of a regulation issued by the Council of Ministers or by the Commission under Articles 87 and 213 (stipulating the Commission's right to collect information[2]). According to Article 192 those decisions in which a payment by individuals and corporations (as distinct from States) is ordered, are instruments authorising execution; this is carried out in accordance with the national law of civil procedure of the State in whose territory it is to take place.[3] Although not expressly stated, administrative decisions will be made by the Commission, at least as a rule, since the administration of the Community is the task of the Commission.

Lastly, Article 189 lists recommendations and opinions which shall have no binding force. Both the Council of Ministers and the Commission (cf. Article 155) are competent to act in this way.[4]

---

[1] One may assume that the Council and the Commission will take account of the constitutional law of the Member States according to which a measure adopted by the State against an individual (including a corporation), or a limited number of individuals in a particular case, will as a rule be carried out by means of an administrative act and only exceptionally be a statute ("administrative act in the form of a statute"). This practice is in principle at variance with that in the United Kingdom where "private bills which relate to some matter of individual, corporate or local interest" (see Wade & Phillips, *Constitutional Law*, 6th ed., 1960, pp. 130, 141 ff.) are a normal and frequently used instrument of government.

[2] This is one of the competencies in respect of which the E.E.C. will have to develop an administrative law of its own.

[3] For further details of this enforcement, see paragraphs 2 and 3 of Art. 192. Whether on the enforcement of a judgment by the European Court (Arts. 187, 192) or of a decision under Art. 192 its compatability with the Member State's *ordre public* can be examined is not free from doubt but should have to be answered in the negative (see Schuetze, *NJW* 1964, p. 2204).

[4] Certain other enactments and orders for the implementation of Treaty provisions need not comply with the categories set forth in Art. 189, *e.g.*, the Rules of Procedure of the Organs of the Community, including those of the European Court of Justice (Art. 188), see Wohlfarth a.o., *op. cit.*, Art. 189, ns. 18, 19, pp. 521/522.

The regulations, directives and decisions of the Council and of the Commission shall be fully reasoned and shall refer to the proposals and opinions which have to be obtained in accordance with the Treaty.[1] While regulations must be published in the *Journal Officiel* of the Community, directives and decisions have only to be notified to those to whom they are addressed and take effect upon such notification but need not be published; frequently, however, they are also published in the *Journal*.

In the case of the Rules of Competition, Article 87 enables the Council of Ministers – on a proposal by the Commission and after consultation with the European Parliament – to issue regulations or directives which are appropriate for carrying into effect the principles set out in Articles 85 and 86 so that it was thought prudent to give the Council an express power to legislate. It must, however, be emphasised that this authorisation does not give the Council a free hand to act in a manner that would affect the basic principles which have been laid down in these Articles.[2] Secondly, it has been maintained that the competencies which the Council now possesses by virtue of Article 87 could not be exercised on the strength of Article 189 directly since this Article only contains provisions as to the form and effect of the legislative measures, whereas the substantive authority for them must be found elsewhere in the Treaty; in the words of this Article, they must be taken "in accordance with the provisions of this Treaty" (Fr. *"dans les conditions prévues au présent Traité"*).

This means that as far as the implementation of the Rules of Compe-

---

[1] By a judgment of July 4, 1963 (in Matter 24/62) the European Court declared a decision of the Commission invalid on the ground that it had not been sufficiently reasoned as prescribed by the above Article (*Recueil*, Vol. IX, p. 129; (1963) 2 C.M.L. Rep., p. 347).

[2] Wohlfarth a.o., *op. cit.*, Art. 87 ns. 4 and 5, p. 254, comment on (2) b) that the Council may determine which agreements *etc.* can be generally exempted from the prohibition or be permitted in individual cases and, further, that the application of Art. 85(3) might be governed by the principle of mere abuse (instead of the principle of prohibition). As regards c) they say: "The Council may grant exemptions from Articles 85 and 86 or from parts thereof for some economic sectors. This authority permits to a limited extent a substantive alteration of Arts. 85 and 86; as distinct from other cases (see n. 1 [where in regard to paragraph 1 the authors deny the legality of substantial alterations]), Articles 85 and 86 do not in this particular instance constitute an absolute barrier to an alteration by means of a regulation. However, having regard to the purpose of this provision, one will have to assume that such "area exemptions" can only be permitted in so far as extraordinary conditions prevail in a particular economic sector – *e.g.*, on account of State control – so that the application of Art. 85 would be inappropriate. Yet even by such an exemption the substantive nucleus of Arts. 85, 86 must not be encroached upon. Such exemptions are already envisaged for agriculture, traffic and public utility undertakings in the Treaty itself. Further possible examples are, for instance, banks and isurance companies."

tition is concerned, Article 87 circumscribes the substantive powers of the Council to issue regulations and directives, whereas their form and effect is laid down in Articles 189 et seq.

2. THE LAW APPLICABLE BY THE ORGANS OF THE E.E.C.

It might appear from the foregoing lines that the law which the organs of the E.E.C. apply is merely that of the Treaty itself. Such a view is indeed justified and derives support from several decisions of the European Court.[1] But this law does not consist of the Articles of the Treaty alone. First, two Articles of the Treaty itself contain references to other, extraneous law. Article 215(2) refers to the general principles common to the laws of the Member States. Although these are only mentioned as the standard of making good damage done by the Community in the case of non-contractual liability, this special reference is now understood to express a general principle to be observed in the supplementary interpretation of the provisions of the Treaty.[2] In Article 234 the basic principle of international law, *pacta sunt servanda*, is expressly safeguarded, subject only to the Member States' duty to bring their obligations under international treaties concluded prior to the establishment of the E.E.C. into accord with their duties under the latter Treaty (Article 234(2)). But even without such special authority the organs of the Community have to observe the general rules of international law, a principle which has found explicit expression in Article 25 of the Basic law of the German Federal Republic, in paragraph 14 of the Preamble of the French Constitution of 1946 to which paragraph 1 of the Preamble of the 1958 Constitution refers, and in Art. 10 of the Italian Constitution of 1948; it prevails in this country by virtue of the common law doctrine that the law of nations is part of the law of the land.[3]

Much more difficult is the question whether the organs of the Community are bound by the constitutions of the Member States, especially

---

[1] Of February 4, 1959, *Recueil*, Vol. V, p. 42; of July 15, 1960, *ibid.*, Vol. VI, p. 662 (both concerning the E.C.S.C. Treaty).

[2] See Ehle, *AWD*, 1963, pp. 157/158, and *NJW*, 1963 p. 2197; Wohlfahrt, *Juristen-Jahrbuch*, Vol. 3, 1962/63, pp. 241, 270. The European Court has ruled in this sense in the interpretation of the E.C.S.C. Treaty: a) the principle of justice and certainty of the law, Matter 17, 20/61, *Recueil* Vol. VII, p. 319; b) the extensive interpretation of provisions granting protection by law, Matter 6/60, *ibid.*, Vol. VI, p. 1125; c) the principle of estoppel *(venire contra factum proprium)*, Matter 17, 20/61, *ibid.*, Vol. VII, p. 319. See thereon Wenner, *AWD* 1963, pp. 33/34.

[3] See Oppenheim-Lauterpacht, *op. cit.*, pp. 39 ff.

if these contain basic rights.[1] At least in Germany the opinion prevails that these basic rights and the fundamental principles of the constitutions of the Member States must not be violated by the Community. It appears that the European Court will not directly apply national constitutional law but would interpret the Treaty in conformity with the constitutions of the Member States.[2]

II. The Relation between Community Law and National Law

This chapter should not be concluded without a brief reference to the important and much discussed question of the relationship between Community law on the one hand and the national law of the Member States on the other hand. This question is a general one which occurs in many instances of the application of the Treaty and has therefore to be examined as a matter of principle. As regards the subject-matter of this book, it would seem that the special provisions of Article 88 have not simplified but complicated its solution for that part of the Treaty with which we are concerned.

The general principles can be stated fairly briefly. In so far as a subject-matter belongs to the exclusive competence of the Community, only Community law is valid and only the Community can legislate. Immediately binding (primary) law is automatically effective in the Member States or becomes effective through a regulation of the Council independent of national law which is superseded if it exists and must not be re-enacted.[3] Community law which becomes effective through legislation by the organs of the Community in the form of directives and decisions has the same force once the Member States concerned have acted in compliance with these legislative measures of the Community.[4] Since no subject-matter, at least at the present stage of the Community, is in the exclusive jurisdiction of the Community,[5]

[1] For instance the "*Grundrechte*" of the German Basic Law, Arts. 1–19 which are inalienable and cannot be made the object of a change of law. (Art. 79(3) of the Basic Law).
[2] Judgments of February 4, 1959 (Matter 1–58), *Recueil*, Vol. V, p. 42, and July 15, 1960 (Matter 20–59), *ibid.*, Vol. VI, p. 662. See on this problem in relation to the German Basic Law, Ehle, *AWD* 1963, pp. 157–161, *NJW* 1963, pp. 2193–2198, and *NJW* 1964, p. 321.
[3] See Government Justification of the E.E.C. Treaty, German text, *Bundestagsdrucksache* 3440/2. *Wahlperiode*, p. 150.
[4] In the event of a Member State refusing or neglecting to act, the Commission may refer the matter to the European Court (Art. 169).
[5] This legal position will also in future remain the exceptional one; the only instance of the Community's exclusive jurisdiction will probably be the legislation on customs duties after the establishment of a common customs tariff (Art. 3(a), 23(3)), see Wohlfarth a.o., *op. cit.*, Preliminary Observations preceding Art. 189, n. 3, p. 513.

both the Community and the Member States possess what has been called "concurrent legislative competence." The Member States are therefore free to maintain existing law or to introduce new law in regard to all those economic sectors which are regulated by the Treaty until the Community has exercised the right to legislate in accordance with the Treaty; once the Community has lawfully done so, incompatible and even concordant law becomes invalid. A striking example of such concurrent legislative competence is cartel law. The Member States are still entitled to maintain their own restrictive trades practices law or create a new one for their internal national economy, but they have lost this power in so far as trade between Member States could be affected thereby (Articles 85, 86)[1] in which case Community law prevails. Finally, in so far as the Member States have retained full jurisdiction in such fields as are also subject to the Community's power to legislate with binding effect, Community organs can nevertheless intervene for the purpose of furthering the integration of the Community either by an unanimous resolution of the Council (e.g., Article 100)[2] or by recommendations and opinions (e.g., Article 118)[3] and Article 5 requires the Member States generally to co-operate in the implementation of the Treaty.

In the special case of the Rules of Competition, Article 88 tries to regulate the relationship between Community Law and the national law of the Member States for the transitory period. Article 87(2,e) authorises the Council of Ministers to determine the relationship between the national restrictive trade practices laws of the Member States on the one hand and the provisions contained in the Rules of Competition of the Treaty and Regulations made thereunder on the other. So far the Council has not taken any step in this direction, except perhaps the enactment of Article 9(3) of Regulation No. 17 which will be referred to presently.[4] When discussing Article 88, one has to distinguish its significance before and after the enactment of Regulation No. 17 and the judgment of the European Court in the *Bosch* case by which it was established that the prohibition of Article

---

[1] See thereon the detailed exposition in Schwartz, *op. cit.*, pp. 5–14, with further reference to legal practice and literature.

[2] Concerning the approximation of legislative and administrative provisions of Member States.

[3] Concerning the promotion of close collaboration between Member States in the social field.

[4] Caution must be exercised in referring to the prohibition of restrictive trade practices in Art. 65 of the E.C.S.C. Treaty as these provisions also apply to restraints on competition within the Member States in the field of production and distribution of coal and steel.

85(1) (and most probably also that of Article 86) could only become effective through a ruling by national Authorities to the effect that a transaction was governed by paragraph 1, but that this provision could no longer be declared inapplicable by national Authorities.[1] Although Article 88 does not contain a demarcation between Community law and national restrictive practices law (if any), and does not even expressly state that any national laws will remain in force, it is generally understood to confirm the concurrent validity of these two systems of norms.[2] Through Article 9(3) of Regulation No. 17 the function of Article 88 has been newly determined: "As long as the Commission has not initiated[3] any action pursuant to Articles 2, 3 or 6 (of this Regulation) the Authorities[4] of the Member States shall remain competent to enforce Article 85(1) and Article 86 in accordance with the Treaty even if the time limits for notification laid down in Article 5(1) and Article 7 have not expired." Disregarding the legal position as it stood before this Regulation came into force and refraining from dealing with the rather complicated and disputed procedural aspects of this part of the Regulation, the present relationship between Community law and national law on restrictive trade practices may be summarised as follows.

Both Article 85 or Article 86, as the case may be, and a provision in a national law may apply to the same transaction. The Rules of Competition prohibit transactions designed to prevent, restrict or distort competition within the Common Market which are liable to affect

---

[1] See *supra*, p. 23 and *infra*, n. 4.

[2] See Wohlfarth a.o., *op. cit.*, Art. 88, n. 5. p. 260; Baruch, *loc. cit.*, pp. 14 ff.; Clément in *Cartel and Monopoly*, 1961, Vol. I, p. 395. This follows too from Art. 87 (2,e) in which the Council of Ministers is given authority to determine the relationship between the national laws on restrictive trade practices and the Rules of Competition.

[3] This term is not clear. According to Deringer, *op. cit.*, Regulation No. 17, Art. 9, n. 17, the earliest moment is the Commission's adoption of its first measure by manifestly dealing with the case submitted to it, and the latest when it sends an inquiry or issues a request for information (Regulation No. 17, Art. 11).

[4] The question whether this term also comprises Courts of the Member States is doubtful. Present prevailing opinion seems to be inclined to answer it in the negative (see Deringer, *op. cit.*, Regulation No. 17 Art. 9, ns. 18–22). This is of particular importance for France where the (State) *Commission des Ententes et des Positions Dominantes* has only consultative powers, see *supra*, p. 91 n. 1. In the case of *Consten v. U.N.E.F.* (January 26, 1963, *Gazette du Palais* of February 15, 1963 (1963) 2 C.M.L. Rep., p. 176), the *Cour d'Appel* of Paris stayed proceedings on the ground that the plaintiff had asked the Commission to declare its agreement with Grundig prohibited by Art. 85, (see *supra*, p. 113 n. 4 and p. 124). It should be repeated in this connection that a declaration of the inapplicability of Art. 85(1) can now only be made by the Commission (Art. 9 of Regulation No. 17); according to general opinion such a "negative clearance certificate" is not binding either on Authorities or on Courts but national Authorities are indirectly bound by virtue of Art. 9(3) of Regulation No. 17 unless and until new facts come to light.

trade between Member States, whereas a national law against restraints on competition shall in principle protect free competition on the home market of the Member State concerned. Several cases of conflicts in the operation of these two legal systems are possible. Firstly, a transaction may under a national law be lawful *ipso iure* or after permission has been granted but may nevertheless be prohibited under Articles 85 or 86 – as regards Article 85, subject to a declaration in accordance with paragraph 3 thereof. Secondly, in the converse case, a transaction may be unobjectionable under Article 85, possibly after a ruling by the Commission under paragraph 3, or under Article 86, but be prohibited under a national law or lawful only with governmental approval. Thirdly, the facts and/or legal set-up of a transaction may be of a kind that affects both inter-state and home market trade in such a manner that its component elements cannot reasonably be separated. The solution of conflicts occuring in instances one and two are fairly simple. Each respective part of a transaction will have to be judged under the applicable Community law or national law, irrespective of a determination by the Commission whether a declaration in accordance with Article 85(3) is in point or whether national Authorities are called upon to render a decision. Thus, even if the Commission has exempted a transaction under Article 85(3), a national Authority may still apply its own prohibiting law to the same transaction in so far as it is considered as restrictive of internal trade.[1] More complicated and of greater significance in view of the growing integration of the Common Market is the third instance.

A case in point would be a cartel whose participants are enterprises situated in several Member States. Although it has recently been argued that such a situation may provoke conflicting rulings by the Commission and national Authorities and that an exemption granted by the Commission under Article 85(3) should be respected by national Authorities also in regard to the application of their national laws, at least for the time being,[2] no such effect need be attributed to a decision

[1] The decision of the *Cour d'Appel* of Amiens in the case of *Etat Français v. Nicolas et Société Brandt, supra*, pp. 124 f. The Court pointed out that the European Court's power (under Art. 177) is limited to the application of Community Law and does not extend to the settling of conflicts between that law and internal law, questions raised by the disparity of laws being the subject of a special procedure laid down in Arts. 100 to 102 of the Treaty which do not provide for the intervention of the European Court. This view may, however, be rather sweeping since that Court might in a given case also have to pronounce upon the incompatibility of a national law (or a judicial interpretation) with overriding Community law.

[2] See Schumacher in *Die Aussprache*, 1963, p. 44 (with reference to Art. 5 of the E.E.C. Treaty) and against this view, Deringer, *op. cit.*, Art. 87, n. 43, 44.

of the Commission as provided for in Articles 101 and 103.[1] *De lege ferenda*, it would seem that such conflicts could not entirely be resolved by the exercise of the power given to the Council by Article 87(2,e), because such determination would necessarily be confined to the principles laid down in Articles 85 and 86,[2] so that the only way to achieve the desired result would be the approximation of the national laws by the machinery provided in Article 100 of the Treaty.

---

[1] If the integration of commerce and industry in the Common Market proceeds, the development in the field of cartel law will, *mutatis mutandis*, probably be similar to the history of antitrust law in the United States. Although federal jurisdiction is in principle limited to intervention if inter-state commerce is affected, the factual creation of a common market covering the whole of the United States has led the Courts to assume that inter-state commerce was adversely affected in the great majority of all cases with which they were seized (see Oppenheim, *op. cit.*, pp. 54–57; Neale, *op. cit.*, pp. 10 f.). However, in so far as States of the Union have State antitrust laws (which are with a few exceptions considered as of little effect, see Oppenheim, *ibid.*, and Neale, *ibid*), the State Authorities and State Courts have retained jurisdiction to administer them.

[2] See Deringer, *op. cit.*, Art. 87, ns. 45–47.

APPENDICES

UNITED STATES

Sherman Act

Sec. 1. Every contract, combination in the form of trust or otherwise, or conspiracy, in restraint of trade or commerce among the several States, or with foreign nations, is declared to be illegal: *Provided*, That nothing herein contained shall render illegal, contracts or agreements prescribing minimum prices for the resale of a commodity which bears, or the label or container of which bears, the trademark, brand, or name of the producer or distributor of such commodity and which is in free and open competition with commodities of the same general class produced or distributed by others, when contracts or agreements of that description are lawful as applied to intrastate transactions, under any statute, law, or public policy now or hereafter in effect in any State, Territory, or the District of Columbia in which such resale is to be made, or to which the commodity is to be transported for such resale, and the making of such contracts or agreements shall not be an unfair method of competition under section 45 of this title: *Provided further*, That the preceding proviso shall not make lawful any contract or agreement, providing for the establishment or maintenance of minimum resale prices on any commodity herein involved, between manufacturers, or between producers, or between wholesalers, or between brokers, or between factors, or between retailers, or between persons, firms, or corporations in competition with each other. Every person who shall make any contract or engage in any combination or conspiracy declared by Sections 1–7 of this title to be illegal shall be deemed guilty of a misdemeanor, and, on conviction thereof, shall be punished by fine not exceeding fifty thousand dollars, or by imprisonment not exceeding one year, or by both said punishments, in the discretion of the court.

Sec. 2. Every person who shall monopolize, or attempt to monopolize, or combine or conspire with any other person or persons, to monopolize any part of the trade or commerce among the several States, or with foreign nations, shall be deemed guilty of a misdemeanor, and, on conviction thereof, shall be punished by fine not exceeding fifty thousand dollars, or by imprisonment not exceeding one year, or by both said punishments, in the discretion of the court.

Sec. 3. Every contract, combination in form of trust or otherwise, or conspiracy, in restraint of trade or commerce in any Territory of the United States or of the District of Columbia, or in restraint of trade or commerce between any such Territory and another, or between any such Territory or Territories and any State or States or the District of Columbia, or with foreign nations, or between the District of Columbia and any State or States or foreign nations, is declared illegal. Every person who shall make any such contract or engage in any such combination or conspiracy, shall be deemed guilty of a misdemeanor, and, on conviction thereof, shall be punished by fine not exceeding fifty thousandi dollars, or by imprisonment not exceeding one year, or by both said punishments, in the discretion of the court.

Sec. 4. The several district courts of the United States are hereby invested with jurisdiction to prevent and restrain violations of this act; and it shall be the duty of the several district attorneys of the United States, in their respective districts, under the direction of the Attorney General, to institute proceedings in equity to prevent and restrain such violations. Such proceedings may be by way of petition such violation shall be enjoined or otherwise prohibited. When the parties complained of shall have been duly notified of such petition the court shall proceed, as soon as may be, to the hearing and determination of the case; and pending such petition and before final decree, the court may at any time make such temporary restraining order or prohibition as shall be deemed just in the premises.

Sec. 5. Whenever it shall appear to the court before which any proceeding under section four of this act may be pending, that the ends of justice require that other parties should be brought before the court, the court may cause them to be summoned, whether they reside in the district in which the court is held or not; and subpoenas to that end may be served in any district by the marshal thereof.

Sec. 6. Any property owned under any contract or by any combination, or pursuant to any conspiracy (and being the subject thereof) mentioned in section one of this act, and being in the course of transportation from one State to another, or to a foreign country, shall be forfeited to the United States, and may be seized and condemned by like proceedings as those provided by law for the forfeiture, seizure, and condemnation of property imported into the United States contrary to law.

[*Sec. 7.* was repealed by act July 7, 1955, c. 283, § 3, 69 Stat. 283; the section is now covered by section 4 of the Clayton Act.]

Sec. 8. That the word "person," or "persons," wherever used in this act, shall be deemed to include corporations and associations existing under or authorized by the laws of either the United States, the laws of any of the Territories, the laws of any State, or the laws of any foreign country.

Federal Trade Commission Act

Be it enacted by the Senate and House of Representatives of the United States of America in Congress assembled, That a commission is hereby created and established, to be known as the Federal Trade Commission (hereinafter referred to as the commission), which shall be composed of five commissioners, who shall be appointed by the President, by and with the advice and consent of the Senate. Not more than three of the commissioners shall be members of the same political party. * * * The President shall choose a chairman from the Commission's membership. No commissioner shall engage in any other business, vocation, or employment. Any commissioner may be removed by the President for inefficiency, neglect of duty, or malfeasance in office. A vacancy in the commission shall not impair the right of the remaining commissioners to exercise all the powers of the commission.

The commission shall have an official seal, which shall be judicially noticed.

* * *

Sec. 5. (a) (1) Unfair methods of competition in commerce, and unfair or deceptive acts or practices in commerce, are hereby declared unlawful.

(2) Nothing contained in this Act or in any of the Antitrust Acts, shall render

unlawful any contracts or agreements prescribing minimum or stipulated prices, requiring a vendee to enter into contracts or agreements prescribing minimum or stipulated prices, for the resale of a commodity which bears, or the label or container wich bears, the trademark, brand, or name of the producer or distributor of such commodity and which is in free and open competition with commodities of the same general class produced or distributed by others, when contracts or agreements of that description are lawful as applied to intrastate transactions under any statute, law, or public policy now or hereafter in effect in any State, Territory, or in the District of Columbia in which such resale is to be made, or to which the commodity is to be transported for such resale.

(3) Nothing contained in this Act or in any of the Antitrust Acts shall render unlawful the exercise or the enforcement of any right or right of action created by any statute, law, or public policy now or hereafter in effect in any State, Territory, or the District of Columbia, which in substance provides that willfully and knowingly advertising, offering for sale, or selling any commodity at less than the price or prices prescribed in such contracts or agreements whether the person so advertising, offering for sale, or selling is or is not a party to such a contract or agreement, is unfair competition and is actionable at the suit of any person damaged thereby.

(4) Neither the making of contracts or agreements as described in paragraph (2) of this subsection, nor the exercise or enforcement of any right or right of action as described in paragraph (3) of this subsection shall constitute an unlawful burden or restraint upon, or interference with, commerce.

(5) Nothing contained in paragraph (2) of this subsection shall make lawful contracts or agreements providing for the establishment or maintenance of minimum or stipulated resale prices on any commodity referred to in paragraph (2) of this subsection, between manufacturers, or between producers, or between wholesalers, or between brokers, or between factors, or between retailers, or between persons, firms, or corporations in competition with each other.

(6) The Commission is hereby empowered and directed to prevent persons, partnerships, or corporations, except banks, common carriers subject to the Acts to regulate commerce, air carriers and foreign air carriers subject to the Federal Aviation Act of 1958, and persons, partnerships, or corporations insofar as they are subject to the Packers and Stockyards Act, 1921, as amended, except as provided in section 406(b) of said Act, from using unfair methods of competition in commerce and unfair or deceptive acts or practices in commerce.

Clayton Act

Be it enacted by the Senate and House of Representatives of the United States of America in Congress assembled, That "antitrust laws," as used herein, includes the Act entitled "An Act to protect trade and commerce against unlawful restraints and monopolies," approved July second, eighteen hundred and ninety [The Sherman Antitrust Act, supra]; sections seventy-three to seventy-seven, inclusive, of an Act entitled "An Act to reduce taxation, to provide revenue for the Government, and for other purposes," of August twenty-seventh, eighteen hundred and ninety-four; an Act entitled "An Act to amend sections seventy-three and seventy-six of the Act of August twenty-seventh, eighteen hundred and ninety-four, entitled 'An Act to reduce taxation, to provide revenue for the Government, and for other purposes,'" approved February twelfth, nineteen hundred and thirteen; and also this Act.

"Commerce," as used herein, means trade or commerce among the several States and with foreign nations, or between the District of Columbia or any

Territory of the United States and any State, Territory, or foreign nation, or between any insular possessions or other places under the jurisdiction of the United States, or between any such possession or place and any State or Territory of the United States or the District of Columbia or any foreign nation, or within the District of Columbia or any Territory or any insular possession or other place under the jurisdiction of the United States: *Provided*, That nothing in this Act contained shall apply to the Philippine Islands.

The word "person" or "persons" wherever used in this Act shall be deemed to include corporations and associations existing under or authorized by the laws of either the United States, the laws of any of the Territories, the laws of any State, or the laws of any foreign country.

Sec. 2. (a) That it shall be unlawful for any person engaged in commerce, in the course of such commerce, either directly or indirectly, to discriminate in price between different purchasers of commodities of like grade and quality, where either or any of the purchases involved in such discrimination are in commerce, where such commodities are sold for use, consumption, or resale within the United States or any Territory thereof or the District of Columbia or any insular possession or other place under the jurisdiction of the United States, and where the effect of such discrimination may be substantially to lessen competition or tend to create a monopoly in any line of commerce, or to injure, destroy, or prevent competition with any person who either grants or knowingly receives the benefit of such discrimination, or with customers of either of them: *Provided*, That nothing herein contained shall prevent differentials which make only due allowance for differences in the cost of manufacture, sale, or delivery resulting from the differing methods or quantities in which such commodities are to such purchasers sold or delivered: *Provided, however*, That the Federal Trade Commission may, after due investigation and hearing to all interested parties, fix and establish quantity limits, and revise the same as it finds necessary, as to particular commodities or classes of commodities, where it finds that available purchasers in greater quantities are so few as to render differentials on account thereof unjustly discriminatory or promotive of monopoly in any line of commerce; and the foregoing shall then not be construed to permit differentials based on differences in quantities greater than those so fixed and established: *And provided further*, That nothing herein contained shall prevent persons engaged in selling goods, wares, or merchandise in commerce from selecting their own customers in bona fide transactions and not in restraint of trade: *And provided further*, That nothing herein contained shall prevent price changes from time to time where in response to changing conditions affecting the market for or the marketability of the goods concerned, such as but not limited to actual or imminent deterioration of perishable goods, obsolescence of seasonal goods, distress sales under court process, or sales in good faith in discontinuance of business in the goods concerned.

(b) Upon proof being made, at any hearing on a complaint under this section, that there has been discrimination in price of services or facilities furnished the burden of rebutting the prima facie case thus made by showing justification shall be upon the person charged with a violation of this section, and unless justification shall be affirmatively shown, the Commission is authorized to issue an order terminating the discrimination: *Provided, however*, That nothing herein contained shall prevent a seller rebutting the prima facie case thus made by showing that his lower price or the furnishing of services or facilities to any purchaser or purchasers was made in good faith to meet an equally low price of a competitor, or the services or facilities furnished by a competitor.

(c) That it shall be unlawful for any person engaged in commerce, in the course of such commerce, to pay or grant, or to receive or accept, anything of value as a commission, brokerage, or other compensation, or any allowance or discount in lieu thereof, except for services rendered in connection with the sale or purchase of goods, wares, or merchandise, either to the other party to such transaction or to an agent, representative, or other intermediary therein where such intermediary is acting in fact for or in behalf, or is subject to the direct or indirect control, of any party to such transaction other than the person by whom such compensation is so granted or paid.

(d) That it shall be unlawful for any person engaged in commerce to pay or contract for the payment of anything of value to or for the benefit of a customer of such person in the course of such commerce as compensation or in consideration for any services or facilities furnished by or through such customer in connection with the processing, handling, sale, or offering for sale of any products or commodities manufactured, sold, or offered for sale by such person, unless such payment or consideration is available on proportionately equal terms to all other customers competing in the distribution of such products or commodities.

(e) That it shall be unlawful for any person to discriminate in favor of one purchaser against another purchaser or purchasers of a commodity bought for resale, with or without processing, by contracting to furnish or furnishing, or by contributing to the furnishing of, any services or facilities connected with the processing, handling, sale, or offering for sale of such commodity so purchased upons terms not accorded to all purchasers on proportionally equal terms.

(f) That it shall be unlawful for any person engaged in commerce, in the course of such commerce, knowingly to induce or receive a discrimination in price which is prohibited by this section.

Sec. 3. That it shall be unlawful for any person engaged in commerce, in the course of such commerce, to lease or make a sale or contract for sale of goods, wares, merchandise, machinery, supplies or other commodities, whether patented or unpatented, for use, consumption or resale within the United States or any Territory thereof or the District of Columbia or any insular possession or other place under the jurisdiction of the United States, or fix a price charged therefor, or discount from, or rebate upon, such price, on the condition, agreement or understanding that the lessee or purchaser thereof shall not use or deal in the goods, wares, merchandise, machinery, supplies or other commodities of a competitor or competitors of the lessor or seller, where the effect of such lease, sale, or contract for sale or such condition, agreement or understanding may be to substantially lessen competition or tend to create a monopoly in any line of commerce.

Sec. 4. That any person who shall be injured in his business or property by reason of anything forbidden in the antitrust laws may sue therefor in any district court of the United States in the district in which the defendant resides or is found or has an agent, without respect to the amount in controversy, and shall recover threefold the damages by him sustained, and the cost of suit, including a reasonable attorney's fee.

Sec. 4A. Whenever the United States is hereafter injured in its business or property by reason of anything forbidden in the antitrust laws it may sue therefor in the United States district court for the district in which the defendant resides or is found or has an agent, without respect to the amount in controversy, and shall recover actual damages by it sustained and the cost of suit.

Sec. 4B. Any action to enforce any cause of action under section 4 or 4A shall be forever barred unless commenced within four years after the cause of action accrued. No cause of action barred under existing law on the effective date of this Act shall be revived by this Act.

Sec. 5. (a) A final judgment or decree heretofore or hereafter rendered in any civil or criminal proceeding brought by or on behalf of the United States under the antitrust laws to the effect that a defendant has violated said laws shall be prima facie evidence against such defendant in any action or proceeding brought by any other party against such defendant under said laws or by the United States under section 4A, as to all matters respecting which said judgment or decree would be an estoppel as between the parties thereto: *Provided,* That this section shall not apply to consent judgments or decrees entered before any testimony has been taken or to judgments or decrees entered in actions under section 4A.

(b) Whenever any civil or criminal proceeding is instituted by the United States to prevent, restrain, or punish violations of any of the antitrust laws, but not including an action under section 4A, the running of the statute of limitations in respect of every private right of action arising under said laws and based in whole or in part on any matter complained of in said proceeding shall be suspended during the pendency thereof and for one year thereafter: *Provided, however,* That whenever the running of the statute of limitations in respect of a cause of action arising under section 4 is suspended hereunder, any action to enforce such cause of action shall be forever barred unless commenced either within the period of suspension or within four years after the cause of action accrued.

Sec. 6. That the labor of a human being is not a commodity or article of commerce. Nothing contained in the antitrust laws shall be construed to forbid the existence and operation of labor, agricultural, or horticultural organizations, instituted for the purposes of mutual help, and not having capital stock or conducted for profit, or to forbid or restrain individual members of such organizations from lawfully carrying out the legitimate objects thereof; nor shall such organizations, or the members thereof, be held or construed to be illegal combinations or conspiracies in restraint of trade, under the antitrust laws.

Sec. 7. That no corporation engaged in commerce shall acquire, directly or indirectly, the whole or any part of the stock or other share capital and no corporation subject to the jurisdiction of the Federal Trade Commission shall acquire the whole or any part of the assets of another corporation engaged also in commerce, where in any line of commerce in any section of the country, the effect of such acquisition may be substantially to lessen competition, or to tend to create a monopoly.

No corporation shall acquire, directly or indirectly, the whole or any part of the stock or other share capital and no corporation subject to the jurisdiction of the Federal Trade Commission shall acquire the whole or any part of the assets of one or more corporations engaged in commerce, where in any line of commerce in any section of the country, the effect of such acquisition, of such stocks or assets, or of the use of such stock by the voting or granting of proxies or otherwise, may be substantially to lessen competition, or to tend to create a monopoly.

This section shall not apply to corporations purchasing such stock solely for investment and not using the same by voting or otherwise to bring about, or in attempting to bring about, the substantial lessening of competition. Nor shall anything contained in this section prevent a corporation engaged in commerce from causing the formation of subsidiary corporations for the actual carrying on of their immediate lawful business, or the natural and legitimate branches or extensions thereof, or from owning and holding all or a part of the stock of such subsidiary corporations, when the effect of such formation is not to substantially lessen competition.

Nor shall anything herein contained be construed to prohibit any common carrier subject to the laws to regulate commerce from aiding in the construction of branches or short lines so located as to become feeders to the main line of the company so aiding in such construction or from acquiring or owning all or any part of the stock of such branch lines, nor to prevent any such common carrier from acquiring and owning all or any part of the stock of a branch or short line constructed by an independent company where there is no substantial competition between the company owning the branch line so constructed and the company owning the main line acquiring the property or an interest therein, nor to prevent such common carrier from extending any of its lines through the medium of the acquisition of stock or otherwise of any other common carrier where there is no substantial competition between the company extending its lines and the company whose stock, property, or an interest therein is so acquired.

Nothing contained in this section shall be held to affect or impair any right heretofore legally acquired: *Provided,* That nothing in this section shall be held or construed to authorize or make lawful anything heretofore prohibited or made illegal by the antitrust laws, nor to exempt any person from the penal provisions thereof or the civil remedies therein provided.

Nothing contained in this section shall apply to transactions duly consummated pursuant to authority given by the Civil Aeronautics Board, Federal Communications Commission, Federal Power Commission, Interstate Commerce Commission, the Securities and Exchange Commission in the exercise of its jurisdiction under section 10 of the Public Utility Holding Company Act of 1935, the United States Maritime Commission, or the Secretary of Agriculture under any statutory provision vesting such power in such Commission, Secretary, or Board.

Webb-Pomerene (Export Trade) Act

Sec. 1. Be it enacted by the Senate and House of Representatives of the United States of America in Congress assembled, That the words "export trade" wherever used in this Act means solely trade or commerce in goods, wares, or merchandise exported, or in the course of being exported from the United States or any Territory thereof to any foreign nation: but the words "export trade" shall not be deemed to include the production, manufacture, or selling for consumption or for resale, within the United States or any Territory thereof, of such goods, wares, or merchandise, or any act in the course of such production, manufacture, or selling for consumption or for resale.

The words "trade within the United States" wherever used in this Act mean trade or commerce among the several States or in any Territory of the United States, or in the District of Columbia, or between any such Territory and another, or between any such Territory or Territories and any State or States or the District of Columbia, or between the District of Columbia and any State or States.

The word "Association" wherever used in this Act means any corporation or combination, by contract or otherwise, of two or more persons, partnerships, or corporations.

Sec. 2. Nothing contained in the Act entitled "An Act to protect trade and commerce against unlawful restraints and monopolies," approved July second, eighteen hundred and ninety [Sherman Antitrust Act, supra], shall be construed as declaring to be illegal an association entered into for the sole purpose of engaging in export trade and actually engaged solely in such export trade, or an agreement made or act done in the course of export trade by such association, provided such association, agreement, or act is not in restraint of trade within the United States, and is not in restraint of the export trade of any domestic competitor of such association: *And provided further,* That such association does not, either in the United States or elsewhere, enter into any agreement, understanding, or conspiracy, or do any act which artificially or intentionally enhances or depresses prices within the United States of commodities of the class exported by such association, or which substantially lessens competition within the United States or otherwise restrains trade therein.

Sec. 3. Nothing contained in section seven of the Act entitled "An Act to supplement existing laws against unlawful restraints and monopolies, and for other purposes," approved October fifteenth, nineteen hundred and fourteen [Clayton Act, supra], shall be construed to forbid the acquisition or ownership by any corporation of the whole or any part of the stock or other capital of any corporation organized solely for the purpose of engaging in export trade, and actually engaged solely in such export trade, unless the effect of such acquisition or ownership may be to restrain trade or substantially lessen competition within the United States.

Sec. 4. The prohibition against "unfair methods of competition" and the remedies provided for enforcing said prohibition contained in the Act entitled "An Act to create a Federal Trade Commission, to define its powers and duties, and for other purposes," approved September twenty-sixth, nineteen hundred and fourteen [Federal Trade Commission Act, supra] shall be construed as extending to unfair methods of competition used in export trade against competitors engaged in export trade, even though the acts constituting such unfair methods are done without the territorial jurisdiction of the United States.

Sec. 5. Every association now engaged solely in export trade, within sixty days after the passage of this Act, and every association entered into hereafter which engages solely in export trade, within thirty days after its creation, shall file with the Federal Trade Commission a verified written statement setting forth the location of its officers or places of business and the names and addresses of all its officers and of all its stockholders or members, and if a corporation, a copy of its certificate or articles of incorporation and by-laws, and if unincorporated, a copy of its articles or contract of association, and on the first day of January of each year thereafter it shall make a like statement of the location of its offices or places of business and the names and addresses of all its officers and of all its stockholders or members and of all amendments to and changes in its articles or certificate of incorporation or in its articles or contract of association. It shall also furnish to the commission such information as the commission may require as to its organization, business, conduct, practices, management, and relation to other associations, corporations, partnerships, and individuals. Any association which shall fail so to do shall not have the benefit of the provisions of section two and section three of this Act, and it shall also forfeit to the United States the sum of $100 for each and every day of the continuance of such failure, which forfeiture shall be payable into the Treasury of the United States, and shall be recoverable in a civil suit in the name of the United States brought in the district where the association has its principal office, or in any district in which it shall do business. It shall be the duty of the various district attorneys, under the direction of the Attorney General of the United States, to prosecute for the recovery of the forfeiture. The costs and expenses of such prosecution shall be paid out of the appropriation for the expenses of the courts of the United States.

Whenever the Federal Trade Commission shall have reason to believe that an association or any agreement made or act done by such association is in restraint of trade within the United States or in restraint of the export trade of any domestic competitor of such association, or that an association either in the United States or elsewhere has entered into any agreement, understanding, or conspiracy, or done any act which artificially or intentionally enhances or depresses prices within the United States of commodities of the class exported by such association, or which substantially lessens competition within the United States or otherwise restrains trade therein, it shall summon such association, its officers, and agents to appear before it, and thereafter conduct an investigation into the alleged violations of law. Upon investigation, if it shall conclude that the law has been violated, it may make to such association recommendations for the readjustment of its business, in order that it may thereafter maintain its organization and management and conduct its business in accordance with law. If such association fails to comply with the recommendations of the Federal Trade Commission, said commission shall refer its findings and recommendations to the Attorney General of the United States for such action thereon as he may deem proper.

For the purpose of enforcing these provisions the Federal Trade Commission shall have all the powers, so far as applicable, given it in "An Act to create a Federal Trade Commission, to define its powers and duties, and for other purposes."

GERMANY

Law Against Restraints of Competition of July 27, 1957

Section 1. (1) Agreements made by enterprises or associations of enterprises for a common purpose and resolutions of associations of enterprises are invalid insofar as they are apt to influence, by restraints of competition, the production or the market conditions with respect to the trade in goods or commercial services. This does not apply as far as this law provides otherwise.

(2) The term "resolution of associations of enterprises" includes resolutions of meetings of the members of a juristic person, provided that such members are enterprises.

Section 6. (1) Section 1 does not apply to agreements and resolutions which serve to protect or to promote export insofar as they are limited to regulating competition in markets outside the area of applicability of this law.

(2) The Cartel Authority shall, upon application, approve an agreement or resolution of the nature described in section 1 if an arrangement within the scope of paragraph (1) covers also the trade in goods or commercial services within the area of applicability of this law, insofar as such arrangement is necessary to insure the desired regulation of competition in the markets outside such area. These provisions are not affected by section 15. The comments of the affected domestic producers and purchasers shall be attached to the application.

(3) No permission pursuant to paragraph (2) shall be granted by the Cartel Authority if the agreement or resolution or the method of its execution.

1. Violates the principles which the Federal Republic of Germany has accepted in international treaties with regard to trade in goods or commercial services, or

2. May lead to a substantial restraint of competition within the area of applicability of this law and if the interest in the preservation of competition is predominant.

(4) The Cartel Authority may authorize the participants to conclude an arrangement falling under paragraph (2) within a framework specified in the authorization.

Section 15. Agreements between enterprises with respect to goods or commercial services relating to markets located within the area of applicability of this law are null and void insofar as they restrict any party to them in its freedom to establish prices or terms in contracts which it concludes with third parties in regard to the goods supplied, other goods, or commercial services.

Section 16. (1) Section 15 shall not apply to agreements made between

1. An enterprise and the purchasers of its trademarked goods which are competing in price with similar goods of other producers or dealers, or

2. A publishing enterprise and the purchasers of its publications,

as far as such agreements impose upon the purchasers directly or indirectly the obligation to maintain certain resale prices or to impose the same obligation upon their own purchasers down to the resale to the ultimate consumer.

(2) Trademarked goods within the meaning of paragraph (1) No. 1 are products whose delivery in equal or improved quality is guaranteed by the price-fixing enterprise if

1. Such goods, or
2. Their wrappings or adornments intended for delivery to the consumer, or
3. The containers out of which they are sold

display some distinctive mark indicating the origin (a symbol indicating the firm, a word, or a picture).

(3) Paragraph (2) shall apply to agreements concerning agricultural products with the proviso that insignificant natural quality fluctuations, which cannot be eliminated by measures that can reasonably be required of the producer, shall be disregarded.

(4) Price agreements pursuant to paragraph (1), No. 1, are valid only if they have been filed with the Federal Cartel Office and if the receipt of the documents filed has been confirmed in writing. Attached to the documents filed shall be complete data on all sales prices charged by the producer or dealer to the subsequent distributors, as well as on trade margins. A further attachment shall contain the wording of the price agreement or the wording of contract terms pertaining to the fixing of prices. In addition, the documents filed must show whether the dealer is bound to render special services to the customers. Subsequent changes of the reported facts must be reported to the Cartel Authority without delay, together with pertinent documents. If the data or wording to be attached are incorrect or incomplete, the filing is considered null and void.

Section 17. (1) Upon its own motion the Cartel Authority may, and upon the application of a purchaser obligated pursuant to section 16 it shall, invalidate any resale price maintenance obligation with immediate effect or with effect from some future date to be determined by it and prohibit the application of a new similar obligation, if it has ascertained that

1. The conditions set forth in section 16 (1), (2), and (3) do not or do no longer prevail, or
2. The resale price maintenance is being abused, or
3. The resale price maintenance as such or in connection with other restraints of competition is apt, in a manner not justified by general economic conditions, to raise the prices of the goods affected, to avoid a lowering of such prices, or to restrict production or sale of such goods.

In deciding whether resale price maintenance is being abused, all circumstances shall be considered.

(2) Prior to a decision according to paragraph (1), the Cartel Authority shall call upon the price-fixing enterprise to discontinue the abuse to which objection is made.

Section 18. (1) With immediate effect or with effect from some future date to be determined by it, the Cartel Authority may invalidate agreements between enterprises with respect to goods or commercial services and prohibit the application of a new similar restriction insofar as such agreements

1. Restrain one of the parties in its freedom to use the received goods or other goods or commercial services, or
2. Restrain one of the parties in the purchase or sale of other goods or other commercial services from or to third persons, or
3. Restrain one of the parties in the resale of the goods delivered to it to third persons, or
4. Commit one of the parties to accept goods or services not related in kind or by trade custom,

and thereby unreasonably restrict the freedom of business activities of that party or of other enterprises; the same action may be taken insofar as the extent of such restrictions substantially restrains competition in the market for these or other goods or commercial services.

(2) The term "unreasonably" within paragraph (1) includes restraints which are unsupported by a reasonable consideration (counterobligation).

Section 19. (1) If the Cartel Authority invalidates a resale price mainetnance obligation or a restraint of the nature described in section 18, the validity of any other provisions of the agreement is determined by general rules of law except as otherwise provided in paragraph (2).

(2) Upon application of a party to the agreement, the Cartel Authority may, simultaneously with the action described in paragraph (1), order that the invalidation pronounced by it does not affect the validity of the other provisions of the agreement. Such order may only be issued if it is necessary to prevent unreasonable hardship to a party to the agreement and if this hardship is not outbalanced by more important interests of another party to the agreement.

(3) If an agreement provides that in the case of paragraph (1) the obligee of a price maintenance obligation or the beneficiary of a restrictive clause may terminate the agreement, or if the agreement provides in such case for an alteration of the contract to the disadvantage of the obligor, especially by increasing his obligations, no rights may be asserted under such agreements unless the Cartel Authority approves an application to this effect. Such application shall be granted if the exercise of these rights does not unreasonably restrict the freedom of economic action of the obligor. The approval may contain restrictions, time limits, or conditions.

Section 20. (1) Agreements concerning the acquisition or the use of patents, registered designs *(Gebrauchsmuster)* or protected brands *(Sortenschutzrechte)* are invalid if they impose upon the acquirer or licensee any restrictions in his business conduct which go beyond the contents of the said privileges *(Schutz-rechte)* ; restrictions pertaining to the type, scope, quantity, territory, or period of exercise of the privilege shall not be deemed to go beyond its contents.

(2) Paragraph (1) shall not apply to

1. Restrictions imposed upon the acquirer or licensee insofar and as long as they are justified by any interest of the seller or licensor in the technically unobjectionable exploitation of the matter protected by the privilege,

2. Obligations of the acquirer or licensee with respect to the price to be charged for the protected article,

3. Obligations of the acquirer or licensee to exchange experiences or to grant licenses for improvements or related inventions if these correspond to reciprocal obligations of the patent owner or licensor,

4. Obligations of the acquirer or licensee not to challenge the protected privilege,

5. Obligations of the acquirer or licensee relating to the regulation of competition in markets outside the area of applicability of this law,

provided that these restraints do not remain in force beyond the expiration of the privilege which is the subject of the acquisition or of the license.

(3) Upon application, the Cartel Authority may approve an agreement of the nature specified in paragraph (1) if the freedom of economic action of the acquirer or licensee or any other enterprises is not unfairly restricted, and if competition in the market is not substantially restrained through the restrictions involved. Sections 11 (3) to (5) shall apply, as appropriate.

(4) Sections 1 to 14 remain unaffected.

Section 21. (1) Section 20 shall apply, as appropriate, to agreements concerning the transfer or exploitation of legally unprotected inventions, manufacturing processes, technical designs, and other technological achievements, as well as legally unprotected achievements toward plant cultivation in the field of plant breeding, if such achievements constitute business secrets.

(2) Section 20 shall apply, as appropriate, to agreements concerning seed brands entered into the special list of sorts (section 37 of the Seed Law) between a plant breeder engaged in the maintenance of parent stock and a multiplier or a multiplying enterprise.

Section 22. (1) As far as an enterprise has no competitor or is not exposed to any substantial competition in a certain type of goods or commercial services, it is market-dominating within the meaning of this law.

(2) Two or more enterprises are considered as market-dominating as far as, in regard of a certain type of goods or commercial services, no substantial competition exists in fact between them in general or in specific markets, and as far as they jointly meet the requirements of paragraph (1).

(3) In regard of market-dominating enterprises the Cartel Authority has the powers set forth in paragraph (4), insofar as these enterprises
1. Abuse their market position in the conclusion of contracts with respect to such goods or commercial services with regard to prices offered or demanded or to terms and conditions imposed, or
2. By abusing their market position, make the conclusion of contracts concerning such goods or commercial services dependent upon the purchase by the other party of goods or services not related in kind or by trade custom.
In deciding whether the market position has been abused all circumstances shall be taken into account.

(4) If the conditions set forth in paragraph (3) exist, the Cartel Authority may prohibit the abuse by market-dominating enterprises and may invalidate contracts; section 19 shall apply, as appropriate. Prior to such action, the Cartel Authority shall call upon the participants to refrain from the abuse to which objection is made.

(5) Insofar as the conditions set forth in paragraph (1) exist in regard of a combine within the meaning of section 15 of the Stock Corporation Law, the Cartel Authority may use its powers under paragraph (4) with regard to each enterprise belonging to the combine.

Section 23. Any consolidation of enterprises shall immediately be reported to the Cartel Authority if as a result of such consolidation the participating enterprises obtain a share of 20 percent or more of the market with regard to a specific type of goods or commercial services, or if one of the enterprises involved has such a share even without the consolidation. The following transactions shall be considered as such consolidations:
1. Merger with other enterprises;
2. Acquisition of the capital of other enterprises;
3. Acquisition of ownership of plants of other enterprises;
4. Contracts providing for the use or management of plants of other enterprises;
5. Acquisition of participations of any kind in other enterprises insofar as such participations, alone or in combination with other participations held by the acquiring enterprise itself or by an enterprise belonging to a com???
Upon receipt of a report pursuant to section 23, first sentence, the Cartel Authority may summon the participants to an oral hearing or may invite them

to submit a written statement with regard to the consolidation, if there is reason to expect that, through the consolidation, the participating enterprises obtain the position of a market-dominating enterprise within the meaning of section 22 (1) or (2), or if a market-dominating position is strengthened by the consolidation.

Section 25. (1) Enterprises or associations of enterprises shall not threaten or cause disadvantages, or promise or grant advantages, to other enterprises in order to induce them to activities which, under this law or under any regulations issued thereunder by the Cartel Authority, may not be made the subject of a contractual obligation.

(2) Enterprises or associations of enterprises shall not coerce other enterprises
　　1. To join an agreement or resolution within the meaning of sections 2 to 8, 29, 99 (2), 100 (1) and (7), 102, and 103, or
　　2. To merge with other enterprises within the meaning of section 23, or
　　3. To act uniformly in the market with the intention to restrain competition.

Section 26. (1) Enterprises or associations of enterprises shall not induce another enterprise or associations of enterprises to block deliveries or purchases with the intention of unfairly harming certain competitors.

(2) Market-dominating enterprises, associations of enterprises within the meaning of sections 1 to 8, 99 (2), 100 (1) and (7), 102, and 103, and enterprises which fix prices pursuant to sections 16, 100 (3), or 103 (1), No. 3, shall not unfairly hinder, directly or indirectly, another enterprise in business activities which are usually open to similar enterprises and shall not directly or indirectly treat them in a manner different from the treatment accorded to similar enterprises in the absence of facts justifying such differentiation.

Section 38. (1) A contravention is committed by any person who
　　1. Willfully disregards the invalidity of an agreement or resolution, the nullity of which ensues from sections 1, 15, 20 (1), 21, 100 (1), third sentence 103 (2), or 106;
　　2. Willfully or negligently disregards the invalidity of an agreement or resolution which under sections 3 (4), 12 (2), No. 3, 17 (1), 18 (1), 22 (4), 102 (2) or (3), or 104 (2), No. 3, was invalidated by the Cartel Authority through a decision that has become final;
　　3. Willfully and in violation of section 14 (1) sells or otherwise disposes of collateral security without a permission;
　　4. Willfully or negligently contravenes a final order of the Cartel Authority issued under sections 12 (2), No, 1, 17 (1), 18 (1), 22 (4), 27, 102 (2) or (3), or 104 (2), No. 1, and which refers explicitly to the provisions of this law regarding administrative fines;
　　5. Willfully or negligently contravenes an interim order issued under sections 56 or 63 (3) and which refers explicitly to the provisions of this law regarding administrative fines;
　　6. Willfully or negligently fails to meet requirements imposed by the Cartel Authority if the order imposing the requirements has become final and refers explicitly to the provisions of this law regarding administrative fines;
　　7. Willfully furnishes or uses incorrect or incomplete information in order to obtain fraudulently a permission under this law for himself or for another person or the registration of a competition rule, or to induce the Cartel Authority to raise no objection in cases under sections 2, 3, or 5 (1);
　　8. Willfully or negligently violates any of the prohibitions in sections 25 or 26;

9. Willfully causes an economic disadvantage to another person for the reason that such person has applied for the issuance of orders by the Cartel Authority or has exercised the rights granted him by section 13.

(2) A contravention is also committed by any person who, by making recommendations, willfully participates in the commission of contraventions specified in paragraph (1). A contravention is also committed by any person who has made recommendations which, through a uniform conduct, have resulted in an evasion of the prohibitions set forth in this law or of orders issued by the Cartel Authority on the basis of this law. This provision shall not apply to recommendations to demand or to offer certain prices or to apply certain types of price-fixing when such recommendations are made by associations of enterprises and are restricted to the circle of the participants, provided that

1. They are intended to create conditions promoting the competition with large enterprises or with similar types of enterprises, and

2. The recommendations are explicitly stated not to be binding and no economic, social, or other pressure is exerted toward their observation.

(3) Administrative fines may be imposed for contraventions in the following amounts:

1. If the violation was committed willfully: Up to DM 100,000, or up to three times the additional proceeds obtained by the contravention, whichever is more;

2. If the violation was committed negligently (paragraph (1), No. 2, 4, 5, and 6): Up to DM 30,000, or up to twice the additional proceeds obtained by the contravention, whichever is more.

Section 98. (1) This law shall also apply to enterprises which are wholly or partly public property or which are managed or operated by public authorities, except as otherwise provided in sections 99 to 103.

(2) This law shall apply to all restraints of competition effective in the area of applicability of this law, also if they result from acts done outside such area.

FRANCE

Price Ordinance No. 45-1483 of June 30, 1945

supplemented and amended by Decrees No. 53—704
of August 9, 1953,
No. 58—545 of June 24, 1958 and
No. 59—1004 of August 17, 1959.
and by Act No. 63—628 of July 2, 1963.

PART II — OFFENCES AND PENALTIES

Article 37. It shall be deemed to be an illegal practice in connection with prices:
1. for any producer, trader, person engaged in industry or craftsman:
a) to refuse to satisfy to the best of his ability and upon the customary trade terms any request for the purchase of goods or the performance of services which has no abnormal character and is made in good faith, and provided that the sale of such goods or the performance of such services is not forbidden by law or government regulation, or habitually to apply discriminatory conditions of sale or discriminatory price increases which are not warranted by an equivalent increase in the cost of production or the cost of performing the service;
c) provided always that such sale or performance is not governed by any special regulation, to make the sale of goods or the performance of a service conditional upon the purchase of other goods or upon the purchase of a stipulated quantity or upon the performance of another service;

3. for any person taking part in concerted action to carry out or procure the carrying out of any practice prohibited by Article 59 bis of this Ordinance;

4. for any person to fix, maintain or impose minimum prices for goods or services or trading margins by means of lists or scales of charges or by means of a combine of any nature or form whatsoever.
Provided that paragraph 4 hereof shall not apply to any goods or services expressly exempted by joint order of the Minister responsible for Economic Affairs, the Minister responsible for Trade and the Minister concerned with such goods or services. Such exemption, which shall in any event be subject to a time limit, may be given on the grounds, inter alia, of the novelty of such goods or services, of exclusive rights under a patent, licence or registered design or of the requirements of a specification which includes a warranty of quality or condition or of an initial publicity campaign.
Any undertaking whose operators or managers being party to any concerted action, convention, combine whether express or implied, or trade coalition having been found guilty under the terms of paragraph 3 of this Article shall be excluded from taking part in any contract made with the State or with any public authority or public undertaking or with any undertaking in which the State or the public authorities have a majority interest, unless they are relieved of such disqualification by joint decision of the Minister responsible for Economic Affairs, the Minister responsible for Trade and the Minister interested in the subject matter.

PART III — SUPPLEMENTARY PROVISIONS

Section IV — Maintenance of Free Competition

Article 59 bis. Subject to the provisions of Article 59 ter, every concerted action, convention, combine, express or implied, or trade coalition in any form and upon any grounds whatsoever, which has the object or may have the effect of interfering with full competition by hindering the reduction of production costs or selling prices or by encouraging the artificial increase of prices, shall be prohibited.

Any engagement or agreement relating to such prohibited practice shall be absolutely void.

Any party and any other person shall be entitled to rely upon such avoidance but no party shall be entitled to rely upon it as a defence against a person who is not a party. Any dispute arising shall be determined by the Courts of Common Law, who shall be notified of the opinion of the Commission where the matter has been brought before the Commission.

The activities of an enterprise of group of enterprises holding on the home market a dominant position that is characterised by a monopoly situation or by the manifest concentration of economic power, where such activities have the object or may have the effect of interfering with the normal operation of the market shall be prohibited in like manner.

Article 59 ter. The provisions of Article 59 bis shall not apply to any concerted action, convention or combine, or to the activities of an enterprise or group of enterprises holding a dominant position:

1. Arising out of the application of a legislative provision or regulation;
2. Whose promoters are able to prove that its effect is to improve and extend the market for their products or to ensure further economic progress by means of rationalisation and specialisation.

Article 59 quater. A technical Commission on Combines and Dominant Positions shall be set up.

The Technical Commission on Combines and Dominant Positions shall enquire into all offences committed against the provisions of Article 59 bis and into any justification relied upon the terms of Article 59 ter. Its decisions and opinions shall be reached by majority vote. Where the votes are equal, the Chairman shall have a second or casting vote.

The persons acting as Rapporteurs to the Commission shall be appointed jointly by the Minister responsible for Economic Affairs and the Minister responsible for Trade. Their reports shall be communicated to the interested parties, who shall be given an opportunity of making their observations to the Rapporteurs. They shall have the powers of investigation provided by Part II of Price Ordinance No. 45—1484 of 30 June 1945. The Rapporteurs shall be entitled to take part in the discussion on the matters which they are reporting.

The Secretariat of the Commission shall be provided by the Minister responsible for Economic Affairs. A representative of the Ministry of Economic Affairs (Directorate-General of Prices) shall in each case submit the observations of the ministerial departments concerned.

On the advice of the Technical Commission on Combines and Dominant Positions, or if the Commission has not delivered its decision within a period of six months from the date when the matter was first brought before it, or in cases of urgency, repeated offences or flagrant offence, the Minister responsible for Economic Affairs may send the papers to the High Court for the purpose of enforcing Ordinance No. 45—1484 of 30 June 1945, on the establishment, prosecution and punishment of offences against economic legislation or of applying Article 419 of the Criminal Code.

PART IV — GENERAL PROVISIONS

Article 62. The provisions of this Ordinance do not apply to exports direct or through an agent.

Act No. 63-628 of July 2, 1963 relating to prohibition of loss leaders and misleading advertising

Article 1. I. Resale of any product without further processing at a price below its real purchase price plus turnover tax on such resale, shall be prohibited. The real purchase price is to be taken as the price less any rebates or discounts, whatever their nature, allowed by the supplier at the time of invoicing.

II.   The foregoing provisions shall not apply to:

Perishable goods when they are in danger of rapid deterioration;

Voluntary or forced sales due to the cessation or alteration of business activity;

Products the sale of which is distinctly seasonal in nature, at the end of the selling season and in the interval between two selling seasons;

Products which are no longer in general demand on account of a change in fashion or the appearance of technical improvements;

Products, stocks of which were renewed or could be renewed at a lower price, the real purchase price being replaced in such event by the price shown on the invoice for the new purchase or by the cost of restocking;

Products, the resale price of which is aligned on the price lawfully quoted for the same products by another retailer in the same sphere of activity.

III.   The exceptions provided for in paragraph II above shall under no circumstances be a bar to the application of Articles 575-5 and 614-6-3 of the Commercial Code.

Article 4. Breaches of the provisions of Articles 1 and 3* of this Act shall be dealt with in the same manner as illegal practices in connection with prices and shall be established, prosecuted and published in the manner laid down in Ordinances No. 45-1483 and 45-1484 of June 30, 1945.

Article 5. Any advertisement shall be prohibited which is made in bad faith and which contains statements that are false or misleading, provided that such statements are specific and relate to one or more of the following items: the nature, contents, origin, basic qualities, date of manufacture or properties of the products or services advertised, the reasons for the sale or the selling methods, the results to be expected from use, the identity, qualities or capabilities of the manufacturer, dealer or supplier of services.

Article 6. Breaches of the provisions of Article 5 shall be punishable with the penalties laid down in Article 1 of the Act of 1 August 1905 on the repression

* Article 3, which amends and supplements Articles 59bis and 59ter of Ordinance No. 45-1483 of June 30, 1945, introduces control of dominant positions. See the amended wording of Articles 59bis and 59ter, *supra.*

of frauds. In addition, the Court may order the cessation of the advertisement complained of the publication of the judgement.

Officials of the Economic Enquiries Department or of the Repression of Frauds Department shall be empowered to establish breaches of the provisions of Article 5 of this Act. They may require the advertiser to produce to them any documents that are material to their enquiries. The investigating officers' official reports shall be sent immediately to the Public Prosecutor (*Procureur de la République*) having jurisdiction in the matter.

UNITED KINGDOM

Patents Act, 1949

37—(1) At any time after the expiration of three years from the date of the sealing of a patent, any person interested may apply to the comptroller upon any one or more of the grounds specified in the next following subsection for a licence under the patent or for the endorsement of the patent with the words "licences of right."

(2) The grounds upon which application may be made for an order under this section are as follows, that is to say : —

(a) that the patented invention, being capable of being commercially worked in the United Kingdom, is not being commercially worked therein or is not being so worked to the fullest extent that is reasonably practicable;

(b) that a demand for the patented article in the United Kingdom is not being met on reasonable terms, or is being met to a substantial extent by importation;

(c) that the commercial working of the invention in the United Kingdom is being prevented or hindered by the importation of the patented article;

(d) that by reason of the refusal of the patentee to grant a licence or licences on reasonable terms—

(i) a market for the export of the patented article manufactured in the United Kingdom is not being supplied; or

(ii) the working or efficient working in the United Kingdom of any other patented invention which makes a substantial contribution to the art is prevented or hindered; or

(iii) the establishment or development of commercial or industrial activities in the United Kingdom is unfairly prejudiced;

(e) that by reason of conditions imposed by the patentee upon the grant of licences under the patent, or upon the purchase, hire or use of the patented article or process, the manufacture, use or sale of materials not protected by the patent, or the establishment or development of commercial or industrial activities in the United Kingdom is unfairly prejudiced.

(3) Subject as hereinafter provided, the comptroller may, if satisfied that any of the grounds aforesaid are established, make an order in accordance with the application; and where the order is for the grant of a licence, it may require the licence to be granted upon such terms as the comptroller thinks fit :

Provided that—

(a) where the application is made on the ground that the patented invention is not being commercially worked in the United Kingdom or is not being worked to the fullest extent that is reasonably practicable, and it appears to the comptroller that the time which has elapsed since the sealing of the patent has for any reason been insufficient to enable it to be so worked, he may by order adjourn the application for such period as will in his opinion give sufficient time for the invention to be so worked;

(b) an order shall not be made under this section for the endorsement of a patent on the ground that a market for the export of the patented article is

not being supplied, and any licence granted under this section on that ground shall contain such provisions as appear to the comptroller to be expedient for restricting the countries in which the patented article may be sold or used by the licensee;

(c) no order shall be made under this section in respect of a patent on the ground that the working or efficient working in the United Kingdom of another patented invention is prevented or hindered unless the comptroller is satisfied that the patentee in respect of that other invention is able and willing to grant to the patentee and his licensees a licence in respect of that other invention onreasonable terms.

(4) An application under this section may be by any person notwithstanding that he is already the holder of a licence under the patent; and no person shall be estopped from alleging any of the matters specified in subsection (2) of this section by reason of any admission made by him, whether in such a licence or otherwise, or by reason of his having accepted such a licence.

(5) In this section the expression "patented article" includes any article made by a patented process.

38—(1) When the comptroller is satisfied, on application made under the last foregoing section, that the manufacture, use or sale of materials not protected by the patent is unfairly prejudiced by reason of conditions imposed by the patentee upon the grant of licences under the patent, or upon the purchase, hire or use of the patented article or process, he may, subject to the provisions of that section, order the grant of licences under the patent to such customers of the applicant as he thinks fit as well as to the applicant.

(2) Where an application under the last foregoing section is made by a person being the holder of alicence under the patent, the comptroller may, if he makes an order for the grant of a licence to the applicant, order the existing licence to be cancelled, or may, if he thinks fit, instead of making an order for the grant of a licence to the applicant, order the existing licence to be amended.

(3) Where on an application under the last foregoing section the comptroller orders the grant of a licence, he may direct that the licence shall operate—

(a) to deprive the patentee of any right which he may have as patentee to make, use, exercise or vend the invention or to grant licences under the patent;

(b) to revoke all existing licences in respect of the invention.

(4) Subsection (3) of section thirty-five of this Act shall apply to any licence granted in pursuance of an order under the last foregoing section as it applies to alicence granted by virtue of the said section thirty-five.

57—(1) Subject to the provisions of this section, any condition of a contract for the sale or lease of a patented article or of an article made by a patented process or for licence to use or work a patented article or process, or relating to any such sale, lease or licence, shall be void in so far as it purports—

(a) to require the purchaser, lessee or licensee to acquire from the vendor, lessor or licensor, or his nominees, or prohibit him from acquiring from any specified person, or from acquiring except from the vendor, lessor or licensor, or his nominees, any articles other than the patented article or an article made by the patented process;

(b) to prohibit the purchaser, lessee or licensee from using articles (whether patented or not) which are not supplied by, or any patented process which does not belong to, the vendor, lessor or licensor, or his nominees, or to restrict the right of the purchaser, lessee or licensee to use any such articles or process.

(2) In proceedings against any person for infringement of a patent, it shall be a defence to prove that at the time of the infringement there was in force a contract relating to the patent made by or with the consent of the plaintiff and containing a condition void by virtue of this section.

(3) A condition of a contract shall not be void by virtue of this section if—

(a) at the time of the making of the contract the vendor, lessor or licensor was willing to sell or lease the article, or grant a licence to use or work the article or process, as the case may be, to the purchaser, lessee or licensee, on reasonable terms specified in the contract and without any such condition as is mentioned in subsection (1) of this section; and

(b) the purchaser, lessee or licensee is entitled under the contract to relieve himself of his liability to observe the condition upon giving to the other party three months' notice in writing and subject to payment to him of such compensation (being, in the case of a purchase a lump sum, and in the case of a lease or licence a rent or royalty for the residue of the term of the contract) as may be determined by an arbitrator appointed by the Board of Trade.

(4) If in any proceeding it is alleged that any condition of a contract is void by virtue of this section, it shall lie on the vendor, lessor or licensor to prove the matters set out in paragraph (*a*) of the last foregoing subsection.

(5) A condition of a contract shall not be void by virtue of this section by reason only that it prohibits any person from selling goods other than those supplied by a secified person, or in the case of a contract for the lease of or licence to use a patented article, that it reserves to the lessor or licensor or his nominees the right to supply such new parts of the patented article as may be required to put or keep it in repair.

58—(1) Any contract for the sale or lease of a patented article or for licence to manufacture, use or work a patented article or process, or relating to any such sale, lease or licence, whether made before or after the commencement of this Act, may at any time after the patent or all the patents by which the article or process was protected at the time of the making of the contract has or have ceased to be in force, and notwithstanding anything to the contrary in the contract or in any other contract, be determined by either party on giving three months notice in writing to the other party.

(2) Where notice is given under this section to determine a contract made before the twenty-eighth day of August, nineteen hundred and seven, the party by whom the notice is given shall be liable to pay to the other party such compensation as may, in default of agreement, be determined by an arbitrator appointed by the Board of Trade.

(3) The provisions of this section shall be without prejudice to any right of determining a contract exercisable apart from this section.

Restrictive Trade Practices Act, 1956

An Act to provide for the registration and judicial investigation of certain restrictive trading agreements, and for the prohibition of such agreements when found contrary to the public interest; to prohibit the collective enforcement of conditions regulating the resale price of goods, and to make further provision for the individual enforcement of such conditions by legal proceedings; to amend the Monopolies and Restrictive Practices Acts, 1948 and 1953; to provide for the appointment of additional judges of the High Court and of the Court of Session; and for other purposes connected with the matters aforesaid.

2nd August, 1956

Registration of Agreements

6—(1) Subject to the provisions of the two next following sections, this Part of this Act applies to any agreement between two or more persons carrying on business within the United Kingdom in the production or supply of goods, or in the application to goods of any process of manufacture, whether with or without other parties, being an agreement under which restrictions are accepted by two or more parties in respect of the following matters, that is to say:—

(a) the prices to be charged, quoted or paid for goods supplied, offered or acquired, or for the application of any process of manufacture to goods;

(b) the terms or conditions on or subject to which goods are to be supplied or any such process is to be applied to goods;

(c) the quantities or descriptions of goods to be produced, supplied or acquired;

(d) the processes of manufacture to be applied to any goods, or the quantities or descriptions of goods to which any such process is to be applied; or

(e) the persons or classes of persons to, for or from whom, or the areas or places in or from which, goods are to be supplied or acquired, or any such process applied.

(2) For the purposes of the foregoing subsection it is immaterial whether any restrictions accepted by parties to an agreement relate to the same or different matters specified in that subsection, or have the same or different effect in relation to any matter so specified, and whether the parties accepting any restrictions carry on the same class or different classes of business.

(3) In this Part of this Act "agreement" includes any agreement or arrangement, whether or not it is or is intended to be enforceable (apart from any provision of this Act) by legal proceedings, and references in this Part of this Act to restrictions accepted under an agreement shall be construed accordingly; and "restriction" includes any negative obligation, whether express or implied and whether absolute or not.

(4) For the purposes of this Part of this Act an agreement which confers privileges or benefits only upon such parties as comply with conditions as to any such matters as are described in paragraphs *(a)* to *(e)* of subsection (1) of this section, or imposes obligations upon parties who do not comply with such conditions, shall be treated as an agreement under which restrictions are accepted by each of the parties in respect of those matters.

(5) Without prejudice to the last foregoing subsection, an obligation on the part of any party to an agreement to make payments calculated by reference—

(a) to the quantity of goods produced or supplied by him, or to which any process of manufacture is applied by him; or

(b) to the quantity of materials acquired or used by him for the purpose of or in the production of any goods or the application of any such process to goods,

being payments calculated, or calculated at an increased rate, in respect of quantities of goods or materials exceeding any quantity specified in or ascertained in accordance with the agreement, shall be treated for the purposes of this Part of this Act as a restriction in respect of the quantities of those goods to be produced or supplied, or to which that process is to be applied.

(6) This Part of this Act shall apply in relation to any agreement made by a trade association as if the agreement were made between all persons who are members of the association or are represented thereon by such members and, where any restriction is accepted thereunder on the part of the association, as if the like restriction were accepted by each of those persons.

(7) Where specific recommendations (whether express or implied) are made by or on behalf of a trade association to its members or to any class of its members, as to the action to be taken or not taken by them in relation to any particular class of goods or process of manufacture in respect of any matter described in the said subsection (1), this Part of this Act shall apply in relation to the agreement for the constitution of the association notwithstanding any provision to the contrary therein, as if it contained a term by which each such member, and any person represented on the association by any such member, agreed to comply with those recommendations and any subsequent recommendations made to them by or on behalf of the association as to the action to be taken by them in relation to the same class of goods or process of manufacture and in respect of the same matter.

(8) In this section "trade association" means a body of persons (whether incorporated or not) which is formed for the purpose of furthering the trade interests of its members, or of persons represented by its members; and for the purposes of this section, two or more persons being inter-connected bodies corporate or individuals carrying on business in partnership with each other shall be treated as a single person.

8—(1) This Part of this Act does not apply to any agreement which is expressly authorised by any enactment, or by any scheme, order or other instrument made under any enactment.

(2) This Part of this Act does not apply to any agreement which constitutes or forms parts of a scheme certified by the Board of Trade under Part XXIII of the Income Tax Act, 1952 (which relates to contributions and payments under schemes for rationalising industry).

(3) This Part of this Act does not apply to any agreement for the supply of goods between two persons, neither of whom is a trade association within the meaning of section six of this Act, being an agreement to which no other person is party and under which no such restrictions as are described in subsection (1) of section six of this Act are accepted other than restrictions accepted—
(a) by the party supplying the goods, in respect of the supply of goods of the same description to other persons; or
(b) by the party acquiring the goods, in respect of the sale, or acquisition for sale, of other goods of the same description.

(4) This Part of this Act does not apply to any licence granted by the proprietor or any licensee of a patent or registered design, or by a person who has applied for a patent or for the registration of a design, to any assignment of a patent or registered design, or of the right to apply for a patent or for the registration of a design, or to any agreement for such a licence or assignment, being a licence, assignment or agreement under which no such restrictions as are

described in subsection (1) of section six of this Act are accepted except in respect of—

(a) the invention to which the patent or application for a patent relates, or articles made by the use of that invention; or

(b) articles in respect of which the design is or is proposed to be registered and to which it is applied,

as the case may be.

(5) This Part of this Act does not apply to any agreement between two persons, neither of whom is a trade association within the meaning of section six of this Act, for the exchange of information relating to the operation of processes of manufacture (whether patented or not), being an agreement to which no other person is party and under which no such restrictions as are described in subsection (1) of section six of this Act are accepted except in respect of the descriptions of goods to be produced by those processes or to which those processes are to be applied.

(6) This Part of this Act does not apply to any agreement made in accordance with regulations approved by the Board of Trade under section thirty-seven of the Trade Marks Act, 1938 (which makes provision as to certification trade marks) authorising the use of such a trade mark, being an agreement under which no such restrictions as are described in subsection (1) of section six of this Act are accepted, other than restrictions permitted by the said regulations.

(7) This Part of this Act does not apply to any agreement between the registered proprietor of a trade mark (other than a certification trade mark) and a person authorised by the agreement to use the mark subject to registration as a registered user under section twenty-eight of the said Act of 1938 (which makes provision as to registered users), being an agreement under which no such restrictions as aforesaid are accepted except in respect of the descriptions of goods bearing the mark which are to be produced or supplied or the processes of manufacture to be applied to such goods or to goods to which the mark is to be applied.

(8) This Part of this Act does not apply to an agreement in the case of which all such restrictions as are described in subsection (1) of section six of this Act relate exclusively—

(a) to the supply of goods by export from the United Kingdom;

(b) to the production of goods, or the application of any process of manufacture to goods, outside the United Kingdom;

(c) to the acquisition of goods to be delivered outside the United Kingdom and not imported into the United Kingdom for entry for home use; or

(d) to the supply of goods to be delivered outside the United Kingdom otherwise than by export from the United Kingdom;

and subsection (7) of section six of this Act shall not apply in relation to recommendations relating exclusively to such matters as aforesaid.

(9) For the purposes of this and the last foregoing section two or more persons being inter-connected bodies corporate or individuals carrying on business in partnership with each other shall be treated as a single person; and any reference in this section to such restrictions as are described in subsection (1) of section six of this Act shall be construed, in relation to any agreement, as not including references to restrictions of which, by virtue of any provision of section seven of this Act, account cannot be taken in determining whether the agreement is an agreement to which this Part of this Act applies, or of restrictions accepted by any term of which account cannot be so taken.

Resale Prices Act 1964

An Act to restrict the maintenance by contractual and other means of minimum resale prices in respect of goods supplied for resale in the United Kingdom; and for purposes connected therewith. [16th July 1964]

BE IT ENACTED by the Queen's most Excellent Majesty, by and with the advice and consent of the Lords Spiritual and Temporal, and Commons, in this present Parliament assembled, and by the authority of the same, as follows:—

Restriction of contractual and other means of
maintaining minimum resale prices

1. [Avoidance of conditions for maintaining resale prices]—(1) Subject to the provisions of this Act with respect to registration and to the powers of the Restrictive Practices Court thereunder, any term or condition of a contract for the sale of goods by a supplier to a dealer, or of any agreement between a supplier and a dealer relating to such a sale, shall be void in so far as it purports to establish or provide for the establishment of minimum prices to be charged on the resale of the goods in the United Kingdom; and it shall be unlawful for any supplier of goods (or for any association or person acting on behalf of such suppliers)—

   (a) to include in any contract of sale or agreement relating to the sale of goods any term or condition which is void by virtue of this section;

   (b) to require, as a condition of supplying goods to a dealer, the inclusion

in any contract or agreement of any such term or condition, or the giving of any undertaking to the like effect;

(c) to notify to dealers, or otherwise publish on or in relation to any goods, a price stated or calculated to be understood as the minimum price which may be charged on the resale of the goods in the United Kingdom.

(2) This section applies to patented articles (including articles made by a patented process) as it applies to other goods; and notice of any term or condition which is void by virtue of this section, or which would be so void if included in a contract of sale or agreement relating to the sale of any such article, shall be of no effect for the purpose of limiting the right of a dealer to dispose of that article without infringement of the patent:

Provided that nothing in this section shall affect the validity, as between the parties and their successors, of any term or condition of a licence granted by the proprietor of a patent or by a licensee under any such licence, or of any assignment of a patent, so far as it regulates the price at which articles produced or processed by the licensee or assignee may be sold by him.

(3) Nothing in subsection (1)(a) of this section affects the enforceability of a contract of sale or other agreement except in respect of the term or condition which is void by virtue of this section.

(4) Nothing in subsection (1)(c) of this section shall be construed as precluding a supplier, or any association or person acting on behalf of a supplier, from notifying to dealers or otherwise publishing prices recommended as appropriate for the resale of goods supplied or to be supplied by the supplier.

(5) References in subsection (2) of this section to patented articles shall include references to articles protected by the registration of a design and articles protected by plant breeders' rights or a protective direction under Schedule 1 to the Plant Varieties and Seeds Act 1964, and references in that subsection to a patent shall be construed accordingly.

2. *[Prohibition of other measures for maintaining resale prices]*—(1) Subject to the provisions of this Act with respect to registration, to the powers of the Restrictive Practices Court thereunder and to the next following section, it shall be unlawful for any supplier to withhold supplies of any goods from a dealer seeking to obtain them for resale in the United Kingdom on the ground that the dealer—

(a) has sold in the United Kingdom at a price below the resale price goods obtained, either directly or indirectly, from that supplier, or has supplied such goods, either directly or indirectly, to a third party who had done so; or

(b) is likely, if the goods are supplied to him, to seel them in the United Kingdom at a price below that price, or supply them, either directly or indirectly, to a third party who would be likely to do so.

(2) In this section "the resale price", in relation to a sale of any description, means any price notified to the dealer or otherwise published by or on behalf of a supplier of the goods in question (whether lawfully or not) as the price or minimum price which is to be charged on or is recommended as appropriate for a sale of that description, or any price prescribed or purporting to be prescribed for that purpose by any contract or agreement between the dealer and any such supplier.

(3) For the purposes of this Act a supplier of goods shall be treated as withholding supplies of goods from a dealer—

(a) if he refuses or fails to supply those goods to the order of the dealer;

(b) if he refuses to supply those goods to the dealer except at prices, or on terms or conditions as to credit, discount or other matters, which are significantly less favourable than those at or on which he normally supplies those goods to other dealers carrying on business in similar circumstances; or

(c) if, although he contracts to supply the goods to the dealer, he treats him in a manner significantly less favourable than that in which he normally treats other such dealers in respect of times or methods of delivery or other matters arising in the execution of the contract.

(4) For the purposes of this Act a supplier shall not be treated as withholding supplies of goods on any such ground as is mentioned in subsection (1) of this section if, in addition to that ground, he has other grounds which, standing alone, would have led him to withhold those supplies.

(5) In any case where, by virtue of this section, it would be unlawful for a supplier to withhold supplies of goods, it shall also be unlawful for him to cause or procure any other supplier to do so.

3. [Exception for measures against loss leaders]—(1) It shall not be unlawful by virtue of section 2 of this Act for a supplier to withhold supplies of any goods from a dealer, or to cause or procure another supplier to do so, if he has reasonable cause to believe that within the previous twelve months the dealer or any other dealer to whom the dealer supplies goods has been using a loss leaders any goods of the same or a similar description, whether obtained from that supplier or not.

(2) The reference in this section to the use of goods as loss leaders is a reference to a resale of the goods effected by the dealer, not for the purpose of making a profit on the sale of those goods, but for the purpose of attracting to the establishment at which the goods are sold customers likely to purchase other goods or otherwise for the purpose of advertising the business of the dealer:

Provided that a sale of goods shall not be treated for the purposes of this section as the use of those goods as loss leaders—

(a) where the goods are sold by the dealer at a genuine seasonal or clearance sale, not having been acquired by the dealer for the purpose of being resold as mentioned in this section; or

(b) where the goods are resold as mentioned in this section with the consent of the manufacturer of the goods or, in the case of goods made to the design of a supplier or to the order and bearing the trade mark of a supplier, of that supplier.

4. [Civil remedies for breach of restrictions]—(1) No criminal proceedings shall lie against any person on the ground that he has committed, or aided, abetted, counselled or procured the commission of, or conspired or attempted to commit or incited others to commit, any contravention of the foregoing provisions of this Act.

(2) The obligation to comply with the said provisions is a duty owed to any person who may be affected by a contravention of them, and any breach of that duty is actionable accordingly (subject to the defences and other incidents applying to actions for breach of statutory duty).

(3) Without prejudice to the right of any person to bring civil proceedings by virtue of subsection (2) of this section, compliance with the foregoing provisions of this Act shall be enforceable by civil proceedings on behalf of the Crown for an injunction or other appropriate relief.

(4) If in proceedings brought against a supplier of goods in respect of a contravention of section 2 of this Act it is proved that supplies of goods were withheld by the supplier from a dealer, and it is further proved—

(a) that down to the time when supplies were so withheld the supplier was doing business with the dealer or was supplying goods of the same description to other dealers carrying on business in similar circumstances; and

(b) that the dealer, to the knowledge of the supplier, had within the previous six months acted as described in paragraph *(a)* of subsection (1) of that section, or had indicated his intention to act as described in paragraph *(b)* of that subsection in relation to the goods in question,

it shall be presumed, unless the contrary is proved, that the supplies were withheld on the ground that the dealer had so acted or was likely so to act:

Provided that this subsection shall not apply where the proof that supplies were withheld consists only of evidence of requirements imposed by the supplier in respect of the time at which or the form in which payment was to be made for goods supplied or to be supplied.

Provision for exemption of particular classes of goods

5. *[Power of Court to exempt classes of goods]*—(1) Subject to the provisions of this Act, the Restrictive Practices Court may, on a reference made by the Registrar of Restrictive Trading Agreements, by order direct that goods of any class specified in the order (being goods of which particulars are entered in the register kept in accordance with those provisions) shall be exempted goods for the purposes of this Act; and where such a order is made—

(a) section 1 of this Act shall not apply in relation to any contract of sale or other agreement relating to exempted goods of the class specified in the order, or anything done in relation to such goods; and

(b) section 2 of this Act shall apply in relation to the withholding of supplies of such goods as if paragraph *(b)* of subsection (1) were omitted, and as if the reference in paragraph *(a)* of that subsection to goods obtained from the supplier did not include any exempted goods so obtained.

(2) An order under this section directing that goods of any class shall be exempted goods may be made by the Restrictive Practices Court if it appears to the Court that in default of a system of maintained minimum resale prices applicable to those goods—

(a) the quality of the goods available for sale, or the varieties of the goods so available, would be substantially reduced to the detriment of the public as consumers or users of those goods; or

(b) the number of establishments in which the goods are sold by retail would be substantially reduced to the detriment of the public as such consumers or users; or

(c) the prices at which the goods are sold by retail would in general and in the long run be increased to the detriment of the public as such consumers or users; or

(d) the goods would be sold by retail under conditions likely to cause danger to health in consequence of their misuse by the public as such consumers or users; or

(e) any necessary services actually provided in connection with or after the sale of the goods by retail would cease to be so provided or would be substantially reduced to the detriment of the public as such consumers or users,

and in any such case that the resulting detriment to the public as consumers or users of the goods in question would outweigh any detriment to them as such consumers or users (whether by the restriction of competition or otherwise) resulting from the maintenance of minimum resale prices in respect of the goods.

(3) On a reference under this section in respect of goods of any class which have been the subject of proceedings in the Court under Part I of the Restrictive Trade Practices Act 1956 the Court may treat as conclusive any finding of fact made in those proceedings, and shall do so unless prima facie evidence is given of a material change in the relevant circumstances since those proceedings.

(4) In this section "necessary services," in relation to goods, means services which, having regard to the character of the goods, are required to guard against the risk of injury, whether to persons or to premises, in connection with the consumption, installation or use of the goods, or are otherwise reasonably necessary for the benefit of consumers or users; and "consumers" and "users" include persons consuming or using for the purpose or in the course of trade or business or for public purposes.

6. [*Registration of goods for exemption*]—(1) It shall be the duty of the Registrar to prepare, compile and maintain for the purposes of this Act a register of goods in respect of which notices are given to him under this section, and to make reference to the Court under section 5 of this Act (subject to such directions as may be given by the Board of Trade with respect to the order in which such references are to be made) in respect of all goods of which particulars are for the time being entered in the register.

(2) Within the period of three months from the commencement of this section, any supplier who supplies goods under arrangements for maintaining minimum prices on resale, or any trade association whose members consist of or include such suppliers, may give notice to the Registrar in respect of goods of any description so supplied by that supplier or those suppliers claiming registration in respect of those goods.

(3) Where a notice under this section is duly given in respect of goods of any description, the Registrar shall cause particulars of the goods, of the person giving the notice and of the arrangements described in the notice to be entered in the register; and until the Court makes or refuses to make an order under section 5 of this Act in respect of a class of goods consisting of or comprising the goods of which particulars are so entered the foregoing provisions of this Act shall apply in relation to those goods as if such an order had been made.

(4) The Registrar shall from time to time publish lists of the classes of goods of which particulars are entered in the register kept by him under this section; and in any legal proceedings (including proceedings under this Act)—
(a) the fact that goods of any description are included in a class specified in a list so published shall be conclusive evidence that they are goods of which particulars are so entered; and
(b) the fact that goods of any description are not included in any such class shall be prima facie evidence that they are not goods of which particulars are so entered.

(5) The Registrar shall also from time to time publish lists of the classes of goods in respect of which the Court has made, refused to make or discharged orders under this Act, and any such list may be combined with a list published under subsection (4) of this section.

(6) For the purpose of compiling the lists described in subsection (4) of this section and, subject to rules made by virtue of section 8(2) of this Act, for the purpose of making references to the Court under the said section 5 the Registrar may combine or divide the goods in respect of which notice is given to him under this section into such classes as appear to him to be appropriate.

7. *[Late applications to, and review of decisions by, the Court]*—(1) The Restrictive Practices Court may, upon application made under this subsection at any time after the expiration of the period mentioned in section 6(2) of this Act, make such an order as is described in section 5(1) of this Act in respect of goods of any class, not being goods of which particulars are entered in the register kept under the said section 6 or goods in respect of which a previous application has been made under this subsection.

(2) The Restrictive Practices Court may, upon application made under this subsection—

(a) discharge any order previously made by the Court directing that goods of any class shall be exempted goods;

(b) make such an order in respect of any class of goods in respect of which the Court has previously refused to make such an order or has previously discharged such an order.

(3) An application under this section may be made by the Registrar, by any supplier of goods of the class in question or by any trade association whose members consist of or include suppliers of such goods.

(4) No application shall be made under this section except with the leace of the Court; and such leave shall not be granted—

(a) in the case of an application under subsection (1) of this section, except upon prima facie evidence of facts upon which an order could be made in accordance with section 5(2) of this Act in respect of the goods in question, or could be so made if any detriment to the public resulting from the maintenance of minimum resale prices were disregarded;

(b) in the case of an application under subsection (2) of this section, except upon prima facie evidence of a material change in the relevant circumstances since the last decision of the Court in respect of the goods in question under the said section 5 or subsection (1) or (2) of this section.

(5) The provisions of section 5(2) and (3) of this Act shall apply with the necessary modifications in relation to proceedings on an application under this section as they apply in relation to proceedings on a reference by the Registrar under that section.

8. *[Supplementary provisions as to registration, references and applications]*—(1) The Registrar may make regulations for the purposes of registration under section 6 of this Act and for purposes connected therewith, and in particular—

(a) for prescribing the manner in which notice claiming registration in respect of goods is to be given under that section;

(b) for prescribing the particulars to be included in any such claim of the descriptions of goods to which it relates, and of any arrangements for maintaining minimum resale prices in respect of those goods, and the documents to be furnished in support of any such particulars;

(c) for applying in relation to the register kept under the said section 6, subject to such modifications as may be prescribed by the regulations, any of

the provisions of section 11 of the Restrictive Trade Practices Act 1956 (general provisions as to the register under that Act); and subsections (2) to (4) of section 19 of the said Act of 1956 (supplementary provisions as to regulations) shall apply to regulations under this subsection as they apply to regulations under that section.

(2) The Schedule to the said Act of 1956 (proceedings of the Restrictive Practices Court) and, so far as applicable, section 23 of that Act (rules of procedure) shall apply in relation to proceedings before the Court on a reference or application under this Act as they apply in relation to proceedings on an application under Part I of that Act, and as if references to agreements in the said section 23 included references to classes of goods:

Provided that notwithstanding anything in the said Schedule the Court may order the payment by the Registrar of all or any of the following costs incurred by any other party, that is to say—

(a) costs incurred on a reference under section 5 of this Act, or on an application under section 7(1) of this Act, in respect of any issue determined in favour of that party, being an issue which in the opinion of the Court substantially corresponds with an issue so determined in proceedings under Part I of the said Act of 1956; or

(b) costs incurred on an application under section 7(2) of this Act in respect of an issue determined in favour of that party.

(3) Rules made by virtue of subsection (2) of this section shall include prosions—

(a) for enabling the Court, on the application of the Registrar or of any party interested, to give directions with respect to the goods to be included in or excluded from any reference or application under section 5 or section 7 of this Act;

(b) for securing that retailers, and trade associations representing employees in the distributive trades, who have given notice to the Registrar within such time and in such manner as may be prescribed by the rules shall, if they have an interest in any such reference or application, be entitled, whether in consequence of a representation order to otherwise, to be represented before the Court in the proceedings.

(4) In section 1(5) of the said Act of 1956 (authentication and proof of documents issued by the Registrar) the reference to Part I of that Act, and in section 34 of that Act (proceedings of the Board of Trade) the reference to that Act, shall include references to this Act.

Supplementary

9. *[Additional judges]*—(1) The maximum number of puisne judges of the High Court shall be increased by three, and accordingly in section 2(1) of the Supreme Court of Judicature (Consolidation) Act 1925 (as amended by the Criminal Justice Administration Act 1962) for the word "fifty-three" there shall be substituted the word "fifty-six."

(2) The maximum number of judges of the Court of Session shall be increased by one, and accordingly in section 1(1) of the Administration of Justice (Scotland) Act 1948 (as amended by the Criminal Justice (Scotland) Act 1963) for the word "seventeen" there shall be substituted the word "eighteen."

10. *[Expenses]*—(1) There shall be defrayed out of moneys provided by

Parliament any expenses of the Registrar under this Act, and any increase attributable to this Act in the sums required to be so defrayed under section 35(1) of the Restrictive Trade Practices Act 1956.

(2) There shall be defrayed out of the Consolidated Fund and out of moneys provided by Parliament respectively any increase attributable to section 9 of this Act in the sums required to be so defrayed.

11. [Interpretation]—(1) In this Act the following expressions have the meanings hereby respectively assigned to them, that is to say—

"dealer" means a person carrying on a business of selling goods, whether by wholesale or by retail;

"the Registrar" means the Registrar of Restrictive Trading Agreements;

"supplier" means a person carrying on a business of selling goods other than a business in which goods are sold only by retail;

"trade association" means a body of persons (whether incorporated or not) which is formed for the purpose of furthering the trade interests of its members or the persons represented by its members.

(2) Where the dealer referred to in section 2(1)*(a)* or section 3(1) of this Act, or the supplier referred to in the said section 2(1)*(a)*, is one of a group of interconnected bodies corporate within the meaning of the Restrictive Trade Practices Act 1956, the reference shall include to any other dealer or, as the case may be, any other supplier who is also a member of that group.

12. [Application to Scotland and Northern Ireland]—(1) In its application to Scotland this Act shall have effect as if for references to an assignment and to an injunction there were substituted references respectively to an assignation and to an interdict.

(2) It is hereby declared that this Act extends to Northern Ireland, but the Parliament of Northern Ireland shall have the same power to pass Acts with respect to any matter as they would have had if this Act had not passed and, in the event of any inconsistency between any Act of the Parliament of Northern Ireland duly passed after the passing of this Act and any provision of or any regulation, rule or other instrument under this Act, the Act of the Parliament of Northern Ireland shall, in Northern Ireland, prevail.

13. [Saving for statutory schemes] Nothing in this Act shall apply to any agreement which is expressly authorised by any enactment, or by any scheme, order or other instrument made under any enactment, or to anything done pursuant to any such agreement, scheme, order or instrument.

14. [Short title, commencement and transitional provisions]—(1) This Act may be cited as the Resale Prices Act 1964.

(2) The provisions of this Act shall come into force as follows, that is to say—

(a) section 8(1) and (4), sections 9 to 13 and this section, on the date of the passing of this Act;

(b) sections 5 to 7 and section 8(2) and (3) on the expiration of the period of one month beginning with that date;

(c) sections 1 to 4, on such date (not less than three months after the expiration of the last-mentioned period) as the Board of Trade may, by order made by statutory instrument, appoint.

(3) The transitional provisions set out in the Schedule to this Act shall have effect in relation to the coming into force of section 1 of this Act.

SCHEDULE

Transitional Provisions

1. Section 1 of this Act, so far as it affects the validity of any term or condition of a contract or agreement for or relating to the sale of any goods, or the effect of notice of any term or condition so relating, shall apply to contracts and agreements made and notices given before, as well as after, the commencement of that section, and accordingly,—

(a) for the purposes of the jurisdiction of any court to grant an injunction in proceedings pending at the commencement of the said section 1, that section shall be treated as if it had come into force before the cause of action arose; and

(b) any injunction granted or undertaking given before the commencement of that section in or for the purposes of any proceedings shall be of no effect in so far as it would operate to require compliance with any term or condition which is void, or notice of which is invalidated, by virtue of that section.

2. Subsection (1)*(c)* of the said section 1 shall not apply to a publication consisting of the issue of goods having any such price as is therein mentioned marked on the goods or their container if that price was so marked before the date of the commencement of that section and the issue is made within the period of twelve months beginning with that date.

3. In relation to any goods, references in this Schedule to the commencement of section 1 of this Act are references to the time at which, by virtue of section 14(2)*(c)* of this Act or of any decision of the Court under section 5 or section 7 of this Act, the said section 1 takes effect in relation to those goods; and the reference in paragraph 1*(a)* of this Schedule to the said section 1 having come into force shall be construed accordingly.

EUROPEAN COMMUNITIES

Treaty establishing The European Coal and Steel Community, Paris, 18th April, 1951

TITLE ONE

THE EUROPEAN COAL AND STEEL COMMUNITY

Article 1. By the present Treaty the High Contracting Parties establish among themselves a EUROPEAN COAL AND STEEL COMMUNITY, founded upon a common market, common objectives and common institutions.

Article 3. The Community's institutions shall within the limits of their respective competence and in the common interest:
(b) assure to all consumers in comparable situations within the Common Market equal access to the sources of production;

Article 4. The following practices are hereby abolished and prohibited within the Community, as incompatible with the common market for Coal and Steel, under the conditions laid down in the present Treaty:
(b) measures or practices which discriminate between producers, between purchasers and between consumers especially as regards price and delivery terms or transport rates, as well as measures or practices which hamper the purchaser in the free choice of his supplier;
(c) subsidies or assistance granted by States or special financial burdens imposed by them in any form whatsoever;
(d) restrictive practices tending towards the sharing or exploitation of markets.

Article 5. The Community shall carry out its duties, as laid down in the present Treaty, with a limited degree of intervention.
To this end the Community shall:
Ensure the establishment, maintenance and observance of normal competitive conditions and only interfere directly with production or the operation of the market when circumstances make it imperative to do so;
Publish the reasons for its actions and take the necessary measures to ensure the observance of the rules laid down in the present Treaty.

TITLE THREE

ECONOMIC AND SOCIAL PROVISIONS

Chapter V—Prices

Article 60. 1. Pricing practices contrary to the provisions of Articles 2, 3 and 4 are prohibited, and in particular:
unfair competitive practices, in particular purely temporary or purely local price reductions tending towards the acquisition of a monopoly position within the common market;

discriminatory practices involving, within the common market, the laying down by a seller of unequal conditions in the case of comparable transactions, especially according to the nationality of the buyer.

The High Authority may define the practices covered by this prohibition by decisions taken after consulting the Consultative Committee and the Council.

2. For the above purposes:

(a) the price-lists and conditions of sale applied by undertakings within the common market must be made public to the extent and in the form prescribed by the High Authority after consulting the Consultative Committee; if the High Authority finds that an undertaking has chosen an abnormal basing point for its price-lists, in particular one which may be covered by (b) below, it shall make the appropriate recommendations to that undertaking.

(b) The methods of quotation used must not have the effect of introducing into the prices charged by an undertaking in the common market, when reduced to their equivalent at the basing point chosen for the price-list:

increases over the price shown by the price-list in question for a comparable transaction; or

reductions below this price of which the amount exceeds:

either the margin making it possible to align the quotation with the price-list, based on another point, which secures for the buyer the most advantageous conditions at the place of delivery;

or the limits fixed for each category of product, taking into account their origin and destination, by decision of the High Authority after consulting the Consultative Committee.

Such decision shall be taken when it appears necessary to avoid either disturbances in all or any part of the common market or imbalances resulting from a difference between the methods of quotation used for a product and for materials which enter into its manufacture. Such decision shall not prevent undertakings from aligning their quotations with those of undertakings outside the Community, provided that such transactions are notified to the High Authority which may, in case of abuse, limit or suppress the right of the undertakings concerned to benefit from this exception.

Chapter VI—Agreements and Concentrations

Article 65. 1. All agreements between undertakings; all decisions by associations of undertakings and all concerted practices tending, directly or indirectly, to prevent, restrict or distort the normal operation of competition within the common market are forbidden, and in particular those tending:

(a) to fix or determine prices;

(b) to restrict or control production, technical development or investments;

(c) to allocate markets, products, customers or sources of supply.

2. However, the High Authority shall authorise agreements to specialise in the production of, or to engage in the joint buying or selling of, specified products if it finds:

(a) that such specialisation or such joint buying or selling will contribute to a substantial improvement in the production or distribution of the products in question; and

(b) that the agreement in question is essential to achieve these results, and is not more restrictive than is necessary for that purpose; and

(c) that it is not capable of giving the undertakings concerned the power to determine prices or to control or limit the production or marketing of a substantial part of the products in question within the common market or of protecting them from effective competition by other undertakings within the common market.

Should the High Authority find that certain agreements are strictly similar, both in kind and effect, to the agreement referred to above it shall authorise such agreements, if it finds that the same conditions apply to them as to the agreements referred to above. When considering such action the High Authority shall pay particular attention to the fact that this paragraph applies to distributive undertakings.

Authorisations may be granted on specified conditions and for a limited period. In such cases the High Authority shall renew authorisations once or several times if it finds that the conditions stated in paragraphs (a) to (c) above still apply at the time of renewal.

The High Authority shall revoke or modify an authorisation if it finds that as a result of a change in circumstances the agreement no longer fulfils the conditions set out above, or that the actual results of the agreement or its execution are contrary to the conditions required for carrying it out.

Decisions granting, renewing, modifying, refusing or revoking an authorisation shall be published together with the reasons therefor; the prohibition contained in the second paragraph of Article 47 shall not apply in such cases.

3. The High Authority may, in accordance with the provisions of Article 47, obtain any information needed for the purpose of this Article, either by a special request addressed to the parties concerned or by means of a Regulation setting out the kinds of agreements, decisions or practices which must be notified to it.

4. Any agreement or decision prohibited by Section 1 of the present Article shall be null and void and shall be inadmissible in evidence before any court of any of the Member States.

The High Authority shall have exclusive competence, subject to appeal to the Court to decide whether this Article applies to any such agreement or decision.

5. If any undertaking shall have entered into an agreement which is null and void in law, or shall have enforced or attempted to enforce, by arbitration, forfeiture, boycott or any other means, an agreement or decision which is null and void in law or an agreement for which approval has been refused or revoked or has obtained an authorisation by means of information which it knew to be false or misleading, or has engaged in practices prohibited by paragraph 1 of this Article, the High Authority may impose upon such undertaking fines and financial penalties not to exceed twice the actual turnover on the products which were the subject of the agreement, decision or practice prohibited by this Article. Moreover if the purpose of the agreement is to restrict production, technical development or investments this maximum may be raised to 10 per cent, of the annual turnover of the undertakings in question, in the case of fines, and 20 per cent. of the daily turnover in the case of financial penalties.

Article 66. 1. Subject to the provisions of paragraph 3 below, any transaction shall require the prior authorisation of the High Authority if it would in itself have the direct or indirect effect of bringing about a concentration, within the territories mentioned in the first paragraph of Article 79, between undertakings of which at least one is covered by Article 80, whether the transaction is carried out by one person or undertaking or a group of persons or undertakings, whether it concerns a single product or different products, whether it is effected by merger or by the acquisition of shares or assets, loan, contract or any other means of control. For the purpose of the above provisions, the High Authority shall, by means of a Regulation drawn up after consulting the Council, define the meaning of control.

2. The High Authority shall grant the authorisation referred to in the preceding paragraph if it finds that the transaction in question will not give to the persons or undertakings concerned, as regards the product or products subject to its authority the power:

to determine prices, to exercise control over or restrict production or distribution, or to hinder the maintenance of effective competition in a substantial part of the market for such products; or

to evade the rules of competition as they result from the execution of the present Treaty, in particular by establishing an artificially privileged position involving a substantial advantage in access to supplies or markets.

In arriving at its decision and acting in accordance with the principle of non-discrimination laid down in Article 4 (b), the High Authority shall take account of the size of undertakings of the same kind existing in the Community, to the extent it considers necessary, so as to avoid or correct the disadvantages resulting from unequal competitive conditions.

The High Authority may make such an authorisation subject to any conditions which it considers appropriate for the purposes of the present paragraph.

Before pronouncing upon a transaction affecting undertakings of which at least one is not subject to Article 80, the High Authority shall obtain the views of the Government concerned.

3. The High Authority shall exempt from the requirement of prior authorisation those kinds of transactions which because of the size of the assets or undertakings with which they are concerned, considered together with the kind of concentration which they bring about, in its opinion are covered by the conditions required by paragraph 2. The Regulation drawn up for this purpose, after obtaining a confirmatory opinion from the Council, shall also fix the conditions to which such exemption is to be subject.

4. Without prejudice to the High Authority's right to make use of the provisions of Article 47, in the case of undertakings over which it has authority, it may obtain from natural or legal persons (personnes physiques ou morales) who have acquired or regrouped, or are about to acquire or regroup, the rights or assets in question any information required to give effect to this Article as egards operations which may produce the effect mentioned in Section 1; it may do this either by a Regulation drawn up after consulting the Council, which shall define the kind of operations to be notified to it or by a special request to the parties concerned and covered by this Regulation.

5. If a concentration should occur, which the High Authority finds has been effected contrary to the provisions of paragraph 1 but which nevertheless satisfies the conditions laid down in paragraph 2, it shall make the approval of this concentration subject to payment, by the persons who have acquired or regrouped the rights or assets in question, of the fine provided for in the second sub-paragraph of paragraph 6; provided that the amount shall not be less than half of the maximum provided for in the said sub-paragraph in any case where it is clear that authorisation should have been requested. If this payment is not made the High Authority shall apply the measures hereinafter provided for concentrations held to be illegal.

If a concentration should occur which the High Authority finds cannot satisfy the general or special conditions to which an authorisation under paragraph 2 would be subject, it shall denounce this concentration as illegal by means of a reasoned decision; after allowing the parties concerned an opportunity to put forward any arguments they wish, the High Authority shall order separation of the undertakings or assets illegally concentrated or cessation of common control as well as any other action which it considers appropriate to re-establish the independent operation of the undertakings or assets in question and to restore normal conditions of competition. Any person directly concerned may lodge an appeal against such decisions under the conditions provided for in Article 33. Notwithstanding the provisions of the said Article, the Court shall have jurisdiction to judge whether the operation effected is a concentration within the meaning of paragraph 1 of this Article and of the Regulations issued in implementation thereof. This appeal shall be suspensive. It may not be lodged until the measures provided for above have been taken, unless the High Authority agrees to the lodging of a separate appeal against the decision holding the operation to be illegal.

The High Authority may at any time, subject to its right to give effect to the provisions of the third paragraph of Article 39, take or cause to be taken such interim measures as it may consider necessary to safeguard the interests of competing undertakings and of third parties and to prevent any action which might impede the execution of its decisions. Unless the Court decides otherwise, appeals shall not suspend such interim measures.

The High Authority shall allow the parties concerned a reasonable period in which to execute its decisions, at the expiration of which it may impose daily financial penalties equal to one-tenth of one per cent, of the value of the rights or assets in question.

Furthermore, if the parties concerned fail to fulfil their obligations, the High Authority shall itself take steps to enforce its decision and in particular may: suspend the exercise, in undertakings over which it has authority, of the rights attached to the assets illegally acquired; arrange the appoinment by the judicial authorities of a receiver for these assets; organise the forced sale of such assets, under conditions which protect the legitimate interests of their owners; annul, with respect to natural or legal persons who have acquired the rights or assets in question as a result of the illegal transaction, the acts, decisions, or resolutions, of the managing bodies of undertakings under illegal control.

The High Authority is also empowered to send the Member States concerned recommendations as may be necessary to ensure the enforcement of the measures provided for in the preceding paragraphs in accordance with their domestic law.

In the exercise of its powers, the High Authority shall take account of the rights of third parties which have been acquired in good faith.

6. The High Authority may impose fines equal to:

3 per cent. of the value of the assets acquired or regrouped or to be acquired or regrouped on natural or legal persons who have failed to observe the obligations provided for in Section 4;

10 per cent. of the value of the assets acquired or regrouped, on natural or legal persons which have failed to observe the obligations provided for in paragraph 1; after the end of the twelfth month following completion of the transaction this maximum shall be increased by one-twenty-fourth for each month which has elapsed before the High Authority discovers the infringement;

10 per cent. on the value of the assets acquired or regrouped or to be

acquired or regrouped, on natural or legal persons which have obtained or
attempted to obtain the benefit of the provisions of paragraph 2 by means
of false or misleading information;

15 per cent. of the value of the assets acquired or regrouped, on undertakings
over which it has authority which have participated in or lent themselves to
the carrying-out of operations contrary to the provisions of this Article.

Persons subject to the penalties laid down in the present paragraph may
appeal to the Court under the conditions provided for in Article 36.

7. If the High Authority finds that public or private undertakings, which,
in law or in fact, have or acquire in the market, in respect of one of the products
over which it has authority, a dominant position which protects them from
effective competition in a substantial part of the common market, are using that
position for purposes contrary to those of the present Treaty, it shall address
to them any recommendations required to prevent that position from being used
for such purposes. If such recommendations are not carried out satisfactorily
within a reasonable time, the High Authority, by decisions taken in consultation
with the Government concerned, and in accordance with the penalties laid down
respectively, in Articles 58, 59 and 64, shall fix the prices and conditions of sale
to be applied by the undertaking in question or draw up programmes of manufacture or of delivery which it must fulfil.

Chapter VII—Impairment of the Conditions of Competition

Article 67. 1. Any action by a Member State which may have appreciable
repercussions on the conditions of competition in the coal and steel industries
shall be brought to the attention of the High Authority by the Government
concerned.

2. If such action is liable to provoke a serious disequilibrium bys subtantially
increasing differences in costs of production, otherwise than through variations
in productivity, the High Authority, after consulting the Consultative Committee and the Council, may take the following steps:

If the action taken by the said State is causing harmful effects for coal or
steel undertakings over which such State has authority, the High Authority
may authorise such State to grant assistance to such undertakings, the amount,
conditions and duration of which shall be determined in agreement with the
High Authority. The same provisions shall apply in case of a variation in wages
and in working conditions which would have the same effects, even if such
variation is not the result of action by the said State.

If the action taken by the said State is causing harmful effects for coal or
steel undertakings over which other Member States have authority, the High
Authority may address a recommendation to the said State with a view to
remedying those effects by such measures as that State may consider most
compatible with its own economic equilibrium.

3. If the action taken by the said State reduces differences in costs of production by granting a special advantage to, or by imposing special burdens on,
coal or steel undertakings over which it has authority by comparison with the
other industries in the same country, the High Authority is empowered to make
the necessary recommendations to the State in question after consulting the
Consultative Committee and the Council.

Treaty establishing The European Economic Community
Rome, 25th March, 1957

Article 1. By the present Treaty, the High Contracting Parties establish among themselves a EUROPEAN ECONOMIC COMMUNITY.

Article 2. It shall be the task of the Community, by establishing a Common Market and progressively approximating the economic policies of Member States, to promote throughout the Community a harmonious development of economic activities, a continuous and balanced expansion, an increased stability, an accelerated raising of the standard of living and closer relations between its Member States.

Article 3. For the purposes set out in the preceding Article, the activities of the Community shall include, under the conditions and in accordance with the time-table envisaged in this Treaty:

(a) the elimination, as between Member States, of customs duties and of quantitative restrictions in regard to the import and export of goods, as well as of all other measures having equivalent effect;

(b) the establishment of a common customs tariff and of a common commercial policy towards third countries;

(c) the abolition, as between Member States, of obstacles to the free movement of persons, services and capital;

(d) the inauguration of a common policy in the field of agriculture;

(e) the inauguration of a common policy in the field of transport;

(f) the establishment of a system ensuring that competition in the Common Market is not distorted;

(g) the adoption of procedures permitting the co-ordination of the economic policies of Member States and the correction of instability in their balances of payments;

(h) the approximation of their respective national laws to the extent required for the Common Market to function in an orderly manner;

(i) the creation of a European Social Fund in order to improve the possibilities of employment for workers and to contribute to the raising of their standard of living;

(j) the establishment of a European Investment Bank to facilitate the economic expansion of the Community by opening up fresh resources; and

(k) the association of overseas countries and territories with a view to increasing trade and to pursuing jointly the task of economic and social development.

Article 4. 1. The achievement of the tasks entrusted to the Community shall be ensured by the following institutions:

—an ASSEMBLY
—a COUNCIL,
—a COMMISSION,
—a COURT OF JUSTICE.

Each institution shall act within the limits of the powers conferred upon it by this Treaty.

2. The Council and the Commission shall be assisted by an Economic and Social Committee acting in a consultative capacity.

Article 5. Member States shall take all measures, whether general or particular, appropriate to ensure the carrying out of the obligations arising out of this Treaty or resulting from the acts of the institutions of the Community. They shall assist the latter in the achievement of its tasks.

They shall abstain from any measures which could jeopardise the attainment of the objectives of this Treaty.

Article 7. Within the field of application of this Treaty, and without prejudice to any particular provisions mentioned therein, any discrimination on the grounds of nationality shall be prohibited.

The Council may, on a proposal of the Commission and after consulting the Assembly, adopt, by qualified majority vote, regulations designed to prohibit such discrimination.

Article 36. The provisions of Articles 30 to 34 inclusive shall not preclude prohibitions or restrictions on imports, exports or goods in transit justified on the grounds of public morality, public order, public security, the protection of health or life of individuals, animals or the preservation of plant life, the protection of national treasures possessing artistic, historic or archaeological value, or the protection of industrial and commercial property. Provided always that such prohibitions or restrictions shall not be used as a means of arbitrary discrimination nor as a disguised restriction on trade between Member States.

Article 37. 1. Member States shall gradually adjust any State trading monopolies so as to ensure that, when the transitional period expires, no discrimination exists between the nationals of Member States as regards the supply or marketing of goods.

The provisions of this Article shall apply to any organisation through which a Member State, *de jure* or *de facto*, either directly or indirectly controls, supervises or appreciably influences imports or exports as between Member States. These provisions shall likewise apply to monopolies delegated by the State to other legal entities.

2. Member States shall abstain from introducing any new measure which is contrary to the principles laid down in paragraph 1 of this Article or which restricts the scope of the Articles dealing with the abolition of customs duties and quantitative restrictions between Member States.

3. The timetable for the measures referred to in paragraph 1 shall be harmonised with the abolition of the quantitative restrictions on the same products, as provided for in Articles 30 to 34 inclusive.

If a product is subject to a State trading monopoly in only one or some Member States, the Commission may authorise the other Member States to impose protective measures until the adjustment provided for in paragraph 1 of this Article has been effected; the Commission shall decide upon the conditions governing such measures and determine the manner in which effect shall be given to them.

4. If a State trading monopoly has rules which are designed to facilitate the

distribution or marketing of agricultural products, the rules contained in this Article shall be given effect to in such a manner that equivalent guarantees are provided, in respect of the employment and standard of living of the producers concerned; account shall be taken of possible adjustments and of necessary specialisations.

5. The obligations on Member States shall be binding only in so far as they are consistent with existing international agreements.

6. At the beginning of the first stage the Commission shall make recommendations as to the manner of effecting the adjustment provided for in this Article and the timetable which shall govern it.

Article 42. The provisions of the chapter dealing with the rules of competition shall only apply to the production of, and trade in, agricultural products to the extent determined by the Council within the framework of Articles 43 (2) and (3) and in accordance with the procedure laid down therein, account being taken of the objectives defined in Article 39.

The Council may, in particular, authorise the grant of aid:

(a) for the protection of undertakings handicapped by structural or natural conditions;

(b) within the framework of economic development programmes.

Article 46. Where in a Member State there is a national marketing organisation for a particular product, or where such product is subject to rules having equivalent effect, and where the competitive position of a similar product in another Member State is affected thereby, Member States shall levy a countervailing duty on the import of the said product from the Member State in which such organisation exists or where there are such rules, unless the latter State levies a countervailing duty on the export of the said product.

The Commission shall set the amount of such duties at the level necessary to redress the balance; it may also authorise recourse to other measures the conditions and details of which it shall determine.

PART THREE

POLICY OF THE COMMUNITY

Chapter 1—Rules of Competition (Articles 85—94)

Section 1
Rules Applying to Enterprises

Article 85. 1. The following practices shall be prohibited as incompatible with the Common Market: all agreements between enterprises, all decisions by associations of enterprises and all concerted practices which are capable of affecting trade between Member States and which are designed to prevent, restrict or distort competition within the Common Market or which have this effect. This shall, in particular, include:

(a) the direct or indirect fixing of purchase or selling prices or of any other trading conditions;

(b) the limitation or control of production, markets, technical development or investment;

(c) market-sharing or the sharing of sources of supply;

(d) the application of unequal conditions to parties undertaking equivalent engagements in commercial transactions, thereby placing them at a competitive disadvantage;

(e) making the conclusion of a contract subject to the acceptance by the other party to the contract of additional obligations, which, by their nature or according to commercial practice have no connexion with the subject of such contract.

2. Any agreements or decisions prohibited pursuant to this Article shall automatically be null and void.

3. The provisions of paragraph 1 may, however, be declared inapplicable in the case of:

any agreement or category of agreement between enterprises,

any decision or category of decision by associations of enterprises, and

any concerted practice or category of concerted practice

which helps to improve the production or distribution of goods or to promote technical or economic progress, whilst allowing consumers a fair share of the resulting profit and which does not:

(a) subject the enterprises in question to any restrictions which are not indispensable to the achievement of the above objectives;

(b) enable such enterprises to eliminate competition in respect of a substantial part of the goods concerned.

Article 86. Any abusive exploitation by one or more enterprises of a dominant position on the Common Market or on a substantial part of it shall be deemed to be incompatible with the Common Market and shall be prohibited, in so far as trade between Member States could be affected by it. The following practices, in particular, shall be deemed to amount to improper exploitation:

(a) the direct or indirect imposition of unfair purchase or selling prices or of any other unfair trading conditions;

(b) the limitation of production, markets or technical development to the disadvantage of consumers;

(c) the application of unequal conditions to parties undertaking equivalent engagements in commercial transactions, thereby placing them at a competitive disadvantage;

(d) making the conclusion of a contract subject to the acceptance by the other party to the contract of additional obligations which by their nature or according to commercial practice have no connexion with the subject of such contract.

Article 87. 1. Within three years of this Treaty coming into force, the Council shall issue the appropriate regulations or directives to put into effect the principles set out in Articles 85 and 86. The Council shall decide on these unanimously, on a proposal of the Commission and after consulting the Assembly.

If such regulations or directives have not been adopted within the specified period they shall be issued by the Council by qualified majority vote on a proposal of the Commission and after consulting the Assembly.

2. The regulations or directives referred to in paragraph 1 shall be designed, in particular:

(a) to ensure, by the institution of fines or penalties, the observance of the prohibitions referred to in Article 85 (1) and in Article 86;

(b) to decide exactly how Article 85 (3) is to be applied, taking into account the need both on the one hand to ensure effective supervision and, on the other hand, as far as possible to simplify administrative control;

(c) to define, where necessary, the extent to which the provisions of Articles 85 and 86 are to be applied in the various economic sectors;

(d) to define the respective functions of the Commission and of the Court of Justice in giving effect to the provisions referred to in this paragraph;

(e) to determine how domestic legislation is to be reconciled with the provisions of this Article and with any rules made thereunder.

Article 88. Until the regulations or directives issued in pursuance of Article 87 shall have come into force, the competent authorities in Member States shall determine to what extent to permit agreements (decisions, concerted practices) or the abusive exploitation of a dominant position on the Common Market. The said competent authorities shall so determine in accordance with their domestic law and the provisions of Articles 85 (especially para. 3) and 86.

Article 89. 1. Without prejudice to the provisions of Article 88, the Commission shall, upon assuming its duties, see that the principles laid down in Articles 85 and 86 are put into effect. It shall, of its own volition, or at the request of a Member State, investigate any alleged infringement of the principles mentioned above. It shall do so in co-operation with the competent authorities of the Member States, who shall give it their assistance. If it finds that such infringement has taken place, it shall propose appropriate measures for bringing it to an end.

2. Should such infringement continue the Commission shall, by means of a reasoned decision, confirm that such an infringement of the principles is being made. The Commission may publish its decision and may authorise Member States to take the necessary measures, the conditions and details of which it shall determine, to remedy the situation.

Article 90. 1. In the case of public undertakings and enterprises to which they grant special or exclusive rights, Member States shall neither introduce nor maintain in force any measure contrary to the rules contained in this Treaty, in particular to those rules provided for in Article 7 and Articles 85 to 94 inclusive.

2. Any undertaking entrusted with the management of services of general economic interest or having the character of a fiscal monopoly shall be subject to the rules contained in this Treaty, in particular to the rules of competition, in so far as the application of such rules does not obstruct the *de jure* or *de facto* fulfilment of the specific tasks entrusted to such undertakings. The development of trade shall not be affected to such an extent as would be contrary to the interests of the Community.

3. The Commission shall see that effect is given to the provisions of this Article and shall, where necessary, issue appropriate directives or decisions to the Member States.

Section 2

Dumping Practices

Article 91. 1. If, during the transitional period, the Commission, at the request of a Member State or of any other interested party, determines that dumping practices exist within the Common Market, it shall send recommendations, designed to end these, to the originators of such practices.

Should such dumping practices continue, the Commission shall authorise any adversely affected Member State to take protective measures of which and for which the Commission shall lay down the nature and the methods to be followed.

2. Immediately this Treaty comes into force, any products which originate in or are entitled to free circulation in one Member State and have been exported to another Member State shall be admitted free of all customs duties, quantitative restrictions or measures having equivalent effect when re-imported into the territory of the first-mentioned State. The Commission shall make appropriate rules for giving effect to this paragraph.

Section 3

Aids Granted by States

Article 92. 1. Except where otherwise povided for in this Treaty any aid granted by a Member State or through State resources in any form whatsoever which distorts or threatens to distort competition by favouring certain enterprises or the production of certain goods shall, in so far as it adversely affects trade between Member States, be deemed to be incompatible with the Common Market.

2. The following shall be compatible with the Common Market:

(a) aid having a social character, granted to individual consumers, provided that such aid is granted without discrimination on the grounds of the origin of the products concerned;

(b) aid intended to make good the damage caused by natural disasters or other extraordinary events;

(c) aid granted to the economy of certain regions of the Federal Republic

of Germany affected by the division of Germany, in so far as such aid is required so as to compensate for the economic disadvantages caused by that division.

3. The following may be deemed to be compatible with the Common Market:

(a) aid intended to promote the economic development of regions where the standard of living is abnormally low or where there is serious under-employment;

(b) aid intended to promote the execution of an important project of common European interest or to remedy serious disturbance in the economy of a Member State;

(c) aid intended to facilitate the development of certain activities or of certain economic regions, provided that such aid does not adversely affect trading conditions to such an extent as would be contrary to the common interest. Any grants of aid to shilbuilding existing as on 1 January, 1957, shall, in so far as they serve only to offset the absence of customs protection, be progressively reduced under the same conditions as apply to the abolition of customs duties, subject to the provisions of this Treaty concerning common commercial policy in regard to third countries;

(d) such other types of aid as may be specified by the Council by qualified majority vote on a proposal of the Commission.

Article 93. 1. The Commission shall, in conjunction with Member States submit to constant examination all systems of aids existing in those States. It shall propose to the latter any appropriate measures required by the progressive development or by the functioning of the Common Market.

2. If, after having given notice to the parties concerned to submit their comments, the Commission find that aid granted by a State or through State resources is not compatible with the Common Market within the meaning of Article 92, or that such aid is being improperly used, it shall decide that the State concerned shall abolish or modify such aid within a time-limit to be prescribed by the Commission.

If the State concerned does not comply with this decision within the prescribed time-limit, the Commission or any other interested State may, notwithstanding the provisions of Articles 169 and 170, refer the matter to the Court of Justice direct.

The Council may, at the request of a Member State, unanimously decide, if such a decision is justified by exceptional circumstances, that any aid granted or planned by that State shall be deemed to be compatible with the Common Market, notwithstanding the provisions of Article 92 or the regulations provided for in Article 94. If the Commission had, as regards the grant of aid in question, already initiated the procedure provided for in the first sub-paragraph of this paragraph, the request made to the Council by the State concerned shall cause such procedure to be suspended until the Council has made its attitude known.

If, however, the Council has not made its attitude known within three months of the said request being made, the Commission shall give its decision on the case.

3. The Commission shall be informed, in sufficient time to enable it to submit its comments, of any plans to grant or modify grants of aid. If it considers that any such plan is incompatible with the Common Market within the meaning of Article 92 it shall without delay initiate the procedure provided for in the preceding paragraph. The Member State concerned shall not put its proposed measures into effect until this procedure has resulted in a final decision.

Article 94. The Council may, by a qualified majority vote on a proposal of the Commission, make any appropriate regulations for carrying out Articles 92 and 93 (3) and may in particular determine the conditions for carrying out Article 93 (3) and the types of aid to be exempted from this procedure.

Chapter 2—Fiscal Provisions

Article 99. The Commission shall consider how to further the interests of the Common Market by harmonising the legislation of the various Member States concerning turnover taxes, excise duties and other forms of indirect taxation, including compensatory measures in respect of trade between Member States.

The Commission shall submit proposals to the Council; the latter shall decide upon the matter unanimously without prejudice to the provisions of Articles 100 and 101.

Chapter 3—Approximation of Laws

Article 100. The Council shall, by a unanimous decision, on a proposal of the Commission, issue directives for the approximation of such legislative and administrative provisions of Member States as directly affect the establishment or operation of the Common Market.

The Assembly and the Economic and Social Committee shall be consulted in the case of directives the implementation of which would involve amending legislation in one or more Member States.

Article 101. Where the Commission finds that a discrepancy between the legislative or administrative provisions of Member States is interfering with competition within the Common Market and consequently producing distortions which need to be eliminated, it shall consult the Member States concerned.

If such consultation does not result in an agreement eliminating the distortion in question, the Council shall issue the necessary directives for this purpose. It shall decide on these on a proposal of the Commission, unanimously during the first stage and thereafter by the qualified majority. The Commission and the Council may take any other appropriate measures provided for in this Treaty.

Article 102. 1. Where there is reason to fear that the introduction or amendment of a legislative or administrative provision may cause distortion within the meaning of the preceding Article, the Member State desiring to proceed therewith shall consult the Commission. After consulting the Member States the Commission shall recommend to the States concerned such measures as may be appropriate to avoid the distortion in question.

2. If the State desiring to introduce or amend its own provisions does not comply with the recommendation made to it by the Commission, no request, in pursuance of Article 101, shall be made to other Member States to amend their own legislative or administrative provisions in order to eliminate such distortion. If the Member State which has ignored the Commission's recommendations is the only one to be adversely affected by the distortion which it has caused, the provisions of Article 101 shall not apply.

Article 155. In order to ensure that the Common Market works efficiently and develops satisfactorily, the Commission shall:
—ensure that the provisions of this Treaty and the measures taken by the institutions by virtue of this Treaty are carried out;
—formulate recommendations or give opinions on matters within the scope of this Treaty, if it expressly so provides or if the Commission considers this necessary;
—have power itself to take decisions and in the circumstances provided for

in this Treaty participate in the shaping of measures taken by the Council and by the Assembly;

—exercise the powers conferred on it by the Council to ensure effect being given to rules laid down by the latter.

Article 172. The regulations enacted by the Council pursuant to the provisions of this Treaty may confer on the Court of Justice full jurisdiction as to the merits in regard to the penalties provided for in these regulations.

Article 173. Supervision of the legality of the acts of the Council and the Commission other than recommendations or opinions shall be a matter for the Court of Justice. The Court shall for this purpose have jurisdiction in proceedings instituted by a Member State, the Council or the Commission on the grounds of lack of jurisdiction, substantial violations of basic procedural rules, infringements of this Treaty or of any rule of law relating to effect being given to it or of misuse of powers.

Any natural or legal person may, under the same conditions, appeal against a decision directed to him or against a decision which, although in the form of a regulation or a decision directed to another person, is of direct and individual concern to him.

The proceedings provided for in this Article shall be instituted within a period of two months, dating, as the case may be, either from the publication of the measure concerned or from its notification to the complainant or, in default of this, from the day on which the latter learned of the said measure.

Article 174. If the Court of Justice considers the complaint well founded, it shall declare the measure concerned to be null and void.

Provided always that if the Court declares a regulation null and void, it shall, if it considers this necessary, declare which effects of the annulled regulation shall be deemed to remain in force.

Article 175. Should the Council or the Commission in violation of this Treaty fail to act, the Member States and the other institutions of the Community may refer the matter to the Court of Justice in order to have the said violation placed on record.

No proceedings arising out of the said reference shall be heard unless the institution concerned has been called upon to act. If within two months of being so called upon, the institution concerned has not made its attitude clear, the said proceedings may be brought within a further period of two months.

Any natural or legal person may bring proceedings before the Court of Justice, under the conditions laid down in the preceding paragraphs, on the ground that one of the institutions of the Community has failed to send him a formal document, such document not being a recommendation or an opinion.

Article 176. An institution responsible for a measure subsequently declared null and void or an institution whose failure to act has been declared contrary to the provisions of this Treaty shall be required to take the necessary steps to implement the judgment of the Court of Justice.

This obligation shall not affect any obligation arising under Article 215, second paragraph.

Article 177. The Court of Justice shall be competent to give preliminary rulings concerning:—

(a) the interpretation of this Treaty;

(b) the validity and interpretation of acts of the institutions of the Community;

(c) the interpretation of the statutes of any bodies set up by a formal measure of the Council, where the said statutes so provide.

Where any such question is raised before any court of law of one of the Member States, the said court may, if it considers that a decision on the question is essential to enable it to render judgment, request the Court of Justice to give a ruling thereon.

Where any such question is raised in a case pending before a domestic court of a Member State, from whose decisions there is no possibility of appeal under domestic law, the said court is bound to refer the matter to the Court of Justice.

Article 189. The Council and the Commission shall, in the discharge of their duties and in accordance with the provisions of this Treaty, issue regulations and directives, take decisions and formulate recommendations or opinions.

Regulations shall have general application. They shall be binding in every respect and directly applicable in each Member State.

Directives shall be binding, in respect of the result to be achieved, upon every Member State, but the form and manner of enforcing them shall be a matter for the national authorities.

Decisions shall be binding in every respect upon those to whom they are directed.

Recommendations and opinions shall have no binding force.

Article 190. The regulations, directives and decisions of the Council and of the Commission shall be fully reasoned and shall refer to any proposals or opinions which this Treaty requires to be obtained.

Article 191. The regulations shall be published in the Official Journal of the Community. They shall come into force on the date provided for in them or, failing this, on the twentieth day following their publication.

Directives and decisions shall be notified to those to whom they are addressed and shall take effect upon such notification.

Article 192. Decisions of the Council or of the Commission which include a pecuniary obligation on persons other than States shall have the enforceability of a Court judgment.

Enforcement shall be governed by the rules of civil procedure in force in the State in the territory of which it takes place. The order for its enforcement shall be stamped on the decision, without more verification than that the document is authentic, by the national authority which the government of each Member State shall designate for this purpose and which shall be notified to the Commission and to the Court of Justice.

When these formalities have been completed at his request, the party concerned may proceed to enforcement by applying directly to the authority which is competent according to domestic law.

Enforcement may only be suspended by a decision of the Court of Justice. Provided always that the proper method of enforcement shall be a matter for the domestic courts.

Regulations of the Council of Ministers of the E.E.C.

REGULATION NO 17
FIRST IMPLEMENTING REGULATION PURSUANT TO
ARTICLES 85 AND 86 OF THE TREATY

THE COUNCIL OF THE EUROPEAN ECONOMIC COMMUNITY,

NOTING the provisions of the Treaty establishing the European Economic Community and especially Article 87 thereof:

NOTING the Commission's proposal,

NOTING the opinion of the Economic and Social Committee,

NOTING the opinion of the European Parliament,

CONSIDERING that in order to establish a system ensuring that competition shall not be distorted in the Common Market, it is necessary to provide for the uniform and balanced application of Articles 85 and 86 in the Member States:

CONSIDERING that in determining the particulars of the application of Article 85 paragraph 3, due account must be taken of the need, on the one hand, of ensuring effective supervision and, on the other hand, of simplifying administrative control to the greatest possible extent;

CONSIDERING that it therefore appears necessary to make it in principle obligatory for enterprises wishes to invoke Article 85, paragraph 3, to notify the Commission of their agreements, decisions and concerted practices;

CONSIDERING however that such agreement, decisions and concerted practices are probably very numerous and cannot therefore be examined at the same time and that a number of them have special features which may make them less of a threat to the development of the Common Market;

CONSIDERING that there is consequently a need to establish provisionally a more flexible system for certain categories of agreements, decisions and concerted practices, without prejudging, however, the question of their validity under Article 85;

CONSIDERING, moreover, that it may be in the interest of enterprises to know whether the agreements, decisions or concerted practices in which they participate, or are contemplating participation, are likely to lay them open to action by the Commission under Article 85, paragraph 1, or Article 86;

CONSIDERING that in order to secure the uniform application of Articles 85 and 86 in the Common Market, it is necessary to fix the rules under which the Commission, working in close and constant liaison with the competent authorities in the Member States, can take the measures necessary for the application of the said Articles;

CONSIDERING that, for this purpose, the Commission must have the cooperation of the competent authorities in the Member States and be empowered, over the whole Common Market area, to require information and take the necessary steps to bring to light the existence of any agreement, decision or concerted practice prohibited by Article 85, paragraph 1, and abuse of a dominant position prohibited by Article 86;

CONSIDERING that if the Commission is to carry out its task of watching over the implementations of the Treaty it must be empowered to address to enterprises or associations of enterprises recommendations and decisions designed to put an end to infringements of Articles 85 and 86;

CONSIDERING that compliance with Articles 85 and 86 and the fulfilment of obligations imposed on enterprises and associations of enterprises under the present Regulation must be enforceable by means of fines and penalties;

CONSIDERING that it is desirable to confirm the right of the enterprises concerned to be heard by the Commission, that it is desirable to give third parties whose interests may be affected by a decision the prior opportunity to submit their comments, and that it is desirable to ensure that the decisions taken are published to a substantial extent;

CONSIDERING that all decisions taken by the Commission under the present Regulation will be subject to review by the Court of Justice under the conditions defined in the Treaty, and that it is moreover desirable to confer on the Court of Justice, under Article 172 full jurisdiction in respect of decisions by which the Commission imposes fines or penalties;

CONSIDERING that the present Regulation can enter into force without prejudice to any other provisions which may be adopted later under Article 87;

HAS APPROVED THE PRESENT REGULATION;

Article 1
Basic provision

The agreements, decisions and concerted practices referred to in Article 85, paragraph 1, of the Treaty and any abuse of a dominant position on the market within the meaning of Article 86 of the Treaty shall be prohibited, no prior decision to this effect being required; Articles 6, 7 and 23 of the present Regulation shall not be affected by this provision.

Article 2
Negative clearance

At the request of the enterprises or associations of enterprises concerned, the Commission may find that, according to the information it has obtained, there are, under Article 85, paragraph 1, or Article 86 of the Treaty, no grounds for it to intervene with respect to an agreement, decision or practice.

Article 3
Ending of infringements

1. If, acting on request or *ex officio*, the Commission finds that an enterprise or association of enterprises is infringing Article 85 or Article 86 of the Treaty, it can by means of a decision oblige the enterprises or associations of enterprises concerned to put an end to the said infringement.

2. A request to this effect may be submitted by:
   (a) Member States
   (b) Natural and legal persons and associations of persons, who show a justified interest.

3. Without prejudice to the other provisions of the present Regulation, the Commission, before taking the decision mentioned in paragraph 1, may address to the enterprises or associations of enterprises concerned recommendations designed to put an end to the infringement.

Article 4
Notification of new agreements, decisions and practices

1. The Commission shall be notified of any agreements, decisions or concerted

practices referred to in Article 85, paragraph 1, of the Treaty which have come into being after the entry into force of the present Regulation and for which those concerned wish to invoke Article 85, paragraph 3. As long as such notification has not taken place, no decision applying Article 85, paragraph 3, may be rendered.

2. Paragraph 1 shall not be applicable to agreements, decisions and concerted practices where:

(i) enterprises of only one Member State take part and where such agreements, decisions and practices involve neither imports nor exports between Member States;

(ii) only two enterprises take part and the sole effect of these agreements is:

(a) to restrict the freedom of one party to the contract to fix prices or condition of trading for the resale of goods which have been acquired from the other party to the contract, or

(b) to impose on an acquirer or user of industrial property rights—particularly patents, utility models, registered designs or trade marks—or on the person entitled, under a contract, to acquire or use manufacturing processes or knowledge relating to the utilization or application of industrial techniques, restraint on the exercise of those rights.

(iii) their sole object is:

(a) the development or the uniform application of standards and types

(b) joint research to improve techniques, provided that the result is accessible to all parties and that each of them can exploit it.

The Commission may be notified of such agreements, decisions and practices.

Article 5

Notification of existing agreements, decisions and practices

1. The Commission must be notified before August 1, 1962*, of any agreements, decisions and concerted practices referred to in Article 85, paragraph 1, of the Treaty which are already in existence at the date of entry into force of the present Regulation and in respect of which those concerned wish to invoke Article 85, paragraph 3.

2. Paragraph 1 is not applicable where the said agreements, decisions and concerted practices fall within the categories referred to in paragraph 2 of Article 4; the Commission may be notified of these.

Article 6

Decisions applying Article 85, paragraph 3

1. When the Commission issues a decision applying Article 85, paragraph 3, it shall indicate the date from which the decision shall take effect. This date shall not be prior to the date of notification.

2. The second sentence of paragraph 1 shall not be applicable to the agreements, decisions and concerted practices referred to in Article 4, paragraph 2, and Article 5, paragraph 2, nor to those which are referred to in Article 5, paragraph 1, and of which the Commission has been notified within the time-limit fixed therein.

* Amended by Council Regulation No. 59 of July, 1963 (see *infra*, p. 218).

Article 7

Spooial provisions for existing agreements, decisions and practices

1. Where agreements, decisions and concerted practices already in existence at the date of the entry into force of the present Regulation and notified before August 1, 1962,* do not meet the requirements of Article 85, paragraph 3, of the Treaty, and where the enterprises and associations of enterprises concerned put an end to them or modify them so that they no longer fall under the prohibition laid down in Article 85, paragraph 1, or so that they then meet the requirements of Article 85, paragraph 3, the prohibition laid down in Article 85, paragraph 1, shall be applicable only for a period fixed by the Commission. A decision by the Commission pursuant to the foregoing sentence cannot be invoked against enterprises or associations of enterprises which have not given their express assent to the notification.

2. Paragraph 1 shall be applicable to agreements, decisions and concerted practices which are already in existence at the date of the entry into force of the present Regulation and which fall within the categories referred to in Article 4, paragraph 2, provided that notification shall have taken place before January 1, 1964.**

Article 8

Period of validity and revoking of decisions applying Article 85, paragraph 3

1. A decision applying Article 85, paragraph 3, of the Treaty shall be granted for a specified period and may have certain conditions and stipulations attached.

2. The decision may be renewed on request provided that the conditions for applying Article 85, paragraph 3, of the Treaty continue to be fulfilled.

3. The Commission may revoke or alter its decision or prohibit those concerned from taking certain courses of action:

(a) where the *de facto* situation has changed with respect to a factor essential in the granting of the decision;

(b) where those concerned infringe a stipulation attached to the decision;

(c) where the decision is based on false information or has been obtained fraudulently; or

(d) where those concerned abuse the exemption from the provisions of Article 85, paragraph 1, of the Treaty granted to them by the decision.
In the cases covered by sub-paragraphs *(b)*, *(c)* and *(d)*, the decision can also be revoked with retroactive effect.

Article 9

Competence

1. Subject to review of its decision by the Court of Justice, the Commission shall have sole competence to declare Article 85, paragraph 1, inapplicable pursuant to Article 85, paragraph 3, of the Treaty.

2. The Commmission shall have competence to apply Article 85, paragraph 1,

---

* Amended by Council Regulation No. 59 of July 3, 1962 (see *infra*, p. 218).
** Amended by Council Regulation No. 118/63 of November 5, 1963 (see *infra*, p. 220).

and Article 86 of the Treaty, even if the time-limits for notification laid down in Article 5, paragraph 1, and Article 7, paragraph 2, have not expired.

3. As long as the Commission has not initiated any procedure pursuant to Articles 2, 3 or 6, the authorities of the Member States shall remain competent to apply Article 85, paragraph 1, and Article 86 in accordance with Article 88 of the Treaty, even if the time-limits for notification laid down in Article 5, paragraph 1, and Article 7 have not expired.

Article 10
Liaison with the authorities of the Member States

1. The Commission shall transmit without delay to the competent authorities of the Member States copies of the requests, applications and notifications together with copies of the most important documents which have been sent to it with the purpose of establishing the existence of infringenemts of Article 85 or Article 86 of the Treaty, or with the purpose of obtaining negative clearance or a decision applying Article 85, paragraph 3.

2. It shall carry out the procedures mentioned in paragraph 1 in close and constant liaison with the competent authorities of the Member States; and these authorities may submit their views on the said procedures.

3. A Consultative Committee on Cartels and Monopolies shall be consulted prior to any decision consequent upon a course of procedure referred to in paragraph 1 and prior to any decision concerning the renewal, the alteration or the revocation of a decision applying Article 85, paragraph 3, of the Treaty.

4. The Consultative Committee shall be composed of officials competent in the field of cartels and monopolies. Each Member State shall appoint one official to represent it, who, if he is prevented from attending, may be replaced by another official.

5. The consultation shall take place at a joint meeting called by the Commission; the session shall take place fourteen days at the earliest after dispatch of the convocation letter. This letter shall be accompanied by an exposition of the case to be considered, indicating the most important documents, and a preliminary draft of the decision shall be enclosed.

6. The Consultative Committee may render an opinion even if some members are absent and have not been replaced by another official. The result of the consultation shall be set out in a written statement which shall be attached to the draft of the decision. It shall not be made public.

Article 11
Requests for information

1. In the execution of the duties assigned to it by Article 89 and by provisions pursuant to Article 87 of the Treaty, the Commission shall have power to seek all necessary information from the Governments and competent authorities of the Member State as well as from enterprises and associations of enterprises.

2. When sending a request for information to an enterprise or association of enterprises, the Commission shall at the same time address a copy of this request to the competent authority in the Member State in the territory of which the principal place of business of the enterprise or the association of enterprises is situated.

3. In its request the Commission shall indicate the legal basis and the purpose of the same, and the penalties for supplying false information laid down in Article 15, paragraph 1, sub-paragraph *(b)*.

4. Information must be supplied on request by the owners of the enterprises or by their representatives and, in the case of legal persons, or companies or of associations without legal personality, by the persons responsible for representing them according to the law or the memorandum or articles of association.

5. Where the enterprise or association of enterprises does not supply the information required within the time-limit set by the Commission, or supplies incomplete information, the Commission's request for information shall be made by means of a decision. This decision shall specify the information requested, fix an appropriate time-limit within which it is to be supplied and specify the sanctions applicable under Article 15, paragraph 1, sub-paragraph *(b)*, and under Article 16, paragraph 1, sub-paragraph *(c)*, and shall indicate that there is a right to institute proceedings against the decision before the Court of Justice.

6. The Commission shall at the same time send a copy of its decision to the competent authority of the Member State in the territory of which the principal place of business of the enterprise or association of enterprises is situated.

Article 12
Inquiries by economic sectors

1. If in any sector of the economy the trend of trade between Member States, price movements, inflexibility of prices or other circumstances suggest that in the economic sector concerned competition is being restricted or distorted within the Common Market, the Commission may decide to conduct a general inquiry in the course of which it may request enterprises in the sector concerned to supply the information necessary for giving effect to the principles laid down in Articles 85 and 86 of the Treaty and for carrying out the tasks entrusted to the Commission.

2. The Commission may in particular request any enterprise or group oj enterprises in the sector concerned to communicate to it all agreements, decisions and concerted practices which are exampted from notification by virtue of Article 4, paragraph 2, and Article 5, paragraph 2.

3. When making inquiries as provided for in paragraph 2, the Commission shall also request enterprises or groups of enterprises whose size suggest that they occupy a dominant position within the Common Market or within a substantial part thereof to supply any particulars relating to the structure of the enterprises and to the conduct of their affairs necessary to appraise their situation in the light of Article 86 of the Treaty.

4. Article 10, paragraphs 3 to 6, and Articles 11, 13 and 14 shall be applied *mutatis mutandis.*

Article 13
Investigations by authorities of the Member States

1. At the request of the Commission, the competent authorities of the Member States shall carry out the investigations which the Commission considers ne-

cessary under Article 14, paragraph 1, or which it has ordered by a decision taken pursuant to Article 14, paragraph 3. The employees of the competent authorities of the Member States carrying out this investigation shall exercise their powers on production of a written warrant issued by the competent authority of the Member State in the territory of which the investigation is to be carried out. This warrant shall indicate the subject and the purpose of the inquiry.

2. The employees of the Commission may, at its request or at that of the competent authority of the Member State in the territory of which the investigation is to be made, assist the employees of this authority in the execution of their duties.

Article 14
Investigating powers of the Commission

1. In execution of the duties assigned to it by Article 89 and by provisions laid down pursuant to Article 87 of the Treaty, the Commission may conduct all necessary investigations into the affairs of enterprises and associations of enterprises.

To this end the employees authorized by the Commission shall be vested with the following powers:

(a) to examine the books and other business documents;

(b) to make copies of, or extracts from the same;

(c) to ask for verbal explanations on the spot;

(d) to have access to all premises, land and vehicles of enterprises.

2. The employees authorized by the Commission for these investigations shall exercise their powers on production of a written warrant stating the nature and purpose of the inquiry and the penalties provided for in Article 15, paragraph 1, sub-paragraph (c), in the event of incomplete submission of the books or other business documents required. The Commission shall, in good time, advise the competent authority of the Member State in the territory of which the investigation is to take place, of this investigation, stating the name and office of the authorized employee.

3. The enterprises and associations of enterprises must submit to the investigations which the Commission has ordered by means of a decision. The decision shall state the subject and purpose of the inquiry, fix the date when it is to begin and call attention to the sanctions provided for under Article 15, paragraph 1, sub-paragraph (c), and Article 16, paragraph 1, subparagraph (d), and shall indicate that there is a right to institute proceedings against the decision before the Court of Justice.

4. The Commission shall take the decions referred to in paragraph 3 after consulting the competent authority of the Member State in the territory of which the investigation is to be carried out.

5. The employees of the competent authority of the Member State in the territory of which the investigation is to be carried out may, at the request of this authority or of the Commission, lend assistance to the Commission's employees in the performance of their duties.

6. Where an enterprise resists an investigation ordered pursuant to the present Article, the Member State concerned shall lend the employees authorized by the Commission the assistance necessary to enable them to carry out their

investigation. The Member State shall, after consulting the Commission, take the necessary measures for this purpose before October 1, 1962.

Article 15

Fines

1. The Commission may by means of a decision impose on enterprises or associations of enterprises fines of from one hundred to five thousand units of account, where, wilfully or through negligence:

(*a*) they supply false or misleading information in an application submitted pursuant to Article 2 or in a notification made pursuant to Articles 4 and 5;

(*b*) they supply false information in reply to a request made pursuant to Article 11, paragraph 3 or 5, or to Article 12, or do not supply information within a time-limit fixed by a decision taken under Article 11, paragraph 5; or

(*c*) they submit in incomplete form, on the occasion of investigations carried out under Article 13 or Article 14, the books or other business documents required, or decline to submit to an investigation ordered by means of a decision taken pursuant to Article 14, paragraph 3.

2. The Commission may be means of a decision impose on enterprises and associations of enterprises fines of from a minimum of one thousand to a maximum of one million units of account; this last figure may be increased to 10 per cent. of the turnover of the preceding business year of each of the enterprises having taken part in the infringement where these enterprises, wilfully or through negligence:

(*a*) have infringed the provisions of Article 85, paragraph 1, or of Article 86 of the Treaty, or

(*b*) have infringed a stipulation made under Article 8, paragraph 1.

In determining the amount of the fine the duration of the infringement shall be considered in addition to its gravity.

3. Article 10, paragraphs 3 to 6, shall apply.

4. The decisions taken under paragraphs 1 and 2 shall have no penal character.

5. The fines provided for in paragraph 2, sub-paragraph *(a)*, may not be imposed for actions taking place:

(*a*) after the notification to the Commission and prior to its decision regarding the application of Article 85, paragraph 3, of the Treaty, insofar as these actions do not go beyond the limits of the activity described in the notification;

(*b*) prior to the notification of, and within the framework of the agreements, decisions and concerted practices existing at the date of entry into force of the present Regulation, provided that this notification has been made within the time-limits laid down in Article 4, paragraph 1, and Article 7, paragraph 2*t*

6. Paragraph 5 shall not apply once the Commission has informed the enterprises concerned that after a preliminary examination it considers that the conditions of Article 85, paragraph 1, of the Treaty have been fulfilled and that application of Article 85, paragraph 3, is not warranted.

Article 16

Penalties

1. The Commission may by means of a decision impose on enterprises or

associations of enterprises penalties of from fifty to one thousand units of account per day of delay, reckoning from the date fixed in its decision, in order to oblige them:

(a) to put an end to an infringement of Article 85 or Article 86 of the Treaty in conformity with a decision taken pursuant to Article 3;

(b) to discontinue any action prohibited under Article 8, paragraph 3;

(c) to supply completely and truthfully any information which it has requested by a decision taken under Article 11, paragraph 5;

(d) to submit to any investigation it has ordered by a decision taken pursuant to Article 14, paragraph 3.

2. When the enterprises or associations of enterprises have fulfilled the obligation which it was the object of the penalty to enforce, the Commission may fix the final amount of the penalty at a figure lower than that which would result from the initial decision.

3. Article 10, paragraphs 3 to 6, shall apply.

Article 17

Review by the Court of Justice

The Court of Justice shall have full jurisdiction within the meaning of Article 172 of the Treaty to adjudicate on proceedings instituted against the decisions by which the Commission has fixed a fine or a penalty; it may cancel, reduce or increase the fine or the penalty imposed.

Article 18

Unit of account

For the purposes of Articles 15 to 17 the unit of account shall be that adopted for drawing up the budget of the Community in accordance with Articles 207 and 209 of the Treaty.

Article 19

Hearing of the parties concerned and of third parties

1. Before taking decisions as provided for in Articles 2, 3, 6, 7, 8, 15 and 16, the Commission shall give the enterprises or associations of enterprises concerned an opportunity to express their views on the points objected to which have been taken into consideration by the Commission.

2. So far as the Commission or the competent authorities of the Member States consider it necessary, they may also hear other natural or legal persons or associations of persons. If natural or legal persons or associations of persons who can show that they have a sufficient interest ask to be heard, their request shall be granted.

3. When the Commission intends to give negative clearance pursuant to Article 2 or to render a decision applying Article 85, paragraph 3, of the Treaty, it shall publish the essential content of the application or notification, inviting all interest third parties to subunit their observations within a time-limit which it shall fix and which shall not be less than one month. Publication shall respect the justified interest of enterprises that their business secrets should not be divulged.

Article 20

Professional secrets

1. Information gathered pursuant to Articles 11, 12, 13 and 14 may not be used for any purpose other than that for which it was requested.

2. Without prejudice to the provisions of Articles 19 and 21, the Commission and the competent authorities of the Member States as well as their officials and other employees may not disclose matters which have come to their knowledge through the application of the present Regulation and which by their nature are professional secrets.

3. The provisions of paragraphs 1 and 2 shall not hinder the publication of general surveys or reviews not containing information relating to particular enterprises or associations of enterprises.

Article 21

Publication of decisions

1. The Commission shall publish the decisions which it takes pursuant to Articles 2, 3, 6, 7 and 8.

2. The publication shall name the parties concerned and give the essential content of the decisions; the justified interest of the enterprises that their business secrets should not be divulged shall be respected.

Article 22

Special provisions

1. The Commission shall submit to the Council proposals to the effect that certain categories of agreements, decisions and concerted practices referred to in Article 4, paragraph 2, and Article 5, paragraph 2, should be subject to the notification provided for in Articles 4 and 5.

2. Within one year from the entry into force of the present Regulation the Council shall examine, on a proposal of the Commission, the special provisions which might be made by derogation from the provisions contained in this Regulation with respect to agreements, decisions and concerted practices referred to in Article 4, paragraph 2, and Article 5, paragraph 2.

Article 23

Transitional system applicable to decisions taken by Member States' authorities

1. Agreements, decisions and concerted practices referred to in Article 85, paragraph 1, of the Treaty to which, before the entry into force of this Regulation, the competent authority of a Member State has declared Article 85, paragraph 1 to be inapplicable pursuant to Article 85, paragraph 3, shall not be subject to the notification provided for in Article 5. The decision of the competent authority of the Member State shall be considered a decision within the meaning of Article 6; its validity shall expire at the latest on the date which the said authority has fixed, but may not exceed a duration of three years reckned from the entry into force of the present Regulation. Article 8, paragraph 3, shall apply.

2. The Commission shall decide in accordance with Article 8, paragraph 2, in regard to applications for renewal of the decisions referred to in paragraph 1.

Article 24

Implementing provisions

The Commission shall have authority to lay down implementing provisions concerning the form, content and other details of applications submitted pursuant to Articles 2 and 3 and of the notification provided for in Articles 4 and

5, and to lay down those concerning the hearings provided for in Article 19, paragraphs 1 and 2.

The present Regulation shall be binding in every respect and directly applicable in each Member State.

Done at Brussels, February 6, 1962
By the Council
The President.

⁎

REGULATION NO. 26
ON THE APPLICATION OF CERTAIN RULES OF COMPETITION
TO THE PRODUCTION OF, AND TRADE IN, AGRICULTURAL PRODUCE

THE COUNCIL of the European Economic Community,

HAVING REGARD to the provisions of the Treaty setting up the European Economic Community, and in particular Articles 42 and 43 thereof;

HAVING REGARD to the proposal of the Commission;

HAVING REGARD to the opinion of the European Parliament;

WHEREAS it follows from Article 42 of the Treaty that the application to the production of, and trade in, agricultural produce of the rules of competition down in the Treaty constitutes one of the elements of the common agricultural policy; and whereas the provisions set forth hereunder will require to be supplemented in the light of the development of this policy;

WHEREAS according to the proposals submitted by the Commission for the framing and implementation of the common agricultural policy certain rules of competition must be made immediately applicable to the production of, and trade in, agricultural produce, in order to eliminate practices contrary to the principles of the Common Market and prejudicial to the objectives set out in Article 39 of the Treaty, and in order to create the necessary conditions for the subsequent introduction of a competitive system adapted to the development of the common agricultural policy;

WHEREAS the rules of competition concerning the agreements, decisions and practices referred to in Article 85 of the Treaty, and those concerning the improper use of dominant positions, must be applied to the production of, and trade in, agricultural produce insofar as the application of such rules does not hamper the working of national organisations of agricultural markets and does not jeopardise the objectives of the common agricultural policy;

WHEREAS it is appropriate to give special consideration to the position of farmers' associations insofar as one of the main objectives is of such association the joint production of, or trade in, agricultural produce, or the use of joint facilities, saving where such joint action excludes competition or jeopardises the objectives of Article 39 of the Treaty;

WHEREAS in order to avoid impeding the development of a common agricultural policy and in order to provide certainty as to the law and non-discriminatory treatment for the undertakings concerned, the Commission must have sole competence, subject to review by the Court of Justice, to decide whether the conditions laid down in the two previous paragraphs are fulfilled with respect to the agreements, decisions and practices refferred to in Article 85 of the Treaty;

WHEREAS, with a view to observance of the Treaty provisions on agriculture and in particular those of Article 39, the Commission must, in the matter of dumping, evaluate all the factors behind the practices complained of, particularly the level of prices at which imports are made from other sources into the market concerned; and whereas, in the light of this evaluation, the Commission must address the recommendations and authorize the protective measures provided for in Article 91, paragraph 1 of the Treaty;

WHEREAS with a view to the implementation, in the development of the common agricultural policy, of the rules concerning aid to the production of, or trade in, agricultural produce, the Commission must be enabled to make an inventory of existing, new or contemplated aids, to make appropriate observations to the Member States and to propose suitable measures to them;

HAS ADOPTED THE PRESENT REGULATION:

Article 1. From the entry into force of the present Regulation and subject to the provisions of Article 2 below, Articles 85 to 90 of the Treaty inclusive and the measures taken for their implementation shall apply to all agreements, decisions and practices referred to in Article 85, paragraph 1 and Article 86 of the Treaty and which concern the production of, or trade in, the products listed in Annex II of the Treaty.

Article 2. 1. Article 85, paragraph 1 of the Treaty shall not be applicable to any agreements, decisions or practices referred to in the preceding Article which are an integral part of a national market organisation or which are necessary for the attainment of the objectives set out in Article 39 of the Treaty. In particular, it shall not apply to any agreements, decisions or practices of farmers, farmers' associations or associations of these associations belonging to a single Member State insofar as these agreements, decisions or practices concern the production or sale of agricultural produce or the use of joint storage, treatment or processing facilities for agricultural produce and impose no obligation to charge a specific price, unless the Commission finds that the effects is to eliminate competition or to jeopardise the objectives of Article 39 of the Treaty.

2. After consulting the Member States and hearing the undertakings or associations of undertaking sconcerned and, if thought fit, any other person or body corporate, the Commission shall have sole competence, subject to review by the Court of Justice, to give a ruling in a decision which shall be published, as to agreements, decisions or practices for which the conditions laid down in paragraph 1 above are fulfilled.

3. The Commission shall give the said ruling either ex officio or at the request of a competent authority of a Member State, or of an undertaking or association of undertakings concerned.

4. Such publication shall name the parties concerned and shall give the essential content of the decision; the interest of the enterprises that their business secrets should not be divulged shall be respected.

Article 3. 1. Without prejudice to the provisions of Article 46 of the Treaty, Article 91, paragraph 1, thereof shall apply to trade in the products listed in Annex II of the Treaty.

2. With due regard to the Treaty's provisions on agriculture, and in particular those of Article 39, the Commission shall evaluate all the factors behind the practices complained of, particularly the level of prices at which imports are made from other sources into the market concerned. In the light of this evaluation, it shall address the recommendations and authorize the protective measures provided for in Article 91, paragraph 1 of the Treaty.

Article 4. The provisions of Article 93, paragraphs 1 and 3 (first sentence) of the Treaty shall be applicable to aids granted to the production of, or trade in, the products listed in Annex II of the Treaty.

Article 5. The present Regulation shall come into force on the day following publication in the Official Gazette of the European Communities with the exception of Articles 1 to 3 inclusive, which shall enter into force on 1 July 1962.*

The present regulation shall be binding in every respect and directly applicable in each Member State.

Done at Brussels,
on the fourth day of April in the year
one thousand nine hundred and sixty-two
by the Council
THE PRESIDENT

*_**

REGULATION NO. 49
AMENDING THE DATE OF ENFORCEMENT OF CERTAIN ACTS
CONCERNING COMMON AGRICULTURAL POLICY

THE COUNCIL of the European Economic Community,

HAVING REGARD to the Treaty establishing the European Economic Community and especially to Articles 42, 43 and 44 thereof;

HAVING REGARD to the Commission's proposal;

CONSIDERING that Council Regulations Nos. 19, 23, 25 and 26 concerning common agricultural policy and the Council Decision concerning minima prices provide for the implementation of their basic provisions on 1 July 1962;

CONSIDERING that Member States should be given a reasonable time for the effective enforcement of the above acts and the implementing regulations

---

* Amended by Council Regulation No. 49 of 29 June 1962 (see *infra*).

adopted by the Council or the Commission, some of which could only be adopted just before 1 July 1962;

CONSIDERING, however, that the cereal marketing season (maize excepted) in the Community begins about 1 July and that ,in consequence, in the case of the 1962–1963 season measures may have to be taken on the internal market as from 1 July 1962;

HAS APPROVED THE PRESENT REGULATION:

Article 1. 1. The date of 30 July 1962 shall be substituted for that of 1 July 1962:

g) In Article 5 of implementing Regulation No. 26 of the Council for certain rules governing competition in the production of and trade in agricultural products;

Article 2. The present Regulation shall come into force on 1 July 1962.

It shall be binding in every respect and directly applicable in each Member State.

Done at Brussels,
June 29, 1962
By the Council
THE PRESIDENT

* *
*

REGULATION NO. 59
AMENDING CERTAINS PROVISIONS OF COUNCIL REGULATION NO. 17

THE COUNCIL of the European Economic Community,

HAVING REGARD to the Treaty setting up the European Economic Community;

NOTING the Commissions's proposal;

NOTING the Parliament's opinion;

CONSIDERING that Regulation No. 17 of 6 February 1962, provides that the agreements, decisions and concerted practices referred to in Article 5, paragraph 1, thereof must be notified before 1 August 1962 in order to benefit from the transitional measures provided for in their favour by Article 6, paragraph 2, and Article 7, paragraph 1, of the said Regulation.

CONSIDERING that in order to facilitate implementation of these transitional measures, it is advisable to extend this time-limit by three months as a general rule and by six months in respect of agreements, decisions or concerted practices in which not more than two enterprises take part.

HAS APPROVED THE PRESENT REGULATION:

Article 1. 1. In Regulation No. 17, Article 5, paragraph 1, the words "before 1 November 1962" shall be substituted for the words "before 1 August 1962".

2. The following sentence shall be added to Article 5, paragraph 1, of Regulation No. 17:

"Provided always that notwithstanding the foregoing provisions, any agreements, decisions and concerted practices in which not more than two enterprises take part must be notified before 1 February 1963."

3. In Regulation No. 17, Article 7, paragraph 1, the words "within the time-limits set out in Article 5, paragraph 1", shall be substituted for the words "before 1 August 1962."

Article 2. The present Regulation shall come into force on the day following publication in the official Gazette of the European Communities.

The present Regulation shall be binding in every respect and directly applicable in each Member State.

Done at Brussels,
July 3, 1962
By the Council
THE PRESIDENT

.

REGULATION NO. 141
PROVIDING THAT COUNCIL REGULATION NO. 17
SHALL NOT APPLY IN THE TRANSPORT SECTOR

THE COUNCIL of the European Economic Community,

HAVING REGARD to the Treaty establishing the European Economic Community and especially to Article 87 thereof;

HAVING REGARD to the First Implementing Regulation pursuant to Articles 85 and 86 of the Treaty of 6 February 1962 (Regulation No. 17), amended by Regulation No. 59 of 3 July 1962;

HAVING REGARD to the Commission's proposal;

HAVING REGARD to the opinion of the Economic and Social Committee;

HAVING REGARD to the opinion of the Assembly;

CONSIDERING that, in the context of the common transport policy and in view of the special features of this sector, it may prove necessary to make regulations governing competition different from those made or to be made in other economic sectors and, in consequence, that Regulation No. 17, should not apply to the transport sector;

CONSIDERING that in the case of transport by road, rail and inland waterways the adoption of regulations governing competition may be expected within reasonably short time, in view of the work which has been done on the preparation of a common transport policy; whereas in the case of air and maritime transport it is impossible to foresee whether and when the Council will enact the relevant provisions and that in consequence the non-application of Regulation No. 17 can be subject to a time-limit only in the case of transport by railway, road and inland waterways;

CONSIDERING that the special features of transport do not warrant the non-application of Regulation No. 17 except in respect of agreements, decisions and concerted practices which directly affect the performance of transport services.

HAS APPROVED THE PRESENT REGULATION:

Article 1. Regulation No. 17 shall not apply to agreements, decisions and concerted practices in the transport sector which have as their object or result the fixing of transport prices or terms, the restriction or control of demand for for transport or the distribution of transport markets or dominant positions, within the meaning of Article 56 of the Treaty, on the transport market.

Article 2. The Council, in the light of any measures taken in the context of a common transport policy, shall adopt the cecessary provisions for the application of regulations governing competition with regard to transport by road, rail and inland waterways. To this effect the Commission shall submit proposals to the Council before 30 June 1964.

Article 3. In the case of transport by rail, road and inland waterways, the provisions of Article 1 of this Regulation shall continue in force until 31 December 1965.

Article 4. The present Regulation shall come into force on 13 March 1962. This provision shall not be relied upon against any enterprises or association of enterprises which before the day following publication of this Regulation in the Official Gazette of the European Communities have renounced the agreements, decisions or concerted practices specified in Article 1.

This Regulation shall be binding in every respect and directly applicable in each Member State.

Done in Paris,
November 26, 1962
By the Council
THE PRESIDENT

**
*

REGULATION NO. 118/63/EEC
MODIFYING THE PROVISIONS OF REGULATION NO. 17

THE COUNCIL of the European Economic Community,

NOTING the provisions of the Treaty establishing the European Economic Community and especially Article 87 thereof,

NOTING the Commission's Proposal,

NOTING the Assembly's Opinion,

NOTING the Opinion of the Economic and Social Committee,

CONSIDERING that under Article 7 of Regulation No. 17 of the Council, the prohibition decreed by Article 85 (1) of the Treaty is only applicable for the period fixed by the Commission to agreements, decisions and concerted practices existing at the date of the coming into force of that Regulation if the Commission has been notified within the time limit laid down and if the enterprises and associations of enterprises concerned put an end to them or modify them suitably; considering that this provision is equally applicable to agreements, decisions and concerted practices existing at the date of the coming into force of such Regulation and falling within the categories referred to in Article 4 (2) thereof, if they are notified before the 1st January 1964;

CONSIDERING that it will be easier to appreciate what modifications are to be made to such agreements, decisions and concerted practices when the investigation of a certain number of agreements, decisions and concerted practices of which the Commission has already been notified makes it possible to give a better definition of the manner of applying Article 85 of the Treaty; considering that in view of this an extension of the time limit, which is at present due to expire on 31 December 1964, under Article 7 (2), is desirable;

CONSIDERING that such an extension will prevent neither the bringing of proceedings for infringements of the provisions of Article 85 of the Treaty under Article 9 (2) of Regulation No. 17, nor the submission at any convenient moment to notification under Article 22 of the said Regulation of those agreements, decisions and concerted practices mentioned in Article 4 (2) which might particularly affect the development of the Common Market,

HAS APPROVED THE PRESENT REGULATION:

Article 1. In Article 7 (2) of Regulation No. 17, the words "before 1st January 1964" shall be replaced by the words "before 1st January 1967".

Article 2. The present Regulation shall come into force the day after its publication in the Official Journal of the European Communities.

The present Regulation shall be binding in every respect and directly applicable in each Member State.

Done at Brussels
November 5, 1963.
By the Council
THE PRESIDENT

Regulations of the Commission of the E.E.C.

REGULATION NO. 8
ADOPTED BY THE COMMISSION IN IMPLEMENTATION OF
PARAGRAPH 2 OF ARTICLE 91 OF THE TREATY ESTABLISHING
THE EUROPEAN ECONOMIC COMMUNITY

THE COMMISSION OF THE EUROPEAN ECONOMIC COMMUNITY

HAVING REGARD to the first sentence of Article 91 (2) of the Treaty, which provides that any products originating in or freed from, or not subject to, customs control in one Member State, which have been exported to another Member State, shall be admitted free of all customs duties, quantitative restrictions or measures with equivalent effect when re-imported into the territory oi the first State;

HAVING REGARD to the other provisions of the Treaty and its annexes, and in particular to the provisions of Articles 33, 38, 42, 91 (1), 95, 96, 97 and 227;

HAVING REGARD to the decision taken by the Commission on 4th December 1958, concerning the use of a certificate for the movement of goods between Member States (Official Journal of the European Communities, No. 33 of December 31, 1958, p. 688/58);

HAVING REGARD to the second sentence of Article 91 (2) of the Treaty;

WHEREAS it is necessary to define the field of application of Article 91 (2) of the Treaty, the conditions under which the goods in question are to be given such treatment and the formalities to be complied with on re-import;

WHEREAS formalities should be reduced to a minimum and measures should be taken to prevent the abuse of duty free re-imports

HAS ADOPTED THE PRESENT REGULATION:

Article 1. The following definitions shall apply for the purposes of the present regulation:

(a) Member States:
the Kingdom of Belgium, the Federal Republic of Germany, the French Republic (Metropolitan, Algerian and Saharan Départements, Départements of Guadeloupe, Martinique, Guiana and Réunion), the Italian Republic, the Grand Duchy of Luxembourg, the Kingdom of the Netherlands in Europe and those European territories whose foreign relations are administered by one of the above-named Member States;

(b) Re-importing Member State:
the Member State into the territory of which the goods can be re-imported free of customs duties, quantitative restrictions or measures with equivalent effect;

(c) Re-exporting Member State:
the Member State to which the goods specified in Article 91 (2) of the Treaty have been exported;

(d) Goods originating in the re-importing Member State;
goods considered as such under the legislation of the Member State concerned, provided that, in the case of goods made up in that Member State wholly or partly from imported products, customs duties and charges with

equivalent effect payable on the said products, but not actually paid or in respect of which a total or partial exemption or drawback has been grated, are paid in full or guaranteed under bond or by payment of a depsoit not later than the date at which the goods are re-imported into the re-importing Member State;

(e) Goods freed, or not subject to, customs control in the re-importing Member State:

1. Goods from other Member States or third countries, in respect of which import formalities have been completed and all due customs duties and charges with equivalent effect have been paid in the re-importing Member State, and in respect of which no total or partial exemption or drawback of such duties and charges has been granted;

2. Goods made up wholly or partly from imported products in the Member State concerned, provided that customs duties and charges with equivalent effect payable on such products, but not actually paid or in respect of which a total or partial exemption or drawback has been granted, are paid in full or guaranteed under bond or by payment of a deposit not later than the date at which the goods are re-imported into the re-importing Member State.

Article 2. The provisions of Article 91 (2) shall apply to trade in the agricultural products specified in Article 38 (3) of the Treaty only in so far as may be decided by the Council in accordance with Article 42 of the Treaty.

Article 3. The re-importing Member State shall impose no customs duty, quantitative restrictions or measures with equivalent effect on the re-import of goods, in respect of which it has been asked to apply the provisions of Article 91 (2) of the Treaty, on condition that:

1. The goods originated in the re-importing Member State concerned, within the Meaning of Article 1 *(d)*, or have been freed from, or are not subject to, customs control in that State, within the meaning of Article 1 *(e)*;

2. The goods are still in the same condition as when they were exported from the re-importing Member State, that is have not been further handled than is necessary for their preservation or for repairs to packaging and

3. In respect of the said goods, all import formalities have been completed, all customs duties and charges with equivalent effect payable have been paid in the re-exporting Member State, and no total or partial exemption or draw-back has been granted. Such may however, have been granted in respect of duties levied, after authorisation by the Commission, under the terms of Article 91 (1) of the Treaty.

Article 4. (1) Proof that the goods fulfil the conditions laid down in Article 3, must be furnished to the customs authorities of the re-importing Member State. For this purpose, it will be necessary to produce to the said authorities:

1. Either the original or a certified true copy or a certified extract of the movement certificate (customs document DD 1) submitted to the customs authorities of the re-importing Member State when the goods in question were previously exported, and duly endorsed as being correct by the said authorities, and

2. A certificate of identity issued by the customs authorities of the re-exporting Member State certifying:

(a) that the goods are the identical goods originally imported and have not been further handled than was necessary for their preservation or for repairs to packaging, and

(b) that, in respect of the goods concerned, all import formalities have been completed, all customs duties and charges with equivalent effect payable in the re-exporting Member State have been paid, and no total or partial exemption or drawback of such duties and charges has been granted, except in the case of duties levied after authorisation by the Commisssion under the terms of Article 91 (1) of the Treaty.

If these documents cannot be produced, any other satisfactory means of of proof shall be accepted.

(2) During the six months following export from the re-importing Member State, the customs authorities of that State and of the re-exporting Member State shall give their assistance to facilitate production of the means of proof specified above.

Article 5. In the re-importing Member State, the proofs specified in Article 4 shall be submitted to the customs authorities in support of the import declaration. The said authorities may require a written translation of such documents and may further require the import declaration to include an undertaking by the re-importer to the effect that the goods fulfil the necessary conditions to benefit from the provisions of Article 91 (2) of the Treaty.

Article 6. (1) For the purposes of Article 3, the customs authorities of the re-importing Member State may apply to re-imported goods only the formalities laid down in Articles 4 and 5.

(2) In particular, the said authorities may not demand an import licence; if a licence is necessary for exchange reasons it shall be issued by the competent authorities on request.

(3) Similarly, no bond or deposit may be demanded by the customs authorities. If, however, the conditions of Article 3 (1) (Article 1 *d*) and *(e)* (2) have not yet been fulfilled at the time of re-import, the re-importer shall be entitled to give a bond or pay a deposit guaranteeing payment of customs duties and charges with equivalent effect on the goods re-imported.

Article 7. If exports of national goods benefit from a drawback of internal charges in the re-exporting Member State, in accordance with Articles 96 and 97 of the Treaty, the same drawback shall be applied by that State to similar goods re-exported under the terms of Article 91 (2), up to the amount of charges actually paid on such goods.

Article 8. (1) In cases where goods covered by the terms of Article 91 (2) were charged against a global quota, established in accordance with Article 33 of the Treaty, when admitted to the re-exporting Member State, the latter shall cancel the relevant charge against the quota when the goods leave its territory;

(2) The re-import of goods covered by the terms of Article 91 (2) may not be charged against any global quota which the re-importing Member State may have established in accordance with Article 33 of the Treaty.

Article 9. The present regulation shall enter into force on April 15, 1960.

It shall be binding in every respect and shall be directly enforceable in all Member States.

Done at Brussels on
March 11, 1960.
By the Commission,
THE PRESIDENT

.

REGULATION NO. 27

FIRST IMPLEMENTING REGULATION PURSUANT TO COUNCIL REGULATION
NO. 17 OF 6 FEBRUARY 1962
(Form, content and other details
concerning applications and notifications)

THE COMMISSION of the European Economic Community,

NOTING the provisions of the Treaty establishing the European Economic Community, and particularly Articles 87 and 155 thereof;

NOTING Article 24 of Council Regulation No. 17 of 6 February 1962 (First Implementing Regulation pursuant to Articles 85 and 86 of the Treaty);

CONSIDERING that by virtue of Article 24 of Council Regulation No. 17 the Commission is empowered to lay down implementing provisions concerning the form, content and other details of applications submitted pursuant to Articles 2 and 3 and of the notification provided for in Articles 4 and 5 of that Regulation;

CONSIDERING that the submission of these applications and notifications may have important legal consequences for each of the enterprises party to an agreement, to a decision, or to a practice; that consequently each enterprise must have the right to submit an application of notification to the Commission; but that where an enterprise avails itself of this right it is necessary that it should inform the other enterprise sparty to the agreement, decision or practice, in order to enable them to safeguard their interests;

CONSIDERING that the onus of submitting to the Commission information on the facts and circumstances supporting applications filed in connection with Article 2 and notifications provided for in Articles 4 and 5 lies with the enterprises and associations of enterprises;

CONSIDERING that it is appropriate to provide for the use of application forms for negative clearance in connection with the implementation of Article 85, paragraph 1 and of notification forms in connection with the implementation of Article 85, paragraph 3, of the Treaty in order to simplify and speed up scrutiny by the competent services in the interest of all concerned;

HAS APPROVED THE PRESENT REGULATION:

Article 1

Persons authorized to file applications and notifications

1. Any enterprise party to the agreements, decisions, or practices coming under Article 84 or Article 86 of the Treaty shall be entitled to file an application

under Article 2 or a notification under Articles 4 and 5 of Regulation No. 17. Where the application or notification if filed by only certain of the enterprises participating, they shall so inform the other enterprises.

2. Where representatives of enterprises, of associations of enterprises, or of natural or legal persons or of associations of persons sign the applications and notifications provided for in Article 2 and in Article 3, paragraph 1 and paragraph 2, subparagraph b) and in Articles 4 and 5 of Regulation No. 17, they must submit written evidence that they are authorized to act in this capacity.

3. Where an application or notification is filed jointly, a joint representative should be appointed.

Article 2
Filing of applications and notifications

1. Applications, notifications and relevant enclosures are to be filed with the Commission, in seven copies.

2. For enclosed documents, either the original or copies may be sent. Copies must be certified as being true copies of the original.

3. Applications and notifications shall be filed in one of the official languages of the Community. The documents shall be lodged in their original languages. Where the original language is not one of the official languages, a translation into one of these languages shall be enclosed.

Article 3
Date from which applications and notifications take effect

An application or notification shall take effect from the time it is received by the Commission. However, where the application or notification is sent by registered post, it shall take effect from the date shown on the postmark of the place of posting.

Article 4
Content of applications and notifications

1. The application provided for in Article 2 of Regulation No. 17 which concern Article 85, paragraph 1 of the Treaty, must be filed on Form A annexed hereto.

2. The notifications provided for in Article 4 or Article 5 of Regulation No. 17 must be filed on Form B annexed hereto.*

3. Applications and notifications must give the information requested in the forms.

4. Several participating enterprises may submit an application or notification on a single form.

5. The applications provided for in Article 2 of Regulation No. 17 which concern Article 86 of the Treaty shall include a complete statement of the facts; this must cover, in particular, the practice in question and the position

* Amended by Commission Regulation No. 153 of December 21, 1962 (see *infra*, p. 227).

occupied by the enterprise or enterprises in the Common Market or in a substantial part of it with respect to the product or service concerned.

Article 5

Transitional provisions

1. Any applications and notifications filed without use of the forms before the entry into force of this Regulation shall be considered as complying with Article 4 of the present Regulation.

2. The Commission may require that a form. duly filed in, be submitted within such time as it shall determine. In this event, applications and notifications shall not be considered as properly filed unless the forms are subjitted within the period so determined and in accordance with the provisions of the present Regulation.

Article 6

The present Regulation shall enter into force the day after its publication in the official gazette of the European Communities.

The present Regulation shall be binding in every respect and directly applicable in each Member State.

Done at Brussels,
May 3, 1962
By the Commission
PRESIDENT

.

REGULATION NO. 153
SUPPLEMENTING AND AMENDING REGULATION NO. 27 OF MAY 3, 1962

THE COMMISSION of the European Economic Community;

HAVING REGARD to the provisions of the Treaty establishing the European Economic Community and especially to Article 85 thereof;

HAVING REGARD to Regulation No. 17 of the Council of 6 February 1962 and especially to Article 24 thereof;

HAVING REGARD to Regulation No. 27 of the Commission of 3 May 1962 and especially to Article 4 thereof;

CONSIDERING that pursuant to Article 24 of Regulation No. 17 of the Council, the Commission is authorized to prescribe implementing regulations concerning the form, content and other procedure of notification laid down in Articles 4 and 5 of Regulation No. 17;

CONSIDERING that Regulation No. 27 of the Commission in application of Article 24 of Regulation No. 17 and especially Article 4, paragraph 2 thereof prescribes the use of Form B for notification;

CONSIDERING that it is desirable to provide for a simplified from of notification for exclusive dealing agreements which contain no clauses particularly likely to distort competition within the Common Market;

HAS APPROVED THE PRESENT REGULATION:

Article 1 A paragraph 2 bis shall be added to Article 1 of Regulation No. 27 as follows:

"Notification may nevertheless be given in the form specified in the simplified Form B 1, reproduced in Annex, provided that the conditions specified in that form are satisfied, in the case of exclusive dealing agreements in which only two entertrises take part and:

in which one party undertakes with the other to deliver certain products solely to such other party for the purpose of resale within a specified area of the territory of the Common Market.

or

in which one party undertakes with the other to buy certain products solely from such other party for the purposes of resale,

or

in which the two enterprises have, for the purposes of resale, made exclusive agreements for delivery and purchase of the type specified in the foregoing two subparagraphs, in respect of certain products.

Notwithstanding the provisions of Article 2 paragraph 1, only one copy of Form B 1 will be required."

Article 2. The present Regulation shall come into force on the day following its publication in the Official Gazette of the European Communities.

The present Regulation shall be binding in every respect and directly applicable in each Member State.

Done at Brussels,
December 21, 1962
By the Commission
THE VICE-PRESIDENT

* *
*

REGULATION NO. 99/63/EEC OF THE COMMISSION
AS TO THE HEARINGS PROVIDED FOR IN ARTICLE 19(1) AND (2)
OF THE COUNCIL'S REGULATION NO. 17

THE COMMISSION of the European Economic Community

NOTING the provisions of the Treaty establishing the European Economic Community and especially to Articles 87 and 155 thereof.

NOTING Article 24 of the Council's Regulation No. 17 dated February 6, 1962 (first implementing Regulation pursuant to Articles 85 and 86 of the Treaty),

CONSIDERING that under Article 24 of the Council's Regulation No. 17 the Commission is empowered to lay down implementing provisions concerning the hearings provided for in Article 19 (1) and (2) thereof;

CONSIDERING that in the majority of cases the Commission will already in the course of the investigation have had frequent contacts with the enterprises and associations of enterprises at whom the investigation is aimed and that by reason thereof the latter will have had an opportunity to express their views regarding any points objected to which have been taken into consideration;

CONSIDERING nevertheless, that in accordance with article 19 (1) of Regulation No. 17 and with the rights of legal defence, it is necessary to ensure that enterprises and associations of enterprises have the right to submit comments at the end of investigations regarding all the points objected to upon which the Commission intends to base its decisions;

CONSIDERING that persons other than the enterprises and associations of enterprises to which an investigation relates may have an interest in being heard; that in accordance with Article 19(2), second sentence, of Regulation No. 17, such persons must have an opportunity of expressing their views if they so request and if they show that they have a sufficient interest;

CONSIDERING that it is expedient to enable any persons who have submitted an application with a view to putting an end to an infringement in accordance with Article 3(2) of Regulation No. 17 to submit comments where the Commission considers the facts before it do not warrant the granting of the application;

CONSIDERING that the various persons authorised to submit comments should do so in writing in their own interests and in the interests of sound administration, subject to there being, if required, oral hearings for the purpose of supplementing the written investigation;

CONSIDERING that it is necessary to define the rights of persons who are to be heard, in particular as regards the conditions under which they may be represented or assisted and the fixing and calculating of time limits;

CONSIDERING that the Consultative Committee on Cartels and Monopolies issues an opinion on the basis of a preliminary draft Decision and ought thus to be consulted in each case once the investigation thereof has been completed; considering, however, that such consultation does not prevent the Commission from re-opening its investigation so far as may be necessary.

HAS APPROVED THE PRESENT REGULATION:

Article 1. Before consulting the Consultative Committee on Cartels and Monopolies, the Commission shall hold a hearing pursuant to Article 19 (1) of Regulations No. 17.

Article 2. 1. The Commission shall give notice in writing to the enterprise and associations of enterprises of the points objected to which have been taken into consideration. The notice shall be addressed to each of them or to the joint representative appointed by them.

2. Nevertheless, the Commission may give notice by way of publication in the Official Journal of the European Communities when the circumstances of the of the case so warrant, and, in particular, when the enterprises are numerous and have no joint representative. Such publication shall respect the justified interest of enterprises that their business secrets should not be divulged.

3. No fine or penalty may be imposed on an enterprise or association of enterprises unless notice of the points objected to was given in the manner provided in paragraph 1 above.

4. When giving notice of the points objected to, the Commission shall set enterprises and associations of enterprises a time limit within which they may express their views.

Article 3. 1. Enterprises and associations of enterprises shall express their views on the points objected to which have been taken into account against them, in writing and within the time limit laid down.

2. They may set out in their written comments any arguments of law or fact relevant for their defence.

3. In order to prove the facts on which they rely they may annex any necessary documents. They may also request the Commission to hear any persons who are in a position to substantiate the facts relied on.

Article 4. In its decisions the Commission may only consider the points objected to upon which the enterprises and associations of enterprises to whom the decisions are addressed have had an opportunity to express their views.

Article 5. Should natural or legal persons who show that they have a sufficient interest ask to be heard pursuant to Article 19 (2) of Regulation No. 17, the Commission shall give them an opportunity to express their views in writing within such time limit as it shall lay down.

Article 6. When the Commission, having been called upon to adjudicate on an application under Article 3(2) of Regulation No. 17, considers that the facts before it do not warrant the granting of such application, it shall inform the applicants of the reasons therefor and shall set them a time limit within which they may submit any comments in writing.

Article 7. 1. The Commission shall grant to any persons who may so request in their written comments an opportunity to expound their views orally if they show they have a sufficient interest in so doing or if the Commission intends to impose on them a fine or penalty.

2. The Commission may also grant any person an opportunity to express his views orally.

Article 8. 1. The Commission shall summon any persons who are to be heard to appear on such date as it shall specify.

2. It shall immediately forward a copy of the summons to the competent authorities of the Member States, who may appoint an official to lake part in the hearing.

Article 9. 1. Hearings shall be conducted by such persons as the Commission shall appoint for the purpose.

2. Persons summoned shall appear in person or by those entitled to represent them in law or by virtue of their rules or articles. Enterprises and associations of enterprises may also be represented by a Member of their permanent staff duly authorised in htat behalf.

Any persons heard by the Commission may be assisted by practising members of the Bar or by professors entitled to appear before the Court of Justice of the European Communities under Article 17 of the Protocol on the Stature of the said court or by other appropriate persons.

3. The hearing shall not be public. Persons shall be heard separately or in the presence of other persons summoned to appear. In the latter case due account shall be taken of the justified interest of enterprises that their business secrets should not be divulged.

4. The essence of the statements made by each person heard shall be entered in a record which shall be read over and approved by such person.

Article 10. Without prejudice to the provisions of Article 2(2), notices from the Commission and summonses to appear before it shall be sent to the addressees by registered letter with acknowledgement of receipt, or handed to them against receipt.

Article 11. 1. In laying down the time limits provided for in Articles 2, 5 and 6, the Commission shall take into consideration the time needed to prepare comments and the urgency of the matter. No time limit may be less than two weeks: it may be extended.

2. Time shall start to run as from the day following receipt or handing over of notices.

3. Written comments must reach the Commission or be despatched by registered letter before expiry of the time limit laid down. However, when such time limit expires on a Sunday or official holiday its expiry shall be postponed until the end of the following working day. For the purpose of calculating such postponement, the official holidays shall be either those set out in the Annex to this Regulation when the material date is that of receipt of the written comments, or those laid down by the law of the country of despatch when the date is that of sending.

The present Regulation shall be binding in every respect and directly applicable in each Member State.

Brussels, July 25, 1963

By the Commission
THE PRESIDENT

Practical Guide' to Articles 85 and 86 of the Treaty of Rome and the Implementing Regulations
A Manual for Firms *)

PREFACE

The present 'Practical Guide' is intended to help enterprises and associations of enterprises to fulfil the formalities necessary to comply with, or to benefit from the protection of, the 'competition rules' laid down by Articles 85 and 86 of the Treaty establishing the European Economic Community, and the implementing regulations.

This Guide attempts to answer the questions which have been most often asked up to now. However, attention is particularly drawn to the fact that the considerations set out are without prejudice to the eventual interpretations of the provisions of the Treaty or of the regulations as may be made in connection with decisions by the Commission or the tribunals in specific cases; statements made in this document are in no way binding.

The provisions in force are:

(a) *Articles 85 and 86 of the Treaty of Rome* or March 25, 1957, establishing the European Economic Community (EEC);

(b) *Regulation No. 17 of the Council*, dated February 6, 1962 (First Implementing Regulation pursuant to Articles 85 and 86 of the Treaty), published in the *Journal Officiel* of the European Communities No. 13 of February 21, 1962 (page 204 *et seq.*) which came into force on March 13, 1962, as modified by Regulation No. 59 of the Council, dated July 3, 1962, published in the *Journal Officiel* of the European Communities No. 58 of July 10, 1962 (page 1655 *et seq.*) which came into force on July 11, 1962;

(c) *Regulation No. 26 of the Council*, dated April 4, 1962 (Regulation applying certain rules of competition to the production of, and trade in agricultural products), published in the *Journal Officiel* of the European Communities No. 30 of April 20, 1962 (page 993 *et seq.*), as modified by Regulation No. 49 of the Council, dated June 29, 1962, published in the *Journal Officiel* of the European Communities No. 53 (page 1571);

(d) *Regulation No. 27 of the Commission*, dated May 3, 1962 (First Implementing Regulation persuant to Regulation No. 17) published in the *Journal Officiel* of the European Communities No. 35 of May 10, 1962 (page 1118 *et seq.*), which came into force on May 11, 1962.

Under Article 85, enterprises must examine whether the agreements, decisions and concerted practices in which they participate are likely to affect trade between Member States, and have as their object or result the prevention, restriction or distortion of competition within the Common Market. Under Article 86, enterprises will be required to examine whether they occupy a dominant position in the Common Market, or a substantial part of the Common Market, whether they are exploiting this position improperly and whether trade between Member States is likely to be affected thereby.

* This Practical Guide was published by the European Community Information Service in October, 1962.

This will doubtless mean that many agreements or practices will have to be modified or suppressed in order to avoid sanctions (fines or penalties) or possible consequences in civil law (particularly actions for avoidance of contracts or for damages); in other cases, a request for a declaration that Article 85, paragraph 1, does not apply will be needed.

Enterprises may request a 'negative clearance' to show that their activities do not necessitate an intervention by the Commission under Articles 85 and 86.

Enterprises wishing to take advantage of Article 85, paragraph 3, may, and in certain cases must, submit a notification to the Commission.

The procedures for notification are not intended to substitute control by administrative and judiciary authorities for the undertaking's own responsibility. It is rather for the enterprises in the first place, on their own responsibility, to see that the prohibitions laid down are observed.

Any person showing a justified interest in objecting to agreements, concerted practices and improper exploitation of dominant positions may lodge a complaint on the basis of Article 3 of Regulation No. 17. Lastly, the procedures to be followed by the Commission and its services in ensuring that the Treaty is observed are also explained in this Guide.

PART I—GENERAL

I. WHAT ARE THE PROVISIONS OF ARTICLE 85 OF THE TREATY?

1. Paragraph 1 of Article 85 prohibits certain *agreements between enterprises certain decisions by associations of enterprises and certain concerted practices* which have *as their object or result the prevention, restriction or distortion* of competition.**

This article gives certain typical, but not exhaustive, examples :
the direct or indirect fixing of purchase or selling prices or of, any other trading conditions (for example, by fixing uniform reductions, discounts or terms of payment),

the limitation or control of production, markets, technical development or investment (for example by allocating production quotas or fixing maximum production capacity),

market sharing or the sharing of sources to supply. (For example: market sharing on a geographical basis or mutual respect of national markets),

the application of unequal conditions to parties undertaking equivalent engagements in commercial transactions, thereby placing them at a competitive disadvantage (for example, by granting to certain customers unjustified advantages to the detriment of the competitive position of other customers),

making the conclusion of a contract subject to the acceptance by the other party to the contract of additional obligations, which, by their nature or according to commercial practice have no connection with the subject of such contract (for example, by obliging customers or suppliers to buy or sell some other merchandise simultaneously, or to accept or provide some other service unconnected with the first).

2. The arrangement must restrict, prevent or distort competition *within the the Common Market* (see Article 227 of the Treaty). If it has these effects only

---

** For convenience the agreements, decisions and concerted practices which have as their object or result the prevention, restriction or distortion of competition will be designated from now on as 'arrangements'.

outside the Common Market and if it has no other effects, the prohibition in Article 85, paragraph 1, does not apply.

3. Lastly, the arrangement must be *likely to affect trade between Member States of the European Economic Community*.

This will generally be the case if the arrangement regulates economic exchanges (of goods or services) across frontiers or if it affects such exchanges (for example an arrangement governing the conduct of participants in trade between two Member States).

4. If all these conditions are satisfied, the arrangements are prohibited without the need for prior decision by any authority, except when a decision is taken in pursuance of Article 85 paragraph 3 declaring the prohibition inapplicable in a specific case. However, as regards arrangements existing when Regulation No. 17 came into force, the prohibition applies only as from March 13, 1962. This results from the decision of the Court of Justice of the European Communities of April 6, 1962, in the Bosch case. (Case No. 13/61, *Journal Officiel* of the European Communities 1962, No. 33 page 108.)

5. Under Article 85, paragraph 3, *the prohibition in Article 85, paragraph 1, may be declared not to apply* to arrangements which simultaneously satisfy two positive conditions and two negative conditions.

The two positive conditions are as follows:

(a) The arrangement must help to improve the production or distribution of goods or to promote technical or economic progress (for example, agreements for rationalization or standardization;); and

(b) The arrangement must at the same time allow consumers a fair share of the profit resulting from such improvement or progress (this might be the case for example, if a fall in prices or improvement in quality or services had resulted).

The two negative conditions are as follows:

(a) The arrangement must not subject the concerns in question to any restrictions which are not indispensable to the achievement of the above objectives;

(b) The arrangement must not enable such concerns to eliminate competition in respect of a substantial part of the goods concerned.

6. In short, an enterprise may conclude:

(a) That the arrangement falls under Article 85, paragraph 1 and that it cannot hope to benefit from Article 85, paragraph 3.

The enterprise then has the choice between suppressing or modifying the arrangement either on its own initiative or under the procedure envisaged in Article 7 of Regulation No. 17 if the arrangement was already in existence on March 13, 1962, (see Part 2, No. III);

(b) That the arrangement falls under Article 85, paragraph 1, but that it is in a position to invoke Article 85, paragraph 3, because it considers that the four conditions cited above are satisfied. In this case, the enterprise must examine whether it needs to fulfil certain formalities set out in Part 2 (No. III), and in particular whether it needs to notify the arrangement to the Commission of the European Economic Community (voluntary notification is always possible);

(c) That it is not clear whether the arrangement falls under Article 85, paragraph 1, but that the enterprise wishes nevertheless to know whether the Commission considers that it is not bound to intervene in the particular case. In this event, the enterprise can ask the Commission for a 'negative clearance' (see Part 2, No. II). This need not however be done, since it is possible to submit a notification 'for appropriate purposes' by completing Part IV and V of Form B provided for by Regulation No. 27.

II. WHAT ARE THE PROVISIONS OF ARTICLE 86 OF THE TREATY?

The four following conditions must be satisfied for the application of Article 86:

1. The enterprises concerned must, alone or with others, *hold a dominant position* on the market for a certain product or service.

2. The enterprises must hold *a dominant position on the Common Market or on a substantial part of it*. A substantial part of the Common Market may also be comprised in single Member States.

Member States.

3. A dominant position as such is not prohibited, but only *the improper exploitation of it*: Thus it is improper action that is prohibited.

According to Article 86, the following practices in particular shall be deemed to amount to improper exploitation:

The direct or indirect imposition of any unfair purchase or selling prices or of any other unfair trading conditions,

the limitation of production, markets or technical development to the prejudice of consumers,

the application of unequal conditions to parties undertaking equivalent engagements in commercial transactions, thereby placing them at a competitive disadvantage,

making the conclusion of a contract subject to the acceptance by the contract of additional obligations which by their nature or according to commercial practice have no connection with the subject of such contract.

4. Lastly, *trade between member states must be likely to be affected*.

If these four conditions are satisfied, the improper exploitation is *prohibited without the need for prior decision by any authority*.

III. WHO ENSURES THAT THE PROHIBITIONS CONTAINED IN ARTICLES 85 AND 86 WILL BE OBSERVED?

The Observance of the prohibitions contained in Articles 85 and 86 is ensured:

1. *By the Commission of the European Economic Community :*

(a) Either on its own initiative, on the basis of its own information or of information communicated to it,

(b) or at the request (complaint) of a member state or any natural or legal person establishing a justified interest.

2. *By the tribunals of member states*, pronouncing on Article 85, paragraphs 1 and 2, and on Article 86 within their own competence.

3. *By the competent administration authorities of Member States*, to whom in particular complaints may be addressed.

IV. WHO MAY DECLARE THE PROHIBITION IN ARTICLE 85, PARAGRAPH 1, INAPPLICABLE BY VIRTUE OF ARTICLE 85, PARAGRAPH 3?

Only the *Commission* of the European Economic Community (Article 9, Paragraph 1, of Regulation No. 17) whose decisions are subject to verification by the Court of Justice of the European Communities (See Part 3, VI).

V. THE APPLICATION OF ARTICLES 85 AND 86 OF THE TREATY TO PUBLIC UNDER-TAKINGS

Articles 85 and 86 of the Treaty apply equally to private enterprises and to public undertakings.

However, under Article 90, paragraph 2 of the Treaty or enterprises under takings—private or public—which are charged with the management of services of general economic interest or having the character of a fiscal monopoly are subject to the rules in Articles 85 and 86 in so far as the application of these rules does not obstruct the *de jure* or *de facto* performance of the specific tasks entrusted to them. The development of trade must not be affected to such an extent as would be contrary to the interests of the Community.

VI. FIELD OF APPLICATION OF ARTICLES 85 AND 86

In the present legal situation, Articles 85 and 86 apply in principle to all branches of the economy, and in particular also to banking, insurance and transport.

There are however certain exceptions:

1. Articles 85 and 86 do not modify the provisions of the treaty establishing the European Coal and Steel Community, in particular Articles 65, 66, 79 and 80 (Article 232, paragraph 1, of the E.E.C. Treaty).

2. Articles 85 and 86 do not derogate from the provisions of the Treaty establishing the European Atomic Energy Community. (Article 232, paragraph 2 of the E.E.C. Treaty).

3. Articles 85 and 86 of the Treaty, and also the provisions made for their implementation (i.e. at present, Regulation No. 17 of the Council and Regulation No. 27 of the Commission) *apply to agreements, decisions and practices* relating to production of and trade in products set out in Annex II of the Treaty *(agricultural products) only with effect* from July 30, 1962.

This follows from Articles 1 and 5 of Regulation No. 26 of the Council as modified by Article 1 of Regulation No. 49.

Article 2 of this Regulation provides however that Article 85, paragraph 1, shall not apply to agreements, decisions and practices relating to production of or trade in the aforementioned agricultural products which form an integral part of a national marketing organization or which are essential for the attainment of the objectives set out in Article 39 of the Treaty.

In particular Article 85, paragraph 1, does not apply to agreements, decisions and practices or farmers, farmers' associations or federations of such associations belonging to a single Member State, in so far as, without entailing any obligation to charge a fixed price, they concern production or sale of agricultural products or the use of shared equipment for storage, handling or processing of agricultural produce, unless the Commission determines that competition is thereby excluded or that the objectives of Article 39 of the Treaty are endangered.

PART II—RIGHTS AND ABLIGATIONS OF ENTERPRISES

The applicable provisions impose certain obligations on enterprises but also give them certain rights.

I. COMPLAINTS

Under Article 3, paragraph 2, of Regulation No. 17, any natural or legal person who shows a justified interest has the right to request the Commission to find that Article 85 or Article 86 is being infringed with a view to putting a stop to it.

Seven copies of the complaint must be submitted to the Commission of the European Economic Community, Directorate General for Competition, Directorate for Restrictive Agreements and Monopolies, 12, Avenue de Broqueville, Brussels 15. The formalities to be observed are set out in Part III (No. 1).

Enterprises are recommended to use form C, copies of which may be obtained in particular from the services of the Commission, from trade organizations and from Chambers of Commerce and Industry in Member States.

The complainant must describe its justified interest in detail; this justified interest in the cessation of the infringement may exist, for example, as a result of damage suffered because of the infringement.

If a justified interest is not established, the complaint is useful as an indication enabling the Commission to begin investigations on its own initiative.

It is in the complainant's interest that the complaint should at the very outset contain enough evidence or serious indications of the existence of an infringement of the Treaty.

II. REQUEST FOR A 'NEGATIVE CLEARANCE'

1. The procedure only operates on request.

The object of the request is that the Commission should state that, according to the information it has received, there are no grounds for it to intervene under Article 85, paragraph 1, or Article 86 with respect to an arrangement, decision or practice (Article 3 of Regulation No. 17).

Such a request must be sent *only to the Commission of the European Economic Community*, Directorate General for Competition, Directorate for Restrictive Agreements and Monopolies, 12, Avenue de Broqueville, Brussels 15.

Any enterprise which is a party to the arrangements, decisions or practices specified in Article 85 or Article 86 is entitled to submit the request. If the request is submitted only by some of the undertakings which are parties to the arrangement, they must inform the other enterprise which are also parties to it (Article 1, paragraph 1, of Regulation No. 27).

If a 'negative clearance' is requested under Article 85, paragraph 1, form A should be sent to the Commission in seven copies duly completed and signed (Article 4, paragraph 1, of Regulation No. 27).

2. After examination, the Commission may grant a 'negative clearance' to the applicant when, according to the information it has received, it is of the opinion that there are no grounds for it to intervene under Article 85, paragraph 1, or Article 86 with respect to an arrangement, decision or practice.

The 'negative clearance' is related to the information available to the Commission at the time when the clearance is given. Fresh information or the subsequent discovery of further facts unknown to the Commission at the time time of its decision will reopen the question of the scope of the clearance which has been granted. It is therefore greatly in the interest of the enterprises concerned to furnish the fullest information possible.

III. REQUEST FOR APPLICATION OF ARTICLE 85, PARAGRAPH 3

1. General

As has already been explained above, arrangements between enterprises, decisions of associations of enterprises and concerted practives which are likely to affect trade between Member States and which have as their object or result the prevention, restriction or distortion of competition within the Common Market, are prohibited without the need for prior decision by any authority.

The prohibition may be declared inapplicable when the conditions set out in Article 85, paragraph 3, of the Treaty (see sections 1–5 of Part I) are satisfied.

Only the Commission of the European Economic Community is competent to declare the provisions of Article 85, paragraph 1, inapplicable (Article 9, paragraph 1, of Regulation No. 17); enterprises wishing to obtain such a decision must therefore approach the Commission.

When the Commission declares a prohibition inapplicable it will state the date from which its decision shall take effect (Article 6 of Regulation No. 17).

The procedure to be followed in order to obtain a decision applying Article 85 paragraph 3, and the effect of the Commission's decision will differ according to whether:

(a) it is a question of arrangements specified in Article 85, paragraph 1, and concluded after March 12, 1962 (these are called hereafter 'new arrangements'*); or were in existence before March 13, 1962 (these are called hereafter 'existing arrangements');

(b) it is a question of arrangements specified in Article 85, paragraph 1, and for which a notification is necessary, that is to say the arrangements *do not fall within* the categories specified in Article 4, paragraph 2, of Regulation No. 17 (these are called hereafter 'arrangements subject to notification'); for which notification is unnecessary, that is to say the arrangements fall within the categories specified in Article 4, paragraph 2, of Regulation No. 17 (these are called hereafter 'arrangements exempted from notification').

2. Categories of arrangements subject to notification

Notification is to be envisaged for arrangements specified in Article 85, paragraph 1, for which the parties wish to obtain either a decision applying Article 85, paragraph 3, or the special treatment provided for in Article 7 of Regulation No. 17 (see point 4 below).

For certain categories of arrangements notification is a *necessary* formality because the prohibition in Article 85, paragraph 1, may only be lifted by the Commission.

(a) if a notification has been made (Article 4, paragraph 1, Article 5, paragraph 1, and Article 7, paragraph 1, of Regulation No. 17);

(b) and, *in principle*, with effect as from the date of notification (Article 6 of Regulation No. 17).

Among the categories of arrangements subject to notification may be mentioned:

international arrangements with participants from different Member States and which have as their object restrictions of competition (price fixing, market sharing, determination of rebates and conditions, rationalization, establishment of standards, types etc.).

arrangements with participants from only one member State and which regulate imports and/or exports between member States,

arrangements in which enterprises in third countries participate, in so far as these may affect trade between Member States.

General exceptions are set out under point 3 below.

* March 13, 1962 is the date of entry into force of Regulation No. 17.

3. Categories of arrangements exempt from notification

The categories of arrangements exempted from notification are set out in Article 4, paragraph 2, of Regulation No. 17; the list applies equally to new and existing arrangements falling under Article 85, paragraph 1 (Article 5, paragraphs 2, of Regulation No. 17).

These categories are exempt from compulsory notification. Although voluntary notification is possible (Articles 4, paragraph 2, and 5, paragraph 2, last sentence, of Regulation No. 17), notification is not compulsory:

(a) (a) because the interested parties may obtain a decision of the Commission by applying Article 85, paragraph 3, even without formal notification, and

(b) because the retrospective effect of the decision lifting the prohibition of Article 85, paragraph 1, is not limited to the date of notification.

On the other hand, the special treatment provided for in Article 7 of Regulation No. 17 is always subject to a notification having been made even if the conditions of Article 85, paragraph 3, are not satisfied (see point 4 below).

Arrangements are exempted from notification when:

1. Enterprises of only one Member State take part and such agreements, decisions and concerted practices involve neither imports nor exports between Member States.

2. Only two enterprises take part and the sole effect of these arrangements is:

(a) To restrict the freedom of one party to the contract to fix prices or conditions of trading in the re-sale of goods which have been acquired from the other party to the contract, or

(b) To impose restrictions on the rights of an assignee or user of rights over ('proprieté industrielle')—particularly patents, petty patents, industrial designs or trade marks—or on the rights of the grantee, under a contract of transfer of, or licence to use manufacturing processes or knowledge relating to the utilization or application of industrial techniques.

3. Their sole object is:

(a) The development or the uniform application of standards and types;

(b) Joint research to improve techniques, provided that the result is accessible to all parties and that each of them can exploit it.

The first group of arrangements exempted from the obligation to notify relates to national arrangements, that is arrangements in which only undertakings within the jurisdiction of a single Member State take part.

Arrangements in which enterprises within the jurisdiction of a third country participate do not benefit from this exception. National arrangements are subject to notification only if they concern imports and exports between Member States. It follows, for example, that purely regional arrangements for specialization or exclusive rights within one country, which only indirectly affect imports and exports, are not subject to notification; nor are price arrangements limiting production between enterprises in a single Member State, provided that these arrangements do not concern either imports or exports. For example, a national arrangement permitting exports but prohibiting re-imports, or a national arrangement for joint buying in another Member State, will therefore be subject to notification.

The second group of arrangements exempted from the obligation to notify relates to certain arrangements in which only two enterprises participate, regardless of the state under the jurisdiction of which they fall.

The first sub-group (Article 4, paragraph 2–2a) includes, for example—provided that they are likely to affect trade between Member States—arrangements fixing prices and conditions of trading for re-sale, as long as they contain no additional clause such as a prohibition on export.

The second sub-group (Article 4, paragraph 2–2b) covers the limitations imposed on the assignee or user (hereafter called more briefly the 'licensee') of the industrial property right or manufacturing processes etc., cited above. In particular the restrictions to which the holder of the right is subject are not included here (for example an undertaking not to carry on a given economic activity in the country of the licensee), as also are the restrictions contained in arangements for common exploitation of patents; so long as they do not fall within one or other of the categories mentioned in Article 4 paragraph 2, these restrictions are covered by the rule in Article 4 paragraph 1, with the consequence that a declaration that Article 85 paragraph 1 does not apply may only be granted on the basis of a notification and with effect as from the day of notification.

As regards restrictions imposed on the licensee, the following observations are necessary:

(a) It is also assumed here that the restriction falls in any case under the provisions of Article 85 paragraph 1. The prohibition laid down by that article does not in general concern those restrictions imposed on the licensee which are covered by the exercise of the industrial property right itself, that is to say, which result from the fact that the holder of the right is exercising his right within the limit prescribed or authorized by national legislation. This will generally be the case in as far as a certain territory (within the area in which the right is valid), a certain duration (within the period covered by the patent), a certain quantity or a certain volume are prescribed for the exercise of the right. These restrictions do not fall under Article 85, paragraph 1, and therefore need neither a decision that Article 85, paragraph 3 applies nor a notification.

(b) Article 4 paragraph 2–2b, therefore concerns only limitations imposed on the licensee which go beyond the framework laid down. These must however be limitations "in the exercise of these rights." The limitations must consequently also bear a real relation to the exercise of the industrial property right that is to say have a direct bearing on the exercise of that right. Limitations which no longer bear any real relation to the exercise of the industrial property right, i.e., those which no longer have a direct bearing on the exercise of the right, are not covered and fall under the rule in Article 4 paragraph 1, in so far as they do not fall into one of the other categories, in Article 4 paragraph 2. Such limitations could for example exist if the licensee:
accepted obligations of longer duration than that of the industrial property right,
could not acquire, make or sell any competitive product,
undertook not to export to another Member State,
undertook to impose on his customers restrictions of competition.

(c) It is however difficult to define the different categories exactly; that will be possible only on examination of each individual case. It will always be necessary to examine whether, over and above the restrictions in the actual licence contract, there are agreements or concerted practices between the different licensees themselves, or between the licensees on one hand and the holder of the right on the other hand, which may fall under Article 85 paragraph 1, and which are not in any case covered by Article 4 paragraph 2–2b.

4. Special Procedure for Existing arrangements

A. Article 7 of Regulation No. 17 provides for a special procedure for existing arrangements which permits their adaptation to the provisions of Article 85 paragraph 1, or of Article 85 paragraph 3, in the sense that the prohibition in Article 85 paragraph 1 may be lifted even for the period during which the conditions in Article 85 paragraph 3 did not exist or were not yet satisfied.

Application of this special procedure is subject to *two conditions :*

(1) Existing arrangements must be notified to the Commission:

(a) if they fall into one of the categories specified in Article 4 paragraph 2 of Regulation No. 17 (i.e., those which are, as a general rule, exempted from notification): before January 1, 1964;*

(b) if they do not fall into one of the categories specified in Article 4 paragraph 2 of Regulation No. 17 (i.e., those which are in any case subject to notification);

before November 1, 1962, when more than two enterprises are involved, before February 1, 1963, when two enterprises only are involved.

(2) The enterprises or associations of enterprises concerned must:

(a) either terminate the arrangements,

(b) or modify them in such a manner that they no longer fall under the prohibition laid down in Article 85 paragraph 1, or that they henceforth satisfy the conditions for application of Article 85 paragraph 3.

B. The combination of this special procedure and of Article 85 paragraph 3, means that it is desirable to notify to the Commission within the periods provided:

not only arrangements specified in Article 85 paragraph 1 and 'subject to notification', when the undertakings concerned hope to benefit by Article 85 paragraph 3, without having to modify their contents (arrangements for specialization, rationalization, etc.),

but also *existing arrangements* specified in Article 85 paragraph 1, when the enterprises concerned, though scarcely hoping to benefit by the Article 85 paragraph 3 because the conditions for applications of that article are probably not satisfied, nevertheless wish to have the prohibition lifted under the conditions set out at A above.

In this last case however if the arrangements were *voluntarily* dissolved, or amended in such a way as to escape completely the prohibition in Article 85 paragraph 1, a notification would be desirable only if it were feared that there might still be civil actions related to the past (as from 13-3-1962).

5. Examination of the various cases

A. First case : New Arrangements Subject to Notifications

(Arrangements made after March 12, 1962, not specified in Article 4 paragraph 2 of Regulation No. 17, and for which the parties concerned wish to take advantage of the provisions of Article 85 paragraph 3.)

Procedure

Any enterprises participating in the arrangements in question is entitled to submit a notification. If the notification is only submitted by some of the

* Now before January 1, 1967 by virtue of No. 118/63/E.E.C. of November 5, 1963, see *supra*, p. 220.

enterprises which are parties to the arrangements they shall inform the or the enterprises which are also parties to them of their notification (Article 1, paragraph 1 of Regulation No. 27).

Forms of Timing of Notification

(a) The notification must be submitted on form B (Article 4, paragarph 2 of Regulation No. 27); it must contain the information requested on this form.

(b) Since the time of notification determines the limit of the retrospective effect of the Commission's decision (Article 6 of Regulation No. 17), the notification must be made before the arrangement comes into force. No enterprise may invoke Article 85 paragraph 3 for the period before notification: the arrangement is null and void.

Effects of Notification

(a) No fine for infringement of Article 85 paragraph 1 may be imposed for the period following notification (provided that the enterprise remains within the limits of the activity described in the notification), so long as the Commission has not advised the parties to the arrangement that it is of the opinion, after a preliminary examination, that the conditions for application of Article 85 paragraph 1 are satisfied and that application of Article 85 paragraph 3 is not warranted (Article 15, paras. 5 and 6 of Regulation No. 17).

(b) The date from which the prohibition is declared inapplicable may be made retrospective to the date on which the conditions in Article 85 paragraph 3 were satisfied and, at the most, to the date of notification (Article 6 of Regulation No. 17).

(c) If the request is rejected because the conditions in Article 85, paragraph 3 are not satisfied, it is assumed that the arrangement falls under Article 85 paragraph 1, and it is prohibited from the start.

Consequences of Late Notification

If a notification is made after the arrangement has come into force, the Commission may impose fines on the enterprises concerned for infringement of Article 85 paragraph 1, for the period before notification and, if it decides to apply Article 85 paragraph 3 it may not declare the prohibition inapplicable for the period before notification. For this period, Article 85, paragraphs 1 and 2 apply.

Consequences of Omission to Notify

As the Commission cannot declare the prohibition inapplicable (Article 4 of Regulation No. 17), the arrangement is prohibited, with all the administrative and civil consequences (fines, nullity, damages, etc.), even if it in fact satisfies the conditions of Article 85 paragraph 3.

B. Second Case : New *Arrangements Exempt from Notification*
Arrangements made after 12th March 1962, specified in Article 4, paragraph 2 of Regulation No. 17 and for which the parties concerned, wish to take advantage of the provisions of Article 85 paragraph 3.)

Procedure

If the enterprises concerned so wish, they may notify the arrangement to the Commission. Notification makes it possible for the Commission to apply Article

85, paragraph 3, with retrospective effect to the date when the conditions in that Article were satisfied, i.e., even before the date of notification (Article 6 of Regulation No. 17).

Any enterprise participating in the arrangements in question is entitled to submit a notification. If the notification is submitted only by some of the enterprises which are parties to the arrangements, they shall inform the other which are also parties to them of the notification (Article 1, paragraph 1 of Regulation No. 27).

This notification must also be made on form B (Article 4 paragraph 2, of Regulation No. 27).

Effects of a Notification

(a) No fine for an infringement of Article 85 paragraph 1 may be imposed for the period following notification (as long as the enterprise remains within the limits of the activity described in the notification).

This advantage ceases to exist as soon as the Commission has informed the enterprises concerned that, after a preliminary examination, it is of the opinion that the conditions for application of Article 85 paragraph 1, are satisfied and that application of Article 85, paragraph 3 is not warranted (Article 15, paragraphs 5 and 6 of Regulation No. 17).

(b) The notification expresses the request of the parties concerned for a decision by the Commission under Article 85, paragraph 3.

(c) If the request is rejected because the conditions in Article 85 paragraph 3 are not satisfied, it is assumed that the arrangement falls under Article 85 paragraph 1 and it is prohibited from the start.

Consequences of Omission to Notify

(a) A fine for infringement of Article 85 paragraph 1 may be imposed by the Commission if the conditions in Article 85 paragraph 3 are not satisfied.

(b) In case of dispute between members of the arrangement or with a third party on the validity of the arrangement, or when a procedure for terminating the infringement has been started by the Commission on its own initiative or after a complaint or by national authorities, the Commission may only give a ruling on the basis of Article 85 paragraph 3 if the parties concerned invoke this provision, which they can do in particular by means of a notification.

If the Commission then declares that the prohibition does not apply, its decision may have retrospective effect to the date from which the conditions in Article 85, paragraph 3, were satisfied. If the request is rejected because the the conditions in Article 85, paragraph 3 are not satisfied the arrangement, falling under Article 85 paragraph 1, is prohibited from the start.

C. Third Case : Existing Arrangements Subject to Notification

(Arrangements already in existence on 13th March 1962, not falling under Article 4 paragraph 2 of Regulation No. 17, and for which the parties concerned wish to take advantage of Article 85 paragraph 3).

Procedure

Any enterprise participating in the arrangements in question is entitled to submit a notification. If the notification is submitted only by some of the enterprises which are parties to the arrangements, they shall inform the other enterprises which are also parties to them in their notification (Article 1 paragraph 1 of Regulation No. 27).

Forms of Timing of Notification

(a) The notification must be made on form B (Article 4 paragraph 2 of Regulation No. 27). It must contain the information requested on the form.

(b) Notification must be made *before November 1, 1962*. However, notwithstanding the above, arrangements in which only two undertakings participate must be notified *before February 1, 1963* (Article 5, paragraph 1, as amended, of Regulation No. 17). This second date for notification affects among others, licence-contracts and sole agency contracts in so far as they fall under Article 85 paragraph 1, even if they form part of a whole series of such contracts.

Effects of a Notification made by the date laid down in Article 5

(a) No fine for infringement of Article 85 paragraph 1 may be imposed for the period before notification nor for the period after notification (provided that the enterprise remains within the limits of the activity described in the notification), so long as the Commission has not advised the parties to the arrangement that it is of the opinion, after a preliminary examination, that the conditions for application of Article 85 paragraph 1 are satisfied and that application of Article 85 paragraph 1 are satisfied and that application of Article 85 paragraph 3 is not warranted (Article 15 paragraphs 5 and 6 of Regulation No. 17).

(b) The date from which the prohibition is declared inapplicable may be made restrospective to before the date of notification. The prohibition in Article 85 paragraph 1 may be declared inapplicable as from the 13th March, 1962, if since that date the conditions in Article 85 paragraph 3 have been satisfied. For the period before 13th March, 1962, it is not necessary to lift the prohibition according to the decision of the Court of Justice in the *Bosch* case (see part 1:4).

(c) Even if the conditions in Article 85 paragraph 3 were not satisfied during a certain period before the decision, the enterprises concerned may still request the Commission to decide that the prohibition set out in Article 85 paragraph 1 applies only for a period fixed by the Commission.

To this end, in conformity with Article 7 of Regulation No. 17, the enterprises must either put an end to the arrangement or modify it in such a manner that it completely escapes the prohibition in Article 85 paragraph 1 or that it in future satisfies the conditions in Article 85 paragraph 3.

However, it would not be right for an enterprise to be able to bring an action on the basis of the provisions of the arrangement against another enterprise formerly party to the arrangement but which it has since denounced. For this reason Article 7, paragraph 1 of Regulation No. 17 lays down that the Commission's decision cannot be invoked against undertakings or associations of undertakings which have not given their express assent at the time of notification.

Comment

A notification does not of itself validate the arrangement notified. Such validity can only exist if the Commission declares the prohibition of Article 85 paragraph 1 inapplicable in the particular case or if the Commission decides to apply Article 7 of Regulation No. 17.

If a declaration of inapplicability or of application of Article 7 of Regulation No. 17 is refused, the arrangement is prohibited where appropriate as from March 13, 1962.

For the period before the Commission's decision, the situation is undecided.

Consequences of Late Notification

When notification is made after the dates provided in Article 5, its effects will be less favourable; it will be necessary to examine whether it should be considered as a notification of a new arrangement. If so, the consequences would be the same as those quoted for the 'first case', i.e., the impossibility of obtaining a decision applying Article 85 paragraph 3, before the date of notification, the inapplicability of the special provisions of Article 7 paragraph 1 of Regulation No. 17 as described under (c) above and the possibility that enterprises may be liable to fines for the period before notification (Article 15, paragraph 2 of Regulation No. 17).

Consequences of Failure to Notify

The arrangement is prohibited as from March 13, 1962, even if it in fact satisfies the conditions in Article 85, paragraph 3, with all the administrative and civil consequences (fines nullity, damages etc.), since the Commission may make the decision retrospective only if notification has been made (Article 5 paragraph 1, and Article 6 of Regulation No. 17).

D. Fourth Case : Existing Arrangements Exempted from Notification

(Arrangements already in existence on March 13, 1962, specified in Article 4 paragraph 2 of Regulation No. 17 and for which the parties concerned wish to take advantage of the provisions of Article 85 paragraph 3).

Procedure

If the enterprises concerned so wish, they may notify the arrangement to the Commission.

Any enterprise participating in the arrangements in question is entitled to submit a notification. If the notification is submitted only by some of the enterprises which are parties to the arrangement they shall inform the other undertakings which are also parties to them of their notification .(Article 1 paragraph 1 of Regulation No. 27).

This notification must also be made on Form B (Article 4 paragraph 2 of Regulation No. 27); it must contain the information requested in the Form.

The date from which the prohibition is declared inapplicable may be made restrospective to before the date of any notification. The prohibition may be declared inapplicable as from March 13, 1962 if the conditions in Article 85, paragraph 3 have been satisfied since that date. According to the decision of the Court of Justice in the *Bosch* case (see Part 1 :4), it is not necessary to lift the prohibition for the period before March 13, 1962.

Effects of Notification

(a) No fine for infringement of Article 85 paragraph 1 may be imposed for that period before notification (provided that the notification has been made before January 1, 1964) nor for the period after notification (provided that the enterprise remains within the limits of the activity described in the notification). These advantages cease to exist as soon as the Commission has informed the enterprises concerned that, after a preliminary examination, it considers that the conditions for application of Article 85 paragraph 1 are satisfied and that application of Article 85 paragraph 3 is not warranted (Article 15, paragraphs 5 and 6 of Regulation No. 17).

(b) Even if the conditions in Article 85 paragraph 3 were not satisfied during the period before the decision, the enterprises concerned may still request the Commission to decide that the prohibition set out in Article 85 paragraph 1 does not apply for a period determined by the Commission.

To this end, in conformity with Article 7 of Regulation No. 17, they must either put an end to the arrangement or modify it in such manner that it completely escapes the prohibition in Article 85, paragraph 1, or that it in future satisfies the conditions in Article 85 paragraph 3.

However, the decision of the Commission may only be invoked against parties to the arrangement who have participated or acquiesced in the notification (Article 7 paragraph 1 of Regulation No. 17).

These facilities are however granted only for arrangements notified *before* January 1, 1964 (Article 7 paragraph 2 of Regulation No. 17)*.

Comment

A notification does not of itself validate the arrangement notified. Such validity can only exist if Commission declares that the prohibition in Article 85 paragraph 1 is inapplicable in the specific instance, or if it decides to apply Article 7 of Regulation No. 17.

If a declaration of inapplicability or of application of Article 7 of Regulation No. 17 is refused, the arrangement is prohibited—where appropriate—as from March 13, 1962.

For the period before the Commission's decision, the situation is undecided.

Consequence of Late Notification

The arrangement may not benefit from Article 7 of Regulation No. 17.

6. *Period of Validity and Revocation of exemption under Aticle 85, paragraph 3. (Article 8 of Regulation No. 17.)*

Exemption under Article 85 paragraph 3 is granted for a limited period which may be renewed on request if the necessary conditions are still satisfied. It may have certain obligations and conditions attached.

The Commission may revoke or modify its decision:

(a) with future effect if the situation changes with respect to a factor essential to the granting of the decision;

(b) with retrospective effect also, if:

the parties concerned fail to fulfil an obligation to which the decision has been made subject.

the decision is based on inaccurate information or has been obtained fraudulently,

the parties concerned abuse the exemption from the provisions of Article 85 paragraph 1.

Subject to appeal to the Court of Justice of the European Communities (see part 3: VI), a decision granting exemption under Article 85 paragraph 3 affects all the interested parties and third parties; it is binding on national administrations and tribunals.

IV. NEGATIVE CLEARANCE AND NOTIFICATION

It is possible to submit an application for 'negative clearance' (Form A) and notification (Form B) to the Commission simultaneously. It is however not necessary to submit an application for 'negative clearance' if it is merely desired to retain the possibility of contesting the applicability of Article 85 paragraph 1.

Indeed, Form B provides expressly under IV for the possibility of showing that Article 85 paragraph 1 does not apply.

The application for 'negative clearance' does not however extend the period for notification.

In addition, the considerations set out in Part 3: VII below should be studied.

PART III: FORMALITIES, PROCEDURES, VERIFICATION AND CONTROL, APPEAL

I. FORMALITIES

Requests to determine an infringement, and applications for the granting of 'negative clearance' must, like notifications, be signed by one of the enterprises concerned, by its representative or by a jointly designated representative; the authority of representation must be proved (Article 1 of Regulation No. 27).

Applications and notifications must be written in one of the official languages of the Community (French, German, Italian, Dutch) and sent with seven copies to the Commission of the European Economic Community, Directorate General of Competition, Directorate of Restrictive Agreements and Monopolies, 12, Avenue de Broqueville, Brussels, 15, Belgium. Since the Commission will send one copy to the national Authorities of each Member State, documents attached must also be sent in seven copies, whether originals or not. Copies must be certified true copies of the original.

If the original language of the documents is not one of the official languages, a translation into one of the official languages should be attached (Article 2 of Regulation No. 27).

Applications and notifications must contain the information requested in the forms when these have to be used. Two or more enterprises being parties to an arrangement may use the same form, (Article 4 paragraphs 3 and 4 of Regulation No. 27).

The Commission is empowered to impose fines ranging from 100 to 5,000 Units of Account on undertakings which, wilfully or through negligence, supply inaccurate or misleading information in applying for a 'negative clearance' or in a notification (Article 15, paragraph 1, of Regulation No. 17).

II. COLABORATION WITH MEMBER STATES

When a request to determine an infringement, an application for 'negative clearance' or a notification is made to the Commission, one copy is sent to the competent Authorities of the Member States.

In a addition, one copy of the most important documents in all proceedings is sent to those Authorities (Article 10, paragraphs 1 and 2 of Regulation No. 17).

The Commission may request information from Member States (Article 11 of Regulation No. 17) and arrange for investigations to be made by the servants of competent Authorities in Member States (Articles 13 and 14 of Regulation No. 17).

The Commission must, before any decision is taken (except concerning a request for information), consult the 'Consultative Committee on Cartels and Monopolies' on which Member States are represented (Article 10 paragraphs 3 to 6 of Regulation No. 17).

The officials and other servants of competent Authorities in Member States are, like those of the Commission, forbidden to disclose information which they

* This date has been changed to January 1, 1967, by Council Regulation No. 118/63 of November 5, 1963 (see *supra*, p. 220).

have gathered in pursuance of Regulation No. 17 and which, by its nature, is subject to professional secrecy (Article 20, paragraph 2 of Regulation No. 17).

III INVESTIGATION AND CHECKING

In the execution of the duties assigned to it, the Commission is empowered to request information from enterprises (Article 11 of Regulation No. 17) and to conduct itself all necessary investigations in the offices and installations of the enterprises and associations of enterprises to which the proceedings relate (Article 14 of Regulation No. 17). It may also request competent Authorities in Member States to carry out certain investigations (Article 13 of Regulation No. 17).

If in any economic sector the development of trade between Member States, price fluctuations, inflexibility of prices or other circumstances suggest that in the economic sector concerned competition is being restricted or distorted within the Common Market, the Commission may decide to open a general in quiry in that sector (Article 12 of Regulation No. 17).

On the basis of their national legislation, States may also carry out investigations and inquireis and request information on their own initiative if the Commission has not initiated any action (Article 9 paragraph 3 of Regulation No. 17).

To simplify administrative formalities, it is provided that requests for information may be addressed to the enterprise concerned simply by means of a letter from the competent services of the Commission.

All information furnished must be correct, on pain of fine—where appropriate—of from 100 to 5,000 Units of Account. (Article 15, paragraph 1b of Regulation No. 17).

If the information required is not provided within the time limit set by the Commission or if incomplete information is supplied the Commission may request it by means of a decision (Article 11 paragraph 5 of Regulation No. 17)-

In this case, the enterprise is obliged to furnish the information requested.

The Commission may also oblige enterprises, by means of decision, to produce the documents necessary for verification and to give free access to their premises and installations (Article 14, paragraph 3 of Regulation No. 17).

To ensure that enterprises fulfil these obligations, the Commission may impose on them fines of from 50 to 1,000 Units of Account per day of delay. (Article 16, paragraph 1 of Regulation No. 17).

IV PUBLICITY

When the Commission intends to grant a negative clearance or to make a decision applying Article 85 paragraph 3, it publishes the substance of the request or notification and invites interested third parties to submit their observations. (Article 19 paragraph 3 of Regulation No. 17).

The Commission publishes the substance of its decisions to apply:

Article 2 of Regulation No. 17 (negative clearance),

Article 3 of Regulation No. 17 (termination of infringement),

Article 85, paragraph 3 (in addition to the renewal, modification or revocation of decisions),

Article 7 of Regulation No. 17.

Publications must respect the legitimate interest of enterprises in not having their business secrets divulged (Article 19 paragraph 3, and 21 paragraph 2 of Regulation No. 17).

V SANCTIONS

The Commission may, by means of a decision, impose *fines* of from 100 to 5,000 Units of Account when, deliberately or through negligence:

(a) an application for 'negative clearance' or a notification contains incorrect or misleading information,

(b) information furnished is incorrect or is not furnished within the time-limit fixed by the decision, or

(c) the trade documents required are submitted in incomplete form or an investigation ordered by means of a decision is refused.

Very heavy fines up to 1 million Units of Account and even 10 per cent of turnover may be imposed on enterprises which, deliberately or through negligence, infringe Articles 85 paragraph 1, or 86, or fail to fulfil an obligation to which the declaration of inapplicability provided for by Article 85 paragraph 3 is made subject (Article 15 of Regulation No. 17).

The Commission may by decision impose *fines* of upto 1,000 Units of Account per day of delay in order to compel enterprises to fulfil the obligations which may be imposed on them by means of a decision taken in virtue of Articles 3, 8, paragraph 3, 11 paragraph 5, and 14 paragraph 3 of Regulation No. 17 (Article 16 of Regulation No. 17).

VI APPEAL

Under Article 164 of the Treaty, the Court of Justice of the Europan Communities in Luxembourg ensures observance of the law in the interpretation and application of the Treaty. To this end, in conformity with Article 173 of the Treaty, it reviews the legality of the acts of the Commission, other than recommendations or opinions.

On the other hand, it will have full jurisdiction as to the merits when adjudicating on appeals brought against any fine or penalty. It may cancel, reduce, or increase the fine or penalty (Article 17 of Regulation No. 17).

Any physical or legal person may make an appeal on grounds of incompetence substantial defect of form, infringement of the Treaty or of any regulation pursuant to its application (for example Regulation No. 17), or abuse of power, against the decisions served on that physical or legal person and against decisions which, although taken under a regulation or decision addressed to another person concerns him directly or individually.

The appeal must be made within a period of two months as from the publication of the action which is contested as, from the date of its notification to the complainant, or, failing that, as from the date on which the complainant learned of it.

Further, any physical or legal person may in conformity with Article 175 of the Treaty, address an 'appeal on the grounds of default' to the Court of Justice accusing the Commission of failing to communicate to that person any act other than a recommendation or opinion.

Such an appeal is only admissible if the Commission has previously been invited to act. If, at the end of two months as from the date of the invitation, the Commission has not indicated its attitude, the appeal may be made within a further period of two months. These provisions of the Treaty are completed by the Protocol on the Statute of the Court of Justice of the European Communities, dated April 17, 1957, which, in virtue of Article 239 of the Treaty, forms an integral part of the Treaty, and also by the Rules of Procedure of the Court of Justice (including Annexes I and II) of March 3, 1959* (*Journal Officiel*

* Amended by the decision of the Court of June 19, 1962, *J.O.* 1962, pp. 1605 ff.

of the European Communities, pages 349/59 and 13/60) and the additional Rules of Procedure of March 9, 1962. (*Journal Officiel* of the European Communities, page 1113/62).

Under Article 17 of the Statutes of the Court of Justice, private parties must be represented by counsel of the Bar of one of the Member States.

University teachers being nationals of Member States whose legislation recognizes their right to plead shall enjoy before the Court the rights recognized for counsel by that Article.

Under Article 19 of the Statute, the Court is approached by means of a petition addressed to the Registrar. The other provisions concerning the content and form of the petition are set out in Article 19 of the Statute and in Article 37 and 38 of the Rules of Procedure.

The petition must be written in one of the official languages of the Community.

VII SIGNIFICANCE OF 'NEGATIVE CLEARANCE' WITHIN THE FRAMEWORK OF ARTICLE 85 AND OF NOTIFICATION; COMPARISON OF THE TWO PROCEDURES

1. An application must in both cases be made by means of a Form.

2. Applications for 'negative clearance' and a notification are subject to the same publicity procedure; in both cases, a copy of the application is sent to the competent Authorities of Member States; in both cases, the Commission must, when it proposes to accede to an application, publish the substance of the application or notification so as to obtain observations from interested third parties.

3. Examination procedures, like the powers of the Commission concerning investigation and checking, are generally speaking the same in both cases. However, as regards applications for 'negative clearance', the Commission will decide on the basis of the facts brought to its notice.

4. The significance of a decision to apply Article 85, paragraph 3, following a notification, is greater in several ways than that following the grant of 'negative clearance.'

The prohibition in Article 85, paragraph 1, may be declared inapplicable only by decision of the Commission taken under Article 85, paragraph 3. This decision is granted for a specified period and may be revoked only on certain conditions.

Interested parties wishing to obtain such a decision should not be, content simply to submit an application for 'negative clearance.' Indeed, the application for negative attestation does not extend the time limits laid down for notification. The same applies if the arrangement falls within the categories specified in Article 4, paragraph 2 of Regulation No. 17 or if the parties concerned consider that their arrangement has no importance.

The 'negative clearance' signifies only that the Commission considers that there are no grounds for it to intervene in respect of an arrangement given the information it has at its disposal when the decision is taken. In general the Commission will decide to intervene at a later stage only if a change in case law or the availability of information unknown to the Commission at the time of its decision makes this necessary.

Lastly, notification suspends the application of sanctions under the conditions envisaged in Article 15, paragraph 5, of Regulation No. 17. Such suspension is not envisaged in the case of a 'negative clearance'.

Announcements of the Commission of the E.E.C.

ANNOUNCEMENT ON PATENT LICENCE AGREEMENTS
(OF DECEMBER 21, 1962)*

I. On the basis of the facts known at present, the Commission considers that the following clauses in patent licence contracts are not covered by the prohibition laid down in Article 85, paragraph 1, of the Treaty:

A. Obligations imposed on the licensee which have as their object:
1. the limitation to certain of the forms of exploitation of the invention which are provided for by patent law (manufacture, use, sale);
2. the limitation:
   (a) of the manufacture of the patented product.
   (b) of the use of the patented process.
   to certain technical applications;
3. the limitation of the quantity of products to be manufactured or of the number of acts constituting exploitation;
4. the limitation of exploitation:
   (a) in time
(a licence of shorter duration than the patent),
   (b) in space
(a regional licence for part of the territory for which the patent is granted, or to a specific factory),
   (c) with regard to the person
(limitation of the licensee's power of disposal, e.g. prohibiting him from assigning the licence or from granting sub-licences);

B. Obligations whereby the licensee has to mark the product with an indication of the patent;

C. Quality standards or obligations to procure supplies of certain products imposed on the licensee—in sofar as they are indispensable for the technically perfect exploitation of the patent;

D. Undertakings concerning the disclosure of experience gained in exploiting the invention or the grant of licences for inventions in the field of perfection or application; this however applies to undertakings entered into by the licensee only if those undertakings are not exclusive and if the licensor has entered into similar undertakings;

E. Undertakings on the part of the licensor:
   1. not to authorize anyone else to exploit the invention;
   2. not to exploit the invention himself.

II. This announcement is without prejudice to the appraisal from a legal point of view of clauses other than those referred to at I(A) to (E).

Moreover a general appraisal does not appear possible for agreements relating to:

* Published on December 24, 1962 (*J.O.* 1962, pp. 2921 ff.).

1. joint ownership of patents,
2. reciprocal licences,
3. parallel multiple licences.

The appraisal of the clauses referred to at I(A) to (E) is confined to clauses of a duration not exceeding the period of validity of the patent.

III. The object of this Announcement is to give enterprises some indication of the considerations by which the Commission will be guided in interpreting Article 85, paragraph 1, of the Treaty and in applying it to a number of clauses often found in certain patent licence contracts. So long as and in so far as such contracts do not contain restrictions other than those resulting from one or more of the clauses mentioned above, the Commission considers that they are not affected by the prohibition laid down in Article 85, paragraph 1. Generally speaking this specific information will remove the incentive for firms to obtain a negative clearance for the agreements in question, and will make it unnecessary to have the legal position established by an individual decision by the Commission; moreover there is no longer any need to notify agreements of this nature.

This Announcement is without prejudice to any interpretation that may be made by other competent authorities and in particular by the courts.

A decision is to be made later on the question of the application of Article 85, paragraph 1, of the Treaty to clauses of the types mentioned above which are contained in contracts relating to joint ownership of patents, to the grant of reciprocal licences or parallel multiple licences, to agreements relating to the exploitation of other industrial property rights or of creative activities not protected by law and constituting technical improvements, and to any clauses other than those mentioned above.

This Announcement is without prejudice to the interpretation of Article 4, paragraph 2, sub paragraph 2(b) of regulation No. 17.

IV. The undertakings listed at A) do not fall within the scope of the prohibition laid down in Article 85, paragraph 1, because they are covered by the patent. They only entail the partial maintenance of the right of prohibition contained in the patentee's exclusive right in relation to the licensee, who in other respects is authorized to exploit the invention. The list at I(A) is not an exhaustive definition of the rights conferred by the patent.

The obligation imposed on the licensee to mark the product with an indication of the patent (point I(B)) is in accordance with the patentee's legitimate interest in ensuring that the protected articles are clearly shown to owe their origin to the patented invention. Since the licensee may also make distinguishing marks of his own choice on the protected article, this provision has neither the object nor the effect of restricting competition.

The licensee's undertakings, mentioned at I(C), concerning the observance of certain quality standards for the protected products or for semi manufactures, raw materials or auxiliary materials, could not restrict competition which has to be protected (*la concurrence à protéger*) to the extent that they are intended to prevent the technically incorrect working of the invention. The undertaking to procure supplies of certain products can be left out of account, except when quality cannot be established by objective standards. In that case, such an undertaking has the same scope as quality standards.

The undertakings give by the licensee and mentioned at I(D) do not in any case have any restrictive effect on competition when the licensee retains the possibility of disclosing experience gained or of granting licences to third parties and is entitled to participate in the licensor's future acquisitions in the field of experience and inventions. With regard to undertakings give by the licensor concerning the disclosure of experience or the grant of a licence, as mentioned at I(D), these seem to be unexceptionable from the point of view of the law relating to competition, even without that limitation. Thus point I(D) only covers the obligation to disclose experience or to grant licences; this is without prejudice to the appraisal from a legal point of view of any restrictions imposed on the interested parties concerning the utilization of such experience or inventions.

By the undertaking mentioned at I(E)—not to authorise the use of the invention by any other person—the licensor forfeits the right to make agreements with other applicants for a licence. Leaving out of account the controversial question whether such exclusive undertakings have the object or effect of restricting competition, they are not likely to affect trade between member states as things stand in the Community at present. The undertaking not to exploit the patented invention oneself is closely akin to an assignment of the right and accordingly does not seem to be open to objection.

*_*_*

ANNOUNCEMENT ON EXCLUSIVE AGENCY CONTRACTS
MADE WITH COMMERCIAL AGENTS (OF DECEMBER 21, 1962)*

I. The Commission considers that contracts made with commercial agents, in which those agents undertake, for a specified part of the territory of the Common Market,

to negotiate transactions on behalf of an enterprise,

or

to conclude transactions in the name and on behalf of an enterprise,

or

to conclude transactions in their own name and on behalf of this enterprise,

are not covered by the prohibition laid down in Article 85, paragraph 1 of the Treaty.

It is essential in this case that the contracting party, described as a commercial agent, should, in fact, be such, by the nature of his functions, and that he should neither undertake nor engage in activities proper to an independent trader in the course of commercial operations. The Commission regards as the decisive criterion, which distinguishes the commercial agent from the independent trader, the agreement—express or implied—which deals with responsibility for the financial risks bound up with the sale or with the performance of the contract. Thus the Commission's assessment is not governed by the way the 'representative' is described. Except for the usual *del credere* guarantee, a commercial agent must not, by the nature of his functions, assume any risk resulting from the transaction. If he does assume such risks his function becomes economically akin to that of an independent trader and he must therefore be treated as such for the purposes of the rules of competition. In such circumstances exclusive agency contracts must be regarded as agreements made with independent traders.

* Published on December 24, 1962 (*J.O.* 1962, pp. 2921 ff.).

The Commission considers that an 'independent trader' is most likely to be involved where the contracting party described as a commercial agent:

is required to keep or does in fact keep, as his own property, a considerable stock of the products covered by the contract, or

is required to organize, maintain or ensure at his own expense a substantial service to customers free of charge, or does in fact organize, maintain or ensure such a service,

or

can determine or does in fact determine prices or terms of business.

II. In contrast to what is envisaged in this announcement about contracts made with commercial agents, the possibility that Article 85, paragraph 1, may be applicable to exclusive agency contracts with independent traders cannot be ruled out. In the case of such exclusive contracts the restriction of competition lies either in the limitation of supply, when the vendor undertakes to supply a given product only to one purchaser, or in the limitation of demand, when the purchaser undertakes to obtain a given product only from one vendor. In the case of reciprocal undertakings there will be such restrictions of competition on both sides. The question whether a restriction of competition of this nature is liable to affect trade between Member States depends on the circumstances of the case.

On the other hand, in the Commission's opinion, the conditions for the prohibition laid down in Article 85, paragraph 1, are not fulfilled by exclusive agency contracts made with commercial agents, since they have neither the object nor the effect of preventing, restricting or distorting competition within the Common Market. The commercial agent only performs an auxiliary function in the commodity market. In that market he acts on the instructions and in the interest of the enterprise on whose behalf he is operating. Unlike the independent trader, he himself is neither a purchaser nor a vendor, but seeks purchasers or vendors in the interest of the other party to the contract, who is the person doing the buying or selling. In this type of exclusive representation contract, the selling or buying enterprise does not cease to be a competitor; it merely uses an auxiliary, i.e. the commercial agent, to dispose of or acquire products on the market.

The legal status of commercial agents is determined, more or less uniformly, by statute in most of the member countries and by case law in others. The characteristic feature which all commercial agents have in common is their function as auxiliaries in the negotiation of business deals. The powers of commercial agents are subject to the rules laid down in civil law on 'mandate' and 'procuration'. Within the limits of those provisions the other party to the contract—who is the person selling or buying—is free to decide the product and the territory in respect of which he is willing to assign those functions to his agent.

Apart from the competitive situation on those markets where the commercial agent functions as an auxiliary to the other party to the contract, one has to consider the particular market on which commercial agents offer their services for the negotiation or conclusion of transactions. The obligation assumed by the agent—to work exclusively for one principal for a certain period of time— entails a limitation of supply on that market; the obligation assumed by the other party to the contract—to appoint him sole agent for a given territory— involves a limitation of demand on that market. Nevertheless, the Commission sees these restrictions as a result of the special obligation to protect each other's interests which exists between the commercial agent and his principal. Thus the Commission does not consider that they involve any restriction of competition.

The object of this Announcement is to give firms some indication of the considerations which will guide the Commission in interpreting article 85, paragraph 1, of the Treaty, as it applies to exclusive distribution agreements made with commercial agents/ Generally speaking, this explanation will remove the incentive for firms to obtain a negative clearance for the agreements in question, and will make it unnecessary to have the legal position established by an individual decision by the Commission; moreover there is no longer any need to notify agreements of this nature. This Announcement is without prejudice to any interpretation that may be made by other competent authorities and in particular by the courts.

Decisions of the Commission of the E.E.C.

DECISION BY THE COMMISSION OF MARCH 11, 1964
ON AN APPLICATION FOR NEGATIVE CLEARANCE SUBMITTED IN ACCORDANCE WITH
ARTICLE 2 OF REGULATION NO 17 MADE BY THE COUNCIL (IV A–0006)
(64 233 C.E.E.) (GROSSFILLEX AND FILLISTORF)

THE COMMISSION OF THE EUROPEAN ECONOMIC COMMUNITY.

having regard to the Treaty establishing the European Economic Community, and in particular Article 85,

having regard to Regulation No. 17 of February 6, 1962, and in particular Article 2,

having regard to the application for negative clearance submitted by the limited company Grosfillex, of Arbent (Ain), France, in accordance with Article 2 of Regulation No. 17, asking the Commission to declare that there is no ground for it to intervene in pursuance of Article 85(1) of the Treaty in respect of the contract made on September 4, 1959 between the applicants and Etablissements Fillistorf, Zurich, Switzerland.

after consulting the Consultative Committee on Restrictive Trade Agreements and Domination of Markets, in accordance with Article 10 of Regulation No. 17,

I

whereas the contact contains broadly speaking the following provisions

The applicants, Grosfillex, who make articles of plastic material, entrust the Swiss firm Fillistorf—by an overall agreement covering the supply of articles in 'household' and 'hygienic' lines—with the sale of those articles in the territory of the Swiss Confederation (Articles I and II of the contract).

Fillistorf distribute the articles, which are sold to them by Grosfillex free and cleared from the Customs at Zurich, to resellers on their own behalf, and are in no way authorized to act as agents for Grosfillex (Article VII of the contract). Fillistorf may engage in the operations provided for in the contract only in the allotted territory (Article VI of the contract); they undertake not to make or sell any article which might compete with articles made by Grosfillex (Article VI of the contract).

In return Grosfillex undertake not to make on Swiss territory any sales of articles in the lines covered by the contract otherwise than through Fillistorf and to take all measures to put an end to any sales of such articles made by third parties on Swiss territory which may be brought to their knowledge (Article VI of the contract). Furthermore Grosfillex must forward to Fillistorf any orders or correspondence received directly from Switzerland (Article IV of the contract).

II

whereas the negative clearance can be issued, in accordance with the provisions of Article 2 of Regulation No. 17, if the Commission finds that on the basis of the information available to it there is no ground for it to intervene in pursuance of the provisions of Article 85 (1) of the Treaty in respect of the contract made between Grosfillex and Fillistorf;

whereas Article 85 (1) of the Treaty stipulates that all agreements between enterprises which may affect trade between member states, and the object or effect of which is to prevent, restrict or distort competition within the Common Market, are incompatible with the Common Market and are prohibited;

whereas the object of the contract made between Grosfillex and Fillistorf is the grant, by a manufacturer established in the Common Market to an undertaking established outside the Common Market, of the sole concession for the sale of his articles for a territory situated outside the Common Market; the object of the contract is not, therefore, 'to prevent, restrict or distort competition within the Common Market';

whereas, however, certain provisions of the contract prohibit Fillistorf from selling in the Common Market countries the articles covered by the contract and articles which might compete with them, whether these are made inside or outside the Common Market; accordingly it is necessary to consider whether as a result of those provisions the effect of the contract is not to prevent, restrict or distort competition within the Common Market, within the meaning of Article 85 (1);

whereas in this respect the following circumstances should be taken into account:

The articles purchased by Fillistorf, since they are delivered to them in Switzerland by Grosfillex, would have to cross another customs frontier when resold to a customer in the Common Market. Hence they are not likely to compete with similar articles supplied directly in the territory of the Common Market. Except in abnormal circumstances it could not be otherwise—and the Commission has no knowledge of any such circumstances. There is, in point of fact, no reason to suppose that Grosfillex's prices on the Swiss market are lower than those quoted by Grosfillex in the Common Market —and this would seem to be borne out by the fact that Swiss purchasers of the products covered by the contract and sold by Fillistorf are not prohibited from reselling them to customers in the Common Market;

In the market for articles of plastic material in 'household' and 'hygienic lines' there are a considerable number of manufacturers established in the Member States or in other countries and in a position to compete in the territory of the Common Market; the same applies on the commercial side;

Finally, no opposition from third parties has emerged as a result of the notice published in pursuance of Article 19 (3) of Regulation No. 17 in the *Journal Officiel des Communautés Européennes*, No. 102, of July 4, 1963.

whereas these circumstances make it clear that competition within the Common Market is not prevented, restricted or distorted to an appreciable extent by reason of the contract in question.

And whereas, in these circumstances, the information available to the Commission does not at present justify the view that the object or effect of the contract in question is to prevent, restrict or distort competition within the Common Market, within the means of Article 85 (1); one of the conditions for Article 85 (1) of the Treaty to be applicable is thus not satisfied; and the negative clearance applied for can accordingly be issued.

HAS TAKEN THE PRESENT DECISION:

Article 1. There is no ground for the Commission, on the basis of the information available to it, to intervene in pursuance of the provisions of Article 85 (1) of the Treaty establishing the European Economic Community in respect

of the agreement made on September 4, 1959, between the Société Grosfillex
and Établissements Fillistorf.

Article 2. This decision is addressed to the Société Grosfillex, of Arbent.
Done in Brussels on March 11, 1964.
By the Commission,
the President,

WALTER HALLSTEIN.

***

DECISION BY THE COMMISSION OF THE E.E.C. OF JULY 30, 1964
ON AN APPLICATION FOR NEGATIVE CLEARANCE SUBMITTED IN ACCORDANCE WITH
ARTICLE 2 OF REGULATION NO. 17 MADE BY THE COUNCIL
(IV A,00095–64,502,C.E.E.), (NICOLAS FRÈRES AND VITAPRO, CO. (U.K.) LTD.))

THE COMMISSION OF THE EUROPEAN ECONOMIC COMMUNITY,

having regard to the Treaty establishing the European Economic Community, and in particular article 85 thereof,

having regard to Council Regulation No. 17 of February 6, 1962, and in
particular article 2 thereof,

having regard to the application for negative clearance submitted by the
limited company Nicholas Frères, 131 avenue Maréchal Foch, Chatou (Seine-et-
Oise), France, in accordance with Article 2 of Regulation No. 17, asking the
Commission to declare that there is no ground for it to intervene in pursuance
of Article 85, paragraph 1, of the Treaty in respect of the contract made on
July 11, 1962 between the applicant and the Vitapro Company (U.K.) Ltd.,
Regina House, Marylebone Road, London, Great Britain,

after consulting the Consultative Committee on Restrictive Trade Agreements
and Domination of Markets, in accordance with Article 10 of Regulation No. 17;

I

whereas the French enterprise Nicholas, who manufacture and sell mainly
cosmetic products, had, on January 12, 1961, acquired the business of the
Vitapointe laboratories, a limited company established at Villeurbanne (Rhône);
whereas, in the field of hairdressing products, Vitapointe held various patents,
trade marks and design registered in their name in several countries; whereas,
for the distribution of Vitapointe products in Great Britain and in other territories outside the Common Market, they had concluded an exclusive licence and
concession agreement with the British firm Vitapro;

whereas, by the contract of July 11, 1962, which is the subject of the application for negative clearance, Nicholas sold Vitapro part of the business bought
from Vitapointe, namely, the goodwill of the Vitapointe Company in the States
which are not members of the EEC, referred to by name in the contract (and
especially the States of the British Commonwealth), the right to use the brand
name Vitapointe in the said States, as well as various patents, trade marks and
designs registered in the said third countries in the name of the Vitapointe
Company or their agents, and the right to use various manufacturing processes,
formulas, knowledge and technical methods (know-how) in those countries;

whereas by this contract the Vitapro Company undertake not to make use, nor to allow the use, outside those third countries, of the brand name Vitapointe, nor of the trade marks referred to in the contract and assigned by Nicholas, to designate the products which they manufacture or sell;

whereas, in return, the company Nicholas undertake not to make use nor to allow the use, in those third countries, of the brand name Vitapointe, nor of the trade marks, registered in their name on the territory of the Common Market, to designate the products which they manufacture or sell;

whereas, in addition, each party undertakes for a period of five years from January 12, 1961, not to manufacture or sell, nor to cause to be manufactured or sold, in the territories respectively reserved for the other party, other hair-dressing products, whether or not bearing the trade marks in question, except in the case of products which have been purchased or are the subject of a licensing contract; whereas Vitapro are, however, authorized to supply the Navy, Army and Air Force Institute (NAAFI) and British ship's stores;

whereas for the same period of five years the parties have agreed to share experience for their mutual benefit;

whereas the company Nicholas notified the Commission of this contract on October 3, 1962, on form **B**;

whereas in point IV of this form they request for this contract the negative clearance provided for in Article 2 of Regulation No. 17 on the implementation of Article 85, paragraph 1, of the Treaty establishing the EEC;

whereas in the event of this application being rejected they wish to avail themselves of the provisions of Article 85, paragraph 3, of the Treaty establishing the EEC;

II

whereas, as to the form, the company Nicholas have not, it is true, used form A, provided for in Article 4, paragraph 1, of Regulation No. 27 made by the Commission, to submit their application for negative clearance, whereas they have, however, supplied on form B, in points I to IV, all the information specified on form A; whereas, moreover, they have clearly indicated in point IV that they are primarily applying for the negative clearance provided for in Article 2 of Regulation No. 17, and that it is only in case this application should be rejected that they have submitted a notification under Article 4 of Regulation No. 17, with a view to obtaining the benefit of Article 85, paragraph 3, of the Treaty establishing the EEC;

whereas, consequently, the use of form B does not in this particular case constitute a ground for rejecting the application; whereas the application for negative clearance must therefore be considered to have been submitted in due form and to be admissible as to form under Article 2 of Regulation No. 17;

whereas, as to the substance, the negative clearance applied for may be issued, in accordance with the provisions of Article 2 of Regulation No. 17, if the Commission finds that, on the basis of the information available to it, there is no ground for it to intervene in pursuance of the provisions of Article 85, paragraph 1, of the Treaty establishing the EEC in respect of the contract made between Nicholas and Vitapro;

whereas, in order to examine whether there are grounds, for the Commission to intervene in respect of this contract or not, its nature and details must be taken into account as well as the conditions of competition existing, to the knowledge of the Commission, for the hairdressing products covered by the contract;

whereas the subject of the contract between Nicholas and Vitapro is the assignment of certain assets which belonged to Nicholas, as a result of the acquisition of the Vitapointe business, in the third countries referred to in the contract; whereas, by this contract, Vitapro have in particular acquired the right to make use and to allow the use outside the Common Market of the trade marks included among such assets;

whereas this contract includes two provisions which concern competition in the Common Market;

whereas the first of these provisions prohibits Vitapro, for a period of five years, from manufacturing and selling hairdressing products and from allowing their manufacture or sale in the Common Market, so that the British company cannot compete with the French company in it during that period;

whereas, however, that provision has only been agreed for a short initial period, expiring on January 12, 1966, and whereas it does not concern the products which the British firm purchase from third parties or which they manufacture or sell in virtue of a licensing contract made with third parties;

whereas, moreover, the second provision mentioned above prohibits Vitapro, without any time-limit, from making use and from allowing the use, in the Common Market of the trade marks assigned;

whereas, however, that provision was agreed at the time of the division of the former Vitapointe enterprise; whereas this division was effected in such a way that Nicholas retained all the assets connected with the territory of the Common Market, and in particular the trade marks registered there, while assigning to Vitapro all the Vitapointe assets in various third countries, without the Common Market being thereby divided into separate zones;

whereas the effect of the prohibition imposed on Vitapro is to prevent the sale under the same trade mark, in the Common Market, of products manufactured henceforward by an enterprise with their registered office in the Common Market and by an enterprise whose registered office is in a third country.

whereas, in addition, in respect of each of the two above provisions of the contract, the hairdressing products which they concern are in competition with a very large number of similar products available in the Common Market; whereas Nicholas, according to the information available to the Commission, are not among the largest enterprises in this sector and are in keen competition with many enterprises manufacturing or selling hairdressing products on the Common Market;

whereas, lastly, no opposition has been put forward by buyers' circles, who might be concerned, as a result of the publication, in implementation of Article 19, paragraph 3, of Regulation No. 17, of the substance of the application for negative clearance in the *Journal Officiel des Communautés Européennes* (No. 102 of July 4, 1963, p. 1853 and 1854);

whereas, taking into account all these circumstances, the Commission is able to issue the negative clearance applied for,

HAS TAKEN THE PRESENT DECISION;

Article 1. There is no ground for the Commission, on the bais of the information available to it, to intervene in pursuance of Article 85, paragraph 1, of the Treaty establishing the EEC in respect of the agreement made on July 11, 1962, between the companies Nicholas and Vitapro.

Article 2. This decision is addressed to the company Nicholas of Chatou. Brussels, July 30, 1964.

By the Commission,
The President,

WALTER HALLSTEIN.

DECISION BY THE COMMISSION OF THE E.E.C. OF SEPTEMBER 23, 1964
CONCERNING PROCEDURE UNDER ARTICLE 85 OF THE TREATY
(IV A 0004–03344 ("GRUNDIG-CONSTEN") 64 566,C.E.E.))

THE COMMISSION OF THE EUROPEAN ECONOMIC COMMUNITY,

having regard to the Treaty setting up the European Economic Community, and in particular Article 85 thereof,

having regard to Regulation No. 17 of 6th February 1962 and in particular Articles 3, 6 and 7 thereof,

having regard to the request, dated 5th March 1962 and completed 15th July 1962, submitted by the limited company under French law UNEF, of Paris, in accordance with Article 3 of Regulation No. 17, to the effect that the Commission should declare that there has been an infringement of the provisions of Article 85 by the company under German law Grundig Verkaufs-GmbH, of Fürth (Bavaria), Federal Republic of Germany, and by the limited company under French law Ets. Consten, of Courbevoie (Seine), France, in that those undertakings concluded an "agency contract" on 1st April 1957 and an accessory agreement concerning the registration and use of the mark GINT in France,

having regard to the notification of the sole distribution contracts of 1st April, 1957, submitted by Grundig Verkaufs-GmbH on the 29th January 1963 in accordance with Article 5 paragraph 1 of Regulation No. 17,

after hearing the enterprises concerned and other persons, in particular the complainants in accordance with Article 19 of Regulation No. 17,

after consulting the Consultative Committee on Restrictive Trade Agreements and Domination of Markets, in accordance with Article 10 of Regulation No. 17,

I

Whereas the main provisions of the contract concluded on the 1st April 1957 are as follows.

Grundig Verkaufs-GmbH ("Grundig") appoint Ets. Consten s. à r. 1. ("Consten") sole agents for France (continental), the Saar and Corsica for receivers, recorders, dictating machines and television sets manufactured by Grundig and for their spare parts and accessories.

Consten undertake to distribute those goods for their own account. They may neither represent other German firms who produce or sell similar goods, nor sell for their own account or for the account of others, products which compete with the products covered by the contract or which might disturb the sale thereof.

In addition Consten undertake, at their own expense, to advertise adequately and sufficiently and to establish a repair shop with an adequate stock of spare parts; they must always ensure that there is a reliable after-sales service for the equipment which they have sold.

Grundig undertake not to supply either directly or indirectly other persons in the territory under contract. That clause is part of a territorial protection system applied to the whole Grundig sales organisation. Exports and re-exports are prohibited for any Grundig buyer whether German or foreign. Accordingly Consten must not supply any goods, whether directly or indirectly from their territory on behalf of or to other countries.

For the duration of the contract Consten are authorised, for the distribution of Grundig products, to use the name of the emblem "GRUNDIG", without being allowed to register that mark. They are forbidden to use that mark after expiry of the contract whatever the reasons for that expiry.

Whereas the mark GINT ("Grundig International") was registered in France on the 3rd October 1957 in the name of Consten; whereas that registration is based on an agreement concluded between Grundig and Consten and partly laid down in writing on the 13th January 1959; whereas Consten have undertaken to transfer the mark GINT to Grundig or to have the registration cancelled from the moment when they are no longer their sole distributors; whereas the said mark is affixed to all equipment manufactured by Grundig including that sold in Germany and whereas it also appears on business letters, trade literature, etc.

Whereas the mark GINT was introduced by Grundig soon after they had lost a lawsuit, in December 1956, against a "parallel importer" in the Netherlands; whereas by that lawsuit Grundig had attempted to ensure territorial protection for the sole Dutch concessionnaire by the mark GRUNDIG; whereas the mark GINT is registered in Germany in the name of Grundig and in several other Member States in the name of the respective concessionnaire;

Whereas, by a lawsuit heard by the Seine Tribunal of Commerce, Consten had invoked the sole distribution contract concluded with Grundig against third parties, "parallel importers" who had imported Grundig products into France, in particular the complainant's UNEF, alleging that those third parties should have respected the contract, since the latter was generally known and the fact of not respecting it constituted an act of unfair competition; whereas in addition Consten filed a suit against UNEF for infringement of the mark GINT;

Whereas, in the first of those proceedings, UNEF claimed that the sole distribution contract was invalid by virtue of Article 85 of the Treaty setting up the European Economic Community and submitted a request to the Commission in a letter received on 5th March 1962, to the effect that the Commission should declare the said contract to be invalid and prohibit it in implementation of Article 85 et seq;

Whereas, in those first proceedings, the Paris Court of Appeal decided, by a decree of 26th January 1963, to reserve judgment until the Commission's decision on the UNEF request;

Whereas, in the second proceedings, the hearing has not yet taken place;

Whereas, besides, the facts may be summarised as follows:

Since the 1st April 1957 Consten have been the sole importers of Grundig receivers, recorders, dictating machines and television sets into France. After the freeing of imports (1) several firms began to buy Grundig equipment directly from German traders. The largest of those parallel importers are the complaintants UNEF of Paris, who, since April 1961, have bought Grundig equipment from German traders, in particular from wholesalers. The latter have therefore supplied goods to them in spite of the prohibition of exports imposed on them by Grundig. UNEF sold that equipment to French resellers at more favourable prices than those asked by Consten. Several traders in the Consten chain complained to Consten about it.

UNEF have declared that the parallel imports carried out by them were a result of the differences in price between Germany and France. Such differences have indeed been observed. They cannot be explained solely by the existing Customs duties or by the fiscal disparities. Thus at the end of 1962 the catalogue price for a certain type of Grundig recorder was 44% higher in France than in Germany, after deduction of Customs duties and taxes. Taking the "actual prices," catalogue price less "discounts," the difference was at least 23%.

In recent years the French prices of Grundig products have tended to decrease which does not alter the fact that, as Grundig and Consten have moreover admitted, the actual French prices for several items of equipment were, at the beginning of 1964, about 20% higher than the actual German prices, again after deduction of Customs duties and taxes. These items of equipment, a portable receiver, a radiogram and a recorder, have been chosen as examples by the parties themselves. At the same time turnover has increased considerably, both for Consten and for UNEF, the latter having already achieved in 1961 about 10% of the sale of Grundig recorders in France.

Besides the Customs duties and taxes mentioned above, there are not any charges imposed by the public authorities in France which could have given rise to differences in price with Germany. Since the Grundig "ex-works" prices to Consten or to a German wholesaler are basically the same it must be concluded that the differences in sale prices are accounted for by divergences in the trade margins. Indeed in the example quoted above the 44% difference in price corresponds approximately to an 89% difference in margin and that of 23% to a 53% difference in margin. Those percentages refer to the margins between the Grundig sale prices and the consumer prices, after deduction of Customs duties and of taxes due at the first stage of distribution (sale by Grundig to the wholesaler or the concessionnaire). Since the retail trade margins are, in absolute figures, basically the same in France and Germany the source of the differences mentioned must be sought at the stage of wholesale trade.

However, the contribution of the wholesale trade differs to the extent that in Germany Grundig pay the publicity and guarantee costs whereas abroad those costs devolve on the sole concessionnaires.

Grundig and Consten have argued that the contracts between them do not fall within the provisions of Article 85 paragraph 1. In their opinion those contracts are not designed to prevent, restrict or distort competition nor do they have this effect and nor are they likely to affect trade between Member States.

On 29th January 1963 Grundig, for any purpose it might serve, submitted notification of the sole distribution contract.

Whereas moreover the relevant facts for the evaluation of the contract from the point of view of Articles 85 paragraph 3 are set out in Section III,

II

Whereas Article 85 paragraph 1 of the Treaty lays down that all agreements between enterprises which are liable to affect trade between Member States and which are designed to prevent, restrict or distort competition within the Common Market or which have this effect are incompatible with the Common Market, and are prohibited.

1. Whereas the agreements under examination have been concluded between enterprises and whereas they are designed to restrict and to distort competition within the Common Market for the following reasons.

Grundig have undertaken not to supply goods directly or indirectly to other firms in the territory laid down in the contract. They are consequently prevented from selling in France the products referred to in the contract to buyers other than Consten. The undertaking not to supply goods indirectly in the territory covered by the contract is embodied in the prohibition of exports imposed on all buyers of Grundig products. The aim of this is to prevent any buyer of Grundig products, established outside France, from selling those products in France.

In the Seine Tribunal of Commerce Consten relied on the case-law on unfair competition to show that the sole distribution contract could be invoked against third parties and that all imports of Grundig products into France by other firms should be prohibited.

---

[1] For recorders, 29th September 1950, For receivers and television sets: 31st March 1961, For battery receivers: 1st January 1962.

Lastly the manner in which Grundig and Consten use the mark GINT constituted a subsidiary means of protecting Consten against competition.

The mark GINT is intended solely for affixing on Grundig products and, on the other hand, *all* the Grundig products in question are already provided by Grundig with the mark GINT. The use of the mark GINT and the division of rights to the marks are mainly intended to protect the sole concessionnaire against parallel imports in that the mark Grundig is registered everywhere in the name of Grundig, whereas the mark GINT is registered in the name of Grundig in Federal Germany but outside Germany in the name of the respective concessionnaires, in this case of Consten. This is also proved by the historical record of the mark GINT.

It is not necessary to examine the question of whether the mark in question also serves other purposes, in particular in the framework of the law on industrial property. It must however be observed that the mark GINT is not necessary for indicating the origin of the goods, since the mark Grundig is adequate for this purpose.

The conclusion that the registration of the mark GINT in France in the name of Consten and its use by them are based on an accessory agreement with Grundig follows on the one hand from the origin of the said mark and from the similar moves by other concessionnaires in the Common Market apart from Germany and on the other hand from Consten's obligation, laid down in writing on 30th January 1959, to transfer the mark to Grundig or to have its registration cancelled as soon as the sole rights contract is no longer in force.

The result is that, other than Consten, no firm established in France and wishing to buy Grundig products can obtain them outside France without running the risk of an action at law. Such firms are entirely dependent on Consten for their supplies and, consequently, are restricted in their choice.

The sole rights contract and the accessory agreement on the registration of the mark GINT in the name of Consten, the latter in conjunction with the fact that all Grundig equipment is provided with that mark, are therefore designed to free Consten from the competition of other firms as far as the import of Grundig products into France or the wholesale trade in them in France is concerned.

Furthermore, Consten or their "business connections" are forbidden, without Grundig's written agreement, to supply goods directly or indirectly from the territory covered by the contract to other countries.

The objection has been raised that competition operates to such a large extent at the production stage that it is impossible for any distortion of competition to result from the appointment of a sole agent.

When the distribution of products takes place in several commercial stages, for there to be restriction of competition within the meaning of Article 85 paragraph 1 it is enough for competition to be prevented or restricted at only one of them. The fact that Article 85 paragraph 1 juxtaposes the terms "prevent" and "restrict" and the wording of sub-paragraph (b) of Article 85 paragraph 3 show that, for the implementation of Article 85 paragraph 1, it is not necessary for all forms of competition at all the stages of distribution to be prevented.

In addition, for branded articles of the kind in question here the products of the various manufacturers are differentiated as to their external and partly also as to their technical, features. For those products, buyers can therefore generally rely on the comparison of their suppliers' offers and especially prices for articles of the same brand only.

When, for example, Grundig products are offered to the consumer at a higher price than that of comparable products it is hardly possible for the consumer to see whether the divergence can be explained by different production costs, perhaps on account of a difference in quality, or by the Grundig sales organisation's higher costs compared with that of other manufacturers. When, on the other hand, Grundig products distributed by the "official" sales network, in this case that of Consten, are dearer, for any reason whatever, than those same products distributed by a parallel sales network the situation is clear to the consumer and he has a real choice.

Competition at the distribution stage, in particular between wholesalers distributing articles of the same brand, is therefore especially important. That conclusion is all the more valid as distribution costs account for a considerable part of the total cost.

Consequently, the established fact that the parties to the contracts wanted Consten to be freed from competition from other importers for the import and wholesale distribution of Grundig products in France is enough for the conclusion to be drawn that competition is restricted within the meaning of Article 85 paragraph 1.

2. Whereas the contracts are liable to affect trade between Member States for the following reasons.

They have been concluded between two firms belonging to two different Member States and, for the products under contract, they govern trade between those Member States for the purpose of reserving it entirely for the parties.

The therefore prevent firms other than Consten established in France from importing Grundig products. The importance of that prevention is shown by the steps, both legal and extra-legal, undertaken by Consten and Grundig against the parallel importers and exporters, particularly against UNEF and their suppliers.

In addition, the sole rights contract prevents Consten from re-exporting Grundig products. Consequently, the integration of national markets into a Common Market is impeded, if not prevented. That effect is clearly shown by the differences observed in the level of prices in various Member States, in particular in Germany and France.

The accessory agreement on the registration of the mark GINT in the name of Consten is also conducive to the isolation of national markets and is therefore liable to affect trade between Member States.

The objection has been raised that the sales organisation did not affect trade between Member States since during its activity German-French trade in Grundig products increased considerably.

However, no weight can be given to that objection, since, for the implementation of Article 85 paragraph 1, it is enough for a restriction of competition within the meaning of Article 85 paragraph 1 to cause trade between Member States to develop under other conditions than it would have done without that restriction and for its influence on market conditions to be of some importance.

Such is the case for the contracts in question.

III

Whereas, in accordance with Article 85 paragraph 3, the provisions of Article 85 paragraph 1 may be declared inapplicable to the agreement if it helps to improve the production or distribution of goods or to promote technical progress, while allowing consumers a fair share of the resulting benefits (or profit) and does not

(a) subject the concerns in question to any restrictions which are not indispensable to the achievements of those objectives;

(b) enable such concerns to eliminate competition in respect of a substantial part of the goods concerned,

1. Whereas notification of the sole rights contract of the 1st April 1957 was submitted on 29th January 1963 in accordance with the provisions of Article 5 paragraph 1 of Regulation No. 17.

2. Whereas the parties Grundig and Consten submitted the arguments set out below, designed to justify the request made by Grundig for any purpose it might serve for Article 85 paragraph 3 to be applied to their sole rights contract;

the facts of trade have shown that, given the present strcuture of the economy of Europe, sole agencies are the only forms of distribution capable of solving the human, financial and linguistic problems, of adaptation to commercial customs, of co-ordinating a policy of expansion and of bearing the commercial risks which result from it;

the sole concessionnaires must watch the market for the manufacturer and in particular inform him of the conditions and technical requirements;

the sales organisation has allowed Grundig to increase production over the years; consequently, the manufacturer has been able to rationalise production and decrease consumer prices; consumers have therefore been allowed a share of the benefits resulting from those improvements in production and distribution;

the sole concessionnaires organise general publicity for the brand, by all available means, and maintain its reputation; a parallel importer, on the other hand, usually sells a number of products of different manufacturers and therefore does not advertise for one single brand;

the sole concessionnaires must make "forecasts" allowing the manufacturer to adapt his production to demand;

Those forecasts are indispensable for the manufacturer's whole programme and therefore also include the products for which there is less demand;

They create a risk since it is not possible to foresee with certainty on what terms the products reserved will be sold;

Consumers also have the advantage, thanks to the presence of a sole concessionnaire, of being able to count on a prompt and reliable after-sales service;

For the marketing of complicated products such as radio sets, television sets, tape recorders and dictating machines, the guarantee and after-sales service play an important part; if the service is not adequate sales fall rapidly; only a sole importer is concerned with providing a good service because in this way he can increase his turnover and derive a profit from his high investments;

If there is a certain number of importers, each one is bound to fear that his competitors will take advantage of his efforts so that no ne has an interest in providing the after-sales service for Grundig products;

parallel importers take an unfair advantage of the efforts of the sole distributor as regards service and publicity, and this allows them to give their customers slightly higher discounts;

only the sole concessionnaires have the necessary literature for the sale and after-sales service of Grundig products.

3. Whereas the system of sole distribution may lead to an improvement in the production and distribution of goods; whereas that may be true of the organisation of an after-sales and guarantee service and of the forecasts which the sole concessionnaire must make, but not of the publicity, since the fact that Consten is responsible for the publicity does not affect improvement in the distribution but only the sharing out of costs between the parties to the contract; whereas, as is the case in Federal Germany, the publicity could also be provided

by Grundig in the territory referred to in the contract, possibly through the medium of Consten or of another French firm.

Whereas the improvement in production and distribution is conceded here as a hypothesis; whereas a closer examination of that question is not necessary since, as will be shown below, the other conditions of Article 85 paragraph 3 are not fulfilled.

4. Whereas, in accordance with Article 85 paragraph 3, consumers must be allowed a fair share of the benefits; whereas, as regards that condition, the following observations must be made.

In the sphere of trade, the term "benefits" must not be taken to mean only improvement in the distribution of products which, if it leads to wider choice or greater buying facilities, also benefits the consumers, in this case the buyers, that is more especially the retailers established in France; it must also be taken to mean the other advantages resulting from rationalisation; the consumers must also have a share in them, in particular in the shape of prices and other conditions of delivery. The determining factor in this respect is to know whether the consumers' share is a "fair" one.

From observations concerning prices as set out in Section I it appears in this connection that there existed a marked difference in price between France and Germany, after deduction of Customs duties and fiscal charges, which are different in the two countries, and that the difference still exists today; it cannot be justified by the higher wages said to prevail in France, nor by the costs borne by Consten as a result of their obligation to provide the publicity and the guarantee service—costs which only amount to about 3% of their turnover.

The possibility that the consumers of the territory referred to in the contract are not getting a fair share of the benefits derived from a lack of competition has decreased on account of parallel imports by UNEF, but nonetheless it still exists.

If the system of absolute territorial protection were fully effective, and this would be accomplished by a declaration of the inapplicability of Article 85 paragraph 1, Consten would again be protected against that competition. And all other wholesalers and all retailers established in France would only be able to buy Grundig equipment from Consten, even if Consten's prices were much higher than, for example, those of German wholesalers buying directly from Grundig.

Against these arguments the alleged *general* decrease in consumer prices is insignificant. To the opinion that the sales organisation in its present form made an *increase in production* by Grundig possible and, consequently, a rationalisation of production and a decrease in consumer prices, the objection must be raised that it has not been established that all this is attributable to the activity of the sales organisation. There is nothing to indicate that a slackening of that organisation's hold, owing to the appearance of parallel importers, results in a reduction of turnover. In particular the appearance of a parallel importer of Grundig products on the French market has not up till now prevented a marked increase in the sale of those products on that market.

The differences in price which are possible as a result of the absolute territorial protection and which have been observed in the present case make it impossible for consumers to be allowed a fair share of the benefits resulting from the improvement conceded above.

5. Whereas the main reason for which the declaration of inapplicability cannot be made is that the restrictions imposed on the concerns in question for the achievement of the improvement in production and distribution of goods are

not all indispensable; whereas therefore the condition of Article 85 paragraph 3 sub-paragraph (a) is not fulfilled.

Whereas in this connection the following observations must be made.

The restriction of competition contained in the sole distribution contract of the 1st April 1957 with the widest scope is the agreement on absolute territorial protection aimed at preventing the import by parallel importers of the products under contract into the territoryreferred to in the contract. Therefore the question of the indispensable nature of the restrictions may be put in concrete form by asking whether an improvement in the distribution of the products through the sole distribution agreement can no longer be achieved if parallel imports are allowed, that is if other wholesalers and retailers established in France are allowed, insofar as they so wish, to buy Grundig equipment from a wholesaler established outside France and whom Grundig supplies directly, or from any other trader established outside France. If, by such a diminution of territorial protection, the objective of improving the production and distribution of the goods could no longer be achieved absolute territorial protection would then be indispensable. But if, even under those conditions, the improvement of production and distribution of the goods was still possible, absolute territorial protection would not be indispensable.

There appears to be no reason why Consten, even without absolute territorial protection, should be able to take full advantage of the French market as sole concessionnaire. For if Consten, as sole concessionnaire in Frenche, sell Grundig equipment with trade margins which are about the same as those of wholesalers established in the countries of the Common Market other than France, no trader established in France will normally have an interest in obtaining those products outside France and in tackling the difficulties involved in any import. Attention may be drawn, in that respect, to the experience of recent years, both in France and in other Member States, for example in the Netherlands, also with references to the Grundig sales organisation. That experience allows the conclusion to be drawn that the possibility of parallel imports may be regarded as a useful corrective to the difference in price between the various countries which does not however to any extent impede a sales organisation in its activities.

If against this Grundig and Consten invoke the need for absolute territorial protection on account of arrangements for making forecasts and the provision of guarantees and after-sales service the following observations must be made.

The argument of Grundig and Consten that absolute territorial protection is necessary for making reliable forecasts could at most be justified if the admission of parallel imports prevented the making of adequately reliable forecasts, But neither Grundig nor Consten allege this; and in fact the practice in the Federal Republic of Germany shows the very opposite. The German wholesale firms who are supplied directly by Grundig do not benefit from absolute territorial protection in their country. Their ability to make reliable forecasts is apparently not affected.

But even independently of that there is no binding tie between absolute territorial protection and forecasting arrangements.

The result of abolishing Consten's absolute territorial protection would be that parallel imports could no longer be hindered by legal measures; consequently closer business relations between parallel importers and their suppliers, in general German wholesalers, would be promoted to a certain extent, so that the orders placed by the parallel importers with the German wholesalers would also lead to "forecasting arrangements."

That forecasting arrangements are also indispensable for products which are less in demand is not relevant for the implementation of Article 85 paragraph 3.

Consequently that argument cannot justify absolute territorial protection.

Nor is absolute territorial protection indispensable for the observation of the market, the results of which, as it happens, are expressed in the forecasts. The argument concerning informing the producer as to conditions and technical requirements in the territory referred to in the contract is not relevant, since there are special organisations for that purpose.

If Grundig and Consten refer in addition to the guarantee service it is advisable, when considering that argument, to start from the fact that a buyer can normally only claim a right to a guarantee from his supplier and on the terms agreed with him. There are consequently no grounds for the sole concessionnaire to fear that possible competitors will take advantage of those guarantee services. This is all the more true as there is no apparent reason why the parallel importer, if he is authorised to effect parallel imports, could not in the same way, if need be with the help of his supplier, provide a guarantee service like Consten. Absolute territorial protection cannot therefore be justified by that argument either. Moreover UNEF also provide the customary guarantee service.

As regards the after-sales service, which is paid for and which is more important by far than the guarantee service, it is of little consequence to know where an item of equipment was bought since the repair costs must be paid by the person who asked for the repair. It is therefore a normal activity for a firm to carry out such repairs and there is no apparent reason why a disadvantage could result for the person engaged in that activity, owing to the fact that he repairs equipment which has not been supplied by him.

The argument that no one has an interest in providing the after-sales service when several traders import Grundig equipment into France is not convincing; quite on the contrary, competition normally forces traders to meet their buyers' demands as regards the after-sales service. UNEF have also organised such a service.

To this it must be added, for the sake of completeness, that outlay on the after-sales service and the guarantee service, which are subject to roughly the same conditions in France as in Germany, only amount for Consten for 1963 to 1.18% of their turnover.

Grundig and Consten apparently fear that parallel imports will reduce the sole concessionnaire's margin to such an extent that the costs of publicity and the guarantee service can no longer be covered. That fear does not appear justified even if Consten continue to bear the general publicity costs which in 1963 amounted to 1.9% of the turnover. It is enough for Grundig to undertake not to supply goods directly to another firm within the territory referred to in the contract. The effect of this is that the parallel importers, who are compelled to get stocks from wholesalers, therefore at second-hand, are bound to be ata disadvantage from the point of view of costs. It is not true that a parallel importer can, taking into account the turnover tax rebate, buy on better terms from such a wholesaler than the sole concessionnaire who gets stocks directly from Grundig. Wholesalers who export are only refunded the taxes which they have paid. In the end by that rebate the product is not freed from the German tax on turnover to a greater extent than the goods supplied of the German producer to the sole concessionnaire abroad. Moreover the parallel importer must offer his products on the same terms or on better terms than Consten if he wants to penetrate the French market.

The assertion by Grundig and Consten that the elimination of parallel imports is justified on account of the fact that only the sole concessionnaires have the necessary literature concerning the sale and the after-sales service bears no relation to the indispensable nature of the absolute territorial protection but is based solely on the fact that Grundig and Consten themselves have tried by every means to prevent UNEF from gaining possession of that literature.

No other reason in favour of the need for absolute territorial protection has been put forward and no other is foreseeable.

Whereas, according to the above, absolute territorial protection is not indispensable and whereas it is therefore not possible to declare Article 85 paragraph 1 inapplicable, in accordance with Article 85 paragraph 3, to the sole agency agreement of 1st April 1957.

6. Whereas it is not necessary, this being so, to consider whether that contract also makes it possible to eliminate competition in respect of a substantial part of the products in question.

IV

Whereas the parties to the contract have continued to apply the sole distribution agreement, and moreover have not modified it so that it no longer falls under the prohibition laid down in Article 85 paragraph 1 or that Article 85 paragraph 1 can be declared inapplicable to that contract in accordance with Article 85 paragraph 3; whereas Article 7 paragraph 1 of Regulation No. 17 cannot therefore be applied.

V

Whereas Grundig and Consten benefit, on account of the notification of their sole distribution agreement, by the provisions of Article 15 paragraph 5 of Regulation No. 17, according to which, in spite of the incompatibility of that agreement with Article 85, no fine can be imposed on them for the past.

VI

Whereas the accessory agreement was not the subject of the notification of 29th January 1963; whereas the question of whether it was implicitly notified at the same time as the main agreement does not need to be decided since even in the case of a notification duly made in the time required, a declaration of inapplicability could not be issued for that agreement for the reasons set forth in Sections III and IV; whereas that agreement only provides additional means of guaranteeing absolute territorial protection the indispensable nature of which has not been proved.

Whereas the question of whether a notification of the accessory agreement has been given is also of no consequence for determining whether a fine for infringement of Article 85 must be imposed since, in any case, it is not advisable, in this instance, to make use of the possibility provided by Article 15 paragraph 2 sub-paragraph (a) of Regulation No. 17; whereas the accessory agreement is indeed too closely linked to the sole distribution agreement since it only completes the absolute territorial protection which is thereby sought.

VII

Whereas absolute territorial protection has proved to be particularly harmful to the achievement of the Common Market by making more difficult or by preventing the adjustment of the market conditions of the products referred to in the common contract; whereas it has led to litigation between Consten and UNEF as a result of the parallel imports carried out by UNEF and has resulted in the submission of a request in pursuance of Article 3 of Regulation No. 17; Whereas the problem of the admission of parallel imports is consequently especially important in this matter; whereas on account of the above it appears advisable to compel Grundig and Consten to refrain from hindering or impeding, by any means whatever, including by the use to that end of the mark GINT, the parallel import of Grundig products into France;

Whereas that compulsion does not prevent Consten from availing themselves of their rights to the mark GINT in respect of third parties as long as there is no question of hindering or impeding parallel imports of Grundig products into the territory covered by the contract.

HAS ADOPTED THE PRESENT DECISION

Article 1. The contract of sole concession of 1st April 1957 and the accessory agreement on the registration and use of the mark GINT, concluded between Grundig Verkaufs-GmbH and Ets. Consten s.a.r.l. constitute an infringement of the provisions of Article 85 of the Treaty setting up the European Economic Community.

Article 2. The declaration of inapplicability provided for in Article 85 paragraph 3 is refused.

Article 3. The enterprises referred to in Article 1 are required to refrain from all measures aimed at hindering or impeding the acquisition by third undertakings, at their own discretion, from wholesalers or retailers established in the European Economic Community of the products covered by the contract with a view to reselling them in the territory of the contract.

Article 4. This decision is addressed to Grundig Verkaufs-GmbH, Fürth, Bavaria, Federal Republic of Germany, and to Ets. Consten s.a.r.l. of Courbevoie (Seine), France.

Done at Strasbourg, the 23rd September 1964.

O.E.E.C. CODE OF LIBERALISATION

Code of Liberalisation - New Edition Brought up to Date - July 1, 1960 - O.E.E.C. - O.E.C.D.

Article 7. Non-Discrimination Relations between Member Countries
 a. Subject to the provisions of Article 8, Article 9 and Article 10 Member countries shall avoid any discrimination as between one Member country and another:
  i) as from 1st January, 1951, in respect of imports of any commodity originating in these countries which has been freed in accordance with the provisions of Article 1; and
  ii) as from 1st February, 1951, in respect of imports of any commodity originating in these countries.
 b. The Organisation shall decide what steps should be taken to extend the principle of non-discrimination set out in paragraph (a) of this Article to imports to which measures of liberalisation of trade do not apply. It shall define the rules for the application by Member countries, on a non-discriminatory basis, of quantitative restriction on imports.

Article 10. Exceptions to the Principle of Non-Discrimination Dumping
 a. If a Member country suffers any prejudice as the result of dumping (as defined in Article 34 of the text of The Havana Charter) practised by another Member country and has been unable to obtain satisfaction by direct negotiation, it need no longer apply, in respect of the other Member country, the provisions of paragraph (a) of Article 7 with regard to the import of the commodities which are the subject of such dumping.
 b. Any Member country invoking the provisions of this Article may depart from the provisions of paragraph (a) of Article 7 for a period not exceeding eight weeks. If, upon the expiration of this period, the Organisation has not arrived at any decision on the action of that Member country, the latter may, upon notification to the Organisation and for so long as such dumping is practised, continue to depart from the provisions of paragraph (a) of Article 7.

INDEX